SHELTON STATE COMMUNITY
COLLEGE
JUNIOR COLLEGE DIVISION
LIBRARY

DISCARD

D1569974

E
259
.C37
1984

Carp, E. Wayne,
1946-

To starve the
army at pleasure

DATE DUE

TO STARVE THE ARMY
AT PLEASURE

TO STARVE THE ARMY
AT PLEASURE

CONTINENTAL ARMY ADMINISTRATION

AND AMERICAN POLITICAL CULTURE

1775 – 1783

E. WAYNE CARP

UNIVERSITY OF NORTH CAROLINA PRESS

CHAPEL HILL AND LONDON

© 1984 The University of North Carolina Press

All rights reserved

Manufactured in the United States of America

Library of Congress Cataloging in Publication Data

Carp, E. Wayne, 1946–
  To starve the army at pleasure.

  Bibliography: p.
  Includes index.
  1. United States.   Continental Army—History.
2. United States.   Continental Army—Supplies and stores.
3. Sociology, Military—United States—History—18th
century. I. Title.
E259.C37   1984   973.3'4   83-19697
ISBN 0-8078-1587-X

To My Parents,

R A Y M O N D   M.   A N D   L O R R A I N E   C A R P

CONTENTS

ILLUSTRATIONS

FIGURES AND TABLES

PREFACE

PARTLY BECAUSE of the increasing specialization in historical studies and partly because of the historical profession's general lack of interest in military history, the War for American Independence has never been fully integrated into the interpretations of the American Revolution. We know much about the origins of the American Revolution and the adoption of the federal Constitution but relatively little about how either of these developments was related to the eight years of warfare in between. The recent works of Don Higginbotham, Charles Royster, and John Shy, however, have begun to close this gap in our historical knowledge.[1] This study is a further effort to integrate the history of the war into the broader aspects of American politics and society during the era of the American Revolution.

This book has a dual purpose. First, I have endeavored to describe and analyze the difficulties of supplying the Continental army with food, clothing, camp equipage, and medical aid. Chapters 1, 2, 7, and 8 tell this story—the beginnings of congressional administration, its failure by 1776 and subsequent efforts at reform, Congress's decision in 1780 to rely on the states to supply the army, and finally in 1780–81 the origins of the Nationalist movement to strengthen the central government—in chronological fashion.

Second, I have attempted to analyze the relationship between the administration of the Continental army and eighteenth-century American political culture. The two were inextricably intertwined, and it is impossible to understand the organization and failure of governmental administration of the war without taking into account colonial political ideals and practices. This heritage is set forth, in some detail, in the Prologue. It is the contention of this book that American revolutionaries instinctively organized and administered the logistical operations of the revolutionary war on the same principles that governed their understanding of the political world. The various effects of this understanding on the administration of the Continental army form the leitmotif of this study and are most prominently discussed in Chapters 3, 4, 5, 6, and 8, in which the problems of supply, impressment, corruption, motivation of staff officers, and the Nationalist movement are explored in depth. This book, then, is a further attempt to fill the lacunae in our understanding of the American Revolution between 1775 and 1783 by describing and explaining the interaction between army administration and the larger political culture in which it took place.

I should add a caution to military historians. Although this study is about military supplies, it is not a treatise on logistics as that term is commonly understood. I have not, for example, assessed the role logistical failures played in determining the outcome of battles. Military strategy and tactics do not figure prominently in the text, except to illustrate broader points of analysis or interpretation. Rather, my purpose throughout is to discuss the impact of American political culture on the administration of the Continental army and the effect of the failure of those administrative policies on America's political culture.

M A N Y P E R S O N S and institutions contributed to the writing of this study. I am grateful for the cooperation and courtesies extended me by the staffs of the Connecticut Historical Society, the Connecticut State Library, the Friends Historical Society, Swarthmore, Pennsylvania, the Historical Society of Pennsylvania, the Library of Congress, the New Jersey Historical Society, the New Jersey State Library, the New-York Historical Society, the University Library at Berkeley, especially the Inter-Library Loan and Newspaper and Micro-copy departments, and the Yale University Library. I would also like to extend a special word of thanks to Arlene Phillips Shy and Barbara A. Mitchell of the William L. Clements Library, University of Michigan, Ann Arbor, whose professionalism and kindness made my first research trip a memorable one. For speedy and efficient processing of my requests for xerox or microfilm copies of manuscript materials, I am indebted to the staffs of the American Philosophical Society, the Library of Congress, the Massachusetts Historical Society, and to Susan A. Kopczynski of the Morristown National Historical Park, Ruth M. Blair of the Connecticut Historical Society, and Wendell Tripp of the New York State Historical Association. Parts of my article "The Origins of the Nationalist Movement of 1780–1783: Congressional Administration and the Continental Army," *Pennsylvania Magazine of History and Biography* 107 (1983), appear in Chapters 4 and 8. I am grateful to the editor for permission to republish this material.

I am pleased to have the opportunity to express my thanks to friends and colleagues who have shared their time and knowledge with me. All or portions of the study have been read and commented upon most helpfully by Ruth Bloch, John Catanzariti, Charles L. Cohen, Lynn Dumenil, Don Higginbotham, Elizabeth M. Nuxoll, Jack N. Rakove, and Richard K. Showman. I am deeply indebted to James Oakes for many useful suggestions regarding organization and style. I would especially like to thank Paula B. Shields for her close reading of the entire manuscript and notes and her constant good cheer. Ken Beeth had the thankless task of hearing each chapter read aloud in addition to reading the completed text. He reacted as only a true friend can: he praised lavishly what was good and criticized unmercifully what was bad. From the very beginning, Charles Royster has contributed to this project—at its inception he gave me his eighty-page bibliography on the revolutionary war—and I am deeply grateful for his continuing friendship, generosity, and encouragement. Over the years, Lucy Kerman listened to my ideas, read each chapter, and offered penetrating and valuable suggestions, many of which I ultimately adopted.

During 1982–83 I spent a thoroughly enjoyable and stimulating year at Princeton University as a National Historical Publications and Records Fellow at the Papers of Thomas Jefferson. I would like to thank members of the Princeton University historical community—Charles T. Cullen, Douglas Greenberg, Louis P. Masur, John M. Murrin, and Eugene R. Sheridan—for their support and constructive criticism. In particular, this book is better for the fact that nothing I wrote ever satisfied Doug Greenberg.

I would like to give special thanks to two readers who directed the early stages of this work. James H. Kettner labored tirelessly on every chapter, made many substantive suggestions, and saved me from numerous stylistic and factual errors. The manuscript has been much improved by his careful scrutiny. Robert Middlekauff first suggested the topic, allowed me the freedom to develop it in my own way, and gave me the benefit of his wise counsel and encouragement. Through the many years I have known him, his scholarly dedication and personal integrity have been a constant source of inspiration to me. I can only hope to emulate his example in the future.

Albert Acena, Michael Brusin, Stuart Cooke, and Barney Woods first introduced me to the life of the mind and made my two years at the College of San Mateo a rich and rewarding experience. Their lives and friendship have influenced my development as a historian. I am also deeply indebted to my parents, whose love and encouragement have sustained me through the years. This book is dedicated to them. Above all, I would like to thank Sofia Galson for her faith in me and her generous financial support over the years. This book would never have been completed without her.

TO STARVE THE ARMY

AT PLEASURE

Congress have left it in the power of the States
to starve the Army at pleasure.

—Major J. Burnett to Jeremiah Wadsworth,
18 March 1780

PROLOGUE:

EIGHTEENTH-CENTURY

AMERICAN POLITICAL

CULTURE

THOMAS MC KEAN was angry. The chief justice of Pennsylvania held in his hand a letter from Nathanael Greene, the recently appointed quartermaster general of the Continental army, requesting McKean to postpone the court appearance of Greene's deputy, Robert Lettis Hooper, Jr. Hooper had long been a thorn in the side of Pennsylvania's radical government. He strongly disapproved of Pennsylvania's Constitution of 1776, refused to swear allegiance to it, and encouraged the inhabitants of Northampton County to follow his example. In addition, although he was unauthorized to do so, Hooper granted safe-conduct passes to those who wished to visit the British then occupying Philadelphia. In October 1777, the state's attorney general, Jonathan Dickinson Sergeant, and a justice of the peace for Northampton County, Jacob Arndt, reported Hooper's activities to the Pennsylvania Supreme Executive Council, which complained in turn to the Continental Board of War. While congressional authorities deliberated, Hooper took matters into his own hands. He first insulted and threatened Arndt and then, at a meeting of the Supreme Court at Reading, severely beat Sergeant. Soon afterward, Hooper promised to do the same to the council members, who, upon hearing of Hooper's threats, promptly issued a writ ordering him to appear before Chief Justice McKean's court.[1]

At this point Hooper asked Nathanael Greene to intercede on his behalf. Writing from Valley Forge in June 1778, Greene pleaded the needs of the army in requesting McKean to delay the case: "As the army is just upon the Wing, and Part of it in all Probability will march through his [Hooper's] district, I could not without great Necessity consent to his being absent as there is no other Person that can give the Necessary Aid upon this occasion." He suggested that Hooper would be willing to enter into a recognizance with ample sureties and appear in court in the near future. And, Greene hastened to assure McKean, he had not "the least desire to interrupt the Course of the Law, or to Screen [Hooper] from its proper operation."[2] Judge McKean responded quickly and minced no words:

> I do not think, Sir, that the absence, sickness, or even death of Mr. Hooper could be attended with such a consequence, that *no other person* could be found who could give the necessary aid upon this occasion; but what attracts my attention most is your observation, that *you* cannot without great necessity *consent* to *his being absent*. As to that, Sir, I shall not ask *your consent*, nor that of any other person in or out of the army, whether my Precept shall be obeyed or not in Pennsylvania. . . .
>
> I should be very sorry to find, that the execution of criminal laws should impede the operations of the army in any instance, but should be more so to find the latter impede the former.

McKean meant what he said. Civil law would take precedence over the demands of the Continental army. Hooper was arrested, brought to trial for libel, sternly lectured, made to apologize, and then released.[3]

McKean's refusal to honor Greene's request came in the midst of the American revolutionary war and less than six months after the Continental army had nearly perished at Valley Forge. Although McKean no longer sympathized with radical politics in Pennsylvania, he was by no means a Tory. In fact, his action was neither extreme nor uncommon—magistrates had refused to cooperate with military officers earlier in the war, and they would do so repeatedly before the victory at Yorktown. Why, then, would a patriot impede the progress of the Continental army? One of the purposes of this book is to answer that question by examining colonial American political culture—a concept defined by Jack P. Greene as "that elusive and shadowy cluster of assumptions, traditions, conventions, values, modes of expression, and habits of thought and belief" that underlay formal political action—and its effect on administering the Continental army.[4] McKean's blast at Greene exemplifies two vitally important aspects of American political culture that frequently hindered the revolutionary war effort: a localist world view and a deep distrust of the military.[5] To understand the origins of the American Revolution and the difficulties revolutionaries had in administering the Continental army it is thus necessary to recapture the values, practices, assumptions, and explicit ideas that shaped eighteenth-century America's political world. Only when we recognize the realities of the imperial relationship, the colonists' localist perspective, and especially the contemporary meaning that Americans attached to the ownership of property, suffrage, elections, representation, liberty, and the exercise of power can we fully understand how the same forces that pushed the colonists into revolution prevented them from effectively fighting the war with Britain.

THE MOST CRUCIAL FACT to keep in mind about colonial America is that most colonists derived their political institutions and culture from Great Britain. Although the dominant theory by the mid-eighteenth century posited that ultimate sovereign power was indivisible, in practice the institutions of imperial control were fragmented at every level of the Anglophone world. In Great Britain the administration of the colonies was divided among the Privy Council, Parliament, secretary of state for the Southern Department, Board of Trade, Treasury Board, Admiralty Board, and Customs Board. Although the colonies were technically under the authority of the king, day-to-day imperial policy was made and enforced elsewhere. Thus no single organ of government maintained centralized or coordinated administration of imperial affairs. As one authority has noted, "Legal questions were divided among the Privy Council, the High Court of Admiralty, and the Exchequer. Matters of trade were shared by the Board of Trade, the Secretary of State, the Treasury, the Privy Council, and the Customs Board. Governmental problems were equally the concern of the Secretary of State, the Board of Trade, and the Privy Council." Before 1763, divided administrative authority, overlapping jurisdictions, and factional politics fueled by patronage combined to make the creation and execution of most imperial policies in the colonies haphazard and ineffectual.[6]

The effect of imperial inefficiency showed itself most perniciously in the appointment of governors to crown colonies. Chiefly as a result of struggles for patronage and metropolitan inattention to provincial outposts, imperial authorities' choices for this high political post were often ill-suited to govern. Lord Cornbury, for example, an avaricious transvestite, became governor of New York in 1701 and served for seven years. Although Cornbury is an extreme case, most royal governors were grasping politicians, untrained in matters of government, whose main interests lay in England, not America. Governorships were bought and sold, and even the best of British officialdom was subject to recall at a moment's notice, a casualty of changes in ministries. As Bernard Bailyn has noted, colonists took away one important lesson from the arbitrary and often venal nature of the imperial patronage system: "The universe of government . . . was essentially a structure composed of two distinct and antagonistic levels, a level of local, internal government that expressed the dominant interests of the local community, and a superior, external authority which was in its nature hostile to local interests."[7]

By the mid-eighteenth century, the structure of colonial politics resembled Britain's imperial administration in its fragmentation of authority and multiple centers of political power. Although no theory of divided sovereignty existed in the eighteenth century, colonial America's political structure was federal in practice. The governor, council, and (except for Pennsylvania) bicameral assembly divided political authority at the provincial level, while county and town governments provided two additional layers to the political structure. And although the politics of every colony except Virginia, South Carolina, and New Hampshire were divisive and factional, political conflict usually occurred between the branches of the provincial government—mostly assemblies against governors—and between competing economic or religious groups—land company rivals or dissenters against church establishments—rather than between local and provincial levels of government.[8]

The relative lack of friction between central and local authorities resulted from a widespread consensus about the limited role of government. Most colonists believed that defense and the maintenance of internal order and religious orthodoxy were the only legitimate objects of provincial government. The small scale of colonial government reflected this belief: "Budgets—and taxes—were low; paid full-time officials few (Massachusetts had six); civil, judicial, and police establishments small, part-time, and unprofessional; and prior to the Seven Years' War, military establishments never large and usually temporary."[9] Thus in an empire where imperial rule was fitful and provincial government limited in scope, power tended to gravitate downward to the county and town levels.

At the local level of the political structure, the justices of the peace, or magistrates as they were commonly called, enforced laws, maintained order, and handled routine litigation. Almost always prominent local leaders from well-to-do, established families, magistrates were unpaid county officials who were usually appointed by the governor. They presided over criminal and civil cases when collectively sitting as a county court or court of quarter sessions and sometimes also exercised administrative duties. In

Pennsylvania, Delaware, and Virginia, for example, magistrates appointed county officials, collected taxes, maintained roadways, and recommended candidates for tavern licenses. Their reputation, wealth, education, family connections, and position on the bench made them men of influence and power within the community. With the addition of town selectmen in New England, who also helped arbitrate minor conflicts and maintain order, magistrates were usually the only government officials with whom most colonists ever came into contact.[10]

The colonies' virtual autonomy from England and their tradition of self-government at the town and county levels reinforced their localist perspective, a frame of mind common to colonists from all walks of life. Localism was both a product of the colonists' English cultural heritage—in New England, especially, opposition to Stuart centralism manifested itself in a deep suspicion of central authority and a desire to preserve a traditional way of life—and a natural result of the fragmentation of power.[11] Regional, religious, and ethnic differences, the isolation of rural life, the distance between seaboard and hinterland, and poor transportation and communication systems reinforced a localist world view. Americans' predilection for localist tendencies made them insular, parochial, and selfish, with all the strengths and weaknesses a narrow vision of the world provides. It contributed to colonial intolerance of strangers, exemplified in New England's system of warning out, and in the mistreatment of religious minorities, such as Anglican persecution of Baptists in Virginia.[12] But it also created the framework within which the colonists launched and nurtured their successful experiment in self-government and defended their liberties against encroachments.

Relations between Great Britain and its colonies, and the inability of the colonies to cooperate with each other, clearly illustrate the dichotomous nature of localism. At the provincial level, it manifested itself in the way that lower houses sought to win constitutional safeguards for local rights and privileges or refused to come to the aid of the neighboring colonies in need of military assistance.[13] At the county and town levels, it emerged during the early phases of the Great War for the Empire, when magistrates refused to impress goods for the British army and urban mobs fought British press gangs in every major port in America.[14] The most striking example of the colonists' inability to cooperate was the fate of the Plan of Union proposed by the Albany Congress of 1754, which every colony refused to ratify for fear that it would diminish provincial freedom and autonomy. Nor did contemporary observers before 1763 believe that an intercolonial union would ever take place. As Massachusetts Governor William Shirley glumly noted, "Different constitutions, situations, circumstances, and tempers, will ever be found an invincible obstacle to their agreement upon any one plan."[15] When colonists spoke of their "country" they still meant their individual provinces, not America.

English electoral practices and deferential political ideas together constituted the second major component of American political culture. In both England and America, voting privileges were tied to property requirements because of the belief that a citizen should have a "stake in society," a permanent economic attachment to the community to ensure he would pursue the public good. More important, economic independence guaranteed political independence because it was thought that anyone economically dependent on an employer or landlord could not vote his own will. The exclusion of slaves, servants, minors, and most tenants and women from the franchise was thus justified by their dependence on the wills of others.[16] Widespread ownership of land fundamentally shaped the political world of colonial America because it allowed most white adult males to meet property requirements for voting. In this respect there were marked differences between America and England. In eighteenth-century England the franchise was restricted to 20 to 25 percent of the adult males; in the colonies between 50 and 80 percent of white adult males were eligible to vote.[17] The connection between property and political rights is crucial to understanding American resistance to British tax measures in the 1760s and 1770s and to impressment during the war. In the eyes of the colonists, the loss of property meant not only impoverishment but also the loss of political rights.

Widespread suffrage should not be equated with democracy. Constitutional and social theory dictated that society was composed of hierarchical ranks in which deference to one's betters was the accepted norm. Eighteenth-century Americans believed in a constitutional system that mirrored the social structure, and they took as their model the British constitution, with its reputed balance among king, Lords, and Commons, as the ideal way to preserve liberty.[18] Just as the British constitutional framework gave the Commons—representing the people—only one place within a tripartite scheme, so American colonial politics balanced its own democratic tendencies with a tradition of deference and elitism.

Deferential political traditions prescribed that the people identify and elect to office the wisest and most virtuous men to administer the commonwealth. But after electing the best men, the role of the populace in the political process diminished greatly. The people were not expected to initiate policy or dictate to their rulers; their only responsibility was to watch for signs of tyranny or unfit representatives.[19]

The experience of Americans in selecting and controlling elected officials reveals the constant tension in colonial American politics between the theory of deference and the practice of democracy. For although deferential social behavior was declining, and in colonies such as New York and Maryland had never been very strong, deferential political behavior remained as strong as ever. At all levels of government, colonists invariably chose men who came from the social and economic elite. It has been estimated that nearly 85 percent of provincial representatives came from the wealthiest 10 percent of society.[20] This trend toward oligarchy was accelerating on the eve of the Revolution, yet it did not cause unrest among the populace nor indicate a powerless electorate. Rather, it underscores the democratic tendencies of colonial representation. The practices of holding frequent elections in most colonies, instructing elected officials in New England, and insisting everywhere on a geographic basis for representation usually reinforced by a residency requirement meant that political control ultimately lay with colonial voters, not elected officials. Deference never meant blind obedience to political leaders, although the degree of confidence varied widely among colonies. The upper classes ruled conditionally: representatives served as long as they did not abuse their authority and as long as the colonists' interests were well served.[21]

But this was not the way most public officials understood their role in American politics. They remained wedded to the elitist/deference model of colonial politics, a belief reinforced by the electoral behavior of colonial voters. Most representatives and magistrates took their responsibilities seriously and responded to constituents' petitions out of desire to maintain their honor, do well by their community, and remain in office. But they did not think of consulting voters. Theirs was a paternalistic ethos that expected citizens to defer to their wisdom, while they reciprocated by performing their duties as "Guardians of the people."[22] It would take the Stamp Act crisis for colonial spokesmen to articulate in theory what Americans had long known from experience: that representation should be direct and actual and that, as Bernard Bailyn has noted, "the people were present through their representatives, and were themselves, step by step and point by point, acting in the conduct of public affairs."[23] And it would take the revolutionary war to make clear to public officials that the balance between deference and democracy had shifted in ways they only dimly understood or approved.

Along with a localist world view and an elitist model of politics, a strand of British political thought of relatively minor significance in England also strongly influenced American political culture. Commonwealth or Real Whig ideology, as it was called, originated during the English Civil War and Commonwealth period in the works of seventeenth-century libertarians such as James Harrington, John Milton, and Algernon Sidney. In the eighteenth century, Commonwealth ideology was transmitted through the writings of John Trenchard, Thomas Gordon, Thomas Hollis, Richard

Price, and James Burgh, who inveighed against the growing corruption of English society and the machinations of three generations of "prime ministers"—from Sir Robert Walpole through the duke of Newcastle to Lord Bute.[24]

Real Whig ideology offered its adherents a critical assessment of English society and politics, and it placed contemporary events within a comprehensive historical framework stretching back through the English past to classical antiquity. The premise of all Commonwealth ideology and the driving mechanism of its historical analysis was a vision of the uncontrollable nature of power and its propensity to destroy liberty. Throughout history, Real Whig writers charged, political rulers had been the natural enemies of liberty, using every means available, especially standing armies, to extinguish their subjects' freedom. They pointed to the example of designing kings who subverted the ancient Gothic constitution and, more recently, the downfall of liberty in Venice, Sweden, and Denmark. As opposition writers Trenchard and Gordon noted in *Cato's Letters*: "All Parts of *Europe* which are enslaved have been enslaved by Armies; and it is absolutely impossible, that any Nation which keeps them amongst themselves can long preserve their Liberties."[25] Englishmen had been spared this fate, it was widely believed, only because of the excellence of their nation's mixed and balanced constitution.

The fear of a professional standing army played a central role in Commonwealth ideology. English antimilitary sentiment was a legacy of two experiences: the New Model Army's refusal to disband in 1647–48 and the rule by the major-generals and new militia during Cromwell's Protectorate. During the Restoration, Whig opposition politicians kept antiarmy attitudes at a fever pitch by identifying Charles II's military policies with Catholicism, French influence, and arbitrary power. Although the Bill of Rights and Mutiny Act of 1689 placed the ultimate authority for the peacetime army in Parliament, acknowledged the right of Protestant citizens to bear arms, and prohibited the billeting of troops on private citizens, Real Whig writers continued to warn of the dangers to liberty of a standing army. In their view, professional soldiers were a source of social oppression because they were riotous, expensive, and morally corrupt. More significantly, Real Whigs viewed the very existence of a professional army as evidence of a corrupted citizenry and an unbalanced constitution. The unwillingness of citizens to bear arms—and thus the need to rely on a standing army—was a sure sign that the body politic was ill, and the crown's control of the army tilted the constitution dangerously toward despotism. The title of one opposition pamphlet succinctly summed up Real Whigs' fear of the military: *An Argument Showing that a Standing*

Army is Inconsistent with a Free Government and Absolutely Destructive to the Constitution of the English Monarchy. Only a vital militia could guarantee the preservation of liberty and constitutional stability.[26]

Opposition writers drew on this body of thought during the reign of the Hanoverians, when they believed they detected a ministerial conspiracy to overthrow the constitution. Real Whigs denounced the management of Parliament through bribery, patronage, and the appointment of "placemen," warned that a permanent standing army was the instrument monarchs used to crush their subjects' liberties, and railed against debt and speculation that sapped the virtue and vigilance of the citizenry. Opposition writers refused to believe that the maintenance of the empire necessitated a large bureaucracy, an increased national debt, and a strong military force. Instead, they looked backward nostalgically to the Commonwealth period, when, they believed, republican virtue and simplicity thrived, and to the Glorious Revolution, when liberty had triumphed.

Although opposition writers devoted much effort to pointing out corruption and the dangers it presented to liberty, they also offered solutions to the problems they diagnosed. To prevent the constitution from becoming unbalanced, power had to be checked and limited. Because the threat to liberty came from ministerial corruption of the House of Commons, Real Whigs advocated the exclusion of placemen from the Commons, annual parliaments, a reduction in the national debt, and the right of constituents to instruct their representatives. Above all, opposition writers urged Englishmen to watch their rulers constantly in order to ensure the protection of liberty. Inspired by classical republican ideals, Real Whigs called for a virtuous citizenry that disdained luxury, a propertied citizenry that shunned debt and speculation, and an armed citizenry enrolled in a county militia.

Real Whig writings proved extremely popular among Americans. Colonial newspaper editors frequently reprinted the works of opposition writers, especially Trenchard and Gordon's *The Independent Whig* and *Cato's Letters*. When defending free speech, religious toleration, and freedom of the press, political pamphleteers, provincial representatives, and leaders of political factions often cited and quoted from this body of writing. Commonwealth ideology made particular sense to the colonists because they witnessed the chronic instability of much of eighteenth-century provincial politics, instability caused by maladroit governors with substantial formal powers and insufficient patronage to placate opposition politicians. The effect of Real Whig ideology on most of the American people was immense and growing. As Bailyn has written, "For it was the opposition press, as much as any single influence, that shaped the political awareness of eighteenth-century Americans; it was the opposition version of politics, past and present, that became the ordinary presumption of informed Americans."[27]

When a series of British ministries began to rationalize imperial administration—a process that required taxing the colonists to pay for their own defense and enforcing long-neglected trade regulations—they ran headlong into an American political culture that diverged significantly from the British. What began with the passage of the Stamp Act in March 1765 as a question of taxation and the nature of representation widened in the late 1760s and early 1770s to a debate about sovereignty. Throughout this period, colonial spokesmen invoked the colonial practice of actual representation, the rights of Englishmen, and a de facto federal political structure in an effort to resist British measures and justify longstanding colonial practices to a disbelieving and uncomprehending British nation. Colonial fears of a ministerial plot against liberty, awakened by the Stamp Act, intensified with each new British effort to enforce trade regulations, raise revenue, or protect royal authority with professional soldiers.[28]

The final blow—the passage of the Coercive Acts in 1774—could not have been designed more perfectly by Parliament to threaten everything colonists held dear in their political culture. There is no question that the colonists were a freedom-loving people, but they did not make a revolution for liberty in the abstract. Liberty was tied to property, which in turn conferred upon its owner a host of political rights. By attacking Americans' liberty, the Coercive Acts struck at tangible economic interests and traditional political practices embedded in the fabric of colonial life for more than a century and a half. The Boston Port Act assailed colonial economic interests by closing down the city's harbor and prohibiting all imports except for fuel and food for the inhabitants. The Administration of Justice Act, or "Murder Act" as George Washington called it, interfered with local administration of justice by allowing the governor of Massachusetts to remove British officials held for trial in capital crimes to another colony or even to England if he thought a fair trial impossible. The Quartering Act stimulated fears of standing armies by allowing the same governor to requisition from local officials uninhabited buildings for the king's troops. The Massachusetts Government Act directly threatened the colonial legal and political structure by unilaterally altering the provincial charter of 1691, eliminating the elective method of jury selection, and radically restricting the frequency and functions of town meetings—the heart of local government in New England. Finally, the Quebec Act, although not framed in response to the Boston Tea Party, exacerbated economic, political, and religious tensions by depriving the colonists of much western land, introducing a feudal system of land tenure, establishing a government without a representative assembly, failing to provide for jury trials in civil cases, and providing for the free exercise of the Catholic religion in Canada. The passage of the Coercive Acts with their threat to economic prosperity, local autonomy, the rights of Englishmen, and the primacy of Protestantism in the colonies finally convinced a majority of Americans that their fears of a ministerial plot were accurate: Britain intended to enslave them.[29]

The American Revolution was more than a struggle to preserve a traditional way of life, to protect property, and to ensure liberty, although these ideals continued to animate colonists throughout the War for Independence. Just as important, as Gordon S. Wood has perceptively observed, Americans' embrace of republicanism "added a moral dimension, a utopian depth, to the political separation from England—a depth that involved the very character of their society."[30] American republicanism had its origins in Commonwealth ideology, which took as its ideal polity the supposedly simple, virtuous republics of classical antiquity and fifteenth-century Italian city-states. In discussing republics, Commonwealthmen constantly stressed two major themes. Republics were inherently unstable and fragile because they rested totally on the spirit and character of the people. And in order to preserve liberty, republics demanded the practice of civic humanism, which meant an active, public-spirited citizenry willing to live a life of frugality and to sacrifice private interests to the public weal. Real Whigs, however, did not focus their attention on a republic's era of glory when liberty flourished, but rather emphasized the later stages of a republic, when it had been enveloped by vice, luxury, and corruption. Among these dangers to republics that Real Whigs identified, corruption occupied a particularly prominent place. In the eighteenth century, corruption meant fraud, bribery, and embezzlement just as it does today. But in addition, it connoted depravity of manners and a commonwealth's declension. Often likened to a cancer eating away at the vitals of the body politic, corruption strongly suggested "the degeneration of a proper government into a more illiberal, less stable form."[31] By stressing the reasons for a republic's decline, Real Whig writers hoped to alert readers to the signs that liberty was in danger.

When American revolutionaries came to construct their republican governments, they demonstrated that they understood these precepts. They knew that written constitutions and the avowed dedication to the principle of popular sovereignty ultimately rested on the virtue of the American people. Cut off from England, Americans embraced republicanism and then immediately began to wonder whether they were sufficiently virtuous and self-sacrificing to maintain a republic. As John Adams confessed, "Virtue and Simplicity of Manners are indispensably necessary in a Republic among all orders and Degrees of men. But there is so much Rascallity, so much Venality and Corruption, so much Avarice and Ambition such a Rage for Profit and Commerce among all Ranks and Degrees of Men even in America, that I sometimes doubt whether there is public Virtue enough to support a Republic."[32] Corruption, private vices, and excessive wealth and luxury became matters of deep public concern because they indicated that the body politic was fundamentally unsound. If Americans were not virtuous, the experiment in republican government would inevitably fail, and liberty would be lost.

THUS WITH THE OUTBREAK of hostilities at Lexington and Concord, the acts of the British Parliament as interpreted through the lens of American practices and Commonwealth ideology had propelled the colonists into war against the strongest imperial power in the world. But the very forces that hurled the colonists into revolution prevented them from waging war effectively. The habits of autonomy and adherence to a localist perspective made colonists suspicious of encroachments by British officials but also made them stubbornly independent of directives from the Continental Congress, the body that had primary responsibility for administering the war. Deferential political behavior gave stability to an often chaotic world, but it also created bonds between magistrates and constituents that ultimately interfered with attempts by Continental leaders and army officers to prosecute the war. Belief in Commonwealth ideology provided a theory of history and politics that convinced most colonists that British imperial measures aimed at enslaving them, but those same tendencies—to be wary of power and to resort to conspiratorial explanations—spilled over into a deep suspicion of the army and of anyone in authority.

Given this political culture, American victory at Yorktown seems a particularly remarkable achievement. Time and time again, as this study will demonstrate, individual citizens, local magistrates, state officials, and members of the Continental Congress refused to accept that a well-equipped army was necessary to win the military victory that would guarantee American independence; that the prosecution of a war required spending money for supplies and manpower; and that long-held and cherished principles of divided political power, local autonomy, civil control over the military, and fear of power would have to give way if Americans were to win the war and preserve liberty. The conflict between the goals of the Revolution—the preservation of property, liberty, and independence—and the means by which those goals would be realized—a standing army, confiscation of property, and centralized political power—is one of the striking ironies of the period. That Americans so often seemed willing to lose the war rather than sacrifice their principles is great testimony to the strength of ideas in history and to the strength of that American political culture as it had evolved over 150 years of settlement. That those ideas and practices made the war extremely difficult to win and that those difficulties led some revolutionaries to alter their ideas about power are two of the principal themes of this book.

CHAPTER 1

WAR ADMINISTRATION

1775 – 1776

We are lost in the extensiveness of our Field of Business. We have a Continental Treasury to establish, a Paymaster to choose, and a Committee of Correspondence, or Safety, or Accounts, or something, I know not what that has confounded us all Day.
    —John Adams to James Warren, 24 July 1775

Much of our time is employed in raising men, making Cannon, muskets, and merely finding out ways and means of supplying our Troops with Cloathes, provisions, and ammunition. We appear to have everything we want. We resolve to raise regiments, resolve to make Cannon, resolve to make and import muskets, powder and cloathing, but it is a melancholly fact that near half of our men, Cannon, muskets, powder, cloathes, etc., is to be found nowhere but on paper.
    —Joseph Hewes to James Iredell, 17 May 1776

DURING THE FIRST twenty months of the revolutionary war, the Continental army suffered a nearly devastating series of defeats. The worst, no doubt, was America's failure to make Canada the fourteenth state. In a campaign that stretched from September 1775 to June 1776, close to five thousand revolutionaries died in battle or from starvation and disease. In August 1776, two months after the disillusioned and defeated survivors of the Canadian expedition straggled back to Crown Point, the British drove the Continental army from Long Island, and in October they humiliated it at Kip's Bay and White Plains. The surrender of Fort Washington, a month later, with its three thousand men and enormous storehouse of supplies, was a staggering loss. Before the victories at Trenton and Princeton in December 1776, Washington confided to his brother, John Augustine Washington, that if recruits were not found for the army quickly, "*I think the game is pretty near up.*"[1]

The demoralizing succession of losses suffered by the Continental army can be traced to three interrelated factors: a lack of discipline, training, and manpower; a paucity of able officers at all levels of command; and Congress's failure to provide sufficient food, clothing, and medical care for its troops.[2] This last factor—the shortcomings of congressional war administration—is the focus of this and succeeding chapters. The first stage of congressional war administration extended from the opening of hostilities at Lexington Green in April 1775 to the series of defeats on Long Island and the retreat across New Jersey in late 1776. A lack of planning and a chain of ad hoc reactions to military necessity were its most salient characteristics. The result was an unsystematic, ill-managed administrative system that divided responsibility for maintaining the army among congressional committees, state authorities, military commanders, staff officers, and civilians. Congress's inadequate administration of logistical operations stood in stark contrast to the more successfully organized supply and medical system of the British army; a comparison of the two systems strikingly highlights the glaring weaknesses of the Continental Congress.

ALTHOUGH RECENT HISTORIANS have emphasized the shortcomings of British administration during the revolutionary war, the British direction of its war effort was the epitome of efficiency and purpose when compared to the Continental Congress's administration of American forces, particularly logistical operations. This difference was especially true during the first years of the war. Much of Britain's administrative superiority stemmed from procedures and departments already in place as a result of three-quarters of a century of war with its imperial rival, France. Owing to this experience, British war administration was distinguished by clear lines of authority and an established command structure.

In the British scheme, the cabinet made policy, the secretaries of state oversaw it, and executive departments carried it out. Four main departments handled military affairs: the War Office, which designed and ordered army essentials such as uniforms, camp equipment, and medical supplies; the Treasury Department, which negotiated provision contracts with London firms and purchased clothing, blankets, and camp equipment; the Board of Ordnance, which supplied the army with arms and ammunition; and the Navy Board, a division of the Admiralty, responsible for supplying maritime troop transport and after 1779 for shipping food and forage. Beneath these executive departments another level of bureaucracy ministered directly to the army: the Quartermaster Department, the Commissary Department, the Medical Department, the Barrackmaster Department, and the Engineer Department.[3]

In contrast, the colonists began the war with no administrative departments and almost no experience in providing logistical support to an army. Though the colonists had joined in Britain's wars against the French, they were only peripherally involved, if at all, in the planning and organization of military administrative services. Of the sixty-five congressmen in attendance at Philadelphia during the first two years of the war, only five had served with the British in military operations.[4] Of those five, only Roger Sherman, who had been appointed commissary for the Connecticut troops at Albany in 1759, had an intimate knowledge of supply matters. For the most part, the only direct contact the colonists had with logistical operations was as subcontractors to colonial governments or London merchants. Only Francis Lewis, the delegate from New York, who had been a clothing contractor to the British at Oswego in 1756, possessed this experience. Nor had any congressmen served with the British in a medical capacity. Only two, New Hampshire's Josiah Bartlett and Connecticut's Oliver Wolcott, had any training as physicians, and neither was appointed to the Medical Committee. That committee did not boast a knowledgeable physician until Benjamin Rush's appointment in August 1776.[5]

Congressmen who did have experience in military matters generally offered advice of limited usefulness. Roger Sherman's suggestion that the army rely on sutlers to provide clothing, as had been done during the Great War for the Empire, is indicative of the restricted understanding most colonists derived from association with British military actions. Because those members with previous military experience had mostly observed and not planned or organized large-scale military operations, Congress could not fall back on knowledge gained from earlier military conflicts. This fact was apparent to John Adams, who, three months after Lexington, ruefully expressed his thoughts about administering a revolutionary war: "It is a vast and complicated System of Business which We have gone through," he wrote James Warren, "and We were all of us, unexperienced in it."[6] Most of his fellow delegates would probably have agreed.

Just as congressional experience was a poor guide to administering a revolutionary army, so, too, the colonists' intellectual heritage provided few clues to waging war. Indeed, the most determinative strand of colonial thought, Real Whig ideology—rooted as it was in a conspiracy mentality and a fear of excessive power—only made it more difficult for Congress to administer the war. Maxims derived from that intellectual heritage, which in another context provided sure guidance to protecting the colonists' liberties, were inappropriate to managing the business of a fighting army. For example, when Congress resolved to allow General Washington to appoint his own quartermaster general, commissary of musters, and com-missary of artillery, John Adams thought it "against every proper Rule and Principle." Fearful of concentrating too much power in the hands of a single individual, Adams denounced the action because, "as these officers are Checks upon the General, and he a Check upon them: There ought not to be too much Connection between them. They ought not to be under any dependance upon him or so great obligations of Gratitude as th[o]se of a Creature to the Creator."[7] Adams's strictures were, no doubt, fueled by his experience with Massachusetts Governor Thomas Hutchinson's practice of filling the colony's top offices with friends and relatives. But from a strictly military point of view, Adams's mistrust was groundless.

An examination of the specific duties of the quartermaster general, by far the most important and powerful officer Washington was permitted to appoint, bears out this conclusion. As the commander in chief's right-hand man and confidant, the quartermaster general's relationship to his superior rested in large part on trust and cooperation, not suspicion and obstruction. Moreover, the major part of the quartermaster general's duties consisted of important but routine activities: gathering informa-tion, assisting the commanding general in planning his marches, laying out the camp, and assigning quarters. In addition, he and his assistants were responsible for procuring camp equipment and transporting the troops and supplies over land and water.[8] None of these functions re-quired the quartermaster general to "check" the commander in chief or vice versa. Adams's suspicions reveal that Commonwealth ideology could misguide or distort congressmen's administrative decisions. They also re-veal Adams's unfamiliarity with the duties and relationships governing various army positions. Indeed, on the very day Adams denounced the appointments, he wrote his correspondents requesting "to know exactly the Duties, and necessary attributes" of all staff officers, aides-de-camp, and even brigade majors.[9] Adams's lack of knowledge about the details of war administration was symptomatic of congressional inexperience. Like Adams, Congress would have to learn how to wage war while fighting it.

Congress's uncertainty over the duration and magnitude of the conflict with Great Britain contributed to the unsystematic, sporadic nature of providing supplies and medical services to the army. Moderate delegates hoped that petitions and conciliatory measures would bring the disagreement with the mother country to a swift conclusion. More militant members pushed for strong defensive military preparations that would persuade the ministry to redress fully the colonists' grievances. Neither group foresaw a protracted conflict; both hoped for its speedy resolution.[10] These hopes partly account for Congress's reliance on whatever means were available to supply the army, whether congressional committees, civilians, military commanders, or state authorities, and they also explain Congress's failure to organize the staff departments properly.

Yet Congress's lack of experience and its expectation that the conflict would be short did not deter it from waging war. Suddenly faced with unexpected demands and concrete needs, Congress spiritedly set out to repulse the British. Its first priority was the importation and manufacture of arms and ammunition. Its single-minded attitude toward acquiring munitions was ably summarized by Massachusetts Congressman Robert Treat Paine, who declared that "Salt petre, Sulphur, lead, cannon, muskets, like our dayly bread should never be out of our attention." Precipitating Congress's great concern and spurring it to action was the extreme gunpowder shortage facing Washington's army at Cambridge in August 1775. Returns revealed less than one-half pound per man. To end the shortage, Congress engaged in an all-out effort to secure, in the words of Samuel Adams, the "unum necessarium."[11]

Congressional efforts to furnish the army with arms and ammunition were notably disorganized. Congress's actions were not confused or purposely experimental but simply reactions to the needs of the moment. Thus no single method characterized the procurement of munitions. Congress entered into contracts with private merchants to procure munitions overseas; it delegated to the Secret Committee of Trade power to contract with merchants to import gunpowder, and it authorized state governments to exchange nonessential commodities for importations of arms.[12]

Supplementing foreign procurement was an unsystematic but ambitious program of domestic gunpowder production. Congress appointed a Cannon Committee, a committee to acquire muskets and promote the manufacture of firearms in America, and a Saltpeter Committee that published various techniques of manufacturing saltpeter in the newspapers.[13] The latter committee also called on state authorities to persuade families to make saltpeter at home. To encourage home production, Congress recommended that the states offer a bounty of half a dollar for each pound of gunpowder produced. Congress capped its domestic program of securing ammunition by requesting state officials to erect public powder mills. This energetic program was too haphazard to yield more than meager results: overly complicated instructions for making saltpeter and small-scale, unsustained efforts by state legislatures made foreign importations the mainstay of America's supply of gunpowder throughout the war.[14]

A similar lack of a unified, centrally controlled supply system characterized Congress's efforts to provide food, camp equipment, clothing, and medical supplies to the army. As in munitions procurement, congressional committees played a large role. Some, like the Secret Committee of Trade, the Board of War and Ordnance, and the Medical Committee, would continue to function for years. The Secret Committee contracted abroad for clothing, blankets, and medical supplies, as well as arms. The Board of War also contracted for clothing, medicines, and military stores and in addition was ordered on occasion to secure shoes and stockings from state authorities. The Medical Committee, originally appointed to supply the army with medicines, accomplished its task by purchasing them both from state officials and from Philadelphia's largest pharmaceutical firm.[15]

Congress also created temporary committees for specific supply tasks. These committees, which purchased a variety of goods including shoes, stockings, caps, and food, used three basic methods of procurement: they purchased supplies directly in the open market; they asked state legislatures for assistance; and they entered into contracts with individuals to furnish supplies to the army. These committees were formed as specific needs arose. Did the soldiers of General Philip Schuyler's Northern Army lack shoes? Congress formed a committee. Did the battalion raised in Pennsylvania require rations? Congress formed another committee. As soon as their tasks were completed, the committees were dissolved.[16]

Congress's employment of civilian suppliers who were neither members of Congress nor military personnel revealed the same tendency to react to crises rather than to forecast the army's needs. Referred to as "commissary" or "continental commissary" but not members of the Quartermaster Department or Commissary Department, men such as James Mease, Thomas Lowrey, and Ephraim Blaine acted under direct congressional authority to purchase every sort of supplies for the troops. Troubleshooters, in a manner of speaking, these men were given specific instructions to alleviate shortages and meet the basic needs of the troops. When the First Virginia battalion marched to join General Schuyler's army in New York in the fall of 1776, Congress ordered Mease to provide clothing and other necessities. Similarly, Blaine was called upon to purchase five thousand blankets for the soldiers stationed in Williamsburg, Virginia, and to furnish provisions to the troops gathered in Cumberland County, Pennsylvania.[17]

Congress used several other methods to supply the army. It "desired" commanding generals, such as Schuyler and Richard Montgomery, to purchase clothing and tent material for the soldiers and awarded a contract to Carpenter Wharton to supply food to a Pennsylvania battalion at 7d. per ration. It even published lists detailing the supply needs of the army in Canada and encouraged sutlers to attend the army. Nor was Congress loath to accept attractive supply contracts when opportunity knocked. Thus it approved a contract for camp kettles that had been solicited by one Thomas Bates, an enterprising blacksmith.[18]

Not surprisingly, in light of American political culture with its emphasis on localism and divided power, the states were Congress's primary agents of supply. For the first two years of the war, Congress called upon state governors, legislatures, and committees of safety to provide Washington's and Schuyler's armies with wood, hay, guns, flints, ammunition, medicine chests, rations, blankets, hats, shirts, shoes, tents, and wagons. It also recommended that state legislatures screen and examine medical officers destined for army service. Congress expected state governors to furnish military commanders with money, and it instructed congressional committees to consult with state authorities on supply matters. In addition, Congress often called upon state governments to perform tasks that in the British army would have been handled by the staff departments. For example, it instructed the Convention of New York, not the Quartermaster Department, to take possession of "the King's Stores in New York" and forward them to the Northern Army. Similarly, Congress directed state authorities, not the commissary general, to appoint commissaries to provision the new recruits marching to join Washington's army just before the battles of Trenton and Princeton.[19]

The Quartermaster and Commissary departments slowly supplanted other means of supplying the army until by 1779 they had become the major source of congressional expenditures.[20] But in the first stage of congressional war administration, Congress placed no special emphasis on the staff departments; it used them simply as one among many ways to supply the troops. Staff officers received the same directives to supply the army as congressional committees, military commanders, and state officials.[21] At times, instructions were fairly specific, as when the deputy commissary was ordered to provide "provision for 1,000 men for one month, and keep that quantity in stock."[22] But such explicit instructions were infrequent. Congress's failure to rely on the staff departments as its prime logistical agents again exemplifies its hopes for a quick conclusion to hostilities and its inexperience in military matters.

The inadequacy of Congress's knowledge of logistical operations was nowhere better illustrated than in its rudimentary organization of the staff departments. Of the three major staff departments, only the Hospital Department was provided with some semblance of organization and direction. In contrast, the most striking characteristic of the Quartermaster and Commissary departments was the lack of any structural organization. Aside from designating one quartermaster general and a deputy on 16 June 1775, Congress made no provision for that department. Unacquainted with persons qualified to direct supply matters, it delegated the nomination to General Washington, who on 14 August appointed the thirty-one-year-old aristocratic Pennsylvanian, Thomas Mifflin. The Commissariat was conceived in the same perfunctory fashion. On the same day the Quartermaster Department was established, Congress created the position of commissary general of stores and provisions, filling it two days later with Joseph Trumbull, the eldest son of Connecticut's governor. To provision the troops in the Northern Department, Congress appointed General Schuyler's nephew, Walter Livingston.[23] This, then, was Congress's initial structure for the Quartermaster and Commissary departments: three department heads and one deputy to administer two armies with more than twenty thousand men. Except for intervening to settle conflicts or answer queries, Congress made no other structural provision for either department until they underwent their first reorganization in 1777.

Congress placed the organization of the Hospital Department on a sounder basis than either the Quartermaster or Commissary departments, on the advice of Dr. Benjamin Church, who had been sent by Massachusetts to confer on medical matters.[24] Church and the Medical Committee provided the element that was missing from the other staff departments: definition of the duties of the respective personnel, division of labor, and clear lines of authority. On 27 July 1775, Congress appointed Dr. Church director-general and chief physician of the Hospital Department. He was instructed to purchase and distribute "medicines, Bedding and all other necessaries, to . . . superintend the whole," and to report to and receive orders from the commander in chief. Additionally, he was authorized to appoint four surgeons and the apothecary. These officials were directed to visit and attend the sick. The surgeons, in turn, appointed the mates, who "were to obey the orders of the physicians, surgeons, and apothecaries." Congress also provided for nurses, a matron to supervise them, two storekeepers "to receive and deliver the bedding and other necessaries," and one clerk to keep accounts for the director-general and the storekeepers. The nurses, storekeepers, and clerk were to be appointed by the director-general. Six weeks after Church's appointment on 14 September, Congress chose Dr. Samuel Stringer as director of the hospital and chief physician of the army in the Northern Department to tend to General Schuyler's smaller army (see Figure 1).[25] On paper, at least, the Hospital Department was ready to meet the needs of the army.

FIGURE I.I. *Hospital Department, 1775*

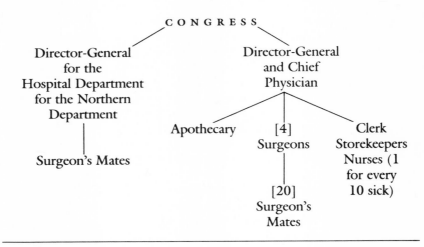

Source: *JCC*, 2:211, 249.

Still the Hospital Department was almost immediately wracked by serious organizational difficulties. The major flaw in its organization was
Congress's omission of any mention of the regimental surgeons in the
Hospital Bill of July 1775.[26] The failure to subordinate the regimental
surgeons to the director-general quickly set Church and his successor,
Dr. John Morgan, at loggerheads with their nominal subordinates. Much
to Church's dismay, the regimental surgeons had turned their infirmaries
into autonomous hospitals. They stubbornly maintained their independence, caring for wounded soldiers who were fearful of being sent far from
the care of family and friends to the General Hospital. Though claiming
they were not subject to the director-general's authority, they loudly insisted he provide them with the General Hospital's medical stores. Church
objected to their independent status. It was clear to him that most of the
regimental surgeons were inexperienced and lacked the necessary medical
training to care properly for the sick. Moreover, the failure to control the
regimental surgeons' freedom to draw on the General Hospital resulted in
their squandering critically short medical supplies.[27]

Church attempted to correct this state of affairs by ordering the regimental surgeons to send their sick to the General Hospital, to provide
better care, and to cut back on the excessive use of medical supplies. In
addition, he denied the regimental surgeons free access to the General

Hospital's stores. This was a serious blow to the regimental surgeons' pretensions of independence, and they charged the director-general with failing to issue medical supplies needed for the sick. Church, in response, complained to the commander in chief that the regimental surgeons spent too much money. Washington, observing that there was "either an unpardonable Abuse on one side, or inexcusable neglect on the other," immediately convened a special court of inquiry. The court met on 9 September 1775 and cleared Church of all charges. In its summation, the court noted that the director-general had never failed to supply medicines if they were available and pointed out that the regimental surgeons should apply to the commissary general, not the director-general, for supplies.[28] Before the court's decision could have any salutary effect, Church was discovered in treasonable correspondence with the British and dismissed. Congress appointed Dr. John Morgan in his place.[29]

Morgan experienced the same problems with the regimental surgeons. They refused to submit to the regulations he formulated for administering the department, balked at submitting to examination, continued to demand supplies from the General Hospital, and noisily complained of his cruelty and negligence when he refused their demands. As with Church, the question of supplies became dominant. Had Congress followed the lead of the British Medical Department, the entire problem might have been avoided. The British withheld a small portion of every soldier's pay and turned it over to the regimental surgeons to purchase medical supplies. In addition, the government provided each regiment with a medicine chest. Unable and unwilling to supply the regimental surgeons, Morgan laid the problem at Congress's door. "They all look to me for supplies of everything they want," Morgan wrote Samuel Adams in July 1776. "I have no authority for that purpose. It is contrary to my judgement to supply them with all they want. . . . I call for orders."[30]

The resolves Congress passed on 17 July 1776 left the basic conflict unsettled. On the issue of the regimental surgeons' independent status, Congress seemed to favor the director-general by ordering the surgeons to make returns to him and by permitting him to inspect and make inquiries about the regimental medicine chests. But on the question of medical supplies, Congress inexplicably ruled "that no regimental surgeon be allowed to draw upon the hospital of his department, for any stores except medicines and instruments." This ruling, in effect, ratified the status quo by allowing the regimental surgeons to continue to draw medical supplies from the General Hospital. Thus the struggle for medical supplies and the charges and countercharges continued. Only after General Washington interceded in late September 1776 did Congress explicitly affirm "that all regimental surgeons and mates, as well as those of the hospitals, be subject to the directions and controul of the directors in the several departments." Nevertheless, as the most able student of the subject, Whitfield J. Bell, Jr., notes, Congress's subordination of the regimental surgeons was "too weak and too late to be effective."[31]

Two features in this conflict stand out. The first is the inordinate length of time it took Congress to respond to the pleas of the directors-general. Church had complained as early as August 1775, and yet Congress did not finally rule on the matter until July 1776, nearly one year later. The second is Congress's ineffectiveness in handling the problem. It is evident from the congressional resolve of 17 July 1776 that committee members did not understand the source of the problem; otherwise, they would never have ordered Director-General Morgan to continue to supply the regimental surgeons. The combination of congressional slowness and ineptitude weakened the director-general's authority and undermined the efficiency of the Hospital Department.

Congress soon became aware of additional problems in the staff departments, which were also the result of initial organizational weakness. Because of Congress's failure to instruct its staff officers regularly and formally, they had a very incomplete notion of what their duties were. Dr. Morgan appealed for guidance regarding his specific responsibilities and "to ascertain a little more accurately the Nature and Extent of [his] commission." Other staff officers also earnestly requested Congress's advice: What officers were entitled to forage and in what instances? Was a deputy commissary general allowed a clerk? How much was he to be paid?[32] Though of minor consequence, these and other issues were time-consuming for congressmen and inevitably delayed the smooth flow of supplies to the army. Queries of this sort also reveal that staff officers, like the congressmen who instructed them, were more at home in the countinghouse and courtroom than in the army.

Congress also neglected to provide an adequate level of manpower for the staff departments to function properly. The most obvious example was its failure to designate assistants and other personnel in the Quartermaster, Commissary, and Hospital departments. Mifflin and Trumbull overcame this problem by hiring their own employees, with or without congressional authorization, and few complaints about the lack of deputies emanated from their departments.[33] But from the beginning of the war, top-ranking medical officials vigorously complained of the shortage of Hospital Department personnel. Congress remedied the problem by authorizing an increase in the number of surgeons, proportional to increases in the size of the army. In regard to unskilled personnel, Congress scrapped its policy of limiting the number of workers the director-general could employ and instead allowed him discretion to appoint as many "store keepers, stewards, managers, and nurses, as are necessary for the good of the service."[34] In effect, Congress merely conferred on the director-general the power that the quartermaster and the commissary general had informally assumed.

Congress aggravated these administrative slips by making little effort to supervise the staff departments. Problems went unattended until they were brought to Congress's attention. Only in emergencies, such as the debacle in Canada in 1775, the retreat from Long Island in 1776, and the army's encampment at Valley Forge in the winter of 1777–78, did Congress rouse itself to send committees to confer with military officials, and then usually too late.[35] Judging from the early organization and administration of the staff departments, one may infer that Congress expected them to run themselves.

The difficulties afflicting the staff departments did not stem only from flaws in their basic organizational structure. Some were a product of Congress's preference for keeping overall direction of the war within its own grasp. Robert Morris pinpointed the problem when he observed that when it came to administration, Congress meant well, but "the Fact is they have too many objects and retain too much executive business in their own hands." In truth, Congress confronted a formidable number of important tasks. In February 1776 it was managing more than a dozen problems, including regulating coin and currency matters, supervising the transition from colonial to state governments, mobilizing troops for Canada, encouraging home manufactures, and raising funds. Congress created standing committees to handle many of these tasks but then overwhelmed committee members by assigning too much work for them to operate effectively. For example, although congressmen had high hopes for the Board of War and Ordnance when they created it in June 1776, the very breadth of the board's mandate doomed it to failure. Congress ordered it to keep an accurate register of Continental officers; to keep exact accounts of all artillery, arms, ammunition, and warlike stores; to be a clearinghouse for all correspondence between Congress, the states, and the army; to superintend the raising, filling out, and dispatching of land forces; to oversee the prisoners of war; and to act as the depository for all letters sent to Congress. Characteristically, Congress assigned the board additional tasks as the needs of the army became known. In this fashion the Board of War also became deeply involved in supplying the army with clothing and blankets.[36]

The tiresome nature of committee work is well illustrated by John Adams's description of his stint as chairman of the Board of War: "The duties of this board kept me in continual employment, not to say drudgery, from the 12th of June, 1776, till the 11th of November, 1777, when I left

Congress forever. Not only my mornings and evenings were filled up with the crowd of business before the board, but a great part of my time in Congress was engaged in making, explaining, and justifying our reports and proceedings."[37] The reluctance of many congressmen to continue in office is thus not surprising. A recent investigation into delegates' patterns of attendance revealed that "by the end of 1776 more than half of those who had attended Congress prior to the Declaration of Independence had left its chambers for good." Thus one result of Congress's decision to retain control of war administration and overload its members with work was a high turnover rate of congressmen. In addition, the army suffered from Congress's chronic delays in getting to pressing military matters. Both factors invariably disrupted the continuity of congressional policy making and interfered with the efficient administration of the army.[38]

Congress's disposition to waste time contributed to delays in administration. As early as July 1775, Virginia's Benjamin Harrison blamed the delay in printing money on the example of the national legislature: "Without, an Imitation of the Congress in its Slowness has become fashionable." Within, delegates complained, ridiculed, and chafed at their colleagues' long and repetitive speeches, their procedural wrangling and chicanery, and their failure to distinguish between trivial and important issues. "We could only harrangue against the misapplication of time and harrangues consumed more time," fumed John Adams in 1776. Members of Congress ascribed their untidy proceedings to everything from a lack of leadership to the wiles of lawyers and the need to compromise a wide diversity of interests and views.[39] But whatever the cause, the effect of Congress's dilatory behavior was usually injurious to the army.

Congressional pay policy offers a good example of how its failure to respond quickly to staff officers' grievances aggravated a difficult situation. Most of Congress's reluctance to increase wages stemmed from its concern with keeping down the costs of war. Though Congress would issue more than $226 million by the end of 1779, it remained tightfisted when it came to paying its employees. In general, before 1778 Congress preferred fixed salaries to commissions for staff officers. Initially, the director-general received $4 per day; the commissary general $80 per month; his deputy $60. The quartermaster general received a basic salary of $80 per month and, by virtue of a congressional resolution of September 1775, a special 5 percent commission on clothing sold to the soldiers.[40] As a rule, congressional delegates thought commissions extravagant. Their aversion reflected most revolutionaries' pervasive distrust of the mercantile community and their moral repugnance at the idea of profit-making in wartime.

At the top level of the staff departments only Commissary General Trumbull was dissatisfied with congressional pay policy. Trumbull felt the compensation he received inadequate to the risk he ran and the services he provided. Moreover, he resented the fact that the quartermaster general and others also engaged in procuring supplies received a commission while he did not. Consequently, Trumbull often lobbied Congress to change to the more traditional and lucrative commission system.[41]

The majority of complaints about pay, however, came from the middle and lower levels of the staff departments, not from the top. Beginning in the spring of 1776, Congress received letters and petitions from commissaries and medical personnel complaining that their pay was "by no means proportional to the share of Duty" and that expenses and the increase in prices swallowed up the small sum allotted them. Heads of departments agreed and warned Congress that without an increase in pay they would be unable to retain the personnel now employed or attract new employees. The Hospital Department was particularly hard hit. Morgan was unable to hire badly needed nurses because they refused to work for the congressionally authorized wage of fifty cents a week. At the same time, he had to contend with disgruntled surgeons, storekeepers, and mates who were demanding additional pay and threatening to quit.[42]

Congress had not foreseen the harmful effect that currency depreciation and the concomitant increase in prices would have upon salaries. Having chosen to finance the war by emissions of paper money, Congress issued $31 million by the end of 1777. The depreciation of the currency began in late 1776, coinciding with the rise in prices and the complaints of the staff officers. Such early doubts about the soundness of America's currency reflected the economic impact of Washington's retreat from Long Island in the summer of 1776 and the attendant British threat to Philadelphia. With state governments refusing or failing to collect taxes—the prescribed method by which the currency was to be taken out of circulation—and congressional presses continuing to spew forth money to fight the war, depreciation worsened.[43]

Congress sought to alleviate the grievances of staff officers by increasing their wages. In May 1776, Congress raised Trumbull's salary by $40 a month. Two months later it increased the pay of the hospital surgeons and mates.[44] All staff officers subsequently received salary boosts in the reforms of 1777. Thus, after two years of war, the director-general was receiving $6 a day and nine rations; the commissary general was receiving $8 a day and six rations; and the quartermaster general was receiving $166 per month (excluding commission). Congress also increased the pay of lower-echelon personnel, but it balked at granting commissions to anyone in the staff departments.[45]

Congress responded in good faith to the complaints of staff officers. But because of its reluctance to run up the costs of the war, its fear of the corrupting power of large salaries, and its inherent slowness in conducting business, pay increases never caught up with the rate of inflation. Once again, congressional action was too little, too late.[46]

A L L O F C O N G R E S S ' S administrative actions during 1775–76 were responses to crises. Congress rarely planned supply and medical operations in advance; instead it waited on military events and reacted to the suggestions and complaints of military commanders and staff officers. The result was an ineffective, uncoordinated administrative system at odds with itself. Contributing to this chaotic state were congressmen's inexperience in military administration and their belief that the war would be over quickly. When these factors were combined with tendencies inherent in all large deliberative bodies—a propensity to react slowly and an insistence on total authority and control—the results were disastrous. As Congress began to recognize that this state of affairs was intolerable if the war was to be won, it attempted to set its own house in order and to reorganize the staff departments along more workable lines.

CHAPTER 2

REFORM AND

REORGANIZATION

1777–1780

*Congress has lately been employed in regulating the several departments
of the army, that the business may be properly conducted and frauds
and abuses prevented.*
   —Roger Sherman to the governor of Connecticut,
      14 May 1778

*We proceed now to state the Arrangement which we propose to make,
promising that it is upon the character of Men principally, and not your
Paper Systems that our Success must depend.*
   —Committee of Congress at Camp to Henry Laurens,
      25 February 1778

CONGRESS'S ABILITY to anticipate the logistical needs of the Continental army did not improve during the second stage of congressional war administration, which lasted from December 1776 to early 1780. Congress continued to react to crises as they developed, tailoring its reforms to the needs of the moment. But out of the jumble of administrative decisions made in this period, some broad trends may be discerned. First, Congress increasingly relied on the staff departments to bear the major responsibility of servicing the army. It called upon congressional committees, civilians, and military commanders much less frequently than before to purchase supplies or provide food to the troops. The reduced reliance upon state authority, the mainstay of army logistics in the early war years, was particularly noticeable. Second, congressional reform and reorganization of the staff departments and its own administrative apparatus dominated this period. Reform began at the executive level of congressional war administration.

A "RAGE FOR REFORMATION" was how Virginia's Richard Henry Lee characterized the mood of congressmen during 1777, and his phrase does justice to their efforts to remodel the administrative machinery. By 1777, Congress had curtailed its earlier practice of forming a committee for every crisis. Ad hoc committees gave way to standing committees, such as the Board of Treasury and the Board of War and Ordnance. Nevertheless, the heavy work load and the resulting high turnover rate made standing committees slow and inefficient. Congress gradually realized that it had neither the manpower nor the knowledge to perform both legislative and executive functions and proposed a solution to this problem as early as March 1776: it recommended that standing committees be staffed by people other than members of Congress. Although congressmen were reluctant to relinquish their control of war administration and thus remained on most committees, they did take steps in late 1776 to place a few noncongressmen on administrative boards.[1]

The Board of War and Ordnance was the first committee to feel Congress's reforming impulse. Fortunately, the indefatigable research of Edmund C. Burnett permits us to follow the tortuous process by which Congress reconstituted the Board of War. Nine months after reform was first suggested and in the wake of the army's defeat at Kip's Bay and White Plains, on 26 December 1776 Congress instructed a committee "to prepare a plan for the better conducting the executive business of Congress, by boards composed of persons, not members of Congress." Five months later, on 8 April 1777, the committee submitted a plan for the new Board of War, which was postponed and recommitted for revision. On 6 June, Congress gently prodded the committee to present its revised report as soon as possible. Finally, on 18 July, the committee submitted the new plan, which Congress accepted: a Board of War was to be created, composed of three men from outside of Congress. Appointment of the men was set for 22 July but was postponed. Inexplicably, the committee did nothing for almost three months. Finally, on 16 October it reconsidered the plan and the next day amended and approved it for the second time. Three weeks later, on 7 November, Congress appointed former Quartermaster General Thomas Mifflin, Adjutant General Timothy Pickering, and Robert H. Harrison to the new Board of War. When Harrison declined to serve, Joseph Trumbull, who had resigned as commissary general on 19 July 1777, was nominated to fill the position. Rounding out its work, Congress on 27 November appointed Major General Horatio Gates chairman of the Board of War and made Richard Peters secretary. Placing Mifflin, Pickering, Trumbull, and Gates on the Board of War demonstrated congressional resolve to use experienced military personnel in positions of administrative responsibility. With their appointment, the Board of War at long last was ready to operate. It had taken Congress eleven months to set up one committee.[2]

In the name of economy and efficiency, Congress tinkered with the machinery of administration at the executive level through 1778–80. It reorganized the Board of War and the Board of Treasury; it modified the Board of Treasury again in 1779. It also recast the Marine Committee, which reemerged in 1779 as the Board of Admiralty. But delays thwarted Congress's efforts to make its administrative process more efficient.[3] In an attempt to correct its dilatory habits, congressmen circulated among themselves in April of 1778 an "Engagement of Members to Meet Punctually." Even that effort met with little success. As Maryland's Charles Carroll of Carrollton remarked, "We murder time, and chat it away in idle impertinent talk." Although Congress acted with the best intentions to reform its committee system by adding noncongressional, experienced military personnel to run the administration of the war, delays caused by overworked, habitually wrangling, and time-wasting congressmen frustrated the effort. As Jack N. Rakove observes, "Congress, in short, was too inefficient to correct its own inefficiency."[4]

As Congress was reforming the Board of War and Ordnance in 1777, it was also wrestling with the problems of the staff departments. The gradual realization that the war was not to be won quickly, coupled with the military defeats on Long Island in late 1776, galvanized Congress to create new staff departments and reorganize existing ones. Like the reform of its own committee system, Congress's reorganization of the staff departments in 1777 was another indication that the supply and medical problems of the army could not be solved by temporary committees or by the inadequate staff departments already in existence.

Such a conclusion had not been anticipated and was, like many congressional actions, a product of necessity and the pressure of military defeat. In this respect Congress continued to react to events and crises. John Adams saw this tendency as a virtue. Commenting on a series of letters received by the Marine Committee, "pointing out Defects, Abuses and Mismanagements and proposing Plans of Improvement, Redress, and Reformation," Adams concluded: "This is the Way to have things go right; for Officers to correspond constantly with Congress and communicate their Sentiments freely."[5] There is, of course, much truth in Adams's reasoning: congressional administrators needed an accurate picture of staff conditions to facilitate planning and management of the war, and the best source of that information was obviously officials in the field. But by waiting for disaster to strike and not anticipating logistical problems, Congress created many hardships for Continental soldiers.

The changes initiated in the staff departments during 1777 closely reflected the complaints and suggestions Congress received from military officials in the field, such as General Washington and Quartermaster General Mifflin. Congress responded by tailoring its solution to the problem. Outcries at the lack of bread, shoes, and clothing led Congress to name a superintendent of bakers and a commissary of hides and to authorize the commander in chief to appoint a clothier general. Demands for administrative regularity and for increased discipline in the army prompted the creation of two other positions: the commissary general of musters and the inspector-general. All five of these new positions set apart or rationalized functions that had been either under the direction of multiple authorities—committees, states, and military commanders—or neglected.[6]

The major reforms of 1777, however, occurred in the Commissary, Quartermaster, and Hospital departments. Reports from the field stressed two major problems in these departments. The first was the extensiveness of staff responsibilities. There was simply too much work. Frustrated by their inability to carry out or even to supervise all aspects of their respective departments, high-ranking staff officers such as Mifflin and Dr. William Shippen, Jr., devised schemes creating new positions to lighten the work load and submitted them to the commander in chief and Congress. General Washington agreed that the duties of the heads of departments were too demanding and in letters to Congress vigorously endorsed their suggestions. The second serious problem that came to the attention of Congress was corruption in the Commissary Department. Confirming earlier reports, a congressional committee returned from army headquarters detailing the squandering of public money and the fraudulent increase of prices by a number of individuals in the Commissariat. With these reports in hand, Congress set out to correct the deficiencies of the staff departments.[7]

Two basic principles guided all the subsequent reforms of 1777: specialization of staff functions and public accountability. Congress finally realized that the sprawling, undifferentiated staff departments it had established in 1775 were unmanageable. Areas of responsibility had to be reduced to lessen the excessive work load of administrative officials. In addition, untrustworthy staff officers had to be controlled to prevent fraud and embezzlement.

Congress began its task of rationalizing the staff departments by totally reorganizing the Hospital Department in April 1777. For administrative purposes, the Hospital Department was divided into four geographic areas, with the director-general in charge of only the hospitals between the Hudson and Potomac rivers and the three deputy directors-general in charge of the hospitals east of the Hudson River, south of the Potomac, and to the north. Each district was assigned a full complement of subordinate officials and staff (see Figure 2.1). On 11 April 1778, William Shippen, Jr., a wealthy Philadelphia physician, was appointed director-general. Congress placed Shippen in charge of "all the military hospitals which shall be erected for the continental army in the United States" but effectively undercut the director's authority and kept control of the department by retaining the power to appoint all subordinate medical officials outside of his district (see Figure 2.2).[8]

Congress took similar action in reforming the Quartermaster and Commissary departments. To reduce the burden of the quartermaster general, Congress ordered Mifflin in May 1777 to appoint a commissary of forage and a wagonmaster general and allowed him also to appoint deputies and assistants (see Figure 2.3). Likewise, in June 1777 Congress split the office of commissary general in two: the commissary general of purchases and the commissary general of issues (see Figure 2.4). By this action, Congress achieved both of its goals in a single stroke: dividing the office of commissary general made the position more manageable, and each official could "check" the other, thereby preventing fraudulent practices. Also reflecting Congress's suspicions of the commissary general and its fear of concentrating power in a single individual was its refusal to allow the commissary general of purchases the power to appoint his own assistants. Instead, Congress reserved the right to appoint deputy commissaries, who in turn were authorized to appoint as many assistants as were necessary (see Figure 2.5).[9]

Congress's desire to decentralize authority, to lessen the power and

FIGURE 2. 1. *Hospital Department, 1777*

CONGRESS
|
Medical Committee
|
Director-General[a]
|

Deputy Director-General	Deputy Director-General	Deputy Director-General
Assistant Deputy Director	Assistant Deputy Director	Assistant Deputy Director
Apothecary General and Mates	Apothecary General and Mates	Apothecary General and Mates
Commissary of Hospitals and Assistants	Commissary of Hospitals and Assistants	Commissary of Hospitals and Assistants
Physician General	Physician General	Physician General
Surgeon General	Surgeon General	Surgeon General
Physician and Surgeon General[b]		
Matrons	Matrons	Matrons
Stewards	Stewards	Stewards
Nurses	Nurses	Nurses
Clerk and Assistants	Clerk and Assistants	Clerk and Assistants

Source: *JCC*, 7:231–37.

a. The director-general with his staff presided over the fourth district. He was not authorized a deputy director-general.

b. One to each army.

F I G U R E 2. 2. *Appointments in the Hospital Department, 1777*

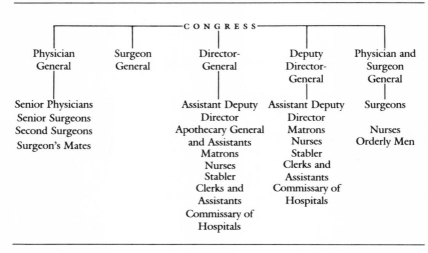

Physician General	Surgeon General	Director-General	Deputy Director-General	Physician and Surgeon General
Senior Physicians Senior Surgeons Second Surgeons Surgeon's Mates		Assistant Deputy Director Apothecary General and Assistants Matrons Nurses Stabler Clerks and Assistants Commissary of Hospitals	Assistant Deputy Director Matrons Nurses Stabler Clerks and Assistants Commissary of Hospitals	Surgeons Nurses Orderly Men

Source: *JCC,* 7:231–37.

F I G U R E 2. 3. *Quartermaster General Department, 1777*

CONGRESS
|
Quartermaster General
|
Wagonmaster General
Commissary of Forage[a]
Assistant Quartermaster General
Deputy Quartermaster General[a]
Assistant Deputy Quartermaster General
Assistant Commissary of Forage
Foragemasters
Wagonmasters
Clerks

Source: *JCC,* 7:355–59.
a. One for each military district.

F I G U R E 2. 4. *Commissary Department, 1777*

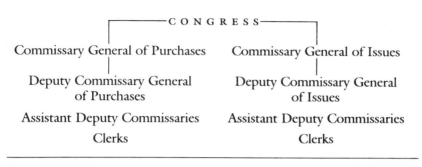

Source: *JCC*, 8:434.

F I G U R E 2. 5. *Appointments in the Commissary Department, 1777*

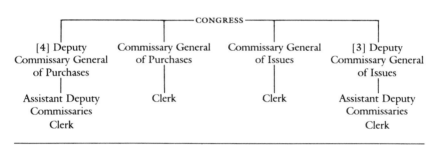

Source: *JCC*, 8:434.

responsibility of department heads, and to keep military officials under close scrutiny was the outstanding characteristic of its reform of the major staff departments. In the Hospital and Quartermaster departments Congress explicitly followed plans submitted to it by Shippen and Mifflin because the military situation dictated that changes be instituted and because the plans were in harmony with Congress's general orientation toward the decentralization of power. In contrast, Commissary General Joseph Trumbull's repeated and insistent requests that he be given complete control over his department went against the ideological grain of Congress and so were rejected.

Another manifestation of Congress's fear of corruption and desire to control the administrative process was its introduction of systematic procedures to make staff officers more accountable for public funds. In a sharp departure from previous practice, Congress issued detailed directives governing administrative procedures. The instructions for the Commissary Department alone filled fifteen pages of the *Journals of Congress.*[10] The main thrust of these new directives, especially in the Quartermaster and Commissary departments, was not to control day-to-day management but to prevent fraud. To achieve its goal of strict public accountability, Congress placed enormous emphasis on the written word and recordkeeping. When goods changed hands, receipts were to be issued specifying the item, quantity, and quality; some supplies, such as forage, were not to be issued except by written order of commanding military officials; and monthly reports of all transactions were to be made to department heads, who would forward the information to Congress.

To facilitate the accountability of military officials, Congress ordered the quartermaster general to furnish all his personnel with preprinted forms to aid in keeping accurate records. Similarly, it ordered the commissary general of purchases to issue his deputies and assistants a book of ten-column pages into which every purchase was to be entered with the following information: date of purchase; seller's name; place purchased; species and quantity of provisions; the number, color, and natural or artificial marks of livestock; price paid; total amount of purchase; and weight. Elaborate recordkeeping was instituted primarily to prevent embezzlement of public property and outright fraud, but it also had the effect of systematizing army administration.[11]

Congress legislated additional measures to check corruption in the staff departments. Two strategies were employed to prevent staff officers from deliberately raising prices: the commissary general of purchases was to assign purchasing agents clearly defined areas of operation to prevent them from bidding against one another, and he was to instruct his deputies to keep themselves and their assistants apprised of prices so as not to exceed the current price level. Congress hoped to enforce these regulations by stipulating that deputies guilty of fraud, misconduct, or neglect of duty were to be suspended without pay. Four months later, Congress mandated that assistant deputy commissaries had to give bond for $5,000 to the president of Congress for the faithful performance of their duties. Finally, Congress raised the salaries of staff officers, though it still balked at commissions.[12]

From Congress's point of view, 1777 was a banner year in its administration of the war. The year witnessed the creation of a new Board of War staffed by noncongressional, experienced military personnel and the complete overhaul of the staff departments: new positions were created; new departments formed; existing ones reorganized; new guidelines issued to clarify duties and to prevent fraud; staff department salaries increased. Congress had acted forthrightly. The result was Valley Forge.

Paradoxically, both congressional action and inattention played major roles in the disaster that overtook the Continental soldiers in the winter of 1777–78. In particular, congressional reform of the Commissariat resulted in a host of resignations at all levels of the department, leaving it demoralized and unprepared for the army's winter encampment at Valley Forge. The commissary general, Joseph Trumbull, had two major objections that led him to resign. The first was Congress's refusal to pay him a commission. Trumbull had insisted he be paid .5 percent commission on purchases and his deputies 2.5 percent as a condition of accepting the office of commissary general of purchases.[13] The second was Congress's refusal to allow him to appoint his own assistants yet holding him responsible for their behavior in office. Trumbull believed that the head of every department ought to retain complete control. Because he was forced to operate the department with divided authority, Trumbull complained that "an Imperium in Imperio [was] established," an intolerable logical absurdity. Consequently, Trumbull resigned.[14] Congress appointed William Buchanan, a Baltimore merchant, to replace Trumbull on 5 August 1777, but Buchanan proved unequal to the task. The absence of forceful leadership at this critical juncture contributed to the disorganized efforts made to supply the troops at Valley Forge.[15]

Subordinates joined Trumbull in demanding payment on a commission basis. Though Congress had raised their pay, compensation continued to lag behind the increase in prices. Deputy commissaries claimed they had no choice but to resign. The alternative to quitting, according to Deputy Commissary William Aylett, was to be impoverished by the "great decrease of the value of our Current money or the great rise of the Articles of life—take it which way you will." Resignations became the order of the day.[16]

The new regulations governing the Commissary Department supplied additional grounds for discontent among lower-ranking staff personnel. A group of deputy commissaries protested that the strict accounting procedures called for by Congress made no allowance for common wastage or accidental losses, unless proven under oath. Because provisions were "sometimes Embezzled by the Soldiery and that in the Most private Manner," the issuing commissaries claimed they were unable to make such proof. To be held accountable for what they could not prevent they believed was "the Height of Folly" and, more important, injurious to their reputation. They, too, resigned.[17]

The difficulty of securing replacements for the men who resigned added to the Commissary Department's disorganized state. Men of business refused public office unless paid on a commission basis; others refused to give bond. Worse yet, the men who were persuaded to join lacked experience. "The whole Race of Commissaries," Deputy Quartermaster Hugh Hughes remarked caustically, "Look like Cats in a strange Garret at one another, and not one of them knows what he is about.—Such are the happy Effects of shifting Hands in the Midst of a Campaign." The situation only worsened. Two months later, in October 1777, Deputy Commissary Peter Colt lamented that "no person knows how to act or what to do. Every kind of Commissary Business is here entirely stopped."[18] Thus as the army prepared to go into winter quarters at Valley Forge, Congress's new regulations had the injurious effect of returning the Commissary Department to the inexperienced and inefficient days of 1775.

Congress contributed to the breakdown of the supply system in other ways. Historians agree that the major cause of the dearth of food at Valley Forge was not its scarcity—crops were abundant that year—but the lack of wagons to transport it to camp.[19] Both congressional action and neglect were largely responsible for the unavailability of drivers and wagons. In an effort to hold down the cost of labor, Congress had limited the price of hiring a wagon, driver, and four horses to thirty shillings a day. Teamsters, however, demanded and received three to four pounds a day from private contractors. Consequently, military officials were unable to procure transportation, and deliveries of food and supplies were delayed.[20] Contributing to the overall disorganization of the Quartermaster Department was Thomas Mifflin's resignation on 10 October 1777.[21] Thoroughly disliking the job and angered at Washington's failure to heed his advice to defend Philadelphia, Mifflin claimed he was sick and retired to Reading, Pennsylvania. Though General Washington repeatedly urged Congress to appoint a successor, it did not fill the post until 2 March 1778. The delay of nearly five months almost proved fatal to the army.[22]

There can be no doubt that in the wake of Congress's reforming zeal the Commissary and Quartermaster departments fell apart, partly because of a lack of leadership and partly because of the inexperience and demoralization of deputies and assistants. In addition, congressional inattention greatly exacerbated many of these problems, particularly its failure to appoint a quartermaster general following Mifflin's resignation, its neglect to appoint a deputy commissary for the Middle Department, and its sluggishness in clarifying its resolves. In the latter case, the deputy commissaries who had resigned in July 1777 over the risk to their reputations had in fact misinterpreted Congress's intent to hold them responsible for unavoidable losses. A timely response might have prevented the resignations. Instead, Congress waited four months to assuage the commissaries' fears and correct their misapprehension, but by October 1777 the deputies had already left camp.[23]

It would be inaccurate, however, to place all the blame for the suffering at Valley Forge on congressional shoulders. It was not Congress's fault that during most of the winter the Schuylkill River was frozen solid or was too shallow for boats to bring provisions down from Reading, the army's major supply depot. Nor can Congress be censured for the miserable roads, dishonest teamsters, or state militia laws that depleted the ranks of available wagon drivers. But though these factors certainly retarded supply operations at Valley Forge, their effect on supply operations can be over-estimated.[24]

When Congress was made aware of these problems, its initial reaction was to fill the breach with temporary expedients that would prevent the army's disbandment. In November 1777 Congress reminded Washington of his power to impress military supplies and urged him to exercise it in the surrounding counties to feed the army. A month later, it called on Connecticut and Virginia to forward cattle and salt to Valley Forge and recommended that Pennsylvania and Maryland appoint officials to seize food for the army. A measure of success greeted state procurement efforts and Washington's impressment orders, and although the soldiers' diet continued to be spare and unappealing throughout the winter of 1777–78, the army did not disband.[25]

In order to assign responsibility for the Valley Forge disaster, Congress in January 1778 dispatched a committee to Washington's headquarters with broad powers to investigate and reform the staff departments.[26] In forceful and comprehensive reports, the Committee at Camp attempted to impress upon Congress the crucial importance of filling the quartermaster general's position, explaining that neglect of "this great Wheel in the Machine" jeopardized the army's existence and American independence. The absence of strong leadership in the Quartermaster Department was evident everywhere. With no one at the helm, negligent deputies made little effort to supervise quartermaster operations. The committee reported that though wagons were in short supply, "not an encampment, Route of the Army or Considerable Road, but abounds with Waggons to the Mercy of the Weather and the Will of the Inhabitants." A similar situation existed with military equipment. Tents, entrenching tools, spades, and shovels were to be found lying on the roads and abandoned in farmers' barns. Deputies were not only inattentive and indolent but fraudulent and corrupt: "The number of little, piddling, pilfering, Plunderers in the Character of Deputies and Deputies Assistants is sufficient almost to form an Army." The committee pointed out two examples: deputy quartermasters charged enormous commissions on "Capitol purchases," and they transported private property in public wagons.[27]

As a result of the disorganized state of the Quartermaster Department and the consequent suffering of the troops, committee members lost faith in the efficacy of congressional regulations to direct supply operations. In effect, the committee recognized that it was not possible for Congress to legislate the staff departments into efficiency. The solution the committee envisaged was as simple as it was radical. It required Congress to abandon the decentralized system by which it had organized the staff departments and to place its trust in individuals by concentrating power and authority in "Characters of known and approved abilities." The committee reached this conclusion by observing that divided authority inevitably led to controversies and confusion among staff officers. The committee assured Congress that these problems would be eliminated if the Quartermaster Department was placed "under one controlling, superintending, Power, whose Authority and Influence may regulate, pervade, and animate the whole System."[28]

After justifying its proposal to increase the power of the quartermaster general, the committee presented Congress with a specific plan of action, which called for congressional appointment of a new quartermaster and two assistants. The committee had considered General Schuyler and Baron von Steuben for the post but had rejected Schuyler because he was not in favor with Congress and could not recommend the baron because he was a mercenary and a "Foreigner." Instead, the committee proposed General Nathanael Greene as quartermaster general and John Cox and Charles Pettit as his assistants. Under the committee's arrangement, Greene would direct the purchases and supervise the distribution of military supplies; Cox would make all the purchases and examine all the goods; and Pettit would take charge of the bookkeeping, accounts, and dispersal of cash. The great merit of the plan, in the committee's opinion, was that it did away with the need for inefficient congressional regulations and consigned the operation of the Quartermaster Department to the discretion of superior individuals.

The committee also called for a radical change in the manner in which the quartermaster and his assistants were paid. Committee members were convinced that a salary commensurate with the importance of the offices and the great labor involved must be offered to anyone who undertook these positions. Thus Greene, Cox, and Pettit should divide a 1 percent commission on all money issued in their department. The committee fully shared Congress's dislike of paying commissions to staff officers, acknowledging that they were a temptation to peculation and should be avoided. To justify its divergence from conventional wisdom, committee members urged that Congress place its faith in men, not systems, and drove its point home by observing fatalistically that there was "an infinity of Ways, in spite of every Check which the Ingenuity of Man can devise," by which dishon-

47

Reform and Reorganization, 1777–1780

est men could defraud the public. Another point in favor of the commission system, according to the committee, was the ease by which peculating staff officers could be identified: "Of all the Means of defrauding, the Swelling of Commissions by great Expenditures, is the most liable to Detection." In short, the committee reluctantly rejected Congress's long-standing objections to paying staff officers on a commission basis.[29]

The committee did not restrict its report to the Quartermaster Department. Turning to the Commissary Department, the committee confessed it was unable to pinpoint the causes of the failure of provisions at Valley Forge. Nevertheless, it recommended the same solution for the ineffectual Commissariat as for the Quartermaster Department: "A Man of Abilities, extensive Connection[s], and Influence" must be placed in charge and given the power to direct the department as he saw fit. The man the committee proposed was the Connecticut merchant Jeremiah Wadsworth. The committee took little notice of the Hospital Department except to lament the high mortality rate among the troops and to assure Congress that the soldiers expressed no complaints against their surgeons or physicians.[30]

From its top medical officers, however, Congress received a different and highly critical picture of the Hospital Department. Criticism focused on the position of the director-general and echoed the strictures voiced at the Quartermaster and Commissary departments in 1777. In particular, medical officials denounced the all-embracing duties of the director-general, objected to the concentration of so much power in a single individual, and voiced fears of the potential to abuse that power for personal profit. Dr. William Brown, surgeon general of the Middle Department, warned Congress that "the present Establishment lays duties on the Director-General, which, for so large an army as ours . . . are too extensive and diversified for any individual to bear the charge of, and also are incompatible with the power that ought to be exercised by the Director-General." According to Dr. Brown, the incompatibility lay in the director-general's uncontrolled authority to purchase medical supplies without any formal supervision of his expenditures. Dr. Benjamin Rush, who had been strongly influenced by John Adams's pamphlet on government, arrived at a similar conclusion. Commenting to Adams, Rush drily noted the empyreal quality of the director-general's authority: "Such unlimited powers and no checks would have suited an angel."[31]

Both doctors cited reputable British medical authorities to justify their objections to the extensive powers of the director-general. That patriot physicians had recourse to the teachings of the enemy is not as unusual as it may first appear. It is simply testimony that revolutionaries such as Rush and Brown—who had studied in Edinburgh and London, the medical capitals of the Atlantic community, and who believed the British medical system "the most perfect in the world"—did not let their hatred of the enemy blind them to the merit of the British army's Medical Department.[32] Thus it is not surprising that both doctors quoted from the eminent British physician, Dr. Donald Monro, whose work on military hospitals counseled that "the *directing* and *purveying* branches ought N E V E R to be entrusted to the *same* person, as the temptation for accumulating wealth has at A L L times and in A L L services given rise to the grossest abuses."[33] For these medical officers the problem was not the director-general's character but the system that authorized him such a large measure of control over medical operations. Their solution, which mirrored the reforms suggested in 1777, was to transfer the director-general's control over purchasing medical supplies to other hands. Thus Dr. Brown suggested that a purveyor-general with deputies responsible for medicines, hospital stores, and provisions be appointed to correct the problem. The benefits arising from such a plan were clear: it would both reduce the director-general's duties and decrease his opportunity to defraud the public.[34]

The emphasis of the reports Congress received from the field on the corruption and negligence of staff officers struck an ideological chord among a small but growing number of congressmen. The reports strongly reinforced Congress's general distrust of the military, its suspicion of merchants, and its distaste for wartime profiteering. Therefore, the reports both shaped and confirmed the suspicions of some congressmen about who was to blame for Valley Forge. Indicative of Congress's mood was President Henry Laurens's angry attack on one of the congressmen sent to headquarters for soft-pedaling the responsibility for the debacle at Valley Forge: "You intimate good Sir, that most of the Evils which have attended our camp flow from the gross neglect and abuse in the department of Quartermaster general. If it be so, and I am inclined to believe it, why are we so Courtly and mincing? Is there a name under Heaven that shall sanctify the peculation or screen the man whose neglect of Duty has brought thousands to Misery and Death? forbid it torpid patriotism of 1775—No! let the Offender be dragged forth, and the people told, this is the Man!" No matter that the lack of food and supplies could be attributed to everything from the unusually cold weather to miserable roads and unreliable teamsters. Or that the high rate of mortality among the troops was the result of overcrowding in the hospitals, the shortage of medical supplies, and the lack of clothing and blankets, rather than the negligence and peculation of medical officers. These congressmen reduced the entire logistical problem of the army to incompetent and dishonest staff officers, especially in the Commissariat. Rhode Island's Congressman William Ellery summed up the feelings of many of his colleagues in Congress when he asked: "If Diogenes were alive and were to search America with candles would he find an honest man?"[35]

Fears of excessive power and corruption were uppermost in Congress's mind when it reorganized the Hospital Department on 6 February 1778. Three features of the reform stand out. First, alarmed at the concentration of power in the office of the director-general, Congress effectively decentralized the Hospital Department by making the deputy directors-general virtually autonomous within their districts. Second, it stripped the power to purchase medical supplies from the director-general and distributed this power among the deputy directors-general. Finally, Congress extended the bookkeeping system designed in 1777 to make the Quartermaster and Commissary departments more accountable for the outlay of public money to the Hospital Department. Medical officers were directed to issue written orders for supplies, to produce vouchers and receipts proving expenditures and delivery, and to make returns directly to the director-general, who would transmit them to Congress. Failure to do so was punishable by suspension from office.[36]

But if many congressmen believed that corruption was at the root of the collapse of logistical operations at Valley Forge, far more blamed congressional reorganization of the Commissariat in 1777 as the real source of the army's distress. Typical was New Hampshire's Nathaniel Folsom's matter-of-fact explanation: "My Predecessors in Congress made some alterations in the Commissary generals Department in the midle of a Campaign which has given us an infinite Deal of trouble."[37] Similarly, Commissary General William Buchanan, once the object of Congress's wrath, was now viewed in a more sympathetic light. As Elbridge Gerry noted, though Buchanan did not fulfill his duties, "neither could it be expected from a better officer whilst Regulations prevented him from appointing his Deputies."[38]

The lessons congressmen learned from the failure of the staff departments at Valley Forge were so vivid that they set aside their earlier fears of centralization and commissions when they came to reform the Quartermaster and Commissary departments. The experience of wartime failure was beginning to make inroads on the ideological assumptions of many congressmen. Consequently, in a remarkable break with the dominant pattern of reform—decentralization and public accountability—Congress threw caution to the winds and adhered strictly to the Committee at Camp's recommendations. Men of character and ability were installed at the head of the Quartermaster and Commissary departments and given free rein to direct them as they saw fit. On 2 March 1778, Congress appointed General Nathanael Greene quartermaster general and on 9 April designated Jeremiah Wadsworth commissary general of purchases. Congress ensured Wadsworth's control of the department by relinquishing its claim to appoint the commissary general's deputies and granted him "full power to appoint and remove every officer in his department." To attract these men, Congress reversed its longstanding opposition to paying staff officers on a commission basis. Greene and his two assistants, Charles Pettit and John Cox, were granted a 1 percent commission on all funds expended in their department.[39]

Subsequently, Greene established commissions for deputy quartermasters, although no formal congressional resolve granted him that power. In most cases, Greene offered his deputies salaries ranging from $50 a month plus 1.5 percent commission on purchases and other disbursements to a flat fee of 2 percent commission on purchases, out of which the deputy was to pay an assistant.[40] Similarly, Wadsworth was allowed .5 percent on all monies the department disbursed; his deputies were to receive .5 percent on the money they distributed to the purchasing commissaries, who in turn were to receive a commission not to exceed 2 percent on the monies they expended. Connecticut's Eliphalet Dyer succinctly summed up the reason for Congress's *volte-face*: "They Wish to have the Army supplied at any rate."[41]

By April of 1778, congressional war administration had moved from one extreme to another: from parsimony and strict control to a determination to pour money into supply operations and not to interfere with heads of departments. Congress would make no other structural or organizational changes in the chief staff departments for approximately the next two years. Only time would tell if the expectations of the reorganization would be realized.

In the meantime, members of Congress were optimistic about the radical changes instituted in the staff departments. Even congressmen who might have been expected to bemoan the fate of decentralization exulted at the prospect of staff officers acting without restraints. James Lovell approvingly wrote Samuel Adams that "we have got Col. Wadsworth at the Head of the commisariate *unfettered* strictly so. Had the same steps as now been taken with Trumbull a year ago amazing Sums would have been saved and Howe [would] have been reduced to the greatest Extremity last fall."[42] Other radical congressmen such as Josiah Bartlett, Abraham Clark, Elbridge Gerry, Eliphalet Dyer, Daniel Roberdeau, and Richard Henry Lee either championed centralizing the staff departments and switching to commissions or lambasted Congress's reform efforts of 1777.[43] Thus even those members who epitomized the republican spirit of the Revolution approved the new measures. That these radicals did approve strongly suggests the danger of interpreting congressional actions solely in ideological terms. The course of action they followed is also an indication of how pragmatic congressional decision making was: in 1778 revolutionary ideology gave way to military necessity.[44] Nor were congressional hopes totally misplaced. Initially, Greene and Wadsworth substantially improved the army's supply operations. But relief was temporary. By late 1779 the army was once again short of clothing, camp equipment, food, and medical supplies.[45]

CONGRESS NEVER DID, and never would, understand why the army always complained that it was inadequately supplied. In 1775–76, Congress muddled through, supplying the army by unsystematically calling upon a variety of sources. The results were predictably unsatisfactory. In 1777, Congress rationalized supply operations by decentralizing responsibility and introducing a system of public accountability. That approach also failed. In 1778, Congress reversed itself by centralizing the Quartermaster and Commissary departments, abandoning restraints on department chiefs, and handsomely remunerating staff officers. When this system also proved deficient, Congress would wrongly blame failure on corrupt and faithless staff officers. But before examining in detail congressional reaction to the problem of corruption in the staff departments, it is essential to inquire into the day-to-day difficulties with which staff officers contended throughout the war. Shifting from Congress's perspective to that of the ordinary staff officer will provide the background for understanding the future acrimonious relations between Congress and staff officers and will also afford an insight into the complexities of waging war in the eighteenth century.

CHAPTER 3

PROBLEMS OF SUPPLY

If, indeed, the business of the quartermaster general were confined to a few objects, and those only with the army, as in some foreign services; if the supplies of all things necessary in the department were complete; if the various kinds of water craft; if materials for building and other uses; if artificers; if the numerous teams with their conductors and drivers; if forage, straw, fuel, camp equipage, and all the variety of stores required in the American army were provided and brought to his hand, with scarcely a thought of his about them;—the burthens of his office would then be essentially lessened and perhaps be equal only to those of three or four general officers.
    —Timothy Pickering to the president of Congress,
       4 December 1782

[Everyone] think[s] it is a Neglect of mine, and none Considers that my power only is confined to writing, and making seasonable applications.
    —Deputy Quartermaster H. L. Lutterloh to Hugh Hughes,
       20 March 1781

HENRY LAURENS, president of Congress, was thinking of Valley Forge when he confessed in January 1778 that he was at a loss to explain the failure of the staff departments. He could only guess the reason was "some unaccountable deficiency." Laurens was not alone in his bewilderment. The inability of staff officers to provide the army with food, clothing, camp equipment, and medical treatment baffled other revolutionaries. Puzzlement quickly gave way to anger and accusations. After 1778, the alleged fraudulent practices of staff officers became a popular explanation for the army's deficiencies in providing medical treatment and supplies. But although critics differed over the reasons for the failure of army logistics, they refused to entertain the possibility that at the heart of these problems lay difficult terrain, bad weather, fallible individuals, and economic and military forces beyond staff officers' control.[1]

NUMBERS PROVIDE a stunning guide to the magnitude of supplying the Continental army. To take a low point in the Revolution, consider the amount of food consumed by the army at Valley Forge. During the winter months of December 1777 and January and February 1778, revolutionary soldiers consumed more than 2,225,000 pounds of beef, 2,297,000 pounds of flour, and 500,000 gills of rum and whiskey.[2] In the same year—1778—the army's horses ate 253,000 bushels of grain and 2,500,000 tons of hay.[3] The Quartermaster Department operated on a comparable scale. Congress expected it to have on hand more than 240 different items ranging from naval stores, wagon equipment, and ship carpenter's tools to camp equipage, stationery, and "iron mongery."[4] Even in the best of circumstances, the task facing staff officers was nearly impossible, and the best of circumstances was rarely present.

One of the greatest obstacles facing staff officers was America's terrain, for the revolutionary war was primarily a land war. Even though the British blockade failed to deter coastal shipping or foreign trade—shiploads of clothing and ammunition continued to arrive from the West Indies and Europe—supplies still had to be carried from seaports and supply depots overland to the army.[5] Mountains, unfordable rivers, swamps, and large unbroken tracts of wilderness blocked the way, making supply operations difficult and slow.

The supply route needed to provision General Schuyler's Northern Army in the summer of 1775 provides an excellent example of the difficulties inherent in America's natural terrain. Schuyler was preparing an expedition into Canada, and food and camp equipment had to be sent to Lake Champlain, the Northern Army's jumping-off point. Martin H. Bush has ably described the geographical difficulties in supplying Schuyler's troops:

Goods had to be shipped from Albany to Half Moon by batteau. From there they were transferred by wagon to Stillwater on the Hudson, then they were placed in another batteau for a trip to Saratoga Falls. There they were taken across a small portage and on to Fort Miller Falls. At this point they were moved overland and then again by water to Fort Edward. From Fort Edward they could either be shipped on to Ticonderoga via Fort George or by way of Fort Anne. In the former case they were taken overland to Fort George at the southern tip of Lake George, then by water to the north end of the lake, where they were shipped overland to a place on Lake Champlain called the Saw Mills, and finally across the lake to Fort Ticonderoga. The route from Fort Anne appears to have been more manageable. Provisions were moved overland to Fort Anne and then down Wood Creek by batteau to Skene's Falls. There the batteaux were rolled across a small portage to the south end of Lake Champlain where they sailed over to Fort Ticonderoga.[6]

Not all supply routes servicing the army were as cumbersome and laborious as this one, but no matter where the army was stationed supplying it was always a difficult task. Most supply shipments had to be carried overland by wagon and oxcart because the principal waterways crossed rather than followed the main supply routes. Military supply officials had no alternative but to ship goods over rough, unrepaired roads and across rivers lacking bridges or adequate ferry service. The army's dependence on overland transport resulted in delayed, damaged, and lost supplies.[7] Nor were there any simple solutions to overcoming these natural barriers; only time and perseverance were effective.

Adverse weather conditions sometimes caused the army's food shortages. The meteorological conditions affecting the northern states in the summer and fall of 1779 clearly illustrate the direct effect of weather on food production. A drought dried up normally full streams, shutting down the mills and preventing farmers from grinding their wheat. Milling was halted again when a severe winter froze streams. As a result, General Washington was forced to reduce the soldiers' flour ration by 25 percent at the onset of the army's winter encampment at Morristown in 1780. Soldiers blamed the commissaries.[8]

Overland transport was particularly vulnerable to the vagaries of the weather. Winter was always troublesome: heavy snowfalls, frost, and ice on the roads often delayed supply deliveries. For example, a shipment of one thousand barrels of flour sent from Providence, Rhode Island, was held up for three weeks because of icy roads. Rainy weather interfered with the delivery of supplies by making roads impassable and flooding rivers. Military officials anticipated these problems, warned their assistants, and attempted to provide for emergencies, but there was little recourse against the ravages of nature.[9]

But geography and climate were only a small part of the problems delaying the delivery of supplies. Just as pervasive but far more frustrating and unpredictable was the human element. Logistics are generally understood to encompass all the activities and methods connected with the supply of armed force organizations, including storage requirements, transport, and distribution, but such a definition fails to recognize that at the heart of logistical operations, at least in the eighteenth century, were people.[10] The supply of the Continental army depended upon the farmers who grew the crops, milled the wheat, and provided the wagons and horses that transported the goods. Supplies also depended upon the teamsters who drove the wagons and the many skilled artisans who built the boats, sewed the clothing, repaired the wagons, and constructed the barrels in which goods were shipped. And at the head of logistical operations were more people—staff officers—directing and supervising all the others.

Competent personnel were necessary to ensure the free flow and distribution of supplies. By 1779, military supply officials agreed on the ideal qualifications for their men. Most administrators would have concurred with Quartermaster General Nathanael Greene that the model staff officer "should have a proper Knowledge of the forms of business; be a man of activity and good judgment; [and be] of a fair character and of good repute."[11] Owing to the general disorganization of supply services throughout the war, staff officers frequently had to use good judgment in making decisions. But what constituted good judgment? Often it meant flexibility, knowing when to obey instructions and when not to. And because the line between the two courses of action was never clear-cut, some staff officers always followed instructions even when the result was to deny the army needed supplies. For example, a barrackmaster refused General Lee's request of ten beds for sick soldiers by claiming he lacked the authority: "Sir—As my appointment to the office of barrack-master extends only to the city of New York, I have it not in my power to comply with your Excellency's request in regard to the supply of troops in another county, unless a special order be obtained for that purpose from the Congress."[12] Nor was the barrackmaster's "ruinous punctillio" unusual. Positions went unfilled, salt lay undelivered, clothing remained unissued, shoes were not procured, and carters refused to transport supplies beyond the boundary of their districts, "even if the other district ha[d] not the means to carry the goods to the final destination." In one form or another fastidious staff personnel defended or explained all these actions with a simple formula: "As I was not authorized, I declined."[13]

Although administrative legalism frequently obstructed military operations, strict adherence to orders was often the best policy, especially when dealing with Continental line officers, who regularly interfered with supply shipments. Proud, vain, and quick to anger, these officers prided themselves on their superior patriotism, virtue, and courage. Such character traits meant trouble when staff officers denied supplies to officers who felt they and their men were entitled to them. Frustrated with and angry at quartermasters who obstinately refused to obey his orders, General William Heath denounced them to the commander in chief. Sounding like Governor Thomas Hutchinson in 1773 lecturing the Massachusetts General Court on the necessity of a single sovereign authority in a state, Heath enjoined military discipline and the importance of maintaining the military chain of command. Quartermasters must be under the authority of local military commanders. If such principles were denied, Heath wrote, "will not this be imperium in imperio . . . a two headed Monster whose offspring must be confusion and disorder?"[14]

Heath's principles were sound in the abstract, but by 1781 Washington had good reason to suspect that the general's invocation of military discipline was simply an excuse to interfere with supply shipments. In the past, Continental officers faced with supply shortages had not scrupled at intercepting supplies destined for Washington's army. The fate of several wagonloads of clothing sent in July 1777 from Fishkill, New York, to the army at Morristown, New Jersey, was typical. Even before they left Fishkill, the clothing packages were opened on General Israel Putnam's orders and distributed to soldiers who needed a full set of clothes. Once on the road, the wagons were stopped by General John Sullivan, who also diverted a sufficient quantity to clothe his troops. Though the commander in chief, the Board of War, and sundry staff officers vigorously objected to Continental line officers' interference with supply deliveries, the practice continued throughout the war.[15]

State authorities also had a hand in disrupting logistical operations and in frustrating staff officers' efforts to supply the army. Though by 1777 Congress had ceased calling on the states for supplies except in emergencies, state legislatures had on their own initiative assumed a considerable role in procuring and transporting supplies to the army. By 1779, most states had appointed county commissioners to purchase clothing, state commissaries to procure food, and wagonmasters to call out teams and drivers.[16] But no uniform procedures governed the supply operations between the states and the army. Some states forwarded supplies directly to their own troops. Others sent them to Continental supply officers for general distribution to the army. Because no real effort was made to coordinate state supply officials' actions with Continental supply agents, friction and misunderstandings became common. Problems arose when state officials vigorously competed with staff officers for scarce supplies and usually succeeded in besting them.[17] By monopolizing supplies of clothing and tents for the use of their own troops, state officials deprived needier soldiers of these scarce items and made long-range planning almost impossible. Conversely, because of the lack of communication, staff officers imagined some state troops to be well supplied and refused to issue clothing to soldiers in need. According to Pennsylvania line officers, a supply official informed them: "You have a State Clothier of your own, apply to him."[18] The lack of cooperation between staff officers and state supply officials fed on itself.

In their efforts to provide for their own soldiers, state authorities almost equaled Continental line officers' impetuous interference with supplies en route to Washington's army. Certainly they acted with as much panache. For example, speaking on behalf of the Convention of New York, James Livingston, chairman of the Fishkill Committee of Safety, described how it was "with the utmost Satisfaction" that clothing earmarked for Continental troops was discovered stored at Fishkill. To the New York delegates, the apparently superfluous clothing offered an immediate solution to the problem of making good its promise to clothe the state's new recruits. Livingston apologized to General Washington for causing hardship to the army but did not offer to return the clothing. In similar fashion, other states, such as Massachusetts, Rhode Island, and Connecticut, appropriated supplies passing within their borders. Clothing was usually the main target of state officials' raids on supply wagons and magazines, but occasionally food was also diverted. Staff officers rightly complained that such actions "tend[ed] to throw everything into confusion," but even after Congress resolved against the practice, state authorities were usually undeterred. Their native sons were their first priority.[19]

Competing for purchases with staff officers and diverting supplies for their own troops were not the only ways in which the states and the army worked at cross-purposes. Another source of contention was the refusal of state authorities to exempt staff personnel from militia duty. Manpower was at a premium throughout the war. Though state and national officials offered bounty money to attract recruits, and when that failed, drafted citizens, the Continental army, state militia forces, and staff department operations were always in need of additional personnel.[20] In the conflict between staff officers and the states over who would receive the benefit of a recruit's services both sides had merit. Staff personnel complained that key workers employed as assistant deputy quartermasters, wagonmasters, and teamsters were called upon by state authorities to perform militia duty and threatened with fines if they failed to comply, thereby disrupting supply services. The fines levied on Commissary General Ephraim Blaine's assistants for nonperformance of militia duty were so prohibitive that the men quit the army and returned home. The consequences of their departure from Philadelphia in 1780 were severe: without the assistants, according to Blaine, "I must be under the necessity of shutting up my office, and all Business cease." Similarly, Colonel Benjamin Flower, commissary general of military stores, protested to Pennsylvania's President Thomas Wharton, Jr., that a contract entered into for "a large quantity of Shott and Shells" would go unfilled because all of the furnace's workmen had been drafted into the militia. Although in this regard Pennsylvania was the worst offender, the identical problem existed in most of the other states. To avoid state interference with supply personnel, staff officers wanted their men exempted from militia service. Exemption would not only protect current workers but, staff officers believed, would also encourage others to volunteer for employment in the staff departments.[21]

State authorities viewed the matter differently. They claimed they did not object to exemption from militia duty per se but only to abuses of the exemption policy. A few states could even point to statutes already on the books exempting artisans, wagon drivers, postmasters, and postriders as evidence of their support for the army. State officials said they disapproved of attempts to evade militia service and avoid payment of a substitute by serving as staff personnel for as little as a month or two. One solution, proposed by the Pennsylvania Council, was to prescribe a fixed term of enlistment—anywhere from nine months to a year—for men who served in the staff departments. Though a reasonable idea, it was never enacted. Instead, in their zeal to meet their militia quotas and apprehend shirkers, state officials continued to disrupt Continental supply operations by depriving staff officers of needed personnel. Although motivated by the best intentions, state policies undermined the war effort in the name of the war effort.[22]

Clearly, the army's supply lines were at the mercy of geography, prey to the elements, and easy targets for both Continental officers and state officials, making overland transportation at all times an expensive and inefficient means of provisioning the army. The weakest link, however, in the entire complicated system of transportation services, was the Wagonmaster Department.

There were so many interdependent aspects in operating the army's overland transport system efficiently that failure in any one often resulted in the nondelivery of supplies to the army. Wagons were often in short supply, and, without wagons, military officials were unable to ship food, shoes, clothing, or forage. Without forage, the animals used to pull the wagons and oxcarts were forced to remain inactive. Without the horses and oxen, clothing and food remained at supply depots rotting in idled wagons.[23] And, of course, without drivers, supplies did not move.

Throughout the war the army's shortage of wagons remained a problem for many reasons. Their constant use, day in and day out, during inclement weather, over miserable roads, and by careless drivers kept many wagons out of service. Farmers gave priority to the harvest and were reluctant to part with their wagons and eager to reclaim them. At least one state, Maryland, passed legislation restricting the use of wagons to carrying army baggage, thus effectively reducing the number available for shipping supplies. Enemy attacks also took their toll. The worst blow occurred when Lord Cornwallis routed General Horatio Gates at Camden in 1780: the British captured or destroyed almost all of the Southern Army's wagons. Many of General Greene's supply problems during the southern campaign of 1780–81 may be traced to this American defeat and the consequent shortage of transport.[24]

A lack of drivers severely hindered the delivery of supplies to the army. Wagoners were generally unwilling to enlist, in part because of the onerous nature of the job. As Quartermaster General Greene remarked, "The Duty is disagreeable in itself." Indeed, theirs was not an enviable lot. Eighteen-year-old Joseph Joslin of South Killingly, Connecticut, knew these hardships firsthand. In 1777–78, he carried barrels of flour, beef, pork, and rum and hauled loads of pressed hay between Washington's army on the Hudson and various supply depots in Connecticut. During the day, he was at the mercy of adverse weather: cold and snow in winter, rain and heat in summer. The end of a thirteen- or fourteen-hour day brought little relief. After arriving at his destination at nine o'clock in the evening Joslin noted: "It begun to Rain and then there was no fire and nothing to Eat But Dry Bisket and So it goes." At night, he slept on the floors of barns and stables if he was lucky; under the stars on some farmer's haystack, if not. Unlike other drivers, Joslin did not suffer abuse at the hands of line officers, "who from a mistaken opinion, think every body has a right to correct a Waggoner." But the arduous routine eventually took its toll on the stoic Connecticut revolutionary. Thirteen months after he began, Joslin had had enough, and he recorded his decision to resign in his journal: "I Don't Intend to Drive a team for my Continent anymore . . . good-bye."[25]

If revolutionaries quit the Wagonmaster Department because "the Waggoners' duty has no end Day or Night," the low wages prescribed by Congress also made it difficult to attract or keep drivers. Joslin had enlisted in 1777 for $15 a month and was actually paid $96 at the end of six months. By 1779, wagoners received £10 per month in addition to a bounty of a suit of clothing, but these incentives had little effect in preventing shortages of drivers. As at Valley Forge in 1777–78, competition from the private sector overwhelmed staff officers' ability to match the bidding for drivers' services. According to Deputy Quartermaster General Thomas Chase, stationed at Boston in 1779, "the principal reason the Teamsters prefer Carting private before public stores" was that civilian contractors "will give any price, and make the teamsters presents into the Bargain, and pay the money down, which is not in my power to do."[26] Drivers responded with irrefutable logic to staff officers' pleas to continue: "Who Would Drive horses for 80 dollars a Month when [we] Can get 20 Dollars a Day" during the upcoming harvest?[27] Even when wagoners were willing to stay on, the inability of staff officers to pay them and drivers' refusal to accept certificates in lieu of cash resulted in their quitting the service. Constrained on the one hand by congressional limitations on wages and a chronic lack of money and on the other by solvent merchants and farmers who outbid them for drivers' services, staff officers were at a distinct disadvantage in the contest to attract and retain drivers.[28]

Sometimes Quartermaster General Greene and Wagonmaster General James Thompson must have wondered if the game was worth the candle: the presence of wagoners was almost as much trouble as their absence. From almost any point of view they were a self-centered, untrustworthy, irresponsible group who regularly failed to deliver supplies to the army. At times the nondelivery of goods assumed almost comic proportions. In April 1778, Henry Williams of Salem, Massachusetts, explained to Commissary General Jeremiah Wadsworth why he had failed to receive the twelve barrels of flour Wadsworth had sent him. Outside of Hartford, the driver carrying the flour crossed the path of a fellow driver coming from Boston with a cannon bound for the Southern Department. The driver of the cannon, a resident of neighboring Westborough, desired to stay near home and suggested they exchange loads. No sooner said than done. Wadsworth's driver confessed he had not the faintest idea whom the flour was for, but he told the other driver not to worry: "If he could not find the Owner he might sell the flour and Pay him Self hansomly for his trouble."[29] The needs of the army were far from the thoughts of either driver.

Exchanging loads in midjourney was not a frequent occurrence during the war, but the drivers' lack of trustworthiness and their strong sense of self-interest were widespread. Drivers embezzled supplies and used their wagons to carry private goods. They refused to take heavy loads and sometimes lightened their burden by draining the brine from salt pork, thus spoiling the meat. They worked infrequently, maltreated the equipment and horses, and spent much of their time drinking and gambling. Wagoners' unreliability was more often revealed in their habit of dumping their loads on roadsides. Many civilian wagon owners simply jettisoned their loads over the side of the wagon when the roads became uncommonly miry or deeply rutted. Other drivers, according to General Gates, threw their goods overboard from "villainy [and] laziness." Whatever the reason, the results of this irresponsible behavior were manifest everywhere: tools and camp equipment scattered along the countryside, parcels of clothing and blankets left moldering in barns for more than a year, and hundreds of barrels of flour abandoned in towns along supply routes. To prevent these abuses, military and state officials proposed everything from a complex system of holding drivers accountable through bills of lading and written receipts to providing armed escorts with every wagon convoy.[30] None of these proposals was effective or maintained for long. Systematic bookkeeping presupposed the discipline and responsibility it was instituted to enforce and was thus doomed from the start. Nor could Washington's undermanned army spare the large number of soldiers necessary to oversee wagoners. But the problem went deeper. The army's absolute dependence on wagoners made the issue of keeping them in line almost irrelevant, for by 1779, the question was not disciplining unreliable wagoners but finding and keeping anyone who would agree to drive for the army.

Labor difficulties were not confined to the Wagonmaster Department. Staff officers in all departments were unable to retain lower-echelon workers. As with the drivers, insufficient pay was the main sticking point. In April 1779, when $25 bought a pair of shoes in Philadelphia, assistant issuing commissaries received a mere $30 raise, their first in two years, to $90 a month. In the Quartermaster Department, wages had not been increased since 1777. By 1779, the combined effects of inflation and depreciation had destroyed the purchasing power of wage earners. Consequently, salaried staff department workers were unable to support themselves and their families and petitioned their superiors for relief. They usually met with failure because neither Congress nor the heads of staff departments had any money.[31]

Artisans employed by the Quartermaster Department are a case in point; their efforts to increase their wages shed light on the primitive state of eighteenth-century labor relations and reveal the sensitivity of the Quartermaster's Department to popular opinion. In January 1779, artisans employed by Deputy Quartermaster Udny Hay at Fishkill, New York, petitioned Quartermaster General Greene for an increase in their $1.50-a-day wage. The memorialists contended that they would be forced to quit the service unless they received a raise. Greene denied their request, stating that he would not allow the Quartermaster Department to be held for ransom. In what was probably one of the earliest attempts in American history to blacklist workers, Greene sent the names and occupations of

Hay's dissatisfied laborers to Deputy Quartermaster Morgan Lewis and ordered him not to employ them. "The different Agents in the Quartermaster Department must endeavor to support each other," Greene advised Lewis, "in keeping down the wages of the Artificers for they are rising to an intolerable height." The artisans, however, were too important to the army to dismiss outright. Some agreement had to be reached. On the same day he wrote Lewis, Greene instructed Hay to fix the artisans' wages on some reasonable footing. But if they refused to work, Greene swore he would lock them out from employment in the Quartermaster Department.[32]

The raise apparently was not sufficient for the artisans brought up the issue again in November 1779, and Greene again refused to countenance their petition. As before, Greene's main objections to the artisans' "combination" were that it smacked of blackmail, it would lead to more demands, and it rendered quartermaster operations precarious and expensive. But Greene also anticipated a "universal outcry" when citizens heard of the wage increase. He wrote to Hay, "People cannot or will not attend to the current depreciation, indeed they cannot bring their minds to it at once; and therefore where they see the wages of people rising very fast they suppose it to proceed from a want of oeconomy, address, or good management in the public agents." When Greene was assured that the artisans "mean not to abide a combination dangerous to the public service," he reversed his decision and advised Hay to raise their wages. But by November 1779, Hay was in no position to pay the artisans, much less raise their salaries. Like all the other staff officers, he had no money and was deeply in debt. Men in all the staff departments threatened to resign or gave notice of quitting because of inadequate wages. Deputy Quartermaster Moore Furman's complaint exemplifies staff officers' difficulties in retaining workers: "I am very likely to be very soon in a worse Situation than ever. All my assistants and Foragers say they must leave the Service. [Their] Wages [are] so low that they are obliged to spend in one day [what they earn in] four."[33]

Transporting supplies and retaining workers were difficult tasks, but procuring food was easily the most frustrating and exhausting logistical problem confronting military supply officers. At the heart of the problem was the reluctance of many farmers to sell their goods to the army. Some refused to part with their produce, sell their livestock, or grind their wheat or corn because they were disaffected with the American cause. Others, angered at state imposition of price controls on farm products, refused to sell their crops to military supply officials at the stipulated prices. In May 1778, Commissary General Jeremiah Wadsworth reported that ever since Connecticut's Regulating Act went into effect, "a universal withholding prevail[ed]" among that state's beef producers. Nor was Connecticut unique. Wherever state authorities established price ceilings, farm goods disappeared from the open market. Consequently, state officials refused to enforce price control laws or quickly repealed them. As Thomas Burke, North Carolina's congressional delegate noted, it was impossible "to regulate prices in a country where the holders are under no necessity of selling."[34]

Although disaffection and state price control laws obstructed the procurement of food for the army, the speculative practices of countless farmers overshadowed these problems. Their greed took a variety of forms. Rather than sell wheat and other grains to the army, farmers distilled the grain into alcohol for quick and profitable sale to the troops. But the most common problem, especially between 1777 and 1779, was that a great number of farmers sold their crops to merchant speculators or held on to them in the hope that prices would continue to rise. As Assistant Foragemaster Owen Biddle reported: "All the commissaries [give] unpleasing Accounts of the raised price of Grain and the unwillingness of the Farmers to part with it while there is a prospect of a still greater advance in the Price[.] The vast Number of Persons who are speculating in that Article [makes] it almost impracticable to get any considerable Quantity."[35] The speculative practices of farmers delayed the shipment of supplies to the army and made staff officers' tasks more laborious. Nevertheless, staff officers did find a way to solve the problem: they simply had to meet farmers' stiff demands. When they did, the army fared tolerably well. But by paying extortionate charges, staff officers laid themselves open to the accusation that they were purposely raising prices to increase their own commissions.

Civilian theft intensified supply shortages. Some inhabitants carried away from camp almost anything not tied down. Others, impersonating soldiers, drew rations for themselves and forage for their horses. But the worst offenses occurred outside of camp. With teamsters scattering goods all over the country, citizens could not resist the temptation to appropriate army supplies. Indeed, according to Quartermaster General Greene, they considered it their due: "It being a received opinion among many that whatever public property shall by accident or otherwise fall in their way, they have a right to apply to their own use. Thousands of arms and all kinds of public stores have been conveyed away upon this principle." General Washington suggested that guards accompany wagon shipments, and staff officers threatened to prosecute "persons backward in delivering up the property belonging to the public," but nothing appears to have deterred the practice.[36]

The thievery of civilians and the avarice of farmers were matched, if not surpassed, by the negligence and fraud of contractors and suppliers.

Goods that arrived in camp were often shoddily constructed and of inferior quality. Contractors delivered axes without heads. Beef arrived spoiled, flour sour and unwholesome. Leather pack saddles could be torn with "thumb and small finger." Soldiers discovered blankets to be but one-fourth their proper size. Shoes went unused because they were too small, and those that fit fell apart in a day or two because they were made of cheap materials and poorly constructed. Commissaries found that casks of meat contained stones and tree roots and that barrels of flour had "the Center Scooped out and the sides standing." Even gunpowder was debased and unusable. "The people at home," observed one Continental officer in 1778, "are destroying the Army by their conduct much faster than Howe and all his army can possibly do by fighting us."[37]

It would be misleading to suggest that the sharp practices of persons outside the army caused all, or even most, of the army's supply problems. Continental soldiers and militia troops were just as negligent, greedy, and dishonest as their civilian counterparts. Few opportunities to misuse Continental property escaped their notice. They wasted ammunition by needlessly firing their guns in camp; threw away their camp equipment when it became too heavy to carry; deliberately destroyed their weapons and tools; and sold their clothes, ammunition, and accouterments. General Washington railed against their unprofessional behavior, and state authorities prohibited their citizens from purchasing goods from the soldiers, but with little effect.[38]

Washington did more than complain. In March 1778, he nominated Baron von Steuben inspector-general with the expectation of "introducing a regular System of Discipline and Manoeuvers into the Army." But Steuben was not able to turn his attention away from drilling the Continentals to devote time to a systematic inspection of the men and equipment until the spring of 1779. In the interval, the army's wasteful practices continued. Undoubtedly, the baron's inspections and detailed recordkeeping helped improve the soldiers' treatment of military equipment. But the improvement was ephemeral. In October 1780, Washington ordered Steuben to assist Greene, who had resigned as quartermaster general and now commanded the Southern Army. With his transfer to the Southern Department, Steuben dropped all thoughts of the inspectorate.[39] Fulfilling the baron's methods rested on the shoulders of subinspectors and junior officers, who without his forceful presence inevitably neglected their duties. The army then reverted to its old ways. Not until after the victory at Yorktown in October 1781 would the army again benefit from Steuben's administrative expertise.[40]

A further measure of the failure of Steuben's inspectorate to discipline Continental troops was the persistently high level of theft in the army.

Soldiers serving as brigade quartermasters and regimental commissaries embezzled army supplies and sold them for profit. The Continentals also stole military goods and sold them to inhabitants for liquor and cash. Soldiers robbed one storehouse so frequently that the constant comings and goings of the thieves left a well-worn path between the camp and the supply center.[41] Another form of theft that seriously depleted military supplies was soldiers' persistent habit of walking off with the army's equipment after serving only six or twelve months. General Washington and Quartermaster General Greene roundly denounced the militia in particular for this practice.[42] Pennsylvania's President Joseph Reed believed that most of the militia deliberately left their weapons at home in the hope they could draw new ones at Continental expense. General George Weedon claimed that militia troops from the New England states acquired guns "by hook or by crook. . . . It was a kind of common law amongst them to filch arms." To cut down on the embezzlement of military equipment, General Washington, in June 1776, ordered the quartermaster general to stamp all tools with the insignia "*CXIII*" denoting the Continent and the thirteen colonies. A year later, with independence declared, the mark was changed to " U N I T E D   S T A T E S" and was later shortened to "U.S."[43] Though sound in theory, these efforts to institute property control failed to restrain soldiers or civilians from appropriating public property for their own use.

The war itself, of course, consumed an immense amount of war matériel and was a primary cause of the Continental army's recurrent supply shortages. Washington's Fabian strategy of avoiding a major engagement and usually moving out of the reach of the enemy took a frightful toll on soldiers' shoes. The British raids at supply depots in Danbury, Connecticut, in April 1777 and Point of Fork, Virginia, in 1781, resulted in heavy losses of military equipment. Battle defeats also cut deep into army supplies: a British victory usually meant a corresponding loss of badly needed equipment and ammunition. When the British captured Fort Lee in November 1776, for example, they also acquired three hundred tents, one hundred barrels of flour, and most of the Americans' cannon. Close-quarter battles often ended with revolutionary soldiers fleeing from the British. In their haste to escape, they threw away anything that slowed their retreat. In 1776, Private Joseph Martin returned to the spot where earlier the Americans had been fired upon during the Battle of Kip's Bay and observed that "the ground was literally covered with arms, knapsacks, staves, coats, hats, and old oil flasks."[44] The Continentals would eventually learn to hold their ground in battle, but the militia continued to divest itself of military equipment when pressured by the enemy.

Shortages fed on themselves as soldiers cannibalized goods acquired for one purpose and made them serve another. They cut up blankets to make clothing and flour bags; tents became blankets or clothing; cartridge boxes were converted into shaving mugs and their flaps used to mend shoes. And, of course, the ersatz goods fell apart even more quickly than the originals. Erratic and uncoordinated supply deliveries aggravated the problem. When shipments of stockings arrived, quartermasters distributed them to men without shoes, who, not surprisingly, wore them out in less than a week. Rather than repair shoes or patch clothing, the soldiers threw away the worn-out goods and requisitioned new ones.[45]

Military supply officials could do little about these problems except to redouble their efforts to supply an army that seemed to have an inexhaustible capacity for food, clothing, and ammunition. If these had been the only problems confronting staff officers, it is possible that in time the difficulties might have been overcome. But between late 1778 and 1780 the steep increase in prices and the rapidly depreciating currency created an entirely new set of problems that threatened to overwhelm the ability of staff officers to supply the army. After 1778, the financial crisis overshadowed almost every other problem.

The effects of the high rate of depreciation are graphically illustrated in the growth in the annual expenditures of the staff departments, especially in the Quartermaster and Commissary departments, as shown in Table 3.1. Compared with the beginning of the war, expenditures in the Commissary Department had increased twenty-five-fold, and those for the Quartermaster Department had climbed more than fortyfold. As prices rose, Congress printed even more money, which in turn depreciated, causing prices to rise ever higher.

The value of Continental currency plunged in 1779. At the beginning of that year $1 in specie was equal to $6.84 in paper currency. By December 1779 the ratio was 1 to 42.2; in December 1780, 1 to 99.54. By the end of 1780, Connecticut's Congressman Oliver Wolcott was not exaggerating when he noted that Continental currency was "fit for little else but to make the tail of a paper kite with." The most noticeable effect of depreciation was the drastic drop in the purchasing power of Continental currency between 1778 and 1780. In April 1778, £100 in paper money purchased 63 hundredweight of flour, or 308 pounds of sugar, or 1,321 pounds of iron, or almost 10 barrels of beef. One year later, the same amount purchased only 7 hundredweight of flour, or 94 pounds of sugar, or 297 pounds of iron, or slightly less than 2 barrels of beef.[46]

Congress was aware that its enormous emissions of paper money were responsible for devaluing the currency and took measures to halt the presses. On 3 September 1779, Congress resolved to place a ceiling of $200 million on the amount of currency to be issued, but this ceiling was

T A B L E 3. I. *Congressional Expenditures, 1775–1779*

	1775–76	1777	1778	1779
Pay of the army	$9,371,302	$9,633,351	$14,730,073	$15,788,372
Commissary of Provisions	2,539,555	5,755,307	21,003,016	52,761,773
Commissary of Military Stores	——	256,390	504,623	3,044,837
Quartermaster Department	756,553	3,133,302	17,806,571	56,585,666
Clothing Department	657,874	1,053,182	3,742,985	7,710,523
Hospital Department	18,150	482,050	1,145,000	1,496,144
Barrackmaster General	——	25,000	75,000	773,000
Miscellaneous	6,712,233	6,087,751	7,958,001	11,543,543
Total	$20,055,667	$26,426,333	$66,965,269	$149,703,858

Source: General Estimate of the United States from the first Sitting of Congress in 1775 to the End of the Year 1779, PCC, reel 41, item 34, p. 223. I have followed the format used by Robinson, "Treasury Administration," 100, who believes these figures were compiled in 1781.

reached shortly afterward because $160 million was already circulating. The final step in combating depreciation was taken in March 1780, when Congress essentially declared bankruptcy, repudiated its own currency, and resolved to retire its outstanding bills at the ratio of forty to one. In a single stroke, Congress reduced its debt from $200 million to $5 million.[47]

The resulting scarcity of money, coupled with yet another reorganization of the Board of Treasury in July 1779, left congressional fiscal policy in shambles. When finally completed, the reorganization placed men from outside Congress on the board. But Congress, preoccupied with the usual crush of business, waited until 9 November to elect board members, who then did not begin their work until the twenty-ninth of the month. In the interim, the old board improvised as best it could but fell far short of the demands made upon it. The board's chief shortcoming was its lack of foresight. According to Charles Pettit, the Quartermaster Department's liaison with Congress, the board failed "to look forward with due caution so as to provide for probable events; so that every demand comes upon them as it were by surprise. . . . Like an improvident housewife who takes no care to have bread before hand, Cake is generally to be made by way of expedient at dinner time."[48]

The new board's foresight was little better, and its unreliability was increased by its dependence on funds from sources over which it had no control. When John Chaloner and John White, purchasing agents for Commissary General Jeremiah Wadsworth, requested $6 million, the Board of Treasury had little choice but to recommend that twelve separate warrants be drawn upon eight state treasurers, one state governor, two loan officers, and the Continental treasurer.[49] With state legislatures as hard-pressed for money as Congress, the board's action was almost tantamount to nonpayment. The board's recourse to "creative financing" to accommodate the requests of supply officials reveals the damaging but inescapable consequences of stopping the presses.

Because there was never enough money to go around, the staff departments usually wound up on the short end. Assistant Quartermaster General Charles Pettit's experience was typical. On 30 October 1779, Pettit requested $10 million from the Treasury Board. Aware of the financial difficulties confronting the board, he suggested that if the entire sum could not be furnished immediately, $3 million would suffice initially. Two weeks later, on 15 November, the Treasury Board replied that it would issue Pettit the $3 million, but he received only between $100,000 and $200,-000. Nor could the treasurer inform Pettit when he would receive the remainder. For the next three months, the board never came close to furnishing Pettit with the sums he requested. By March 1780, Pettit was forced to accept that "all avenues to the Treasury are shut; or at least the fountain is dried up, and not a dollar is now to be obtained for any purposes whatever."[50]

In the field, staff officers had long been operating under the Board of Treasury's parsimonious regime. Beginning as early as the summer of 1778 and increasing in number over the next twelve months, demands for cash emanated from every purchasing district. "Intirely out of money," "The want of Money is another subject not a little distressing," "Money-Money-Money, for god's sake . . . send me what Cash you can," were typical pleas between 1778 and 1780.[51] When their appeals went unanswered, staff officers turned to other means to supply the army.

In lieu of money, military supply officials issued certificates—drafts upon their respective departments—in exchange for goods. Certificates originated as ad hoc responses to cash shortages and were at first envisioned as merely stopgap measures conferring legitimacy on an essentially credit relationship. By 1778 preprinted forms replaced the handwritten certificates, an indication of their widespread use and the worsening financial situation. Various techniques were employed to encourage inhabitants to accept certificates. In a notice appearing in the *Pennsylvania Packet*, the chief officers of the Quartermaster Department—Greene, Pettit, and Cox —assured would-be recipients that "in every state where these certificates are distributed persons will be appointed to attend and pay them off at certain short periods, and at such places as will best accommodate the inhabitants." Readers were also assured that certificates could be used as money. Both Congress and staff officers pledged their word that certificates would be redeemed quickly and equitably. Additional encouragement came from Pennsylvania's state government, which legislated that certificates were to be accepted for militia fines. Initially, given these reassurances and incentives as well as the high prices they were demanding, farmers willingly accepted Quartermaster and Commissary certificates in place of money.[52]

Sound credit relations and the active cooperation of inhabitants were crucial to supplying the army. If staff officers failed to make good their obligations, farmers would refuse to accept certificates, and the army would suffer accordingly. To maintain the credit-worthiness of certificates, to uphold their own credit and reputation, and to further the cause of American independence, staff officers, with remarkable uniformity, spent their own money first and then borrowed from friends and moneylenders to keep the army supplied. Assistant Deputy Commissary James Reed wrote that he first used £4,000 of his own money, "then took to borrowing of my neighbors till they were all Dry." John Moore sold his property to discharge public debts. Deputy Quartermaster Udny Hay begged the governor of New York to lend him money for which he would "enter into any Bond . . . if it can in the smallest Degree tend to procuring such a sum as may be requisite for getting the army a proper supply of Provisions."[53] Other staff officers borrowed sums ranging from $10,000 to $130,000 on their own personal credit. Assistant Deputy Foragemaster David Duncan's experience was common: "I have borrowed, and laid out my own Money till I have left myself One Hundred Dollars in the World."[54] When their money and their friends' money ran out, staff officers gave their word in exchange for supplies. According to Assistant Foragemaster Owen Biddle, by November 1779 forage for the army rested "chiefly on the Credit of the Officers of the department, [and] unless their Credit is supported . . . with competent supplies of money it must fail." By the end of 1779, military supply officials were deeply in debt: Andrew Bostwick, a deputy foragemaster, alone owed $2,162,405, and Deputy Commissary General Henry Champion owed more than £2 million. Collectively, the Commissary Department was $22 million in debt.[55] Generally speaking, between 1778 and 1779, farmers accepted staff officers' good money or good word.

In the spring of 1779, the credit bubble collapsed. Creditors' patience with staff officers' inability to settle their public and private accounts snapped after delays in some cases of more than a year and a half. "Promises will not answer to pay debts any longer," Assistant Deputy Foragemaster Duncan reported. "[The people] say they would not Trust their Father if in public service."[56] As mistrust of military supply officials spread, those who did business with the army took measures to protect themselves. Many farmers began refusing to part with any more goods until they were paid. Others demanded cash immediately. Deputy Quartermaster Archibald Steel's experience was typical: "My Credit is nearly sunk with the people here from my not being able to comply with my promises to them. They now declare they will not part with their property in future to the public without the Money laid down to them." Merchants also refused to extend credit, and supplies were sold from under military supply officials who could not pay cash. Deputy Commissary General Peter Colt lost 4,400 gallons of molasses because of delays in receiving money. Not only did the army not get the goods, but Colt calculated that by the time he could contract for a similar amount, the price would have doubled, costing the public an additional $30,000. Similarly, wagons remained unbuilt or were sold when contractors realized staff officers could not pay for them. As Quartermaster General Nathanael Greene observed in November 1779, "We can no more support the Army without cash, than the Israelites could make brick without straw."[57]

The presumption that cash could solve the army's supply problems, however, was rudely shattered by the rapidly depreciating currency. As early as March 1779, it was reported from York, Pennsylvania, that "People are now so afraid of the money that it is almost impossible to Purchase Grain at any rate."[58] By December 1779, the people's refusal to accept Continental currency was the main reason for staff officers' inability to supply the army. Reports from the field echoed the same refrain: "I can neither Send on any more stores or procure any thing from my department as the money depreciates so fast no body will trust the Continent one day."[59] By the beginning of 1780, with Congress bankrupt, staff officers indebted for millions of dollars, public credit annihilated, and paper currency growing more worthless every day, the Quartermaster and Commissary departments were incapable of adequately supplying the army. As a result, Washington's army encamped at Morristown, New Jersey, nearly starved and disbanded in the winter of 1780.[60]

All of these problems—the natural impediments to transporting supplies, the interference in supply shipments by Continental officers and state authorities, the administrative legalism of staff officers, the shortage of manpower in the staff departments, the difficulty of securing food from farmers, the fraud and theft by civilians and soldiers alike, and the financial crisis of 1779—led to shortages of supplies that were partially alleviated through channels other than the staff departments. State supply organizations and committees of safety were the second most important source of supply for the army. Civilian volunteer efforts also lent a helping hand. The selectmen of Ipswich, Massachusetts, set the women of the town to making breeches for the soldiers. On a much wider scale, a nationwide women's relief committee, the Ladies Association, headed by Esther De-Berdt Reed, the wife of the president of Pennsylvania, collected money and linen for the army. Launched in Philadelphia in 1780, its initial fund drive netted $7,500. Also responding to the plight of the army in 1780, Philadelphia merchants set up the Bank of Pennsylvania, whose main purpose was to buy food and ammunition for the army. But with the exception of the state supply organizations, which operated throughout the war, civilian volunteer efforts were short-lived and made only a minimal contribution to supplying the army.[61]

To remedy the lack of food and military equipment, army officers and enlisted men resorted to numerous ad hoc solutions. General Gates, commander in chief of the Southern Army, authorized an officer to visit every North Carolina county with a list of the names of the men who lived there and collect clothing and other necessities from their friends and relatives. General William Smallwood established a shoe factory, used his own troops to run it, and kept his men amply supplied with footgear. Light-Horse Harry Lee kept his men supplied by capturing British supply wagons. Continental soldiers also employed more traditional methods. Clothing was sent home to wives for mending, and families supplied soldiers with warm clothing, paper, and candles.[62] When driven by necessity, many soldiers stole food and clothing from their compatriots and plundered neighboring inhabitants to keep from starving.[63]

In addition, victorious battles—at Trenton, Saratoga, and Stony Point, for example—meant captured equipment that augmented American supplies. When the British evacuated Boston in 1776, they left behind nearly thirty thousand pounds of military stores. Both America's small navy and its numerous privateers added to the army's meager supplies by capturing British supply ships.[64] But none of these temporary and unpredictable sources, whether civilian or military, successfully alleviated the army's food, clothing, and equipment shortages. To meet the needs of the army, military officials reluctantly resorted to impressment.

CHAPTER 4

IMPRESSMENT

Tho' dire necessity has obliged us, however reluctantly, to make use of the odious oppressive means of impress for obtaining Supplies, we conceive nothing but the same necessity can justify the Continuance of a Mode so injurious to our fellow Citizens.
    —George Webb to Major Richard Claiborne,
        9 November 1781

It is impossible to carry on a war without oppressing the inhabitants in some degree; and however disagreeable and inconvenient it may be to the people, and to those in power, a regard to the common good and general safety will justify the measure.
    —Nathanael Greene to President Joseph Reed, 1 August 1780

You may justly wonder the Flour is not sent according to your order. . . . [The quartermaster] says he has got Warrants for Impressing Teams— had the Warrants Executed; but the Inhabitants laugh at such methods, as they are never called to the least account for their noncompliance.
    —John McArthur to Charles Stewart, 19 December 1779

IMPRESSMENT DURING the revolutionary war provides a unique opportunity to observe the impact of war on society, for by definition impressment involves the seizure of civilian property by soldiers. Popular notions of impressment tend to conjure up images of bayonet-wielding troops coercing defenseless inhabitants into surrendering all their worldly possessions. But before late 1779 such scenes were the exception in most states rather than the rule. With their long tradition of protecting local interests, state legislatures designed impressment statutes to ease the friction between civilians and soldiers by placing major responsibilities for impressment on town and county magistrates. But because state impressment laws and local officials favored the inhabitants' economic welfare over the army's, military officers were often stymied in procuring supplies. Impressment statutes thus created conflict between army officers, state officials, and inhabitants and raised fundamental questions as to the proper relationship between military and civilian authority.

Beginning in 1780, as a result of the nation's deteriorating financial condition and the repudiation of local elites by irate citizens, the military was forced to intervene more directly and frequently to impress goods from civilians. Much to their consternation, military supply officials met outright resistance from defiant inhabitants. In a society in which social and economic developments had already partially eroded deferential attitudes, impressment and military depredations made many Americans even more prone to question constituted authority and more willing to act without consulting the leaders of society.

IN THE EARLY YEARS of the war, military authorities rarely had recourse to impressment. During the first two years, it was an ancillary means to provide for the army, employed sporadically and subject to few abuses or complaints. In the winter of 1777–78, the breakdown of transport and consequent food shortage, "gross confusion" in the Quartermaster Department, and Congress's neglect in attending to these logistical problems forced the army to rely temporarily upon impressment as its primary means to feed and clothe the soldiers at Valley Forge. In 1778, when Congress instituted reforms in the staff departments, there was a brief respite in the army's need to impress goods. After the appointment of Nathanael Greene as quartermaster general and Jeremiah Wadsworth as commissary general, a marked improvement occurred in transport, provisions, and camp equipment.[1]

But the army's good fortune was short-lived. From late 1778 until the end of the war, the depreciation of Continental currency, the spectacular rise in commodity prices, and the shortage of goods neutralized and ultimately undermined the improvements effected by Greene and Wadsworth.

In an effort to provide for the army, state legislatures enacted embargoes, antimonopoly laws, wage and price controls, and other monetary expedients, but to no avail. The inability of the states to legislate supplies into existence coupled with the severe financial crisis of 1779 forced army officials to cast about for an alternate method of supplying the army. In New York and Pennsylvania after 1778 and in the South after the fall of Charleston in May 1780, the armies under the command of Washington and Greene had no choice but to rely more heavily on impressment to support themselves.[2]

Not surprisingly, the increased reliance on impressment brought in its wake abuses and complaints. For example, Pennsylvania newspapers strongly condemned Dr. William Shippen, Jr.'s use of impressed wagons to transport wine and sugar for personal profit while he was director-general of the Hospital Department. Most complaints, however, tended to center on the failure of military officials to act in accordance with civil law. State authorities criticized staff officers for neglecting to secure impress warrants from magistrates and for not paying for impressed goods.[3] Similarly, staff officers were denounced for treating farmers injuriously. Typical was the Pennsylvania Council of Safety's blast at staff officers at the close of 1777: "Contrary to the Policy of free States, Quartermasters, Commissaries and other persons of Character, purely Military, have been left through necessity, to press Wagons and Horses, a practice big with mischief and oppression, such officers regarding merely their own convenience and ease, and burdening chiefly the neighbourhood where they reside, and forcing into Service Carriages carrying the Town food and fuel to the immediate distress of the inhabitants."[4]

But state authorities did not need abuses by the military to cast a jaundiced eye upon impressment. Even before the war, both theory and experience had created a negative reaction to the practice. In common with other revolutionaries, state authorities' distrust of the military in general and impressment in particular was a legacy of seventeenth-century British anti-army ideology. It was further strengthened by Americans' involvement with the British army during the Great War for the Empire. Colonial officials, especially those in New England and New York, had repeatedly quarreled with the British army's claim to the right to impress men and supplies. Because of their tradition of autonomy and localism, colonial Americans vigorously resisted British impressment efforts and, as John Shy has noted, forced the "British government and army command . . . tacitly [to concede] the right of colonial assemblies to legislate on quartering and impressment." Though the colonists were successful in controlling military impressment, the experience did not lead to a more benevolent feeling toward armies but rather reinforced Americans' antimilitary attitudes and their passionate belief in the primacy of the civil government over the military.[5]

Prompted by its memory of earlier wartime experience, the Massachusetts Provincial Congress quickly asserted its authority over impressment. On 24 April 1775, just five days after hostilities had begun, the Massachusetts Congress empowered its Committee of Safety and Committee of Supplies to impress horses and teams. Connecticut, too, reflected Americans' traditional hostility to unfettered military force in 1776 by enacting the first civil impressment law of the war. In "civil impressment," a term used by contemporaries, no soldiers were present, no bayonets leveled. If they were unable to purchase clothing or food from citizens, army officers (usually quartermasters and commissaries) sought out the nearest justice of the peace, who would then issue an impress warrant to the local constable. The constable would locate the goods, have them appraised by two or more disinterested inhabitants, and turn them over to the staff officers for payment.[6]

There were numerous variations on the civil impressment procedure. One simple technique was for the magistrate to accompany the staff officer through a neighborhood searching for available goods. Another method prescribed by law in Rhode Island was to hold an informal trial. One approving eyewitness described such a civil impressment in Rhode Island at the beginning of 1779. According to the newspaper account, a brigade foragemaster, needing provender for the soldiers' horses, applied to the deputy governor, who immediately gave him a letter requesting the Pawtuxet magistrates "to exert themselves," whereupon one of the magistrates sent notices to eight persons to appear before them. All of the men showed up, and the hearing went on all day. Seven of the eight demonstrated convincingly their inability to contribute to the army; the magistrates acquitted them and allowed them to return home. The eighth inhabitant freely acknowledged that he could spare one ton of bog meadow hay. The magistrate ordered him to bring it the following Tuesday. New Jersey magistrates resorted to yet a different system. Rather than hear individual cases, they apportioned specific amounts among the towns. For example, responding to General Washington's plea from Morristown for 1,500 bushels of grain and 150 head of cattle during the winter of 1780, New Jersey's Sussex County justices assigned specific quotas to communities within their jurisdiction. Thus, Knolton was required to provide 150 bushels of wheat and 10 head of cattle while its neighbor to the north, Hardwick, was called upon for 450 bushels of wheat.[7]

As these examples suggest, the justice of the peace was the key to the civil impressment operation. And in the wake of the army's distresses and reports of abuses by military officers, most states followed Connecticut's lead in relying on magistrates to mediate between the army and the people. State officials and their constituents considered justices of the peace—because of their elite status, prestige, and knowledge of local leaders and conditions—ideal instruments for apportioning the burden of supplying the army. A defender of Rhode Island's impressment system emphasized these qualities. He noted that because "levying supplies by strangers had in many instances . . . prove[d] unequal, from their not knowing the particular circumstances of individuals, they [the Rhode Island Assembly] wisely thought that their public magistrates, who were better informed as they were possessed of the power, so they undoubtedly had the inclination of carrying the benevolent Act [to Supply the Army] into full execution." Although civil impressment was designed to produce maximum support for the army with minimum distress to the inhabitants, state impressment laws gave first consideration to the citizens' economic well-being and comfort. One way to ensure fairness was to instruct magistrates to equalize the amount taken from the inhabitants. Thus Maryland's Council of Safety advised the justices of the peace in Frederick County when impressing carriages to do so "in such Manner that the Burthen of the said one hundred Waggons be divided as nearly equal as conveniently may be on the different parts of the said County."[8] Similarly, New York's Assembly admonished its magistrates to give "due respect to the estate and ability of each respective person, and the number of days and times their respective teams, horses, or carriages shall previous thereto have been impressed."[9] State officials also enjoined magistrates to consider the economic status of individuals and to impress only from inhabitants who "can without very great Inconvenience spare the same."[10]

State officials further acted to protect inhabitants from staff officers' abuses by restricting the power of the military to impress. They ordered quartermasters and commissaries to secure impress warrants from magistrates rather than impress goods directly from the people. Failure to do so was punishable in Pennsylvania at £50 and in Delaware at £100 for every offense. State authorities also demanded that staff officers not request "general" impress warrants but have in their possession a warrant describing the item needed and stating the quantity, purpose, and length of time it was required. Several states placed specific time limits on articles impressed by the military. For example, New Jersey prohibited the retention of any carriages, horses, or cattle impressed for public service for more than three days without the owners' consent. State regulation of impressment reached its height in March 1781, when the Virginia Assembly resolved that staff officers impressing horses must list "1st. The Species of Horse impressed, that is, whether a Stone Horse, Gelding, or Brood Mare. 2d. A Description by the Size, Age, and general Appearance. . . . 3d.

The Sum at which they were first valued. 4th. The sum at which they were revalued. 5th. Whose Property. 6th. In what County Impressed. 7th. By whom impressed. 8th. To whom delivered."[11]

Pennsylvania, which bore the brunt of impressment operations during the army's encampment at Valley Forge, did more than pass impressment laws to control military supply officials. To protect citizens from military impressment, Pennsylvania's General Assembly created in January 1778 a separate administrative system to procure wagons for the army. In this scheme, the quartermaster general applied to the state's wagonmaster general, who would in turn issue the necessary orders to his county deputies, thus removing the military from contact with the populace.[12] Later steps taken by Pennsylvania authorities reveal how serious they were about protecting their citizens. When complaints continued, the power to impress in Pennsylvania was lodged solely in the hands of its Council of Safety from which all military officers, even General Washington, had to secure permission to impress.[13] The motives behind all of these state impressment laws were threefold: to provide an orderly procedure for supplying the army; to protect citizens from military coercion and economic hardship; and to assert the preeminence of civil government over military operations.

With the army's increased reliance upon impressment after 1778, state officials' distrust intensified. Impressment, as state authorities never tired of telling army officers, was a temporary expedient and not to be considered the solution to the army's supply problems: it was to be used only when absolutely necessary. Adding to state officials' ire was impressment's expense, its interference with trade and manufactures, and especially its irritating effect on citizens.[14]

The need to consolidate citizen support for the new revolutionary regimes contributed to state authorities' hostility toward impressment. With the commencement of fighting in 1775, the political legitimacy of the new state governments was not in every case automatically conferred; rather, it had to be carefully cultivated. In such states as New York, where loyalists and secessionists in the northeastern counties of the state challenged widespread acceptance of the central revolutionary government, and Pennsylvania, where disagreement over the newly instituted Constitution of 1776 encouraged opposition to the state's revolutionary leadership, impressment added to the instability of the new regimes by increasing the number of disaffected citizens.[15]

Pennsylvania's Council of Safety expressed these fears when refusing to implement a congressional resolution in 1777 urging it to seize blankets for the army. Though the council recognized the seriousness of the army's need for supplies, it feared that the "intrusion upon the private property of individuals [would] be unavoidably resented, as a grievance arising from the Constitution." And by identifying the fundamental law of Pennsylvania with the policy of impressment, state officials were apprehensive "that it will greatly weaken and disable the Council from performing essential services."[16] In this case, state authorities thought it better to strengthen long-term support for the regime than to give short-term aid to the army. Also implicit in Pennsylvania's decision was a recognition of the need to tread lightly on constituents who annually voted on the government's policies. In other states as well, the necessity of keeping an eye on the ballot box no doubt added to state authorities' reluctance to resort to impressment.

Whether undertaken by the state or the military, impressment was anathema to state authorities. First, it threatened to turn patriots and neutral citizens into loyalists. Precariously constituted state governments could ill afford to increase the instability of their new regimes. Nor, if they cared to be reelected, did revolutionary officeholders wish to alienate a broad and politically active electorate. Coupled with Anglo-Americans' traditional fear of the army and the actual abuses by some staff officers, state officials' hostility toward impressment is not surprising. What is surprising is how close this animus came to jeopardizing the cause.

ALTHOUGH MILITARY OFFICIALS shared state authorities' dislike of impressment, they had fewer misgivings and were quicker to act in an emergency. Congress initially delegated the power to impress military supplies to state authorities. Less than seven months after the war commenced, Congress recommended to the New England states that they enact legislation empowering George Washington "to impress carriages, vessels, horses, and other things necessary" and permitting him to delegate the power to impress to the quartermaster general or to any inferior officer.[17] Washington's attitude toward and his implementation of impressment procedures are crucial to understanding the outlook and practices of military men. Although Washington was a veteran of the Great War for the Empire, his perspective on military affairs was shaped as much by his experience as a Virginia planter and member of the House of Burgesses as by fighting the French. Washington's reluctant and circumspect use of the impressment power reflected his recognition of the need to subordinate the military to civilian authority. Only in the most serious emergencies, either to prevent crucial military stores from falling into the enemy's hands or, more commonly, to preserve the existence of the army, did Washington order the use of impress warrants. As his aide, David Humphreys, informed Quartermaster General Timothy Pickering, Washington was "utterly averse to a Military impress except on great occasions, and when no other expedients can be devised to answer the end proposed."[18]

Acting on these convictions, Washington cautioned his officers to impress goods "with the utmost prudence and precaution."[19] He wanted officers to avoid wanton violence, to obey state laws, to give reasonable compensation or certificates in return for property taken, to maintain accurate accounts, and to impress the property of Tories before that of the well-affected. In addition, officers were to consult magistrates and to use them, if possible, to ensure that the burden of supplying the army was shared equally.[20] If magistrates were unavailable and goods had to be seized, Washington repeatedly ordered his officers to do so "with as much tenderness as possible to the Inhabitants, having regard to the Stock of each Individual, that no family may be deprived of its necessary subsistence."[21]

Washington's insistence that impressment not discomfort citizens stemmed in part from his distaste for the procedure. "Nothing in nature can be more repugnant to my inclination," he commented to New Jersey's Governor William Livingston, "than to be obliged to have recourse to military coercion for subsistence." Behind his dislike of impressment lay pragmatic military considerations: impressment endangered the discipline of the army. Washington warned that impressment operations "never fail, even in the most Veteran troops, under the most rigid and exact discipline, to raise in the Soldiery a disposition to licentiousness, plunder and Robbery, difficult to suppress afterwards, and which has proved not only ruinous to the Inhabitants but in many instances to Armies themselves."[22] Though Washington was not successful in preventing his soldiers from repeatedly robbing nearby inhabitants of "every thing moveable," his understanding of the thin line separating military impressment from outright plunder and his insistence that the military respect the civilian population contributed to minimizing the soldiers' lawlessness.[23]

Washington's aversion to impressment received its most powerful impulse from his desire not to estrange the American people from the revolutionary cause. From the onset of the conflict, Washington grasped the central principle of modern revolutionary warfare: the necessity of maintaining a positive relationship between the army and the people. Aware that taking supplies without the owners' consent, even when compensation was made, contradicted revolutionary ideals, Washington pointedly reminded his troops that it was "for the preservation of [their] own Rights, Liberty and Property, and those of [their] Fellow Countrymen" that they had been called upon to fight. Washington also restricted the use of force because he realized that frequent impressment would turn the well-affected against the Revolution and place the army in "the odious character of the plunderers instead of protectors of the people." Should this occur Washington predicted dire consequences. If the American army could no longer contrast its respectful conduct toward civilians with that of the lawlessness of the British, an important principle would be lost. Of greater consequence was the army's need for men and supplies: the lack of popular support would seriously weaken the war effort. Thus he believed that the army must always act as the guardian of the people so as not "to alienate their minds from the Army and insensibly from the cause." A commitment to revolutionary ideals paid military dividends.[24]

Washington, however, also recognized that force might have to be used, injustices committed, and the burden unevenly distributed. He reminded his officers that sometimes "delicacy and a strict adherence to the ordinary modes of application must give place to our necessities."[25] Liberty and independence could not be won without the army.

Military officers shared their commander in chief's dislike of impressment. They, too, were reluctant to impress goods, and their orders and instructions echoed Washington's injunctions, stressing lawful behavior toward inhabitants, using magistrates when possible, impressing only when absolutely necessary, and apportioning the requisition equally among the populace.[26] Those military officials most responsible for impressing supplies, the staff officers, likewise abhorred calling in the army to enforce their will and did so only as a last resort. Commissaries and quartermasters followed a hierarchy of preferred courses of action in supplying the army. Most desirable was voluntary purchase, followed by civil impressment. Military impressment was the least favored method. Assistant Deputy Commissary Royal Flint's instructions to his deputy, Peter Colt, clearly illustrate the officers' preferences. Flint told Colt that each purchaser "should try to obtain the wheat by voluntary Sale; if they fail in the attempt, they must apply to civil government for power to procure it: and should not this prove effectual it must be secured by military force.—(I wish to God we may not be reduced to this necessity)."[27]

Officers shared Washington's view of the Continental army's role in embodying the ideals of the Revolution, and they knew military impressment contradicted those ideals. Most would have agreed with Nathanael Greene that "the fewer instances [of impressment] the better, as it militates with the first principles of civil government by destroying that security and confidence in the public faith plighted to every individual, to protect him in the enjoyment of personal liberty, and the free disposal of his property."[28] But if staff officers disliked employing force to supply the army, they did not hesitate to use it after exhausting all other peaceful methods of procurement. Again Greene spoke for all staff officers in justifying the circumstances under which the use of force was excusable: "I would wish to make the Laws of the State the rule of my Conduct in all Cases where it can be adhered to without ruin to the Service, but a partial evil had much better be endured than a general ruin take place."[29] If the choice was between the destruction of the army or disobedience of the law, the law would have to be broken.

Officers' aversion to impressment was based in part on the troublesome relations it engendered between the army and the inhabitants, but, more frequently, military supply officials deplored the inherent slowness of civil impressment. These delays caused Greene to grumble that impressing wagons was "little less tedious than the Jews' passage thro' the wilderness." Especially for an army like Washington's, which often changed positions suddenly, civil impressment with its dependence on magistrates and constables was too slow and unwieldy to provide timely support.[30]

It was left to the outspoken New Hampshire General John Sullivan to articulate the dangerous tendency inherent in state impressment statutes: time-consuming impressment laws could, in an emergency, prove fatal to the army and the American cause. Responding to the promulgation of Rhode Island's Act to Supply the Army passed in January 1779, Sullivan described to the state governor a hypothetical case that emphasized the unfortunate results of faithfully adhering to the law during an enemy attack on the coastal towns of Greenwich, Bristol, or Tiverton. Should the army march to oppose the invaders, Sullivan warned, he would first have to call on the magistrate, who would have to issue citations for citizens to attend court and then hold hearings until sufficient supplies were rounded up. Once en route, if the army lacked forage, the same time-consuming process would have to be repeated. Following the logic of the argument to its natural conclusion, Sullivan pointed out that the slightest misfortune—a cracked wheel, a lame horse, or even a broken chain—must delay the entire army until a magistrate was found, "a process formed, a suit commenced, and a trial had." The consequences of these innumerable delays would be devastating. Better to allow a military officer to impress supplies in the first place. For Sullivan, it was simply a matter of common sense, the custom of all armies. A month later, perhaps because of Sullivan's persuasive, if somewhat exaggerated criticism, Rhode Island rescinded its impressment law.[31]

Rhode Island's rescission reveals that state authorities could act quickly to remove unwarranted impediments to supplying the army. Certain provisions of the impressment statutes also suggest the readiness of state legislatures to assist the army. To ensure the enforcement of civil impressment, the Convention of New York allowed the local constable two shillings for his time and trouble in serving each impress warrant. In addition, states prescribed penalties for inhabitants who refused to obey impress warrants, for justices of the peace who failed to execute warrants, and for saboteurs who deliberately destroyed their own impressed property. A few impressment laws contained provisos suspending civil impressment, in part or whole, during emergencies, thus allowing the military to impress directly from the people.[32]

Nevertheless, even after accounting for state responsiveness and statutory incentives and penalties, overwhelming evidence of state officials' deep distrust of impressment remains. The fact that state officials set up systems of civil impressment with their attendant cumbersome regulations clearly testifies to their suspicions and misgivings about military impressment. State authorities also expressed their bias in the different procedures prescribed for impressing goods by state agents and the military. State legislatures allowed state agents to seize goods without consulting magistrates, unlike staff officers, who had to secure permission before they impressed supplies.[33] Distrust of the military was further evident in the reluctant and legalistic attitude displayed by state authorities in issuing impress warrants. New York's Governor George Clinton denied a request to impress horses for garrison duty because "the Law authorizing me to grant Warrants of impress seem to have for its object only sudden moves and emergencies."[34] Pennsylvania went even further by refusing to include in its wagon law of 1778 a clause allowing the army to impress carriages even in an emergency. The convoluted logic guiding the Pennsylvania Council's decision is worth quoting in its entirety to convey the state's deep distrust of military supply officers: "Notwithstanding there is no provision in the Law for cases of real emergency, it is nevertheless the opinion of Council that there may be instances which will fully justify the Quarter Master General, his deputies and the officers commanding detachments in impressing Waggons. If the Law had given authority to the military to impress, there would have been some reason to fear that very little attention would have been paid to the regular mode of calling upon the Farmers, whereby the burthen might possibly be very unequal."[35] In essence, Pennsylvania authorities declared they would not permit the army to impress wagons because the military would abuse the privilege; nevertheless, in emergencies impressment was permissible, even though it was expressly prohibited by statute. Staff officers were thus invited to act without sanction of law, but they risked prosecution should their judgment prove wrong. State laws such as Pennsylvania's contributed to the punctiliousness of military supply officers.

FEW THOUGHT IMPRESSMENT a good idea. All agreed it undercut the war effort by alienating inhabitants from the cause and contradicted revolutionary ideals. All noted its drawbacks, though for different reasons. While military officers chafed at the slowness of civil impressment, state authorities complained of its expense and damaging effect on trade and manufactures. And both agreed that impressment should be infrequent and resorted to only when absolutely necessary.

Despite this consensus, recurrent friction over the issue of impressment characterized military-civil relations, and state authorities continually reined in the army. The crux of their differences lay in conflicting definitions over the circumstances that warranted impressment and specifically over what constituted an emergency. For state officials, the grounds justifying military impressment bordered on a total collapse of the state. Thus Rhode Island allowed the army to disregard its civil impressment law only when "the Enemy actually land upon the Main, and are making Incursions into the Country."[36] In 1777, Pennsylvania, excusing itself from seizing blankets for the army, "however inclined [it] may be, from the Ideas of self-preservation and necessity," apparently would rather have perished than resort to impressment. And Virginia, in 1781, with British troops camped on its soil, its capital, Richmond, partially burned, and its public records destroyed, continued to insist that Greene's officers adhere to irksome, time-consuming impressment regulations.[37] Of course, state officials quickly remedied all of these obstructionist actions. Rhode Island's legislature rescinded its impressment statute within a month. Pennsylvania officials eventually authorized county commissioners to seize supplies for the army; and Governor Thomas Jefferson wrote General Greene privately, criticizing the assembly's resolves and tacitly condoning impressment by Greene's army.[38]

These measures underscore the point that state governments never deliberately or maliciously retarded military operations. Yet state authorities' commitment to the welfare of their constituents, to the sanctity of private property, to the liberties of the inhabitants, and to the primacy of the civil power over the military was so strong that at times it appears they would rather have lost the war than compromise their principles.

The army regarded impressment from a very different perspective, for the army's definition of an emergency hinged primarily on military considerations. Thus Continental officers advanced the need to impress on grounds of the superiority of the enemy, the lack of supplies, or the noncooperation of inhabitants in supporting the army. Behind these justifications stood the specter of the army dissolved or defeated. Preservation of the army was the military officers' main concern, not because of an affection for things military—there were very few career soldiers in the Continental forces—but because upon the army's shoulders rested the outcome of the Revolution. It was a simple but compelling equation: no army—no liberty or property. When impressment forced military officers to make a choice between the two principles, they reluctantly but firmly chose liberty. Property would have to give way temporarily to preserve freedom, the state, and, ultimately, American independence.

General Greene's objections in April 1781 to the Virginia Assembly's resolutions respecting the impressment of horses exemplify this attitude. The issue, according to Greene, was between the rights of individuals ("as dear to me as to any Man") and the welfare of the community, the safety of which was "an object more valuable." Greene reminded Governor Jefferson that a war was being fought and that "in War it is often impossible to conform to all the ceremonies of Law and equal justice." Any effort to do so would produce greater misfortune to the public by the consequent delay than all the inconveniences individuals might suffer as a result of impressment. Greene concluded by laying out the choice as starkly as possible: "If Horses are dearer to the Inhabitants than the lives of Subjects or the liberties of the People there will be no doubt of the Assembly persevering in their late resolution, otherwise I hope they will reconsider the matter and not oblige me to take a measure which cannot fail to bring ruin upon the Army, and fresh misfortunes upon the Country." The assembly did not reconsider its decision, Greene bowed to civil authority, and, if Assistant Deputy Quartermaster Thomas Hamilton's returns are representative, the army attempted to abide by Virginia's guidelines for impressing horses.[39]

THE GENERAL HOSTILITY to impressment that staff officers encountered in executing state laws was more than matched by the magistrates' attitudes. These local officials consistently frustrated the efforts of military supply officers to impress goods. Despite the difficulties, staff officers between 1775 and 1779 routinely resorted to civil impressment when it was necessary to seize private property. With the collapse of the nation's financial structure in 1779–80, staff officers even went outside Congress's mandated supply system and called upon men of influence—socially prominent local leaders—to aid in procuring army supplies. They believed that out of deference to this elite, inhabitants would contribute willingly and generously to the army. Although occasionally successful, this informal supply system frequently failed because inhabitants refused to obey an elite unable to make good its promises or defend its constituents from American and British depredations. By coupling colonial America's traditional social structure—with its notions of hierarchy and deference—to the necessity of army supply, staff officers caused citizens' respect for constituted authority, never very strong, to deteriorate further. Consequently, many Americans would emerge from the war less deferential and more skeptical of rule by men of wealth and social position.

Although staff officers adhered to the law, in practice, state impressment statutes were only partially successful. Until mid-1780, with only a few exceptions, they worked very well to protect the inhabitants from reckless, ill-considered military impressment. As a system for feeding and clothing the army, however, they failed. Staff officers' basic complaints centered on the unexpected delays of the civil impressment procedure and the magistrates' general lack of responsiveness to the needs of the army. The two phenomena were often tied together; staff officers justly suspected that the problems engendered by magisterial footdragging were not accidental.

At almost every stage of civil impressment, staff officers confronted problems. For example, legislators had assumed that justices of the peace would be readily identifiable, but this was not always the case. In some areas, such as New York in 1778, justices had been nominated but had not yet qualified for office by filing the necessary papers and posting bond. Not knowing the identity of magistrates impelled Deputy Quartermaster Udny Hay to request from Governor Clinton "a return of those Gentlemen's names, and particular places of abode" so he could call on them and avoid using military force to impress wagons.[40]

Knowing the name and address of a magistrate was only the first step. Possession of that knowledge did not guarantee that an impress warrant would be issued. Locating the magistrate still remained a problem: he might not be at home, or, if home, he might summarily deny the officer's request. An example of the problems encountered by staff officers is well illustrated by Cornelius Bogart's difficulty in obtaining wagons to carry firewood for the soldiers' barracks: "I went to Justice Wiltsie Last Tues. and Wed., But Could not Find him at home—Thursday I went to Justice Storm at Hopewell, who Refused Giving me . . . A Warrant to impress. I yesterday Hired a Horse and Went to Hackensack. Could not find the Justice At Home, from there I went Again to Justice Wiltsie who Likewise Refused Me A Warrant." Even when a magistrate issued a warrant, however, staff officers' troubles were not over. Delays could occur after the magistrate issued the warrant to the constable, who could be equally unreliable. Using excuses ranging from sickness to ignorance of the law, constables sometimes refused to serve impress warrants on local inhabitants.[41]

For one reason or another, magistrates constantly frustrated staff officers and delayed much-needed supplies for the army by refusing to issue impress warrants. Magistrates sometimes denied requests for a warrant because they feared personal injury to themselves or their property. Especially in areas in proximity to the British army, as in New York and New Jersey, magistrates dreaded retaliation from Tories if they assessed them for army supplies. In September 1778, Hay was forced to request an impress warrant from Washington because the "Justices are in general afraid to put the [impressment] law in force against such as are refractory." Believing no impressment law had been enacted, magistrates in North Carolina refused to issue a warrant because they feared being the object of a lawsuit. Justices also professed themselves ignorant of the impressment law, maintaining they had never received a copy. Without direct knowledge of the law, they refused to cooperate. More than three years after New York passed its first impressment law, Assistant Quartermaster David Wolfe wearily informed his superior Hugh Hughes that military force would have to be used because the magistrates would not enforce the impressment law, "alledging that they have not the laws and therefore do not know how to act agreeable to them."[42]

Magistrates also obstructed the supply process by their fastidious insistence that staff officers comply with every clause of the impressment statutes. These laws stipulated that impressed goods were to be paid for at reasonable prices. As long as staff officers complied with this proviso, there appear to have been few problems with civil impressment. But beginning in 1779, the depreciation of the currency made many farmers distrustful of accepting Continental bills and wary of extending credit to staff officers. Without money and armed only with certificates to give in exchange for goods, staff officers were prevented by magistrates from transacting their business. Greene complained to Samuel Huntington, the president of Congress, that "whenever the law of any state obliges the people to part with their property for the use of the Army, the Magistrates will not put it in execution unless the Public Agents are possessed of money to pay for the same."[43]

In New Jersey, magistrates refused to allow staff officers to impress private dwellings for quartering soldiers. Dislike of this practice originated before the war, when colonial legislatures had vigorously contested Parliament's right to quarter British troops in America. With the British example still fresh in mind, New Jersey's legislators had included a clause in the new state constitution prohibiting military officers from billeting soldiers on citizens. In the wake of abuses by the American army, the New Jersey General Assembly in October 1777 reaffirmed its opposition by passing a statute granting justices of the peace authority to billet soldiers "where it may be necessary, in Inns, Livery Stables, Ale Houses . . . but in no private Houses whatsoever."[44] Thus when New Jersey magistrates refused to allow Greene to quarter officers in private homes during the army's winter encampment at Morristown in 1779–80, they were correct in telling Greene "that the Laws will not support them."[45] Once again magistrates abided by the letter of the law to the detriment of the army.

Some magistrates, of course, readily cooperated with staff officers.[46] But complaints far outweighed praise.[47] By mid-1780, cooperation between magistrates and staff officers was infrequent. So unusual was magistrates' help that in January 1780 Hay expressed surprise at being furnished fifty-seven sleighs from Rambout precinct, Dutchess County, New York, the same week during which he received a total of four sleighs from two other precincts. Writing to another set of justices, Hay quizzically inquired whether the disparity was "owing to the uncommon Exertion of the Justices of Rambout, to the uncommon Zeal of its inhabitants to the Service, or from some accidental cause which I cannot discover."[48] Though Hay never received a reply to his query, his question shows how rare it was to receive aid from magistrates or inhabitants in the later stages of the war.

Even when magistrates did cooperate with staff officers late in the war, their actions were sometimes hedged with stipulations. In November 1781, after agreeing to procure and transport 102 tons of hay, the justices of Ulster County, New York, told Assistant Quartermaster Uriah Mitchell that their exertion was extraordinary and limited to that single instance: "And while we make this voluntary and uncommon venture to relieve the present distress of the Army which has been represented to us to be extremely great, We think ourselves bound in duty to make this public declaration . . . of our first determination to lay no other assessments of this nature but in compliance with the Laws of the State."[49] Ulster County justices had served notice that not even sudden emergencies would deter them in the future from obeying the formalities of the state impressment law.

It is not difficult to explain why magistrates were so legalistic and so reluctant to cooperate with staff officers. Undoubtedly, magistrates shared the traditional ideological dislike of the army. Lending credence to their fear was the army's wanton destruction of private property. At times, soldiers bore a closer resemblance to a plague of locusts than to the defenders of their country's liberties. Certainly that was the impression the magistrates residing near Robert Temple's home in February 1779 must have retained after the army cut down his orchards for abatis; cut up his nursery for fascines and pickets; burned his fences for fuel; pulled down his walls for stones to underpin the barracks; and used his house and outhouses for shelter.[50] By 1780, such occurrences were all too frequent. No wonder magistrates often viewed the army as a destructive force, a troublesome entity to be opposed, outwitted, and, if possible, avoided.

The obstruction of military officers was also a product of magistrates' traditional role as "Guardians of the people."[51] Magistrates' actions frequently reveal that minimizing the war's impact on the citizens within their jurisdiction was their primary task; the well-being of the army was a secondary consideration. Justice of the Peace Ernestus van Harlingen, a New Jersey magistrate presiding over the Somerset Courthouse district, exemplifies this attitude. Quartermaster General Greene had dispatched an officer to secure van Harlingen's help in taking over barns for sick soldiers. The justice refused Greene's request and replied: "Upon examining the Law I find it to be silent in a great degree upon the question; and as the measure requested, is exceedingly disagreeable to the people of the neighborhood; and the Law not explicit, I cannot think myself under any legal or moral obligation, to take upon me a business so opposite to the inclinations of the people; and for which I am not fully authorized; and therefore must decline it."[52] Given the choice between interpreting the statute broadly and aiding the army, or adhering to the letter of the law and protecting the property of citizens, van Harlingen chose the course most congenial to the inhabitants. Van Harlingen's noncompliance only deepened Greene's dislike for magistrates and confirmed his earlier impression that justices were "like the Watchmen upon the Tower to give the cries to the people."[53] Greene's phrase succinctly captures the principal function of magistrates in the revolutionary war.

In fulfilling this role, magistrates used every legal device in their power to prevent staff officers from impressing supplies. Not even warrants issued by General Washington deterred some magistrates from threatening to sue staff officers for trespass, fining them, and even placing them under arrest. As Foragemaster General Clement Biddle worriedly confided to Washington, his deputies wanted assurance that they were justified in impressing forage "as many of them have been sued, confined, and put to a considerable expense the last fall and Summer when acting under your Excellency's warrant." Six months earlier, Greene had outlined to the president of Congress the explanation for the problems afflicting the Forage Department: "A Spirit of competition prevails [among towns, counties, and states] for the benefit of their own inhabitants. . . . So strict are the Laws of some States, and so attentive are the Magistrates to guard the people's property that the Forage officers have been prosecuted and heavily fined for presuming to take forage on the march of the army . . . by virtue of a press-warrant granted by the Commander-in-Chief."[54] Greene's letter illustrates once again the factors hindering the supply of the army by impressment: restrictive impressment statutes, a protective relationship between magistrates and inhabitants, and the use of legal sanctions against staff officers. Upholding the ideals of the Revolution—the protection of life, liberty, and property—ran headlong against supporting the means— the army—by which those ideals would be secured.

In the face of magistrates' intense localism, staff officers continued to obey state impressment laws and made it a conscious practice to avoid oppressing inhabitants. This was especially evident in their efforts to seek out or request the name of "some person well acquainted with the Resources of Every District" to assist them in procuring supplies for the army. "Otherwise," explained Deputy Quartermaster Hay, "we Shall be Apt from our Ignorance of the Country to make our demands Chiefly from the vicinity of the Camp which I am sensible would be an act of Injustice and which by the assistance of such a person as I have described might be easily avoided."[55] Staff officers frequently expressed concern for the welfare of the inhabitants.[56] Underlying their desire not to antagonize citizens was the common-sense belief that inhabitants would be more willing to part with their goods "out of affection than from fear."[57]

Affection had its limits, however. No matter how carefully staff officers tried not to antagonize inhabitants, the collapse of the nation's finances increasingly forced military supply officials to impress goods from citizens. Moved by ideological fears of the military and the loss of their property, citizens after 1779 began refusing to cooperate with staff officers in a variety of ways. After farmers and army contractors refused to extend any more credit, they not only withheld supplies, broke contracts, and demanded cash on delivery but also relentlessly hounded staff officers for payment. In the process, the public held up staff officers to laughter, censure, and ridicule. The experience was deeply humiliating. "I am so plagued for money," Assistant Deputy Foragemaster David Duncan complained, "that I am ashamed to set my head out of doors, and heartily wish to be relieved out of the Commissary Department."[58] Men who took pride in their roles as local community leaders and credit-worthy merchants found being dunned in such a manner psychologically devastating.

Inhabitants were not content with simply demanding repayment. When creditors failed to receive the money owed them, they took the offensive by first threatening and then suing staff officers for debt and nonperformance of contract.[59] To protect themselves from legal proceedings, staff officers took various actions. Quartermaster General Nathanael Greene, taking note of supply agents' fears of being sued, sought legislation from Congress in February 1780 indemnifying them from damages incurred in civil prosecution.[60] But Congress failed to act. Without protective legislation, staff officers had to scramble to make ends meet. Deputy Quartermaster Walter Pynchon was "obliged to borrow Money to replace money where I had borrowed, to prevent a suit." Commissary General Wadsworth also borrowed money "to prevent my People from being sued." Deputy Quartermaster Robert Patton had to leave his post and go to Philadelphia "to pay a Debt of £160 which I must do in ten days or be sued." By March 1781, with complaints mounting, Timothy Pickering, who seven months earlier had replaced Nathanael Greene as quartermaster general, again appealed to Congress to legislate against the principle "*that a public officer is answerable in his private capacity for his public debts.*"[61]

A few staff officers were so unfortunate as to have neither sufficient money to ward off lawsuits nor beneficent friends with money to pay their debts for them; they were arrested for debt. In January 1782, for example, the local sheriff arrested an assistant deputy quartermaster at Albany, who gave bail and was later served with a writ to appear before the Mayor's Court of New York City.[62] Informed of the suit, Congress finally recommended in March 1782 that state authorities pass legislation protecting staff officers from prosecution for debts contracted during public service. In the following year, however, only one state, Pennsylvania, complied.[63]

The failure of the states to act left staff officers at risk. Consequently, on 18 January 1783, the quartermaster general of the Continental army was arrested by a deputy sheriff in Ulster County, New York. Pickering gave bail, contacted a lawyer, and informed General Washington. Fortunately, and probably as a result of Pickering's arrest, the New York state legislature passed a law staying legal proceedings for one year against staff officers for debts contracted during the war. Pickering was confident that the act would be extended and ceased to worry.[64] Nevertheless, staff officers residing in states without protective legislation were sued for debt.[65]

In response to inhabitants' increasing antagonism, staff officers instituted an informal supply system as an alternative to civil impressment. This supply system, initiated without the sanction or knowledge of either congressional or state authorities, was a product of necessity. The bankruptcy of the national treasury, the sharp depreciation of Continental currency, the refusal by numerous farmers to extend credit or accept certificates, and the increasing unwillingness of magistrates to allow the inhabitants to be imposed upon forced staff officers by early 1779 to come up with a solution to the army's supply problems that refrained from using force yet motivated citizens to support the army.

The system that evolved was made up of two components. The first was the increasing emphasis on persuasion and reason. Staff officers began cultivating the confidence of the people by consulting them, responding to their complaints, and offering patriotic and practical defenses of their requests for army supplies.[66] To add persuasiveness to this approach, staff officers instinctively fell back on the second component, which Jeremy Belknap called the "secret bonds of Society": family government, habits of decency, and the examples of influential persons.[67] It was on this last element that staff officers pinned their hopes as the financial crisis deepened. "It has been my opinion for a long time," Nathanael Greene observed to General Washington, "that personal influence must supply the defects of civil constitution."[68]

By "influence" Greene did not mean the sort of power that a governor, by dint of his official position, routinely exercised with the legislature. Nor did Greene's use of the term bear much resemblance to charisma in the

Weberian sense: influence was not a supernatural gift; its possessors were not prophets with messianic missions to perform.[69] Rather, Greene used the term in its specifically eighteenth-century sense, denoting the capacity of some men to affect the behavior of their neighbors through some intangible, personal quality. Influence usually inhered in men who were socially prominent and wealthy and who held public office. But "influence" was also viewed as a distinct attribute of an individual, a quality existing apart from the authority derived from officeholding. Thus George Washington advised General William Irvine "to call upon the Magistrates (not in their official capacity but as men of influence in and knowledge of their neighborhood)."[70] Their role in supplying the army followed from the widely held belief by elites that inhabitants deferred to men of influence, looked to them for guidance, protection, and leadership, and, most important, would follow their advice to contribute to the war effort.

As the financial crisis deepened and the difficulty of securing supplies increased, personal influence became the overriding qualification used in selecting staff officers. As Assistant Commissary General Royal Flint informed his deputy, Jacob Cuyler, he had recommended that Jacob Bailey head the arduous task of erecting magazines along the Connecticut River, "not only because I consider him a Gentleman of integrity and experience in business; but because his long and particular acquaintance with that country and his influence over the people would render his exertions peculiarly serviceable." Similarly, in the war-torn South—where, in addition to the economic chaos, the organization of the staff departments was practically nonexistent—the confidence of the people was indispensable to supplying the army. In offering the post of commissary general of purchases for the Southern Army to the successful North Carolina partisan fighter William R. Davie, Greene emphasized this trait: "Your character and standing in this country lead me to believe you the most suitable person . . . especially as you have an extensive influence among the inhabitants, and are upon a good footing, and much respected in the army."[71] By 1780, securing supplies for the army was no longer a simple economic transaction but involved testing the theory of deference against the reality of America's proto-democratic political culture.

The attempt by Deputy Quartermaster Udny Hay and his assistants in mid-June 1780 to procure pasturage for the army's oxen and horses provides an excellent example of how this auxiliary supply system functioned. The failure of Hay's assistants to acquire sufficient acreage through normal channels and his aversion to using military force on the inhabitants triggered his recourse to persuasion and reliance on the social prestige of local gentry. Hay explained his course of action to Governor Clinton: "I determined to leave no mode unessayed . . . and, therefore, wrote a Circular

Letter to the Inhabitants in General, and another to some of the principal civil officers of the State in particular, requesting their Influence, by signing a recommendation drawn up for the purpose." In appealing to the "Inhabitants on both Sides of the Hudson [River]," Hay used every argument at his command. He appealed to the inhabitants' patriotism by observing that contributing pasturage to the army gave them a singular opportunity to demonstrate "Zeal in the Common Cause." He threatened to expose them to the scorn of the community by publishing the names of noncontributors. He addressed their economic interests by offering to pay them "in hard Money . . . ; no risque, therefore, can arise from Depreciation of Money." He invoked their pride in the past exertions of New York in support of the army by admonishing them not to "sully the reputation" of the state, and he again appealed to their sense of state honor by comparing the energy of the other states with their languor. He impressed upon them the importance of pasturage, though it "may appear of very trifling Consequence to the good of an army." In summing up the alternatives he faced, Hay concluded his address with a veiled threat: he could either acquiesce in "our Country's Ruin at the very moment of approaching Success" or take by force what the army needed.[72]

A copy of Hay's notice was sent to the supervisors, assessors, and justices of the peace requesting "the addition of [their] Influence" by signing a recommendation of Hay's circular, a request the officials promptly fulfilled. On 20 June, Hay's assistant, George Taylor, Jr., went around the countryside with both documents, showing "them to every inhabitant of whom there was the least probability of obtaining any, but all to no purpose; they would not part with a single acre." The next day Hay wrote to Governor Clinton describing the unpleasant alternatives he faced. He could allow the army to suffer, or he could confiscate the supplies by force. Though the choices were clear, Hay still hesitated to seize private property. He had no doubts that the use of force was justified, even "Patriotic," but recognized that such action was ultimately self-defeating. The use of force would destroy any chance of securing the future cooperation of the inhabitants and would also "be productive of the ruin of him who adopted it." In this case, the short-term benefits of impressment would have to give way to the long-term advantages of regaining the inhabitants' confidence.[73]

Staff officers' attempts to rely on the influence of local leaders failed for one basic reason: they fundamentally misread the relationship between magistrates and inhabitants. Expecting the people to defer to their "betters" in accordance with the assumptions of colonial social theory, staff officers failed to understand that inhabitants obeyed local leaders only so long as their interests were served. If before 1779 resistance to impressment was rare, it was as much because impressment was infrequent as because inhabitants were deferential. After 1780, however, the military's increasing reliance on impressment produced a ground swell of violent resistance that neither staff officers nor magistrates could quell.

All over the country, Americans refused to supply the army by means of impressment and, if necessary, defied constituted authority by force. Thus in New York, Deputy Quartermaster Henry Glen, who was also a justice of the peace, rejected the suggestion to impress supplies because the inhabitants "seem to be determined not to suffer their Property to be taken from them any longer at the risque of their lives." Similarly, in Pennsylvania, President Joseph Reed reported that citizens "absolutely refuse to submit to the Impress of anything and particularly their waggons and Horses and have agreed to oppose Force to Force." Whether relying on the trappings of office or their rank in society, both staff officers and magistrates were powerless in the face of inhabitants' defiance. The report Deputy Quartermaster William Keese received from his assistant in the field explaining his failure to forward supplies to the army was typical: "The Justices' Authority was not sufficient to drive out any of the Country People to assist us— they warned them and sent their Constables about to no effect.—I wrote to them at last, that I should be obliged to send the Bayonet among them.—they said they could not force them to come."[74] The people would no longer obey their leaders.

In the South, opposition to supplying the army was even more widespread and similarly eroded citizens' trust in authority. The British victories at Savannah (1778), Augusta (1779), Charleston (1780), and Camden (1780), the ensuing pursuit of Greene by Cornwallis across the Carolinas, and the continuing internecine battles between revolutionaries and loyalists had left the South devastated, its farm lands destroyed, its people war-weary and distrustful of their local leaders.[75] Like their counterparts to the north, southerners had supplied the army by accepting certificates and responding to the appeals of "Gentlemen of interest and influence." But after 1781 their patience also ran out. As Richard Claiborne, Continental quartermaster for the state of Virginia, noted: "There is such a General dissatisfaction and Suspicion among the people that they are determined not to suffer themselves to be deceived any longer, by being connected with contracts on public account. I can assure you . . . that faith in general among the people towards the Public is totally lost."[76]

Unable to procure supplies by purchasing, issuing certificates, or relying on the prestige of local leaders, military supply officials attempted to impress goods on their own. Here, too, they met with stubborn resistance. Claiborne told Virginia's chief supply official, Colonel William Davies, that "impressing is out of the Question with me, because I have no force."[77] Even when force was available, however, impressment was often thwarted because inhabitants hid their wagons and goods in the nearby woods.[78] If impressment was successful, it sometimes was a Pyrrhic victory: southern resistance turned to sabotage. Reported County Lieutenant Francis Peyton, "In procuring wagons for the service, I have been much perplexed, for after having impressed them, the owners of some . . . have taken in the night a Wheel or something to render them useless." Deference was becoming a casualty of the war.[79]

In the South, the inability of local leaders to protect inhabitants from the depredations of either the American or the British armies further eroded respect for authority. When the war shifted to the South in 1780, there was practically no Continental supply organization in place, nor were sufficient staff personnel available to manage logistical operations. Left to fend for itself, Greene's army was forced to live off the surrounding countryside. Commissary General Ephraim Blaine estimated that perhaps as much as 50 percent of the food the Southern Army consumed was secured through impressment. The British army inflicted far more damage on the southern countryside. As a result of Cornwallis's army eating and pillaging its way through the Carolinas up into Virginia, and destructive raids by Generals Alexander Leslie, Benedict Arnold, and William Phillips in Virginia between October 1780 and June 1781, southern inhabitants continuously felt the wrath of British troops. In small Saint David's Parish in King William County, Virginia, property losses totaled more than £13,000. The inability of the southern gentry to restrain or prevent the plundering of the two armies was further evidence of their failure to live up to their half of the social contract: in return for their esteem, deference, and political office, citizens expected local leaders to protect their lives and property. Magistrates' ineffectiveness was evident to everyone.[80]

CHAPTER 5

CORRUPTION

Business in the civil departments of any army, is like making dictionaries; if any errors are committed there is the severest criticism and blame; but the merit of the performance passes off with little notice and no honor.
    —Royal Flint to Nathanael Greene, 10 December 1781

A charge against a quartermaster-general is most like the cry of a mad dog in England. Every one joins in the cry, and lends their assistance to pelt him to death.
    —Nathanael Greene to Henry Marchant, 15 October 1788
      [1778]

THE SUSPICION OF corruption acted as a corrosive on the social order, ate away at the moral legitimacy of the army and Congress, and undermined Americans' faith in their leaders. Although the charges were largely untrue, the acid of corruption could not be neutralized. Allegations of indolence and fraud weakened the ability of military supply officers to provide for the army by destroying their credibility as "influential" and virtuous revolutionaries. Similarly, the charges of corruption that emanated from the Deane-Lee affair in 1779 spilled over into the public press and seriously damaged the prestige of Congress. The overall effect of this atmosphere of backbiting and recrimination was further to erode Americans' respect for constituted authority. The army's military supply officials bore the brunt of these accusations.

FEW GROUPS OF revolutionaries were more reviled than staff officers. Even within the army, there were many who thought there was something unsavory, even despicable, about staff department personnel. That conclusion at least must be drawn from the sentence handed down by a brigade court-martial. Captain David Dexter of the Second Rhode Island was drummed out of the army for frequently associating with a brigade wagonmaster—conduct judged unbecoming an officer and a gentleman.[1] Similarly, Colonel John Laurens complained of the indiscriminate bestowal of military rank on the likes of "waggon masters, regimental quarter masters etc.," declaring that "titles . . . cease to be honorable when possessed by such personages."[2] Outside the army, by 1780 the very word "quartermaster" had become a term of disparagement. When Congress slighted one of its own committees, a member of the committee, South Carolina's John Mathews, indignantly noted that "regardless of our characters as members of their own body, I find we are to be considered as Quarter-Masters, etc., and liable to equal insults."[3]

Members of the staff departments were denounced and vilified beginning in 1777 in the wake of the scarcity of food and medical supplies at Valley Forge and reaching a crescendo during 1779–80. Americans took to the newspapers and condemned agents in the Commissary and Quartermaster departments as "a herd of monopolizing, extortionate and peculating traders," "those greasy, money-making fellows," and "harpies which have preyed upon our vitals."[4] In Pennsylvania, hostility to commissaries rose to such heights that Deputy Foragemaster Owen Biddle reported that they were "considered as a Common Enemy." Nor was the Hospital Department exempt from similar criticism. The purveyor general of the American hospitals was compared to "Judas . . . the Purveyor General of the Apostolic Board . . . the father of all speculators."[5]

The low opinion Americans had for members of the staff departments resulted from a variety of real and imagined abuses committed by army administrators. Revolutionaries commonly complained that staff departments contained too many idle staff officers. Though undoubtedly exaggerated, there was a measure of truth in an aide's complaint to General Washington that "there is not a Cross Road or Village of three houses but a deputy Commissary and Quartermaster is fixed there—to do nothing." Critics of the staff departments pointed out that pay and rations allocated to these idlers deflected scarce financial resources from the fighting army. In addition to the unnecessary expense, the multiplication of staff personnel was also perceived as needlessly clogging and delaying critical deliveries of food and equipment to the army.[6]

Taking note of the problem, Congress recommended on 9 February 1778 that state executive authorities investigate the conduct of all Continental officers within their jurisdiction and suspend staff officers who were guilty of misconduct or neglect of duty or who were unnecessary to the business. New Jersey's William Livingston was one of the few state governors who acted on the congressional resolution. Uncovering what he described as "unparralleled mismanagement," Livingston boasted to Washington that he had reduced the costs of running the hospital at Princeton from £64 10s. 3d. to £21 15s. 2d. "by removing the supernumeraries, and regulating a few abuses" in the Quartermaster and Commissary departments. For his public service, Livingston was voted a resolution of thanks from Congress.[7]

But the shrillness of the denunciation was far out of proportion to the actual abuse—Livingston saved the republic a mere £42 15s. 1d.—and may in part have been the result of the sheer increase in the number of public officials occasioned by congressional reform of the staff departments in 1777.[8] The creation of state supply and transportation systems, which grew up alongside the army's staff departments, also added to revolutionaries' perception of an extraordinary number of public officials.[9] Some critics disapproved of this duplication of effort and complained that state supply officials made staff officers superfluous and expensive.[10] Others probably did not distinguish between the two sets of officeholders and lumped all idle government officials together.

Given the exigencies of making a revolution and fighting a war, much of the public denunciation of overstaffing may be discounted as uninformed or exaggerated. Quartermaster General Nathanael Greene believed that most of the people in the country failed to appreciate that the normal demands of waging a successful war necessitated employing large numbers of men in auxiliary positions, especially in the Quartermaster Department. The army's need to manufacture and repair tents, to build and repair boats, to provide boards for erecting barracks, and to construct ammunition wagons and carts for carrying entrenching tools required the hiring of hundreds, even thousands, of men. An occupational breakdown of the personnel employed in one of the larger quartermaster camps in New York—that of Deputy Quartermaster Morgan Lewis—clearly reveals the purposes for which it existed. There were eighty-seven carpenters, twenty-seven blacksmiths, seventeen wheelwrights, eleven bateaumen, ten wagoners, and four nailers.[11]

Because many Americans were unfamiliar with enterprises employing such large numbers of men, they may have suspected that these camps were overstaffed. Contributing to this belief was the unavoidable idleness that periodically gripped army supply operations. Quartermaster camps like Morgan Lewis's required sufficient materials on hand in order to keep functioning. Bad weather, unrepaired roads or bridges, lack of forage for the teams, inability to purchase construction material, and delays caused by mismanagement idled workers for days and sometimes weeks. No doubt revolutionaries passing by or hearing of a camp's inactivity pursed their lips and shook their heads at such goings on, but the reasons for workers' idleness frequently lay in circumstances beyond their control.

Given the inevitability of slack time, the public's conclusion that idle men indicated overstaffing or neglect of duty is understandable. Other circumstances contributed to this suspicion. For example, at the army's encampment at Morristown in March 1780, a local inhabitant complained that wagoners arrived for duty late in the morning and left early in the afternoon. But, as Deputy Quartermaster Joseph Lewis explained to his superior, the situation was not what it seemed. Yes, the workers put in a short day, Lewis admitted, and he wished it were possible to stop the practice or hire other wagoners. "But," he elaborated, "here lies the evil which is not in our power to remedy—the farmers serve no longer but from Courtesy. We have neither Money or Forage to induce them to continue, or others to come in, if we should discharge these."[12] In short, without pay the wagoners came and went as they pleased. What looked to the public like flagrant neglect of duty was in reality a voluntary contribution to the war effort.

Administrators rarely addressed the issue of overstaffing. Nathanael Greene was one of the few staff officers who put his thoughts about this problem on paper, and his pragmatic response was probably shared by almost everyone connected with the staff departments. Greene agreed with the critics in principle. He believed that "it may be considered a misfortune either in public or private life to be obliged to employ a great number of Agents. The want of capacity in some, and industry and fidelity in others, naturally multiplies expense." He differed from those who found fault only in the conclusion he drew from this premise: "But where the nature of the business renders these [men] indispensably necessary, the inconveniences must be borne with."[13] The top priority for Greene and most other staff officers was to supply the army and win the war.

To recognize the difficulties involved in supplying the army is not to suggest that every individual employed in the staff departments was a diligent and productive worker. Undoubtedly, the multiplication of staff positions by Congress and the creation of state supply systems provided ample room for deadwood to collect. Thus, to some degree, revolutionary critics of the staff departments were correct in lambasting excessive and idle staff personnel. But it is also important to appreciate that the bulk of those employed were needed to fulfill the army's mission and that laggards were not as prevalent as critics imagined. Far more important than over-staffing and idleness for understanding the disrepute in which staff depart-ment personnel were held was the charge of corruption.

IN THE YEARS 1778–80 the American economy underwent a tre-mendous war boom that brought financial gains to farmers, merchants, and some laborers. Fueled by Quartermaster and Commissary department expenditures of more than $109 million in 1779 alone, wealthy Americans, especially in urban areas, purchased imported luxury goods, held fancy balls, and enjoyed lavish entertainments. With a few exceptions—civil ser-vants, artisans, and those on fixed incomes—the country appeared more prosperous in 1779 than before the war had begun.[14]

Rapid depreciation of the currency and the steep rise in prices, however, seriously threatened whatever good fortune Americans experienced be-tween 1778 and 1780. It was evident to many that the times were out of joint. As one writer in the *New Jersey Gazette* stated, it seemed almost as if "some malignant disorder ha[d] seized upon our body politic." The public spirit and patriotism needed to maintain a republic were fast disappearing; in their place "dissipation, venality and luxury" predominated. Taxes were rising, money was becoming worthless, and the cost of goods was skyrock-eting.[15] Who was to blame for the depreciation of money and the high prices, for the dismal condition of the army, for the loss of republican simplicity and virtue? The search for answers to these perplexing questions began in earnest in 1779.

We now know that an increase in the money supply was the fundamental cause of the depreciation of the Continental currency. Until 1780, Congress issued approximately $226 million in paper money, more than half that amount—$124 million—in 1779 alone.[16] Some revolutionaries recognized that the quantity of money issued was the "principal cause of the depreci-ation." Others placed the responsibility for the country's financial woes on the "greediness of avaricious merchants, monopolizers, farmers, sharpers, forestallers, mushroom traders . . . outdoing one another in raising the price of everything." These groups, critics charged, "act as tho' they had agreed to plunder the State between them, each exerting himself to get the greatest share of the booty."[17] A large segment of the public also blamed staff officers, in addition to speculating farmers and merchants, for the many problems that afflicted the country.

Revolutionaries' belief that staff officers were responsible for the nation's financial woes rested on irrefutable cause-and-effect logic. Staff officers were rich and corrupt; ergo, they were rich because they were corrupt. That they were wealthy no one doubted. There was a widespread belief among revolutionaries that employment in the Commissary and Quartermaster departments was highly lucrative.[18] Inflammatory newspaper accounts gave substance to these beliefs. Benjamin Rush, writing as "Leonidas" in the *Pennsylvania Packet*, reported that when attending a public auction, he witnessed an assistant quartermaster's clerk consistently outbid the most prominent landed gentlemen. Rush testified the clerk laid out tens of thousands of dollars for a farm.[19]

The case of John Fitch illustrates the pervasiveness of these beliefs. Fitch was a deputy commissary who was not making a penny in office and in fact was quickly sinking into debt. Yet when writing to Nathanael Greene, he contrasted his financial condition with that of officers in the Quartermaster Department, "where everyone was making a fortune." Thus even those who should have known better, whose own experience belied the generalization, subscribed to the tenet that staff officers became wealthy in office. If most staff officers did not look particularly prosperous, that, too, could be explained: they concealed their riches to deny the assessor his rightful due.[20]

As to the manner in which staff officers acquired "the fortunes of Nabobs or Sultans," most revolutionaries agreed that they did it dishonestly. A writer in the *New Jersey Gazette* asked, "Can we otherwise account for the sudden rise of some agents from penury to affluence? from precarious subsistence to luxury and voluptuousness?" Few revolutionaries could. They believed staff officers were corrupt, and their logic isolated the means by which commissaries and quartermasters had both the opportunity and incentive to depreciate the currency, raise prices, and grow rich. Critics grounded their indictment of staff officers upon the practice of paying them on a commission basis.[21]

Many revolutionaries, agreeing with congressional opponents of the commission system, believed that the logic linking commissions with corruption was compelling. The new policy was perceived as inherently corrupt by one writer in the *Virginia Gazette*. He could suggest no other reason for the change to the commission system than that "fixed salaries give these gentlemen not such favorable opportunities for embezzling the public money as the other." The granting of commissions also explained the nation's high prices and rapidly depreciating currency. Both factors suited quartermasters and commissaries because "in proportion therefore as the expense increases or the depreciation of the money proceeds, the greater will be the profits arising to them."[22] In sum, revolutionaries were convinced that staff officers raised prices to reap higher profits.

There can be no denying that prices increased during the war; after late 1776 they climbed steadily upward. In the Philadelphia area, between January and April 1777 the price of pork increased 80 percent. The largest price surge, however, occurred in the fall and early winter of 1779. Wheat that had sold for four shillings per bushel between 1774 and 1776 was selling for 150 shillings per bushel in May 1779. By the end of the year prices were seven times higher than at the start. Nor was Philadelphia unique.[23]

But revolutionaries erred in blaming staff officers for these rapidly rising prices. Rather than encourage price increases, most staff officers did everything in their power to limit them. They explicitly instructed agents in the field to purchase forage and provisions as cheaply as possible and admonished them not to raise prices. Deputy Commissary General Ephraim Blaine's injunction to his assistant to exercise "every prudent means to reduce as much as possible the price of every Article wanted for the Army" was commonplace.[24] Concerned about bidding competitively against each other, a practice not always successfully avoided, heads of departments advised purchasing agents to correspond with each other to prevent driving prices upward.[25] Though higher prices would increase their profits, commissaries consistently acted against what contemporaries perceived as their own self-interest and resolutely refused to purchase goods at prices higher than stipulated. When the price of wheat rose "beyond belief," army purchasers often refused to buy or were directed by their superiors to suspend purchasing.[26]

These actions had little effect on the avaricious practices of some farmers. Recognizing that the demand for food and forage was equal to if not greater than what they could produce, many farmers raised the price of goods to whatever the market would bear, withheld their crops from sale to enhance their value, and energetically speculated in farm products. Failing in his effort to purchase some beef for the army, one deputy commissary grimly noted the reason: "Every Man buys in order to sell again." With speculators giving half as much again for grain as staff officers, farmers refused to sell to army purchasers and instead chased after the higher price from one county to another. Carrying their crops "*from* the Army to carry [them back] *to* the Army" was how Deputy Quartermaster Moore Furman characterized the farmers' action.[27]

Reacting with various degrees of alarm, confusion, and disbelief, deputies in the field deplored the inhabitants' demands for higher prices. Typical was Deputy Quartermaster James Burnside's complaint: "The farmers are determined to keep a Head of us do as we will; for Example, when 15 shillings [per bushel] was *our* price for corn they demanded 18s. 9d.; when we offered *that* they asked 20s; now we offer 20s and [the] price is between three and four dollars [i.e., 22s. 6d. and 29s. 11d.]." Reluctant to pay that price, Burnside coupled his complaint with a plea for instruction.[28]

Staff officers sometimes engaged in subterfuge to prevent price increases. Thus in October 1778, in response to the Committee of Secret Correspondence's order to purchase three hundred thousand bushels of corn in Maryland and Virginia for the French, Deputy Foragemaster Owen Biddle advised his assistants to keep the project secret so that buying the supplies could be accomplished more cheaply. Biddle went on to suggest the best mode for transacting the business and the likely benefits: "If you were to employ private Gentlemen in the several Counties to make the purchases, perhaps it could be done to better advantage and prevent a rise in the price, which should be guarded against as much as possible, otherwise the Mines of Peru and Mexico would not afford Money enough to support the present campaign." Likewise, Deputy Quartermaster John Mitchell, when ordering his assistant to purchase a large quantity of forage, insisted that "on no account suffer it to be known that you are on such business, as it might tend to rais[e] the price of those Articles and be of bad consequence to the publick."[29] These instructions reveal that the public good and the army's welfare—and not personal profit—were these staff officers' main priorities.

Despite instructions to hold prices down, to suspend purchasing, and to employ secrecy, staff officers fought a losing battle. If the purchasing agents failed to meet a farmer's demands, he refused to sell, and consequently no supplies were purchased for the army. Faced with the choice of impressing the goods—a time-consuming, inefficient, and difficult process—or meeting the farmers' prices, military officials usually capitulated. Staff officers reluctantly advised their deputies "to give the *current* price for Grain and Corn, for forage, let them be what they may, rather than the Army should suffer."[30] The conflicting claims upon staff officers—the public's demand for less spending, the farmers' demand for higher prices, and the army's often desperate need for food—and their reactions to these problems are well captured by Deputy Quartermaster Moore Furman's description of conditions prevailing in Sussex County, New Jersey, in 1779: "The high Prices giving in that County, throws me into the greatest confusion and obliges me to raise the price so much higher throughout the whole State which will not only make a very great noise and bring on a little greater Clamour against the Department or if I don't raise the Price I cannot get even what Forage is to spare."[31] It was impossible to supply the army and simultaneously keep the price of provisions down.

Permission to raise prices according to market demands did not mean that purchasing agents had license to give any price they desired. The men who headed the staff departments were as concerned about the depreciation of money as anyone in the country. They were equally conscientious about maintaining the good name of the staff department they supervised. Regard for such considerations compelled these officials not to countenance purchasers who irresponsibly exceeded market prices. After detecting Anthony Broderick "buying Cattle all over the World" and paying enormous prices, Commissary General Wadsworth insisted on his immediate arrest and ordered him to camp to stand trial. Speaking of the incident, Wadsworth remarked, "This affair of Broderick's has disgraced the Department and injured the Currency more than every Evil that has happened in my affairs."[32]

Unable to hold down the cost of supplies in the field, staff officers sought legislation to control prices. Quartermaster Greene, disturbed at "the growing extravagance of the people," strongly recommended to Rhode Island's governor, William Greene, "the immediate interposition of legislative authority to fix some limits to the price of articles taken for the use of the army." Though Governor Greene doubted the efficacy of limiting prices, he thought a partial regulation necessary to ensure the army its supplies.[33] Other highly placed officials, including Assistant Quartermaster General Charles Pettit, also favored state intervention to halt the rise of prices.[34] So desperate was the army's need for food in October 1778 that even Jeremiah Wadsworth, who had made the suspension of Connecticut's price-regulating act a condition for accepting the position of commissary general, looked kindly upon Congress's resolution recommending price controls to the states.[35] But by 1779, most officials had reversed themselves and were denouncing controls on prices. The counterproductive effects of price control in Connecticut and other states convinced them of its futility.[36] Not the lure of profits but the unavailability of supplies for the army and the universal discontent price control occasioned were responsible for staff officers' change in position.

Although staff officers did everything in their power to keep prices down, they were sometimes responsible for unnecessarily raising prices when they competed against one another for the same commodities. In April 1777, a congressional committee authorized to inquire into the conduct of commissaries found several of them "raising the prices of the articles they purchase by bidding upon each other, under an idea of receiving commissions or compensations proportioned to the sums they expend."[37] Such practices, however, were not common. They were condemned by superiors and subordinates alike and usually resulted from a purchaser's overzealousness to provide for the army or from a breakdown in communication. When heads of departments discovered staff officers competing for goods and driving up prices, they quickly took steps to eliminate the practice.[38]

Competitive bidding by military purchasers constituted only a tiny fraction of the sources of inflationary pressure. International economic conditions caused the prices of some commodities to rise. For example, between 1777 and 1779, the cost of West Indian molasses and sugar climbed sharply owing to the rise in world prices. Crops damaged by the Hessian fly or destroyed by drought, frost, or harsh winters created scarcities of foodstuffs and invariably raised prices, as did Britain's naval blockade of American ports and state embargoes.[39] The presence of too many soldiers in one section of the country, although a rare occurrence, also created local scarcities and had serious repercussions on prices. As Richard Buel, Jr., observes, "the concentration of four armies east of the Hudson from July to November 1778: Washington's at Westchester, Sullivan's at Rhode Island, Burgoyne's in Massachusetts, and D'Estaing's expeditionary force at Boston" inevitably had this effect.[40]

The speculative practices of Americans also had a dramatic effect on the price of farm products. As early as August 1775, Washington complained of an "Artificial scarcity" of firewood and forage, caused "by some persons who are monopolizing those Articles, in order to advance the Price." In 1776, "avaricious, ill designing men" exorbitantly raised the price of salt, and in New York merchants combined to keep wheat prices at an artificially high level.[41] News of the arrival of the French fleet in American waters in July 1778 set off a fresh round of speculation and profiteering. By easily outbidding staff officers, speculators in Delaware, Maryland, and Virginia cornered the flour market and raised prices enormously. John Dorsey, Maryland Congressman Samuel Chase's business partner, was prominent among these speculators. After Chase tipped him off about the fleet's impending arrival, he frantically purchased all the flour he could.[42] Three months after the French arrived, Deputy Commissary Peter Colt described the problems he faced in Connecticut, a key state for supplying the army with beef: "A great Number of unprincipled men—are going thro' every part of this State, engrossing, & buying up, on *Speculation*, every Article that the Country affords for the Subsistence of the Army—and then sell them again to the stationed Commissary—or transport them out of the State, as best suits their interest—as these people are always in *Cash*, and are under no *controuls*, they have the advantage of those who are employed to purchase for the Army."[43]

Americans hardly needed the French forces to stimulate speculators. At no time during the war was the country free of war profiteers, and with each passing year they seemed to multiply. The problem of speculation was so severe that by 1779 every state had passed legislation prohibiting and punishing those "who make it a practice to go from place to place purchasing . . . cattle and every other kind of provision, for no other purpose but to make extravagant gain, and thereby are constantly raising the price of every article of provision."[44] By 1779, Wadsworth estimated that army purchasers were outnumbered by speculators three to one.[45] As a result, commissary agents were forced to give exorbitant prices for food.

In addition to raising prices, some speculators passed themselves off as army purchasers, thereby contributing to the public's perception that staff officers offered unnecessarily high prices for goods. To prevent the "many" persons who "falsely call themselves publick officers in some Department[s]," Congress recommended in January 1778 that the states require staff officers to produce certificates attesting to their appointment. Ten months later, Colt was still plagued by the duplicity of private purchasers: "These Jobbers pretend to be employed as Agents to the Commissaries or for the French fleet."[46] As Colt's testimony demonstrates, legislation had little effect on speculators.

Scarcity and speculation were not the only factors pushing prices upward. Military commanders who acted independently of the Continental army's staff structure also had an adverse effect on prices. The French were especially prone to bypass American supply channels and give excessive prices for provisions. From the very start, the French had no faith in American supply procedures. The actions of French officials under the French commander Comte d'Estaing, after the inconclusive sea battle with British naval forces in August 1778, were typical. His ships damaged by cannonball and a violent storm, d'Estaing sailed to Boston for repairs and refitting. In Boston he requested three months of reserve supplies for his men. Unable to secure the provisions, the intendant of the French fleet hired James Price, a merchant, who proceeded to disrupt the Continental army's food supply operations in Massachusetts and New York by offering prices for flour and beef 25 percent higher than the current market price.[47] Nor was the intendant's recourse to private merchants a rare occurrence. Wary of relying on Continental army commissaries and dismayed by the incompetence of America's state governments, French authorities throughout the war interfered with American efforts to supply Continentals by outbidding staff officers for provisions and by offering to pay in specie. By 1781, French gold had become so attractive to Americans that the mere rumor that the French would make an appearance sent the price of commodities skyrocketing.[48]

French military authorities were not the only ones fond of circumventing the American supply system and raising prices. High-ranking American officers also gave up depending upon staff officers and sent out their own men or hired merchants to alleviate their food and equipment shortages. As General Anthony Wayne observed, "We shall be like Mahomet and the Mountain—if the Clothing won't Come to us—we will go to the clothing."[49]

Though motivated by genuine concern for their men, Continental officers' interference with supply operations often had disruptive and costly consequences. The actions of Major-General John Sullivan are a case in point. His behavior was unique only in its unabashed defiance of military administrators. Like the French, Sullivan disregarded the Continental army's victualling system because he lacked confidence in the American army's commissaries. "They lead us along by Promises from Day to Day," Sullivan complained to Washington in November 1778, "till our Stores are completely exhausted and then leave us to provide for ourselves or Starve." According to Sullivan, even though he had applied to the commissaries, he received no food and was forced to borrow provisions from the Massachusetts Board of War in Boston. When the board demanded that Sullivan return the foodstuffs, he discovered his magazines empty, his troops three days in arrears of food, and his small army on the point of disbanding. Sullivan again applied for assistance to the commissaries and, failing to secure relief, took matters into his own hands by employing the eminent Rhode Island merchant firm of Clark and Nightingale to feed his soldiers. They quickly provided the necessary flour and meat, but as a result prices rose at least 25 percent and the provisioning of Washington's army was badly disrupted. Deputy Commissary Peter Colt pointed out to Sullivan the adverse effect of the merchants' interference and pleaded with him to desist, but to no avail. Though Sullivan was aware that he had run afoul of state and congressional regulations, he justified his action by vowing that "it is a Maxim older than the Congress that Necessity has no Law."[50] Only a direct command from Washington put a stop to Sullivan's disregard for conventional supply channels. In addition to revealing another reason for price rises and the confusion endemic to the army's supply system, this incident illustrates the powerlessness of staff officers when confronted by an adamant military commander.

Competition between state and national purchasers of army supplies also drove prices up. On a few occasions such increases occurred when purchasers for the Committee of Secret Correspondence, the Marine Board, and other Continental bodies competed with state purchasing agents for provisions to export.[51] Another example more directly related to securing food for the army took place in the wake of Washington's plea for food and clothing in the winter of 1777–78 at Valley Forge. Upon hearing of the soldiers' plight, Pennsylvania's legislators appointed two commissioners in each county to purchase supplies at prices set by the state government. This action by itself was inflationary because the state commissioners were authorized to give prices for food well above what army commissaries were permitted to offer. To complicate matters further, the Board of War, acting on a recommendation from Congress, appointed purchasing superintendents to aid the army. The board assigned three of its appointees to purchase in Pennsylvania's Northampton, Berks, Bucks, and Philadelphia counties. Although given instructions not to exceed state limitations on prices, the overzealous superintendents paid higher prices than authorized by Pennsylvania law.

Outraged state officials complained to the Board of War, which suspended the superintendents. But before the Board of War could correct the damage, Pennsylvania was the scene of inadvertent competition among three sets of appointed officials—regular army commissaries, state commissioners, and Continental purchasing superintendents—that drove prices upward. In addition, because Robert L. Hooper, Jr., one of the purchasing superintendents, was also a deputy quartermaster in Pennsylvania and had refused to take the oath of allegiance to the state constitution, the growing spirit of recrimination between Pennsylvania authorities and staff officers increased. Undoubtedly, this case was extreme. But competition between two sets of officials, usually state agents and army purchasers, was commonplace throughout the war.[52]

Loyalists were also responsible for raising prices. Those not steadfastly attached to the British had no scruples about selling to revolutionaries if the price was right. The experience of Maryland's Joseph Dashiell, leader of Somerset County's militia, provides an illustration of the expediency of Tories. He reported to state authorities that his failure to secure a larger quantity of shoes arose from price gouging by the disaffected: "As soon as they heard the shoes was wanted for the army they raised the price from five to fifteen shillings." A more common practice was trading with the enemy. Especially along the New York–New Jersey border, Tories deliberately purchased supplies for the British at excessively high prices in order to depreciate Continental currency.[53]

Like many of his contemporaries, Caesar Rodney, president of Delaware, firmly believed that quartermasters and commissaries gave extravagant prices for the goods they purchased. Rodney wondered why they did so "when there is no other Market for those articles."[54] Rodney's statement reveals his ignorance of the conditions under which staff officers operated. Like many revolutionaries, Rodney had the erroneous impression that the army's purchasing agents constituted the only outlet available to sellers of foodstuffs. It is clear, however, that staff officers competed with a host of rivals: Tories, national and state purchasers, merchants, farmers, the French, and even each other. Revolutionaries who accused staff officers of raising prices to enhance their commissions suffered under an equally erroneous impression. The real causes of the rising prices lay in the excessive quantity of money issued by the Continental Congress, the speculative practices of Americans, and the lack of coordination between military and civil officials.

THE MOST FREQUENT charge against staff officers was un-doubtedly that they deliberately raised prices in order to enhance their commissions. Accusations that they engaged in various schemes to defraud the public were almost as common. Critics claimed that sloppy accounting procedures and lax supervision allowed military officials the opportunity to steal public property and sell it as private property.[55] Revolutionaries also thought that medical officers maintained hospitals without patients "by way of pretext of sending wagon-load after wagon-load of stores" for later resale.[56] And detractors accused commissaries of entering into secret partnerships to engross necessities for the army, selling them when the price rose, and pocketing the profits. New York's Governor George Clinton described the modus operandi in some detail: the deputies "have agents informally appointed in every Part of the State, who Purchase up large Quantities of Flour & Grain, of which no Regular Returns & of Course no immediate Entries are made in the Commissary Book. If the Articles purchased by these Agents rise, as Flour did this year in one Month from £3–4 to £8–10, they are converted to the Purposes of Trade and Sold for the Benefit of the Parties concerned. If they continue the same or fall they are delivered into the public Magazine & the Purchaser of Course intitled to his Commissions."[57] Last, many revolutionaries believed that persons employed in the staff departments applied public money to their own business and investment interests.[58]

These accusations alarmed and angered staff officers, who generally believed the charges false and felt themselves unjustly held up to public calumny. Fearful that their reputations, their ability to provide for the army, and the honor of the department were seriously compromised by such charges, staff officers took a hard line toward corruption within the ranks. Wadsworth's handling of the Broderick case illustrates the treatment dishonest assistants could expect. It is no surprise that when Deputy Foragemaster Owen Biddle was apprised that one of his agents was selling goods privately, "instead of supplying the necessities of the forage department," he ordered Colonel Francis Wade to dismiss him immediately "and make him account for the money put into his hands without delay."[59]

Sensitive to the charges of corruption, staff officers tried various methods of placating the public and vindicating their honor. Recognizing that "the great Clamours against the purchasing Commissaries" were interfering with his ability to procure foodstuffs for the army, Wadsworth made two suggestions to New York's Governor Clinton. First, under the assumption that the people would have more confidence in commissaries appointed by their state officials, Wadsworth suggested that Clinton assume that responsibility. In addition, because "it is impossible for me to be everywhere and inquire into all the doings of my people," Wadsworth proposed that state legislatures initiate strict inquiries into citizens' complaints and punish wrongdoers. Other staff officers, concerned about their personal reputations, also insisted that their conduct be investigated.[60]

Staff officers infrequently met their accusers head-on by defending themselves in the newspapers. Between February 1779 and February 1780 only three staff officers—Deputy Quartermaster Udny Hay, Deputy Commissary William Aylett, and Deputy Commissary Azariah Dunham—responded directly to the public's accusations of widespread corruption. Of the three, Hay's pieces were probably the most effective: at least they attracted no rebuttal—no mean feat given the tenacity and vituperation that characterized most revolutionary quarrels. Hay began a series of letters to the *New York Journal* by conceding that some staff officers deserved censure, but he strenuously objected to the public's blanket condemnations. Such criticism, he wrote, made recruiting good people more difficult, made staff officers' tasks more burdensome by reducing the people's confidence, and made resignation an attractive alternative for public servants "wearied with the labors and fatigues of office, the principal rewards of which are insult and abuse." Hay closed by calling for specific investigations to redress abuses and to exonerate the innocent.[61]

Aylett and Dunham took a different tack. Not content with claiming that they were innocent of advancing prices or speculating with public funds, they defended "all who purchase for the public on commission." They then tried to reason logically with their critics. Aylett pointed out that the depreciation of the currency harmed everyone, including commissaries: "What advantage can result to a Commissary to raise the price of an article in order to increase his commissions when all things rise in due proportion? Wh[y] is £10 better than 10 shillings, when it will purchase no more?" Dunham also pointed to the severe sanctions that could be wielded against dishonest staff officers. They were subject to court-martial for misapplying public money; they could be suspended by state legislatures for misconduct; and they would forfeit the bonds they had given as security for good conduct.

Even more important were inner constraints. Thus "the solemn obligations of an oath, the regard to our own reputation, the pleasure that arises from well doing, the desire of avoiding the censure of a vigilant people, must be sufficient to check us from dishonest practices." In an effort to be scrupulously honest with his readers, Dunham admitted that when purchases had been suspended, he had bought a few hogsheads of rum and small quantities of salt. But, he hastened to add, he had bought the goods with his own money, thus entitling him to sell them for his own profit. Dunham concluded by detailing the many personal sacrifices he had made to keep the army supplied.[62]

Critics had a field day with the two commissaries. By attempting to vindicate everyone in the Commissary Department, Aylett and Dunham had trapped themselves into defending the impossible proposition that there were no dishonest purchasing agents. Opponents were quick to ridicule this point: "Among the twelve Apostles one was capable of being a traitor," wrote "A True Patriot" in the *New Jersey Gazette*. "But you seem to insinuate that the whole of your fraternity are incapable of having any influence on our present evils complained of. So you attribute a greater degree of sanctity to them than [the] twelve Apostles."[63] To Aylett's logical assertion that depreciation hurt everyone equally, "Agricola" pointed out several ways that depreciation could be advantageous. "Is he a landmonger?" By charging twice as much for goods, a commissary could double his commission and purchase twice as much land as he might otherwise. "Has he a turn for trade? A few strokes of this kind furnish him with capital."[64] Likewise, critics made short shrift of Dunham's admission that he had purchased goods for resale. "Timoleon" simply hoisted Dunham with his own petard.[65] Significantly, neither commissary replied to his detractors.

The difference between Hay's defense and Aylett's and Dunham's is instructive. Hay's was effective because his argument allowed his critics few easy targets. Most important, he admitted that wrongdoing existed in the staff departments and invited scrutiny into the conduct of military officers. In contrast, Aylett and Dunham were not skilled polemicists. Partly because of their desire to defend their compatriots and partly because of their candor, Aylett and Dunham left themselves open to ripostes which effectively repudiated their claims to be honest public servants. Writing to newspapers to defend their honor was simply fetching the tarbaby another lick. Consequently, the public was now probably even more convinced of staff officers' dishonesty.

The public did not confine its dissatisfaction with staff officers to spreading rumors and leveling accusations. Citizens also proposed solutions. Once again putting to use the methods of agitation they had used so well against the British, revolutionaries gathered in town and county meetings, passed resolutions, petitioned state legislators, and wrote to newspa-

pers, suggesting methods to control corruption. One committee representing Hanover Precinct met in Ulster County, New York, and petitioned
Wadsworth to publish the names of the deputies operating in the county
so that the inhabitants would know who was authorized to purchase and
be able to prevent the forestalling of provisions.[66]

Few settlements followed Hanover's example of policing staff officers
through community vigilance. Most suggestions called on Congress to
act. One writer in the *Pennsylvania Gazette* defended staff officers and
blamed Congress for the nation's financial woes. He argued that it was
superficial to blame "the ill management or tricks of Quartermasters and
Commissaries for the depreciation of the currency." Either the system was
defective or the personnel incompetent or unfaithful. In either case, because Congress created the staff departments and hired the agents, Congress was responsible for reforming the system or firing the untrustworthy
servants. Placing the blame on staff officers was only a smokescreen "to
draw off the public attention from [its] own mismanagement."[67] But the
voice of the *Gazette* writer was a cry in the wilderness. Other proposals
ranged from setting fixed terms for high-ranking staff officers to demanding that state legislatures investigate the staff departments and forward
their findings to Congress. By far the most popular remedy proposed,
however, was for Congress to end the commission system and instead pay
staff officers a liberal but fixed salary.[68] Mirroring their constituents' alarm
at widespread corruption in the staff departments, congressmen in 1779, as
was their custom in emergencies, turned to the states.

CONGRESS'S APPROACH to corruption reveals the same suspicious attitudes toward staff officers and the same republican beliefs as
those held by the general public. Elected representatives believed staff
officers were corrupt, blamed them for depreciating the currency, and
accused them of jeopardizing the nation's experiment in republicanism.
Various preventive and punitive measures to stop fraud in the staff departments failed to have the desired effect. Congress naturally turned to the
states and conferred upon them the task of investigating staff officers.
Although state authorities also failed to discover any large-scale fraud in
the staff departments, congressmen continued, even years after the war, to
harbor deep suspicions of staff officers' honesty. Military supply officials
would discover that virtuous republics demanded standards of accountability that would prevent all but a very few staff officers from making a
profit from wartime public service.

BEFORE 1778, forceful denunciations, appointment of investigative
committees, and legislation designed to prevent or punish malfeasance in

the staff departments characterized Congress's attempts to prevent corruption. Reports of severe supply problems at Valley Forge stimulated Congress to initiate further action on several fronts. In January 1778, a committee was dispatched to army headquarters empowered to remove officers in the staff departments for misconduct or incompetence and to appoint others in their place. Congress also called upon state governments to lend their assistance. In February 1778, it recommended that they begin investigations into the conduct of staff officers and gave the states power to suspend for misconduct any officer not appointed by Congress. In addition, Congress promulgated new regulations to prevent fraud and to hold prices down. Bond for army supply purchasers was raised to $20,000. Each assistant deputy commissary was now required to take an oath before a magistrate promising not to raise prices, to use his best judgment when purchasing, and to inform the commissary general of any wrongdoing in his district of which he was aware. To encourage honesty, Congress offered assistant purchasing commissaries 10 percent of the money saved by buying provisions at prices lower than those fixed by state legislatures. Congress also ensured that those responsible for the suffering at Valley Forge would be punished. In June 1778, General Washington was directed to begin an inquiry into the conduct of former Quartermaster General Thomas Mifflin and, if warranted, to initiate court-martial proceedings. Two months later, the same procedure was set in motion against the clothier general, his deputies, and his agents.[69]

In the six months following the army's encampment at Valley Forge, Congress had moved quickly to reform the Quartermaster and Commissary departments. The new leadership proved especially effective. But it became evident during the following year that bonds, oaths, monetary incentives, and state investigations did not stop complaints of corruption in the staff departments. Instances of wrongdoing were reported regularly. One congressman received a letter detailing "sundry evils and abuses in the hospitals in the eastern district." Another member recounted a number of "frauds and abuses" in the Quartermaster Department. Pennsylvania's President Reed bitterly complained that General Benedict Arnold and Deputy Quartermaster Robert L. Hooper, Jr., used public wagons for private gain.[70] Preoccupied with other affairs, Congress reacted conventionally and perfunctorily: it ordered heads of departments to conduct investigations or appointed congressional committees to inquire into the abuses. Both responses brought few malefactors to justice. Two events, however, roused Congress from its relative lethargy toward the staff departments. The first was the Deane-Lee affair; the second, the growing evidence of national bankruptcy.

The story of the Deane-Lee imbroglio is familiar to historians.[71] Its significance for the topic of corruption is twofold: it sharply undermined the prestige of Congress and, ironically, increased Congress's hostility to corruption in the staff departments. The constant reiteration of the charges and countercharges against Silas Deane—in the halls of Congress, in private letters, and especially in the newspapers—and the repeated accusations of stockjobbing, profiteering, and misapplication of funds destroyed the widespread deference hitherto accorded Congress and increasingly made it the object of ridicule and disrespect. The acrimonious debate over Deane also heightened the sensitivity of both Congress and the public to corruption in the army.[72] Thus, beginning around April 1779, a majority of congressmen came to link malfeasance of staff officers to the high cost of the war. Richard Henry Lee, for example, related how a request for a million dollars for the Hospital Department was cut in half because of the allegations of fraud: "On a late motion to give a million to the Hospital department much violent debate took place and it was insisted on that infinite abuses prevailed and demanded immediate enquiry—It was alledged that great quantities of Stores were charged for Geese, ducks, chickens, etc., etc., etc., etc.,—that the wine was all drank by the well, and not by the sick—All this ended in reducing the sum to 500,000 dollars."[73]

Within the next two weeks several reports from the Board of Treasury strongly reinforced these beliefs. To explain the spiraling costs of the war, the board singled out the ruinous expense of the staff departments, a result, it believed, of allowing commissions on purchases. Economy became the watchword. According to the board, the remedy lay in reform and retrenchment: staff departments had to be restructured and the number of personnel reduced. Failure to do so, it warned, would plunge the nation into bankruptcy.[74] The Board of Treasury's alarming reports augmented Congress's impression of a connection between corruption in the staff departments and the country's deteriorating financial condition. When, upon the conclusion of the Deane affair, congressmen were able to give full attention to the staff departments and were joined by revolutionaries out-of-doors clamoring for control of quartermasters and commissaries, Congress promulgated the most significant resolve to date in its fight against corruption: on 9 July 1779 it called on the states to investigate staff officers.

Taking as its model the legislation of 9 February 1778, the 9 July resolution called on the executive powers of each state "instantly" to "make the strictest enquiry into the conduct of every person" in the Quartermaster and Commissary departments and in the case of any sort of misbehavior "or strong suspicion thereof," the official was to be suspended from office. Further, executive authorities were ordered to investigate the number of persons employed in the staff departments within their jurisdiction; those judged superfluous were to be discharged. As in the resolve of 1778, there was also a provision directing staff officers to swear an oath to promote the service and report fraud and abuses. What was radically new in the oath-taking section and the subject of two additional sections were provisions forbidding staff officers from engaging in private trade.[75]

In effect, Congress had made its first attempt to prohibit conflicts of interest. Paragraph two stated that no staff officer in the Quartermaster or Commissary departments "shall keep, own or be in any manner whatever interested in any boat, shallop, vessel, waggon or cart . . . engaged in any manner in the transportation of public supplies of any kind." The penalty for disobedience was to suffer being "discharged with infamy" and to forfeit all pay from the day of entrance into the army. The statute also required staff officers to swear that while employed they would not "engage in or carry on any kind of trade or traffic whatever," nor use their position to make profits greater than those allowed them by law. To keep staff officers faithful to their oath, Congress mandated that they file detailed monthly reports with state executive officials, "particularizing all the vessels, boats and carriages employed, the names of the owners, the time they were employed and the supplies removed in them, and regular returns of all the articles of supply and the prices with the names and places of abode of the persons from whom, and the days on which they were purchased, exactly mentioning the sorts, the number . . . and quality thereof." These provisions suggest that Congress was serious about the enforcement of the conflict of interest section of its resolution. Passage of the 9 July resolution was noteworthy in another respect. It clearly demonstrates that at least on one issue—the belief that corruption was widespread in the staff departments—there was little disagreement. Remarkably, in a Congress divided by two bitter, wrangling factions, the 9 July resolution passed almost unanimously.[76]

At first glance, the 9 July resolution appears to be an abdication of responsibility by Congress. Since Congress appointed all the top officials in the staff departments, it, not the states, should have been accountable for investigating and weeding out corrupt Continental military officials. In fact, Congress did not hand over total control to the states. The 9 July resolution explicitly gave states the power to remove or suspend only officers "not . . . immediately appointed by Congress," thus preserving Congress's authority over at least the heads of the staff departments. More important, although Congress was at least theoretically responsible for policing staff officers, it was impractical, if not impossible, to conduct state-by-state investigations. Congress had neither the personnel nor the time to carry out such investigations. It had no choice but to rely on state authorities.[77]

An additional argument can be made for Congress's reliance on the states. Though the immediate response by state executives to Congress's resolution of 9 February 1778 was not overwhelming—only New Jersey's Governor William Livingston seems to have responded to it—in the following year and a half, several states removed staff officers for "Mal-Practice and Peculation."[78] In addition, both New York and Delaware enacted legislation "to prevent and punish the Frauds and Abuses in the Quartermaster and Commissary Departments." Aimed at staff officers who used public funds for personal profit, this legislation subjected violators to fines of £1,000 in New York and £500 in Delaware.[79] Thus Congress had some reason to believe that state officials were concerned about the issue and would take a hard line against corrupt military officials.

New Jersey's tax law provided further evidence of the states' stiffening attitude toward staff officers. In June 1779, New Jersey approved a tax to raise a million dollars. One of its provisions stipulated that, in addition to being assessed at the regular rate of taxation, assistant and deputy quartermaster generals were liable to an assessment of "not under *One Thousand Pounds* nor above *Ten Thousand Pounds.*" This added tax enraged Greene. "Indeed I cannot think of the Law to this moment with out falling into a passion," he confided to Pettit a month after its passage. "Are staff officers necessary to the operations of the army," he demanded of the president of Congress; "if they are why are these embarrassments thrown in their way? If they are not, why is the public burthened with an unnecessary expense?"[80]

Since the statute appeared to single out Greene's assistants, Pettit and Cox, all three remonstrated with Congress to counteract what they perceived to be New Jersey's discriminatory tax law. Although Greene's letter roiled the waters of Congress by reflecting on the New Jersey legislature in "a very insolent" fashion, it was referred, along with Pettit's and Cox's protest, to a committee for study. The committee's report, adopted by Congress and delivered the day before the 9 July resolution passed, accepted the principle of state sovereignty by acknowledging New Jersey's "undoubted right" to tax property "however or wherever acquired." But because the committee feared the tax was "inconvenient and prejudicial to the service and interest of the Untied States," it recommended that the law be repealed. There the matter rested uneasily.[81]

New Jersey's tax law and the response to it again revealed to Congress the tension and animosity that persisted between members of the staff departments and state authorities. The situation reaffirmed what Congress had long known: that military-civil relations arising from conflicts over impressment and quartering soldiers in private houses were precarious. In both areas, state officials railed against what they considered the arbitrary, unjust, and oppressive actions of staff officers. Additionally, some state executives had their own bêtes noires in the staff departments with whom they no doubt wanted to settle scores. Congress was especially aware of the rancor between Pennsylvania's President Joseph Reed and Deputy Quartermaster Robert L. Hooper, Jr.[82] Perhaps Congress decided to use state officials' hostility toward the staff to its own advantage. What better way than to throw the sheep to the wolves?

Both the tone and the content of state authorities' response to the 9 July resolution suggest that Congress chose well. Pennsylvania informed its congressional delegation that they "shall most chearfully co-operate" and made several additional suggestions for granting the states more extensive powers and for widening the investigation to include the Hospital Department. Other states also reacted quickly, revealing the seriousness with which they regarded the resolution. New Jersey's Governor Livingston issued a proclamation calling on its citizens with knowledge "or strong suspicion" of misbehavior in the staff departments to inform the local justice of the peace, who would forward the information to him. President Rodney of Delaware prepared to hear complaints against Deputy Quartermaster Francis Wade at the next council meeting held at Dover on 27 July. The Rhode Island and Connecticut legislatures both formed committees to investigate the staff departments. Leaving nothing to chance, the legislatures guided committeemen in their investigations by providing them with dozens of detailed questions covering accounts, staffing, fraud, and negligence. It was clear that no stone would be left unturned in ferreting out corruption in the staff departments.[83]

Staff officers reacted to Congress's 9 July resolution with dismay and intense anger. Their first impulse was to resign. Deputy Quartermaster Udny Hay's attitude was typical: "Upon reading the resolve of Congress (to which I dare venture to affirm the Annals of Despotism does not afford an equal) that rage which I had with difficulty smothered broke out with a flame, and I wrote General Greene, accompanied with my resignation."[84] Staff officers' perception of the 9 July resolution "as degrading to their honors and betray[ing] a want of confidence in their integrity" provoked this extreme reaction.[85] Significantly, not one staff officer protested the resolution's prohibition against engaging in private trade.

Given staff officers' loud insistence that their conduct be investigated, their denunciation of the 9 July resolution appears hypocritical. Their opposition, however, was not to an investigation per se, but to being subjected to a biased judicial proceeding. Initially, at least one deputy commissary misinterpreted the resolution and objected to it because it permitted "the lowest executive officer—even a tithing Man— . . . to displace me, without my having committed the least Fault and order me to be prosecuted . . . ; as if we were felons." But far more commonly staff officers protested the 9 July resolution because they were suspicious of the motives of the measure's designers and of those who would conduct the investigations. Some feared that a small coterie within Congress was conspiring to ruin the staff departments and bring disgrace upon their members. Others worried that state authorities held grudges against staff officers and would conduct the hearings unfairly either by admitting the testimony of anonymous accusers or by not allowing staff officers to testify in their own defense.[86]

Nathanael Greene was primarily responsible for preventing staff officers from quitting. Concerned that mass resignations would seriously interfere with support of the army, Greene informed Congress of the demoralizing effect of the resolution, predicted dire consequences, and suggested the establishment of two national investigatory boards as alternatives to the state bodies. Congress, however, ignored Greene's suggestions. More important, Greene counseled offended staff officers to submit to state investigation and assured them that state authorities would be fair (though privately he did not believe they would be). He also gently reminded them that failure to appear or cooperate with state authorities would lend credence to the idea that staff officers were afraid to be investigated because they had something to hide. In addition, Greene and Governor Trumbull assured misinformed commissaries that the 9 July resolution empowered only the highest-ranking state officials, not local town or county dignitaries, to conduct investigations. As a result of these efforts, few staff officers resigned and the remainder cooperated with state investigations.[87]

The 9 July resolution and the generally hostile climate toward staff officers intensified their determination to eradicate corruption from the staff departments. Chief administrative officials imposed even stricter standards of conduct upon their assistants. Clearly recognizing the need to avoid further controversy, they warned staff officers to shun situations that could give cause for believing them corrupt. Assistant Quartermaster General Charles Pettit admonished one of his deputies:

> I would wish that all in our department would be careful to be not
> only blameless but unsuspected; for not only every fault that is com-
> mitted, but every one that is suspected to be committed by even the
> lowest Officer in the department gives weight and force to the gen-
> eral clamor against the whole and works a real injury to the public.
> It is therefore not enough that a man does not commit actual fraud,
> he should also be prudent enough to avoid the most distant appear-
> ance of it and exercise the greatest circumspection and caution in all
> his conduct.[88]

Similarly, Greene warned: "It is not enough to be honest in the quarter Masters Dept but you must be like Caesar's wife free from suspicion."[89]

Qualifications for staff officers underwent a significant change as a result of the post–9 July morality. Whereas experience, initiative, and influence had earlier been thought the prime requisites for service in the staff departments, under Quartermaster General Timothy Pickering's leadership, trustworthiness became the most prized quality. Furthermore, the importance of family connections gave way to a more meritocratic method of selecting staff officers. Pickering explicitly requested his assistants "to pay no regard to families or connections, but to select men of unsullied integrity."[90] Earlier it had been acceptable to employ brothers or father-and-son combinations—the presumption was that they would act honestly until proven otherwise—but staff officers abandoned this practice after 1780 to avoid any hint of nepotism. "It somehow or other wears an unfavorable Aspect," remarked Deputy Quartermaster Hugh Hughes in refusing an assistant's request to employ his brother at the same post, "and if any suspicions should happen it might look much worse."[91] High-ranking staff officers were clearly determined to weed out corruption within their own ranks.

While the uproar among staff officers subsided and stricter standards of conduct appeared, state authorities carried out their investigations. In Connecticut, state officials completed a thorough investigation that supported staff officers' denials of wrongdoing and corroborated their claims that speculators raised prices. These conclusions, derived from an inherently hostile source, need to be stated in full:

> It appears that the most capital Abuse which has prevailed in the purchasing Department is that the Assistant Purchasers of Cattle have in very many Instances and in large Proportions purchased Cattle of Speculating Jobbers that have infested the various Parts of the State, during the present War, who have been indefatigable in purchasing under various false Pretexts All the Cattle in their Power. This has been a principal Cause of the Rise of Provisions but it does not appear these People have in any one Instance been employed by the Purchasers and those Purchasers have very often been necessitated to purchase of them.[92]

The records of other state investigations have been destroyed or lost, but indirect evidence suggests that they uncovered only a few relatively minor offenses. Delaware proceeded against Deputy Quartermaster Francis Wade, but because he was continued in office, it seems safe to assume that the charges proved groundless. Investigations conducted before 9 July also revealed no significant cases of corruption and generally found those accused of fraud and negligence innocent. Of the sixteen men who held the top position in the various staff departments, only two, Dr. William Shippen, Jr., and Clothier General James Mease, conformed to the public's conception of staff officers conspiratorially engaged in premeditated criminal behavior for personal gain.[93]

The decision by state authorities to retain many prominent middle-echelon staff officers and their assistants after Congress turned over total responsibility for supplying the army to the states in February 1780 adds weight to the claim that corruption among staff officers was, on the whole, insignificant. Thus such men as Udny Hay, Hugh Hughes, and Henry Champion continued to direct quartermaster and commissary operations as they had when Congress was in charge of the administration of the army.[94] Judging from these facts and others, it is difficult to escape the conclusion that contemporaries, although not wrong about the existence of corruption in the staff departments, exaggerated its extent and severity. What requires explanation, therefore, is why the public believed that staff officers were universally corrupt and why they were denounced with such frenzied rhetoric.

A FUNDAMENTAL CAUSE lay in revolutionary Americans' propensity to resort to conspiratorial interpretations of events. This mode of thought was deeply rooted in the presuppositions of eighteenth-century culture, in the way educated people understood the metaphysics of causation. Most eighteenth-century Americans were incapable of assigning impersonal, abstract, causal forces to events. Instead they imputed the causes of events to the voluntary actions of free and morally responsible individuals; events were the product of human intentions. As a result, as Gordon S. Wood has written, "Never before or since in Western history has man been held so directly and morally responsible for the events of the world." When events produced consequences that could not be understood or were inimical to the public good, Americans sought explanations in the hidden designs of individuals or groups of men. Indeed, "American secular thought was structured in such a way that conspiratorial explanations of complex events became normal, necessary, and rational."[95] Just as Americans in the 1760s and 1770s tried to decipher the purpose of British legislation and concluded that British officials were engaged in a conspiracy to enslave them, so, too, revolutionaries found it easy to explain why commodity prices rose to unprecedented heights during the war. Logically, almost inevitably, they singled out a group of men—staff officers—and blamed them for conspiring to raise prices to enrich themselves.

The choice of staff officers was not random. Conspiratorial explanations focused on staff officers because many of them were merchants, and from the earliest days of settlement colonists were predisposed to believe the worst of the mercantile community. Whether directed at wealthy New England importers or the omnipresent Scottish factors of the Chesapeake tobacco trade, colonists suspected merchants of encouraging unnecessary consumption and viewed them as parasites, living off products they did not produce. Colonial Americans resented merchants' propensity for speculation and, although they tolerated and recognized the need for merchants, viewed them as less honorable and beneficial to society than farmers or artisans. Edmund S. Morgan has labeled this bundle of suspicions and resentments of commercial activity the Puritan Ethic. Its major tenets "encouraged frugality and frowned on extravagance . . . , viewed the merchant with suspicion and speculation with horror . . . , [and] distrusted prosperity."[96] Reinforced by the illegal activities of merchants and fraudulent schemes of army contractors during King George's War (1744–48) and the Great War for the Empire (1754–63), these beliefs prepared revolutionaries to expect the same behavior from those involved in supplying the Continental army. On the eve of the revolutionary war, most colonists would probably have agreed with the earl of Loudoun's assessment that "every one concerned in supplying the army finds means, in doing so, to fill his own pockets."[97]

Once the war was under way, staff officers lent credence to these suspicions by continuing to engage in private trade. This practice is not surprising given the dominant pattern of eighteenth-century mercantile activity. In most urban areas diversity was the key to commercial success. A prosperous merchant was not only an importer of goods but was also a retailer, shipper, insurance agent, and government contractor.[98] Staff officers such as Quartermaster General Nathanael Greene and Commissary General Jeremiah Wadsworth fit this category of large-scale merchant. Greene's business enterprises while quartermaster general ranged from investing in commercial ships and privateering to having an interest in the Batsto Furnace, which supplied the army with ammunition.[99] But Greene and Wadsworth were the exception, not the rule. Nor was it the staff officer as large-scale merchant that roused the suspicions and cries of critics. Rather, it was the activities of the more common small retailer. The practice among some staff officers of selling commodities to private persons from the same location from which they issued supplies to the army particularly damaged their credibility. Although the transactions were legal, and though most staff officers made a rigid distinction between their private and public accounts, their actions were naturally suspect and, in some cases, rightly so.[100]

Just as important for understanding revolutionaries' conviction that staff officers were corrupt were the numerous petty crimes committed by personnel at the brigade and regimental levels of the army. Brigade issuing commissaries embezzled provisions and sold them for private gain; regimental quartermasters committed fraud and embezzled clothing; butchers extorted money from soldiers in exchange for meat; bakers sold flour to the surrounding countryside; and regimental surgeons falsified commissary reports and sold medical discharges.[101] These men were not technically staff officers. Butchers and bakers were usually enlisted men; brigade and regimental quartermasters and commissaries were line officers who received extra pay for performing the thankless task of issuing food and equipment to the troops. None of these men were appointed by staff officers or came under their purview, yet soldiers referred to them by the same nomenclature used in the staff departments. When soldiers went home and told family or friends of the widespread corruption among quartermasters and commissaries, it is doubtful whether any distinction was made between a deputy quartermaster general who was a staff officer and a regimental quartermaster who had been appointed by the colonel of the regiment: all were quartermasters, and all were tarred with the same brush. The conflating of the two sets of men by the public did much to sustain the belief that staff officers were thoroughly corrupt.

The constant reiteration of these accusations strengthened the public's belief in them. Rumor, word of mouth, and newspaper accounts reinforced one another and gave plausibility to every new allegation. But contemporaries and modern scholars have erred in accepting these charges at face value. Individuals with unscrupulous motives as well as those with the common good in mind accused staff officers of being corrupt. Thus Wadsworth discovered, to his dismay, that "in some instances" the clamor against his assistants was "raised by designing men who at the instant they were Complaining were purchasing flour etc. on speculation and raising the Dust to conceal their own evil practice."[102] Sometimes ambition and personal animosity were at the bottom of vicious rumors. Regimental surgeons and administrative rivals, for example, deliberately spread charges of negligence and corruption in a successful campaign to oust Dr. John Morgan from his position as director-general of the Hospital Department. In other instances, simple greed was behind some of the denunciations. Thus one staff officer complained that charges were leveled at him in order that the accuser might take his place.[103] The spectacle of social inferiors growing rich at the expense of the public also prompted accusations. "Only think of a two penny Jack," implored Pennsylvania's Congressman William Shippen, Jr., to Richard Henry Lee, "who never in his life was capable by any business he had been engaged in, of making a Shilling more than maintained his family and that in a very so so manner shall now be making 40,000 or 50,000 per annum."[104] Had the staff officer in question been a member of the colonial aristocracy, one wonders if Shippen's denunciation would have been so shrill.

There were also many revolutionaries to whom it mattered little whether or not staff officers actually engaged in illegal practices. Steeped in the Puritan Ethic, they looked upon the presumption of making money during the war, even if earned honestly, as immoral. Indicative of this attitude toward prosperity and wealth was New Hampshire Congressman William Whipple's statement that "he who increases in wealth at such times as the present, must be an enemy to his Country, be his pretentions what they may."[105] The conviction that profiting during wartime was evidence that the body politic lacked virtue, not the dollars and cents of the matter, lay at the heart of these denunciations. This belief provided the basis for much of the frenzied rhetoric against staff officers.

Republican theory proclaimed that virtue was the cornerstone in maintaining liberty and property. Republics were founded on the virtue of the people, and the lack of virtue not only presaged the failure of America's experiment in self-government but also struck at an emerging national identity.[106] Considerations of this sort prompted Governor William Livingston to represent the small amount of corruption he uncovered at Trenton as "the most unparralleled mismanagement" and motivated Congressman William C. Houston to denounce staff officers as "the very Fagend of the Species who are rolling and wantoning in the hard-earned substance of their neighbours."[107] Though such rhetoric may reveal, as Wood puts it, "the deepest interests and passions" of the revolutionary generation, it is important for historians to begin to realize that rhetoric may prove to have no factual value in gauging the extent of corruption.[108]

Finally, the timing of the charges against staff officers is important. They coincided almost exactly with the deterioration of the country's financial health. Thus both the depreciation of the currency and the accusations against staff officers gained momentum in late 1778, both reached their peak in late 1779, and both subsided by late 1780. It is hard to believe this was mere coincidence. More likely, staff officers became a necessary and convenient surrogate upon which revolutionaries displaced their frustrations. For congressmen, as Jack N. Rakove has noted, "the reputed vices of these officials offered a much easier target for attack than the complexities of public finance."[109] For Whigs of all persuasions, the crimes of staff officers explained the army's lack of military success. For conservative Whigs in particular, staff officers' "criminal behavior" helped to account for the troubling social upheaval they found threatening. For speculators, denouncing staff officers provided a cover for their nefarious business transactions. For merchants, farmers, and other revolutionaries who made money at the army's expense, blaming staff officers assuaged their own guilt and allowed them to maintain the conviction that they themselves were virtuous and patriotic.[110] In short, staff officers became scapegoats for all the ills—military, financial, and psychological—that beset American society during the revolutionary war.

THE PROBLEMS that staff officers faced in convincing the public and government officials that they were honest did not end with York-town. In the years after the war, staff officers attempted to recover money that was rightfully theirs. But adverse economic conditions, the exigencies of war, and the republican component of American political culture pre-vented all but the most fortunate or the most farsighted military supply officials from making money. Of course, to demonstrate that many staff officers failed to profit financially from public service does not prove they were honest. The cynic would say they simply miscalculated. But because contemporaries were convinced and modern historians believe that staff officers made fortunes, it is important to assess the accuracy of the charge.

To suggest that staff officers did not profit from the war is not to say that they did not care whether they received compensation for their ser-vices. They did. Staff officers wanted to be paid as much as anybody else and became angry when they were not. In 1780, for example, when Con-gress ignored their pleas for pay or failed to reimburse them for the per-sonal loans they had made to the government, some staff officers threat-ened to withhold or sell the supplies in their possession. Similarly, after the war, they petitioned the national government for the money they had never been paid and requested compensation for the depreciated currency they had received. Threats and petitions, however, had little effect on either Congress or the Board of Treasury.[111]

By 1780, Congress had resolved that it would pay staff personnel either a fixed salary or a commission on the money passing through their hands. Staff members who received fixed salaries did not profit from their service. To hold costs down, Congress skimped on wages and failed to adjust for the currency depreciation. Adding to the distress of salaried workers, Con-gress rarely met its payroll on time. Issuing commissaries, foragemasters, and physicians complained to their superiors, who in turn beseeched Con-gress for more money, but usually to no avail. After 1778 Congress's penury made it extremely difficult for the army to hire or retain lower-echelon personnel. Many of these workers, unable to support their families on such meager wages, quit the army to work at more lucrative civilian jobs. As for those staff members who remained in the army, their pay, even when Congress increased their wages, barely kept pace with the rampant price inflation. For those on fixed salaries, the war was a losing proposition.[112]

The financial situation of staff officers paid by commission was potentially far more lucrative. Congress had allowed them a commission ranging from 1 to 5 percent on all money passing through their hands. These men thus stood to gain much from public service because they handled great sums of money. Those who profited from this system included Deputy Quartermaster Udny Hay, who made £1,500, Deputy Quartermaster Donald Campbell, who received $4,260, and Quartermaster General Nathanael Greene, who allegedly made $170,000.[113] But these military supply officers were exceptions; only a handful profited from public office.

Staff positions were not profitable for many complicated reasons, and Congress's failure to stipulate how and when commissions were to be paid makes the matter difficult to untangle. Were staff officers to deduct their percentage before purchasing goods, or were they to wait until the end of their service, settle their accounts, and receive a lump-sum payment from Congress? Staff officers never discussed these questions. But their actions—spending their own money to purchase goods and then borrowing to pay for additional supplies—suggest that even if they took their commissions off the top, they did not use the money to enrich themselves but to further the war effort. Indeed, most staff officers ended the war indebted either to farmers who had extended them credit or to friends who loaned them money. Quartermaster General Greene accurately summed up staff officers' financial circumstances at the close of the war: "The number who have benefitted by their appointments are very small, while hundreds have suffered, both in character and fortune from their employment and are now loaded with heavy debts, without the remotest prospect of being able to pay them."[114]

The only way staff officers could get out of debt—aside from repudiating it by ignoring clamorous creditors—and the only way they could receive their commissions was to account fully for the public funds with which they had been entrusted. Settling their accounts, Deputy Quartermaster Moore Furman succinctly noted, was "the road to their money." In addition to the profit motive, there were other strong incentives for staff officers to settle their accounts. Many hoped that by accounting for public money they would give congressmen an accurate indication of the expense of supplying the army and alleviate their exaggerated distrust of staff officers. Quartermaster General Greene strongly exhorted his deputy, John Davis, to obtain returns from his assistants, adding that "I hope our accounts will sufficiently prove that the plan of the war and the nature of the service entail the expense, and that it is not owing to any misapplication of public money."[115] Staff officers' concern for their reputation was as important as making a profit.

But whatever their incentive, they found it extremely difficult to settle their accounts. By September 1788, 65 of approximately 133 staff officers in the Quartermaster and Commissary departments who handled public funds—almost 50 percent—had failed to appear before national auditors. Another 25 staff officers, 19 percent, had presented their vouchers and receipts but had not been able to reach a settlement. Thus by the end of the Confederation period nearly 70 percent of military supply officers had not closed their accounts.[116] The main reason why many staff officers failed to settle their accounts and therefore failed to profit from public service was their inability to verify their claims against the government. Although they made every effort to gather the relevant documents, adverse circumstances thwarted their best intentions. In 1780, for example, Quartermaster General Greene devised a plan to determine the exact amount of money the department owed its creditors. Advertisements were placed in the newspapers, and deputies were advised to encourage citizens who held receipts for goods not paid for to come forward and exchange those documents for certificates. It was hoped that this procedure would not only give the Quartermaster Department an accurate picture of its indebtedness but also the documentation to prove it.[117]

The plan failed. Many inhabitants were angered at the idea and refused to travel the forty or fifty miles necessary unless they were going to receive the money owed them. Deputy Quartermaster Morgan Lewis noted that at least a third of the people to whom he owed money would "certainly not bring in their accounts . . . to receive nothing more than a promise of payment, the Expense of obtaining which will probably cost them one half the Debt." Some farmers refused to bring in their vouchers because they feared they would be defrauded. Others preferred to hold onto the original receipts in the shrewd belief that it would be easier to sue a staff officer than the United States government.[118] Failure to gain creditors' cooperation meant that final settlement would be delayed or never accomplished.

When accounts were slow to arrive, heads of departments badgered, cajoled, and threatened to sue their subordinates to force them to settle their accounts. These entreaties had little effect. As early as 1780, for example, Commissary General Ephraim Blaine called on his deputies to settle their accounts. Using the carrot-and-stick approach, he appealed first to their sense of honor by noting "the Injury done your own Reputation by thus delaying" a settlement and then warned them that unless they rendered their accounts immediately he would "Commence Actions in behalf of the United States against you." Two years later, Blaine complained to Robert Morris that he was unable to collect the money due him because of his failure to get the needed documentation from his assistants. Throughout the 1780s Blaine continued to admonish and demand accounts from his assistants. Finally, in 1787, in desperation he petitioned Congress to direct state attorneys general to sue "each and every delinquent," for without a proper settlement he was "being deprived of the benefit he is entitled to . . . by the detention of a great part of his commission." Congress forwarded Blaine's memorial to the Board of Treasury, which postponed taking any action.[119] As long as his deputies failed to bring in their accounts, Blaine could not collect a single dollar owed him.

Lower-echelon staff officers failed to comply with their superiors' injunctions for a variety of reasons, many of them the result of wartime conditions. When deputy quartermasters and deputy commissaries called for their assistants' accounts they discovered that some would not be forthcoming because several men had been killed in battle, captured by the enemy, or died of natural causes.[120] Complete accounts were also impossible to collect from men who issued supplies during the heat of battle and did not take receipts or from men who were simply overwhelmed by the amount of work forced upon them.[121] Particularly damaging to good recordkeeping was the shortage of paper that developed around 1780, preventing staff officers from recording their transactions.[122] Other factors, including staff officers' negligence and ignorance, obstructed them from rendering their accounts.[123] Nor can one rule out the possibility that some military supply officers refused to be audited because they had embezzled public funds.

After the war, new difficulties arose that prevented military supply officials from achieving a final settlement. The process of settling accounts was delayed by the expense and time involved. Top- and middle-echelon staff officers were forced to purchase numerous reams of paper, hire two or three clerks, and travel around the country or employ additional men to examine claims on the spot—the expense of which came directly out of their own pockets. Because many had left the army broke or in debt, this expense constituted a hardship few could afford. Many thus requested funds to hire a clerk or two or to support themselves while settling their accounts. When no money was forthcoming, it is probable that some staff officers gave up trying and went about the business of making a living. Not only was settling accounts expensive, it was also immensely time-consuming. For those who had the leisure, it was not unusual to have to work full time for six months to a year or more to get their accounts into shape. Not many staff officers could spare that much time, and as a result it is not surprising that the settlement process dragged on for years.[124]

Certain aspects of American political culture exacerbated staff officers' difficulties. The settlement of accounts touched a raw nerve in the new nation by forcing Americans to confront the ever-present question of whether they possessed the proper character for republican government. The ideal of a virtuous republic demanded that private interest be subordinated to the public good and that its people be industrious, frugal, selfless, and patriotic. The reality of American society fell short of the ideal. The war revealed to many revolutionaries another America in which private interest, greed, profiteering, and extravagance were dominant.[125] Settling accounts gave revolutionaries in Congress who were determined to suppress luxury and ferret out corruption the opportunity to reassure themselves that Americans were fit for republican government. It is only within the context of republican ideology that Congress's strict and inflexible auditing policies can be understood.

The differences between England's accounting practices and those of revolutionary America are instructive, for they reveal one of the effects of republican ideology on the new nation. In England, Parliament permitted public money to stay in the possession of public officials long after its purpose had been served. Although the money earned at interest remained in private hands, it was considered a perquisite of public service. Hence Parliament was slow in auditing the public accounts. As late as 1783, no treasurer of the navy or paymaster of the army had rendered his accounts since 1767. Consequently, a total of £171 million (not including the expenses of the American revolutionary war) had yet to be examined by government auditors.[126]

In contrast, the government of the United States perceived public service through the eyes of republican morality, a world view that demanded strict accountability for public funds. On 3 May 1780, less than three months after the system of specific supplies made the Quartermaster and Commissary departments superfluous, the Board of Treasury demanded that staff officers settle their accounts by 1 June or be prosecuted as delinquents and advertised as public defaulters.[127] And from the beginning of the settlement process until well into the 1790s, staff officers were held to strict, uncompromising standards of accountability. One of the first indications of the United States government's hard line occurred in January 1780, when the Board of Treasury refused to grant any additional money to staff officers without written documentation of their previous expenditures.[128] Similarly, the auditor general, James Milligan, questioned Assistant Quartermaster Charles Pettit's right to pay his deputies on a commission basis. Congress had passed no resolve permitting such action, Milligan informed Pettit, and if Congress had not authorized it, Pettit could not do it. Milligan's legalistic reasoning both angered and surprised Pettit. He protested that he was vested with the authority by virtue of his appointment, that he had exercised the power prudently, and that Congress had tacitly agreed to the practice by not objecting when informed. Milligan, though unconvinced, agreed to allow Congress to rule on the issue.[129]

The settlement of accounts, however, reveals the Board of Treasury's adversarial attitude most fully. In addition to an underlying assumption that all staff officers were corrupt, the board seemed oblivious to the fact that the nation was at war and that its financial structure was collapsing. When informed by Pettit that he had no written records of certain transactions, the president of the Board of Treasury, John Gibson, was incredulous. He told Pettit that "he was at a loss to conceive how Debts should exist against the Quarter Masters Department of which no returns can be made." Ignoring the reality of wartime conditions, Gibson demanded that Pettit submit vouchers showing "dates when contracted, for what supplies, and with whom, or from whom the supplies were obtained, in what quantities, and at what prices." No less would do, nor would the board allow partial settlements. When Pettit brought several of his assistants' accounts to the auditor general for inspection, the board ordered him away and told him that it would not audit incomplete accounts. Only the "general account of the department" would be accepted. Under such restrictions, Pettit "despaired of living long enough to get them settled."[130]

Despite its blustering, the Board of Treasury made little progress toward settling the public accounts. The war kept getting in the way. But after Yorktown, Congress rationalized the settlement process by directing the superintendent of finance, Robert Morris, to appoint five commissioners to audit the accounts of the Quartermaster, Commissary, Hospital, Clothier, and Marine departments. The settlement of accounts could now begin in earnest. Before they assumed their duties, Morris reminded the commissioners that "the public Officers in the several Departments have been charged with Peculation, Fraud, and speculating with public money."[131] Their subsequent actions suggest they never forgot the superintendent's words.

Throughout the Confederation period, the commissioners' decisions reflected Morris's and the nation's deep mistrust of staff officers. They continued the Board of Treasury's strict standards of accounting and were unsympathetic to staff officers' explanations for missing vouchers and requests for payment. When several issuing commissaries who had received no pay for several years petitioned in 1783 for a speed-up in the auditing process, the commissioner of the Commissary Department, Jonathan Burrall, rejected it. The faithful and meritorious service of staff officers would have no effect on him, he told Morris, for "it would ill become me to deviate from the limited province of a Public Servant, in order to rejudge the judgments of Congress, and thus indulge the visionary hope of gratifying every man who may fancy himself an object of compensation."[132] Nor did staff officers find a more understanding forum when they petitioned

Congress. The Board of Treasury, to which Congress referred their memorials, repeatedly rejected them because they did not conform exactly to congressional resolves.[133]

Even if staff officers managed to gather the necessary documentation, it did not follow that they would be paid. Republican ideology, bureaucratic indifference, and plain bad luck prevented many staff officers from ever collecting their money. The case of Deputy Quartermaster Hugh Hughes clearly illustrates these problems. He had settled his accounts with his assistants in early 1783 and sent them to his superior, Timothy Pickering, who then forwarded them to Robert Morris. Morris rejected Hughes's claim. In July 1784, Hughes again wrote Pickering defending his claim and again was rebuffed. Pickering explained that though he had spoken personally to Morris about Hughes, Morris claimed he was not authorized to make the allowance and suggested that Hughes apply directly to Congress. In 1786, Pickering attempted to smooth the way for Hughes's petition to Congress by writing laudatory letters to the Board of Treasury and to Rufus King, who was then head of a congressional committee considering Confederation finances. In 1788, Hughes sent an affidavit to Charles Tillinghast, a Treasury official, requesting payment of $8,570 for services rendered to the United States as a staff officer between 16 February 1776 and 1 January 1783. Hughes never received a reply.

Then, in January 1789 disaster struck. A fire that destroyed Hughes's house and worldly possessions also consumed all his accounts, along with those of his assistants and clerks. In February 1790, he waited on the secretary and auditor of the Treasury, requesting their advice. They told Hughes to begin collecting his accounts again by contacting all concerned. Hughes did the best he could, advertising in five newspapers and sending out circular letters. But, of course, he could no longer present an exact accounting of his expenditures.

In 1793, Hughes petitioned Congress, asking it to intercede with the Board of Treasury to authorize a special settlement. The House of Representatives referred his petition to Alexander Hamilton, the secretary of the treasury, who, according to Hughes, "stated that he was so much occupied by other concerns, that he could not attend [to me], and, in fact, never did attend to the business . . . though called on and pressed to do so." In 1799, Hughes once again wrote Pickering. He enclosed all his documents and beseeched Pickering to press his claim against the government. Pickering agreed to do so, but his reply gave Hughes cold comfort: "I have for several years noticed the general rejection of old claims by the committee of claims, and that the House of Representatives confirm their reports: yet some *few* claims are allowed." Pickering suggested that Hughes apply to Congress again. In December 1801, eighteen years after he had left public office, Hugh Hughes attended Congress in person and requested the money he still had not received. The Committee of Claims again rejected his petition. In February 1802 Hughes left the capital and "set out for home in a very languishing state." He died shortly thereafter.[134]

SOME STAFF OFFICERS were compensated for their wartime service, but they were a distinct minority. The inherent difficulties of maintaining full and accurate records under wartime conditions prevented many from making their accounts balance. As a result, some did not bother to settle their accounts. Because of America's adherence to republican ideology, Congress's accounting practices were unusually strict for the eighteenth century. Consequently, department heads were made responsible for their subordinates' deficits and so found themselves owing the government money.[135] A second consequence of these ideological convictions was that the Board of Treasury punctiliously enforced Congress's exacting accounting standards. Unsympathetic Treasury officials brushed aside explanations of mitigating circumstances and began audits with the assumption that staff officers were corrupt—an assumption that hardened to conviction when these officers were slow to render their accounts. Although staff officers appealed to Congress when the Board of Treasury denied their claims, their memorials were either ignored or rejected. Thus in the aftermath of the war, zealous republican officials ensured that no money was granted to staff officers unless they could prove their claims beyond a shadow of a doubt. Because few could, few profited from public office.

1. The Method of Refining Salt-Petre *by Paul Revere, 1774 (Courtesy of the American Antiquarian Society, Worcester, Massachusetts)*

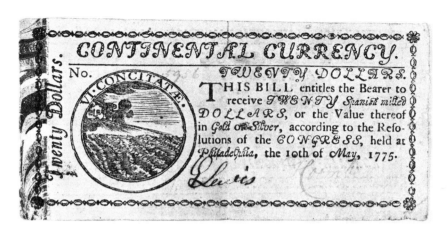

2. *Continental currency, 1775 (Courtesy of The Connecticut Historical Society, Hartford)*

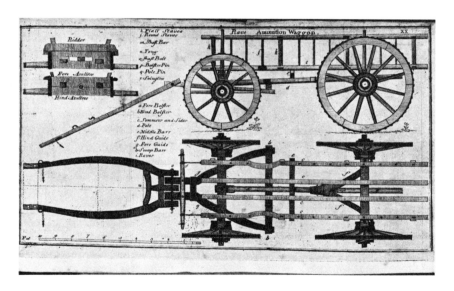

3. *Ammunition wagon by John Norman, from John Muller,* A Treatise of Artillery, *Philadelphia, 1779 (Courtesy of the Library of Congress, Washington, D.C.)*

4. George Washington at Trenton *by John Trumbull, 1792 (Courtesy of Yale University Art Gallery, New Haven, Connecticut)*

5. Thomas Mifflin *by Charles Willson Peale, 1784 (Courtesy of the Independence National Historic Park, Philadelphia)*

140

6. Nathanael Greene *by Valentine Greene, after Charles Willson Peale, 1785 (Courtesy of the National Portrait Gallery, Smithsonian Institution, Washington, D.C.)*

7. Timothy Pickering *by Charles Balthazar Julien Fevret de Saint-Mémin, 1806 (Courtesy of the National Portrait Gallery, Smithsonian Institution, Washington, D.C.; gift of Mr. and Mrs. Paul Mellon)*

By His EXCELLENCY

GEORGE WASHINGTON, Esquire,

GENERAL and COMMANDER in CHIEF of the Forces of the UNITED STATES OF AMERICA.

BY Virtue of the Power and Direction to Me especially given, I hereby enjoin and require all Perſons reſiding within ſeventy Miles of my Head Quarters to threſh one Half of their Grain by the 1ſt Day of February, and the other Half by the 1ſt Day of March next enſuing, on Pain, in Caſe of Failure, of having all that ſhall remain in Sheaves after the Period above mentioned, ſeized by the Commiſſaries and Quarter-Maſters of the Army, and paid for as Straw.

GIVEN *under my Hand, at Head Quarters, near the Valley Forge, in Philadelphia County, this 20th Day of December,* 1777.

G. *WASHINGTON.*

By His Excellency's Command,

ROBERT H. HARRISON, Sec'y.

LANCASTER; Printed by JOHN DUNLAP.

8. Proclamation from George Washington, dated Valley Forge, 20 December 1777, ordering farmers to thresh their grain or have it impressed by commissaries and quartermasters (Courtesy of The Historical Society of Pennsylvania, Philadelphia)

9. Joseph Trumbull *by John Trumbull, 1778 (Courtesy of The Connecticut Historical Society, Hartford)*

10. Jeremiah Wadsworth *by James Sharples, ca. 1795–1800 (Courtesy of the Independence National Historic Park, Philadelphia)*

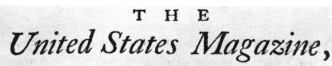

THE
United States Magazine,

New-Hampſhire,
Maſſachuſetts-B
Rhode-Iſland,
Connecticut,
New-York,
New-Jerſey,
Pennſylvania,

Delaware,
Maryland,
Virginia,
North-Carolina,
South-Carolina,
Georgia.

'For JANUARY 1779.

PARTICULARS.

PHILADELPHIA:
Printed and Sold by FRANCIS BAILEY, in Front-Street

11. *Title page of* The United States Magazine, *January 1779, in which fame flies through the archway carrying trumpet and staff with liberty cap; stars representing the thirteen colonies adorn the arch; the pillars also represent the original and the new states (Courtesy of the Library of Congress, Washington, D.C.)*

12. William Shippen, Jr. *by an unidentified artist after Gilbert Stuart, 1798 (Courtesy of the National Library of Medicine, Bethesda, Maryland)*

13. Comfort Sands *by an unidentified artist (Courtesy of The Historical Society of Pennsylvania, Philadelphia)*

14. Alexander Hamilton *by William Rillinson after Archibald Robertson, 1804 (Courtesy of the National Portrait Gallery, Smithsonian Institution, Washington, D.C.)*

15. Robert Morris *by Charles Willson Peale, ca. 1782 (Courtesy of the Independence National Historic Park, Philadelphia)*

150

16. The Resignation of General Washington, 23 December 1783 *by John Trumbull, 1824 (Courtesy of the U.S. Capitol Historical Society, Washington, D.C.)*

CHAPTER 6

MOTIVATION OF

STAFF OFFICERS

The purest treasure mortal times afford
Is spotless reputation; that away,
Men are but gilded loam or painted clay.
. . . .
Mine honor is my life, both grow in one,
Take honor from me, and my life is done.
Then, dear my liege, mine honor let me try;
In that I live, and for that will I die.
     —*Richard II*, I.1

I confess in a republic . . . approbation, honor, and praise, more than
money and emoluments are the reward of faithful services.
     —William C. Houston to William Livingston,
          5 October 1779

THE REVOLUTIONARY WAR was not won by staff officers or even by the Continental army alone. Thousands of Americans, in the army and out, suffered and sacrificed for a cause they believed in. Of course, not all Americans were committed patriots; some practically forgot that the war was still being fought or wished it would go away; others took every opportunity to profit at the army's expense. Yet among American revolutionaries, staff officers exemplified republican virtues: most remained dedicated to the Revolution and were generally honest; some lost money. Such apparently altruistic behavior demands an explanation, and that explanation necessitates quoting extensively from the papers of staff officers. There are three reasons for letting staff officers speak for themselves. To paraphrase Nathanael Greene, who ever heard of Udny Hay, Royal Flint, Ephraim Blaine, Constant Cooper, Moore Furman, Nehemiah Hubbard, Henry Champion, David Duncan, Joseph Lewis, or Hugh Hughes in history? The answer, of course, is very few. Perhaps for that reason alone we should lend a willing ear. Second, in the last quarter of the twentieth century, the mere assertion that staff officers were motivated by patriotism or concern for personal honor seems suspect. But reading their words unselfconsciously set down in the heat of a military campaign or in private correspondence—voicing their deepest fears and beliefs—brings alive and makes convincing a world that was very different from our own. Finally, and most important, staff officers' ideals and behavior can provide insight into why Americans participated in the American revolutionary war. For these men were not members of the highest rank in society: they did not associate on equal terms with a Washington or a Jefferson. Nor were they members of the lower orders: they were often looked up to by Jack Tars, poor artisans, and unemployed laborers. To listen to middle-class staff officers is to hear the voice of a large segment of revolutionary America.[1]

What accounts for the apparently selfless conduct of staff officers? Why did these men join the army, and why did they continue to serve despite economic and psychological hardship? Their motivation cannot be reduced to any single interest or aspiration. Men joined the staff departments for a variety of reasons, including a desire to make money, to preserve their liberty, and to serve their country. As the war continued, however, economic incentives and the fear of British enslavement receded in importance while patriotism remained strong. Increasingly, patriotism was buttressed by a deep sense of loyalty to the staff departments and to other officers that emerged from the war experience. Reinforcing their esprit de corps and providing the most pervasive ideal for keeping staff officers at their posts was their regard for their reputations and the reputation of their departments. Indeed, the question of honor became so important that it led to many resignations. But both reactions—persevering in office and resigning from it—testify to the strength and ubiquity of honor and reputation as motivating forces in the lives of staff officers.

T H E R E   I S   N O   Q U E S T I O N that there were economic reasons for joining the staff departments of the Continental army. During the colonial wars, the staff departments, particularly the Commissary and Quartermaster departments, were often the route by which men made fortunes and founded family dynasties.[2] Thus at the beginning of the revolutionary war it was common knowledge, especially among merchants and others involved in trade and commerce, that serving one's country could also be profitable. Upon hearing in June 1775 that his friend Joseph Trumbull had been appointed by the Continental Congress as the first commissary general of the Continental army, Tristram Dalton observed that the office was "a Place of important Trust, and I dare say will prove of equivalent Profit." Trumbull's subsequent actions—his importuning Connecticut's Congressman Eliphalet Dyer to increase his salary, his constant complaints about expenses, and his resentment at the absence of commissions on his purchases—strongly suggest that profit and loss considerations stood high among the factors prompting his acceptance of office. On the strength of Trumbull's remonstrances, it would appear that, at the highest levels of authority, making money was a powerful incentive to public service.[3]

Trumbull, however, was the exception. More commonly, the question of making a profit had little influence on the decision of high-ranking staff officers to accept or remain in office. Men such as Thomas Mifflin, Timothy Pickering, Jeremiah Wadsworth, and Nathanael Greene were decidedly unenthusiastic about heading up their respective departments. Whether it was because of the lack of opportunity for military glory, of which both Mifflin and Greene complained, or because of the intrinsic difficulties of public service, which were anticipated by Pickering and Wadsworth, these men resisted entering public office and, characteristically, resigned with relief.[4] Writing to the Board of War in 1779, Quartermaster General Greene captured perfectly staff officers' resistance to working in these departments: "I engaged with reluctance and I shall quit it with pleasure."[5] For this group of men the possibility of profit was rarely a factor in accepting office.

Economic self-interest was much more evident among deputies and assistants. The war created economic distress, and some men responded by seeking employment in the staff departments because they needed the money. In applying to the Board of War in 1780 for the position of barrack-master of Philadelphia, Lewis Nicola admitted that the combination of a large family and an inadequate income made him eager for the post.

Nicola justified his request by noting that he saw nothing wrong in making his "private advantage coincide with the public utility."[6]

In addition, the widespread belief that staff officers were amassing fortunes made low-level positions in the Quartermaster and Commissary departments highly desirable. George Olney, a more candid jobseeker than most, though perhaps not otherwise atypical, revealed to Nathanael Greene his reasons for joining the Quartermaster Department: "When I first entered the department as Auditor, it was not the trifling salary that induced me to leave my family; but I honestly confess, it was, principally, the hope of its being an introduction to something more lucrative."[7] Olney did not reveal to Greene what that "something more lucrative" might be, but it can be easily surmised. If he was an honest man, he no doubt had in mind the possibility of making future business contacts or of receiving inside information about investment opportunities. If he was dishonest, an auditor's position would allow him to accept bribes for approving fraudulent vouchers or receipts.

As long as men believed that money could be made in the staff departments, volunteers abounded. The eagerness of some applicants for positions in the staff departments reached an extreme in the opportunism of one Robert McPherson, who, upon informing Ephraim Blaine that "your Deputy Commissary Colonel Eichelberger by the judgment of the Doctors is to leave the world this day," offered himself as the most likely replacement. Given the common belief in the profitability of public office, many prospective staff officers would probably have admitted that economic self-interest played a major role in volunteering to serve. As the assistant commissary general of purchases, Royal Flint, observed, "When an opening to make profit occurs, the purse puts in a claim."[8]

Although staff officers rarely expressed a fear of being enslaved when explaining why they had joined, they, along with a host of other Americans, joined the Continental army believing that, as Bernard Bailyn has written, "nothing less than a deliberate assault launched surreptitiously by plotters against liberty" had culminated with the opening of hostilities on Lexington Green.[9] Closely intertwined with this strand of Real Whig ideology was the third explanation offered by staff officers for joining the service: patriotism.

The patriotism of staff officers was expressed in the three distinct but overlapping ways in which they described their own roles: serving their country, serving the commander in chief, George Washington, and preserving the army. For example, Nathanael Greene, although strongly reluctant to enter the office of quartermaster general in March 1778, gave three reasons for finally accepting the post: the public good, the imminent ruin of the army, and the earnest pleas of Congress and General Washington.

Similarly, when Jeremiah Wadsworth was reluctant to assume the head of the Commissary Department, one of his business partners, Jared Tracy, urged him to heed the summons "when his Country Called and I think those calls were never louder than at this time and unless there is something speedily done we shall be Ruined."[10]

Patriotism was also evident among lower-level officers in the staff departments. John Keese, assistant deputy quartermaster, explained to his superior, Colonel Hughes, why he joined the Continental army: "I was not forced into the service for Bread—I lived easy; and might in all probability, have done so till now; had I not been favored by a kind providence with a manly and patriot Spirit, which scorned to herd with Traitors to my Country." Or as John Moylan, in soliciting the position of clothier general in February 1781, more bluntly put it, "I wish to serve my country."[11] Whether or not Moylan, Greene, or other officers actually joined for these reasons, it is significant that they expressed themselves in this manner and that their compatriots thought such appeals would be effective.

Once in office, staff officers were soon disabused of any hope of material reward. Similarly, those who had harbored misgivings before joining quickly realized that their fears were justified. Much of their dismay was a generalized reaction to low wages, congressional ineptitude, and the lack of cooperation from state authorities and Continental line officers. The charges of corruption that began appearing regularly in late 1779 in newspapers and congressional correspondence also disgruntled military supply officers. Quartermaster General Nathanael Greene explained the problem to a committee of Congress: "One indiscriminate load of censure has been poured out upon every order without regard to their merit or services, or without fixing a single crime upon an individual. The business has been rendered by this policy so odious that every man is determined to quit it."[12]

Crowning staff officers' demoralization were the disorganization and attendant problems engendered by the nation's chaotic finances. These included a lack of money to purchase supplies; debts, lawsuits, and the loss of prestige; and the impossibility of accomplishing their tasks efficiently and honorably. As a result, many staff officers felt anger, despair, and a longing to resign. Commissary General Wadsworth reflected the sentiments of numerous staff officers: "I would not endure the anxiety and trouble one more month to procure the Wealth of the World; my health is bad and will not mend so long as I am in this distressed situation." By 1780, employment in the public realm had become so harrowing that staff officers actually cheered the prospect of early retirement. Nathanael Greene could hardly restrain his joy at learning that Wadsworth had resigned. Upon hearing the news he wrote: "I cannot help congratulating you upon your timely and happy retreat from the Commissary Department. You must be a child of fortune. You have saved your reputation free from reproach, and got out of a scene of perplexity sufficient to exhaust the patience and turn the head of one of the first Philosophers in the World." Not surprisingly, Greene, upon resigning as quartermaster general in August 1780, confessed he felt "happier now than ever I felt in my life."[13] Other staff officers echoed Wadsworth and Greene and with few misgivings left the staff departments.[14]

Although many staff officers refused to serve under these trying circumstances and resigned, many others stayed long after they had just cause to quit. Instead of resigning immediately, they complained loudly and kept working. Ephraim Blaine, who worked his way up through the ranks to become commissary general of purchases, is a good example of a man whose bark was far worse than his bite. He had a never-ending supply of complaints and repeatedly gave notice of quitting. He threatened to resign twice in 1778, once in 1780, and again in 1781. But Blaine remained at his post until 1783, thus serving for seven consecutive years of the war.[15] What kept men such as Blaine from quitting? Explicit statements from those who stayed are rare. Nevertheless, by examining the appeals, inducements, and threats used by these officials to persuade each other and their assistants to exert themselves or not to resign, it is possible to discern what values were most important to the men who stayed in office. These values—patriotism, esprit de corps, and most of all honor and reputation—provide the key to understanding staff officers' willingness to undergo the hardship and strain of public service.

GIVEN THE LOW PAY, the depreciating currency, and the slowness of Congress in compensating its employees, it is not surprising that staff officers rarely stressed economic self-interest in appealing to each other to remain in the army. There was simply little money to be made in the staff departments. The few men who did resort to such an appeal usually were unfamiliar with the state of the Treasury and the economic realities of wartime America. That, perhaps, is one reason why Nathanael Greene, newly appointed quartermaster general, tried to use the lure of financial gain to persuade Deputy Quartermaster Hugh Hughes not to resign. Hughes had declined Greene's written request to remain in office, giving as his reason a desire to settle his accounts with Thomas Mifflin, Greene's predecessor. Greene wrote Hughes again, expressing his surprise and offering what he considered sufficient inducement to remain in office: "I had not the least Idea of your resignation, as you would have the same Command, as heretofore, and continue to enjoy all the profits and Emoluments of the Office."[16] A week later it was Hughes's turn to express surprise: "You speak of Profits and Emoluments. That I am an entire stranger to, I assure you Sir. I never derived any benefit from the Office but my Wages and Rations."[17] Greene eventually discovered for himself that Hughes was telling the truth and never again used the promise of monetary rewards to induce men to work. Speaking from experience a year and a half later, Greene acknowledged that "the emoluments of office in the Quartermaster's department are far from being so inviting as is generally imagined."[18] To understand the reasons why men remained at their posts, we must look beyond economic explanations.

Throughout the war, patriotism remained a potent motivator. Staff officers, in a multitude of ways, frequently used the patriotic appeal of "serving one's country" to spur their men to greater effort. Deputy Foragemaster Owen Biddle, for example, informed his assistant, William Finnie, that "you cannot more essentially serve your country than by giving all possible dispatch to the corn you have purchased." Similarly, Deputy Commissary Blaine wrote Major Robert Forsyth that he was confident Forsyth's "attachment for the General cause of America will surmount all other considerations, and you will use your utmost Exertions in this time of Distress to render me every assistance." In a variation on the same theme, Quartermaster General Nathanael Greene added force to his urgent request for supplies by warning his deputy that "the Safety of America" was at stake if he did not exert himself.[19] Because of the high regard with which the ideal of patriotism was held, staff officers used it as a rationale for settling disputes and for maintaining harmony between officers.[20] They even employed it as a form of praise. Thus George Morton informed one staff officer that besides earning the thanks of Deputy Commissary Blaine and Congress for procuring flour for the army, he would have "the Sweet satisfaction of rendering an important Service to your Country."[21]

Top officials also resorted to patriotic appeals to dissuade subordinates from quitting the service. In October 1779, for example, seven of Deputy Quartermaster Udny Hay's assistants threatened to resign immediately if he did not redress their grievances. Their complaints ranged from dissatisfaction with Congress to grumbling about their pay, which, in their words, was not a fraction of that paid to "those acting in the Diminutive employment of Cooks." Hay acknowledged the legitimacy of his assistants' complaints and complimented them on the fidelity with which they had performed their tasks. He then appealed to them "in the name of your *yet bleeding Country*" to remain at their posts. Warming to this theme, Hay implored his deputies to consider "the duty you owe your Country, [and] the pleasing reflections that must arise from a consideration that you have made so considerable a sacrifice of your interest to that Duty." The response the following day was gratifying. Six out of seven of the men agreed to continue, at least until the campaign ended or Hay could find suitable replacements. Significantly, their initial explanation for remaining was "the strong attachment we feel to the cause of our Country."[22]

In staff officers' hierarchy of values, the army shared place of honor with serving one's country. The link was logical: American independence rested on the army. "The army is the great object on which all political institutions must depend ultimately," observed Nathanael Greene to Pennsylvania's President Joseph Reed, "and therefore you are never to lose sight of its concerns, its interests, or its operations." It was a sentiment widely shared by staff officers. If the army was defeated, the means by which life, liberty, and property were to be defended would be lost. Their strong identification with the army's welfare is evident from the sense of urgency and anxiety they conveyed in their orders and appeals to their subordinates. As Commissary General Jeremiah Wadsworth declared to his deputy: "I am distressed for the Army. . . . I fear nothing but the Army's wanting food, for God's sake let that be prevented, my own Estate I would freely sacrifice rather than let the Army want food."[23]

A sense of personal responsibility to George Washington and, by extension, to the army and American independence also motivated staff officers. As early as 1775, Washington had become, in the words of Douglas Southall Freeman, "a moral rallying-post, the embodiment of the purpose, the patience and the determination necessary for the triumph of the revolutionary cause." Staff officers' love and esteem for their commander in chief often reveals the remarkable reaction that Washington's force of character and symbolic role evoked. The most natural way for military supply officers to show their respect was to keep Washington's table well stocked. Although they often failed, staff officers went to great lengths to supply the commander in chief with raisins, almonds, figs, anchovies, and other foods.[24]

But the deep emotion that staff officers felt for Washington was revealed in more significant ways than in their attempts to procure delicacies for him. When staff officers failed to live up to Washington's expectations, anxiety and guilt consumed them. This was especially true during the first hard winter at Valley Forge. From army headquarters in February 1778, Deputy Commissary Blaine moaned to his superior, Colonel William Buchanan, that no less than three or four times a day during the preceding week, he had faced an angry George Washington "insisting to know the reason why more regular supplies were not laid in to support the army." That experience, according to Blaine, had made him "the most unhappy Man living." Other staff officers, unable to provide Washington with either food for his soldiers or explanations for the failure to fulfill his orders, echoed Blaine's lamentations.[25] To disappoint his Excellency was to fail the cause of American independence.

Staff officers in turn invoked George Washington's name to infuse a strong sense of urgency or importance into the orders they issued. When Ephraim Blaine wanted flour and beef forwarded in a hurry to the troops at Valley Forge, he instructed his agents that it was "the desire of his Excellency. This I trust will suffice to influence you to exert every nerve to forward . . . each and every article above mentioned." Similarly, the merchant commissaries Chaloner and White gave special consideration to a request for money when informed that "a disappointment will defeat the schemes of *His Excellency, George Washington.*"[26] Such exhortations usually were effective because staff officers were sensitive to the threat of losing the respect and approval of the person described by one deputy quartermaster as "the best Man in the World."[27] Jeremiah Wadsworth played on this fear in admonishing his deputy, Ephraim Blaine, to correspond more frequently by warning him that "your own Character with the General shall induce you to answer such parts of my letters as you know he expects to have answered." The desire to uphold one's reputation with the commander in chief was also sometimes responsible for preventing resignations and deflecting resentment at the repeated denial of leaves of absence.[28]

A strong sense of loyalty toward one another also strengthened staff officers' resolve to persevere during the hardest days of the war. For many staff officers the esprit de corps of the staff departments originated in prerevolutionary business and social relationships.[29] But it was staff officers' experience during the war years that revitalized and intensified old associations and created new bonds of allegiance. The day-to-day routine—supplying the army and caring for its sick and wounded—enmeshed these officers in an interdependent operation whose success rested upon cooperation, energy, and dedication. From commonplace occurrences, often punctuated by crisis, arose a respect for each other and a sense of camaraderie. Deputy Quartermaster John Davis's instructions to Robert Patton in response to public criticism of the Quartermaster Department indicates staff officers' regard for one another: "If a majority of the Deputy Quartermasters agree to put anything in the print—I shall cheerfully Acquiesce With them in it. . . . What Ever A majority of the Quartermasters Agree to Shall be a Rule to me."[30] Staff officers' mutual esteem transcended formalities of rank and hierarchy. Heads of departments took pride in their subordinates' sacrifices, praised their unselfish exertions, and defended them against public criticism.[31] Subordinates returned this respect and stood staunchly by their superiors. When Director-General William Shippen, Jr., was accused in 1779 of negligence and corruption, the

Hospital doctors rallied to his side and offered him their support.[32] Similarly, Deputy Commissary Peter Colt assured his chief, Jeremiah Wadsworth, that if Wadsworth continued in office, he would, too, but if Wadsworth quit he would follow.[33]

In addition to everyday operations, a number of other factors contributed to the growth of staff officers' esprit de corps. Business partnerships entered into during the war produced strong bonds of friendship and often continued and prospered after the war's end.[34] Department heads such as Nathanael Greene, believing that the cultivation of "the strictest harmony with one another . . . contributes to the ease and facility of all parties and gives dispatch and success to Business," deliberately fostered a spirit of amity among their deputies for reasons of efficiency.[35] In the Hospital Department, the nascent professionalism of medical men may perhaps have contributed to creating similar bonds of group cohesiveness.[36] The increasingly virulent attacks in the nation's press accusing staff officers of embezzling public money and war profiteering were instrumental in developing what may be most accurately described as a siege mentality. Their defensiveness prevented some staff officers from responding to public criticism with nuanced or qualified statements about their own honesty. Instead, they insisted on the complete innocence of everyone in the staff departments and defended "all who purchase for the public on commission."[37] Although demonstrating staff officers' strong collective identity, such statements did nothing for their credibility.

By far the most powerful and pervasive value motivating staff officers was an inner desire to preserve, defend, and add luster to their individual reputations and the honor of their respective departments. Notions about honor and reputation did not spring full-blown from the soil of the revolutionary war but were derived in part from an inherited aristocratic tradition and in part from the practices of colonial America's deferential society. These ideas, transplanted and nurtured for nearly 150 years in the colonies, were associated with wealth, family, education, and social connections. Reputation denoted character, integrity, honesty, and dependability. It endowed its possessor with standing and influence in society and credit in the world of commerce. Without a sound reputation, an eighteenth-century man could not aspire to public office or a place of influence in the community, nor could he maintain commercial connections for any length of time.[38]

The commercial nexus, however, should not be overemphasized. Wadsworth, Greene, and others were deeply involved in trade before, during, and after the war, and a loss of reputation would have been bad for business. But it is difficult to know whether a concern for their mercantile reputation or a desire for the respect and approval of their fellow citizens lay behind their actions. Both impulses were undoubtedly present. For example, three months after resigning his post as commissary general of purchases, Jeremiah Wadsworth wrote his friend and business partner, Nathanael Greene, regarding the conditions under which he would again agree to serve the cause: "Do not think I mean to withhold my services. No my Country has a right to them. . . . I will now choose my station and serve my country when and where I can do it without loss of reputation, but I will not again risk my character in a situation where every illiberal scoundrel can calumniate with impunity. . . . But whenever I can see an opening where I can serve with a prospect of saving my reputation I shall cheerfully risk everything else." True to his word, Wadsworth engaged as commissary to the French navy until the end of the war, and he also served as a representative from Hartford to Connecticut's General Assembly.[39]

A staff officer's notion of honor and reputation also had much in common with the eighteenth-century neoclassical concept of fame. According to Douglass Adair, the founding fathers—"no angels they but passionately selfish and self-interested men"—viewed their self-interest as identical with the public good. By erecting a republican government and ensuring the preservation of liberty and justice, they planned on paying themselves off in the only coin they coveted: fame, the everlasting applause of contemporaries, and the undying gratitude of generations unborn.[40]

Quartermaster General Nathanael Greene subscribed wholeheartedly to this understanding of fame. Greene, of course, was no Lycurgus or Solon and never pretended to be one. But as assuredly as a Jefferson or an Adams, he hungered for fame and the gratitude of posterity. Instead of attaining fame through statesmanship, however, Greene chose the time-honored route of military glory. It was his feverish desire for laurels above all else that made him so reluctant to serve as quartermaster general.

Greene always resented his decision. From the moment he assumed the duties of the Quartermaster Department, Greene envied his fellow officers' opportunities to lead men into battle. To General Alexander McDougall he lamented, "All of you will be immortallising your selves in the golden pages of History, while I am confined to a series of druggery to pave the way for it." Only in the context of the eighteenth-century notion of fame can we fully appreciate the poignancy of Greene's oft-quoted statement a year later that "nobody ever heard of a quartermaster in history, as such, or in relating any brilliant action." Greene's unhappiness with and dislike of the office never abated. When informing Congress in the spring of 1779 of his intention to resign, Greene made it clear where the Quartermaster's Department stood among his hierarchy of values. "I have ever considered it as derogatory to serve in this office," he informed the president of the Board of Treasury, James Duane, "while I am drudging in an office from which I shall receive no honor and very few thanks, I am losing an opportunity to do justice to my military character."[41] Yet Greene remained in office, grumbling and dissatisfied with his fate, for another full year, not resigning officially until the summer of 1780.

Greene's regard for his reputation kept him from quitting. As he explained to Charles Pettit, his assistant quartermaster general and close confidant, given the disagreeableness of the business—by which Greene meant the country's financial woes and the "chymerical systems" Congress kept proposing—it was in their "interest to retire as soon as there is an opening, in which we can do it without loss of character." In short, Greene reiterated to Pettit, the problem was how to get out of a bad situation "without injury to our reputation."[42] In Greene, fame and reputation were at war with each other. While Greene's quest for military glory tugged at him to abandon his staff position, his concern for maintaining his reputation as a patriot and as a virtuous gentleman kept him at his post.

For Greene and other staff officers the impulse to preserve and add to their reputations represented their highest aspiration in the revolutionary war. It was an ideal that pervaded every facet of army administration. Considerations of the negative effect the nonpayment of debts would have on their reputations often prompted staff officers' fervent pleas for money. Thus Deputy Quartermaster John Mitchell justified his demand for cash because "my Credit and Reputation are at Stake for the Contracts already made and the large sums due."[43] Reputation was also a factor when making appointments to public office because a poor choice redounded upon the appointer's good name. As John Chaloner warned Joseph Trumbull's successor, William Buchanan, "The confidence you have put in Mr. Kennedy has injured your reputation as Purchasing Commissary General."[44] Staff officers invoked reputation to stiffen each other's resolve. Assistant Deputy Foragemaster Owen Biddle, for example, counseled one of his deputies not to give in to defeatism because "we cannot shrink from the burden at this time with reputation to ourselves, nor without great inconvenience to the cause in which we are engaged."[45] Staff officers' hardnosed attitude toward corruption within their own ranks also stemmed in part from this moral calculus. Officers under suspicion of wrongdoing were ordered by their superiors to attend court proceedings punctually because "your own reputation as well as the credit of the department" demanded it.[46] Likewise, staff officers were admonished not to resign "before the end of the campaign at the peril of [their] honor and reputation."[47] In similar fashion, staff officers viewed the making of returns and the settling of accounts from the vantage point of honor and reputation. In demanding returns from his deputy, Samuel Gray, the commissary general of issues, Charles Stewart, resorted to only one rhetorical device:

"I hope I have now only to remind you, that the reputation of every Person concerned in the Issuing Department is at stake, for the speedy settlement of the Public Accounts."[48]

As Stewart's statement reveals, the reputation of individuals could not be separated from that of the department. The desire to bring honor to the department thus spurred the performance of staff officers. The highest compliment Deputy Commissary General Ephraim Blaine could think to bestow upon his assistant for his timely delivery of cattle to the army at Valley Forge was that he deserved "the credit of saving the reputation of the department."[49] Conversely, staff officers feared that their department would be blamed if military expeditions failed, and they dreaded that "the reputation of all concerned in the . . . department [would] fall a sacrifice to the indolence and indulgence of some individuals."[50] Hence staff officers who failed to comply with orders, violated regulations, or neglected their duties were strongly rebuked for bringing "ruin and disgrace" upon the entire department.[51]

Staff officers' concern for reputation, whether for themselves or for the department, was a two-edged sword. At times, it led them to badger and pester their superiors needlessly. Deputy Quartermaster Robert L. Hooper, Jr., for example, recognized that his importuning was excessive and apologetically explained to his boss, Nathanael Greene, that his "anxiety to support the reputation of our Department occasions me to trouble you so much and so often on the Business of it."[52]

But obsessive behavior, bordering on obstruction, was rare. More frequent, and more detrimental to the army's effectiveness, were staff officers' decisions to resign over what they interpreted as matters of honor. Thus, though the lack of pay usually precipitated staff officers' disgruntlement with public service, it was the resulting loss of reputation that really rankled. For example, inadequate pay galvanized the surgeons and mates at Morristown in 1780 to demand from Congress the same compensation as line officers received. If Congress failed to provide a pay increase, they threatened to resign because "whatever may be our Feelings with Respect to our Patriotism we shall be obliged in Defense of our Honour, However unwillingly, to Quit a Service in which we have been treated with such obvious Indifference and Neglect."[53] Similarly, at the beginning of 1779, with Continental currency depreciating wildly, creditors clamoring for money, and Congress unable or unwilling to furnish its agents with funds, staff officers threatened to quit in a last-ditch effort to maintain their reputation. "I have spent my time and Money, and what is worse my Character is now at stake, which I think more of than the whole," explained Assistant Deputy Commissary David Duncan in setting forth his reasons for wanting to be relieved from office.[54] The same story was repeated in the Quartermaster Department; Greene said his deputies were being driven out of the service because they foresaw "no hope of discharging their duty with satisfaction to the Army or with security and reputation to themselves."[55]

Staff officers also threatened to resign when they saw Congress casting aspersions on their honor. Congress's resolution of 9 July 1779 was especially provocative because it empowered state authorities to investigate staff officers. Typical of the angry reaction was Deputy Quartermaster Nehemiah Hubbard's assertion that "every officer in the staff who would wish to save his reputation must resign."[56] Although Nathanael Greene worried that officers "who value their reputation will not serve upon such a precarious footing," he managed to calm their fears and prevented further disruption of logistical operations in the Quartermaster Department.[57]

When staff officers resigned for reasons of honor, illness, or impoverishment, however, it did not always mean they stopped contributing to the war effort. As Hugh Hughes defiantly informed Nathanael Greene in defending his decision to resign: "Tho' I quit the Department, it does not follow, I shall the Country or the cause."[58] Not surprisingly, two years later, Hughes accepted Quartermaster General Timothy Pickering's invitation to act as deputy quartermaster of New York, an office Hughes held until the end of the war.[59] Deputy Commissary General Henry Champion is another case in point. Although Champion resigned in February 1780, he continued unofficially for the next six months to purchase cattle and forward them to the army. In July 1780, the Connecticut General Assembly appointed him superintending purchasing commissary of the state, a position he readily accepted.[60] The examples of Hughes, Champion, and others suggest that resignation from the staff departments did not necessarily signify a lack of patriotism. Staff officers attempted to support the revolutionary war effort and at the same time prevent the sacrifice of their reputation or fortune. When the two goals were incompatible, they resigned and sought positions where these ends were not in conflict.

H O W, T H E N, does one explain staff officers' altruistic behavior? The answer clearly lies in the unique concatenation of political and social ideals—republicanism, esprit de corps, and reputation—that dissolved the distinction between private and public good. For one rare moment in American history, among at least one group of men, self-interest was not at war with the common good; instead, serving the public promoted and enhanced the self. By steadfastly doing their duty—purchasing food, transporting camp equipment, and tending the sick and wounded—staff officers brought honor to themselves, to the staff departments, and in retrospect, to the cause of American independence.

CHAPTER 7

THE STATE SUPPLY SYSTEM

1780 – 1781

Economy in the public expenses is the first object.
    —Report of the Board of Treasury,
      27 April 1779

Where are the Men? Where are the provisions? Where are the Cloaths?
    —George Washington to Gouverneur Morris,
      10 December 1780

CONGRESSIONAL INVESTIGATION of corruption in the staff departments was only the first step in a multipronged effort to cope with the nation's financial crisis. While the Continental army languished at Morristown, New Jersey, during the worst winter of the war, Congress acted on a broad front to cut public expenditures by eliminating superfluous staff departments, reorganizing others, and reducing unnecessary personnel. The centerpiece of congressional reform, however, was the system of specific supplies, a plan by which the states assumed responsibility for provisioning the army. This action signaled Congress's virtual abandonment of its central role in administering the war; in effect, Congress abdicated its power to the states. State legislatures, however, proved unequal to the task. As the war entered its sixth year, logistical problems continued to plague the army, sapping its capacity to launch an offensive, damaging the morale of the soldiers, and setting the stage for the Nationalist movement.

ON A COLD, snowy 1 December 1779, General Washington rode into Morristown, New Jersey, the site chosen by Quartermaster General Greene for the army's winter quarters. The move signaled the end of the campaign of 1779, a campaign on which the general could look with some satisfaction. He had successfully frustrated Sir Henry Clinton's efforts to force the Americans into a general engagement and prevented Sir Henry from driving the army into the Highlands and destroying its communications. Offensively, the troops had demonstrated much resourcefulness and bravery in General Anthony Wayne's storming and temporary occupation of Stony Point, in General John Sullivan's ruthless Indian campaign on New York's western frontier, and in Major Henry Lee's spirited attack on Paulus Hook. In contrast to these bright spots, however, was the bad news Washington received on the evening of 15 November, two weeks before departing for Morristown: the joint French and American assault on British-held Savannah had failed; the allies had been forced to lift the siege; and Comte d'Estaing, wounded twice, had ordered the French fleet to set sail back to the West Indies.[1]

Closer to home the situation was equally bleak. To begin with, General Washington had to contend with the unseasonably severe weather. The snow that greeted him on 1 December fell again on the fifth, the fourteenth, the sixteenth, the eighteenth, the twenty-eighth, and again on the twenty-ninth. Roads were buried under four feet of snow, and it was so cold that New York Harbor was completely frozen over. January's weather was worse. According to the Hospital surgeon, James Thacher, on 3 January the army

> experienced one of the most tremendous snowstorms ever remembered: no man could endure its violence many minutes without danger of his life. . . . Some of the soldiers were actually covered while in their tents and buried like sheep under the snow. . . . The sufferings of the poor wretches can scarcely be described . . . ; at night they now have but a bed of straw on the ground and a single blanket to each man; they are badly clad and some are destitute of shoes. . . . The snow is now from four to six feet deep.[2]

The blizzard continued through the night of 4 January. It snowed again on the sixth and seventh, and much of the rest of the month remained "Intensely cold & freezing."[3] Nor did February's weather show any improvement. Baron de Kalb reported in that month that the ink froze on his pen and that outside the snowdrifts were piled twelve feet high. March brought no relief; elderly residents considered it the worst winter in memory.[4]

The shortage of food compounded the soldiers' misery. The army had been without bread for several weeks before arriving at Morristown. By the middle of December the troops had been on half allowance for five to six weeks. The magazines from which provisions were normally drawn were empty, and the possibility of assistance was remote. Deputy Commissary Royal Flint pronounced the situation "the most critical imaginable: without provisions, without money, the department without credit, without prospect of relief, the patience of the troops worn out, and the army on the point of dissolution."[5] General Washington concurred, declaring that the army had "never experienced a like extremity at any period of the war," and predicted that unless supplies were provided "the army will infallibly disband in a fortnight."[6] Scarcity of meat worsened the situation the following month. "The Army have been reduced to the most Extreme want of provisions," wrote Major John Patten of the Delaware Regiment on 17 January, "having subsisted five days on half a pound of salt Beef and half a pint of Rice without any other kind of support whatever." At other times, the men were without meat for six to eight days. Driven to the edge of starvation, soldiers gnawed birch bark and cooked their old shoes; several officers killed a pet dog and ate him.[7]

The causes of the army's distress were numerous. Almost all of the problems afflicting logistical operations came to a head in the winter of 1779–80: harsh weather blocked roads and froze streams, preventing the delivery of supplies and putting a stop to milling; a fall drought limited crop production; farmers refused to sell their produce for paper money, demanded cash in advance, or charged outrageous prices; and staff employees, unable to support themselves on their meager wages, resigned.

The army was kept from disbanding by erratic but timely impressment of food by military officers and local magistrates. Continental soldiers supplemented these efforts by plundering the surrounding countryside. Throughout this unprecedented crisis, Congress conspicuously failed to provide effective leadership or relief to the army.[8]

IF THE ONLY SOURCE for reconstructing the war's progress were the *Journals of the Continental Congress*, historians would be forced to conclude that the war was drawing to a close in late 1779, for the bulk of Congress's resolves point in that direction. Haunted by the specter of national bankruptcy, Congress single-mindedly began economizing on all facets of logistical operations and delegated the few powers it exercised over war management to the states. Thus in effect, if not intention, Congress began withdrawing from administering the Continental army a full two years before Yorktown.

The impetus for congressional cutbacks came from a series of reports issued by the Board of Treasury in the spring of 1779 concluding that the cost of running the two largest staff departments had increased enormously since the beginning of the war. In 1775–76, the board estimated it cost $5,399,219 to support both the Quartermaster and Commissary departments. By contrast, the board predicted the cost of financing the two departments in 1779 would be $200 million—an expense, it warned Congress, that would strain the nation's financial structure past the breaking point. Citing the widespread belief that the payment of commissions was the major cause of the staff departments' expense, the board called for retrenchment in staff personnel and expenses, a change in the manner quartermasters and commissaries were compensated, and formation of a committee to investigate public expenditures. In the following months, Congress put all of the board's proposals into effect.[9]

In sharp opposition to the Treasury Board's call for economy, Quartermaster General Nathanael Greene defended the staff departments' large expenditures. Writing in July 1779, Greene told the Board of War that logistics was not a science; provisioning the army—whether it be food or camp equipment—was "a Business in its own nature, not reducible to certain modes, but must vary with time and circumstances." He denied that fraud and abuses by staff officers were to blame for the high cost of the war. People who believed that corruption was at the root of the problem, Greene bluntly told Congress, either had no knowledge of the scope of logistical operations or failed to distinguish "between what is incidental and inseparable from the nature of the service and what arises from want of order, method, and due attention to the business. The question is not, whether any abuses prevail, but whether as few exist as are to be expected from the condition and nature of the Service." Greene placed specific responsibility for the war's expense on the unpredictable and fluctuating nature of the conflict, the constant movement of the army, and the extensiveness of the Quartermaster Department's business. His explanation amounted to a logical proof: nations could not wage war without spending money.[10]

Greene's analysis fell on deaf ears. One of Congress's first economy measures—the elimination of minor staff departments—provides a clear example of its penny-wise, pound-foolish policies. On 27 December 1779, Congress moved to dismiss the nation's express riders. Analogous to modern-day special delivery couriers, express riders were eliminated because, according to Connecticut Congressman Roger Sherman, they "involved the public in a very enormous expense." Members of Congress believed that regular mail delivery routes, operating on a twice-weekly basis, would accomplish the same job for less money. Sherman suggested that express riders could be employed "on some extraordinary Occasions," but the wording of the congressional resolve—"that no established express riders be in the future maintained at the public expense"—belied his optimism.[11]

Military officials thought the measure obstructive and ill-conceived. Deputy Quartermaster Udny Hay, complaining that it "cramp'd us in the execution of our duty," interpreted the resolve as another sign of Congress's lack of confidence in staff officers. As a result, Hay again considered resigning. Assistant Quartermaster Charles Pettit criticized Congress for overreacting: its decision to eliminate all express riders went from one extreme to another. For although Pettit agreed with Congress that the number of expresses had become too great and the expense too burdensome, he also noted that "to lop them off at a stroke may work a still greater evil."[12] Pettit's fears were quickly realized. He was temporarily prevented from forwarding much-needed funds to one of the deputy quartermasters because the postmaster refused to be accountable for unauthorized mailings. As a result, Pettit was forced to withdraw the letter containing bills of credit totaling several hundred thousand dollars and wait for the regular mail. Other staff officers also complained that the lack of expresses interfered with their ability to carry out their duties.[13]

General Washington's immediate suspension of the resolve and consequent communication with Congress prevented the army from suffering even further repercussions from Congress's precipitous action. Tactfully but forcefully, Washington instructed Congress on the importance of express riders to the cause. He pointed out that in emergencies "instant communication" was imperative. Delays in military matters often proved fatal. Furthermore, expresses were even more essential to the Continental army than to other armies because of the "multiplied difficulties" afflicting it. Washington also warned that relying on the regular mail made communication between the army and its correspondents predictable, thus increasing the probability that the enemy would intercept messages. Nor did he believe the elimination of expresses would save a large sum of money. Unscrupulous men would recognize the need for urgency and extort extravagant compensation. Rather than dismiss all express riders, he suggested that perhaps only half of them be let go. Congress acknowledged the wisdom of Washington's advice and authorized him to appoint as many express riders as he thought necessary.[14]

Although Congress reversed its decision to discontinue express riders, it adhered to its intention to cut expenses by closing down other unnecessary staff departments and eliminating costly staff personnel. Thus on 11 January 1780, Congress shut down the Mustering Department because its duties duplicated those carried on by the Inspector-General's Department. Nine days later, in a further effort to cut back on public officials, it abolished the Barrackmaster Department.[15] Determined to eradicate the "evil of a numerous Staff department," Congress, in the same month, appointed a committee to investigate staff officers and gave it power to discharge superfluous or delinquent personnel, to break up unnecessary issuing posts, and, in conjunction with General Washington, to "adopt a General Reformation of the Departments."[16] The committee, Congress believed, would "save some millions to this continent."[17]

Congress's economizing temper was also evident in its decision in December 1779 to shift responsibility for supplying the army to the states. This major change in its management of the war marked a return to the earliest days of congressional administration when, as a matter of course, it called upon state authorities to furnish the army with money and supplies. The reform and reorganization of 1777–78 had made the staff departments the mainstays of army supply, but recourse to the states, especially in emergencies, was never far from the minds of congressmen. As early as May 1778, the ineptitude of Clothier General James Mease and subsequent reports by General Washington of the soldiers' distress prompted a congressional committee to recommend that state governments be responsible for clothing their quota of Continental soldiers. After a ten-month delay, in March 1779 Congress acted on the committee's recommendation by dividing responsibility for clothing the troops between a Continental clothier general, whom the Board of War and commander in chief would direct, and state or sub-clothiers, whom the states would appoint. Congress authorized both the Board of War and state clothiers to purchase clothing, the Board of War for Continental soldiers and state clothiers for their own troops. Congress did not coordinate lines of authority between national and local officials. Although under the new scheme state clothiers were instructed to make regular reports to the clothier general, the chain of command was, in practice, separate: the clothier general had no control over state agents, and state agents were answerable primarily to state authorities. The lack of central direction, the four-month delay in appointing a clothier general, and Congress's poor choice for chief administrator of the Clothing Department—James Wilkinson, the social director of Philadelphia high society—ensured that the troops would continue to lack clothing. In short, Congress had created another ineffectual supply system to supplement its own defective one.[18]

As the financial crisis worsened in 1779 and complaints mounted from staff officers about their inability to obtain supplies for the army, Congress increasingly looked to the states to solve its administrative and logistical problems. On 14 June 1779 it strongly recommended that state governments enact legislation to limit the spiraling prices of commodities needed for the army. On 9 July it called on state authorities to investigate the staff officers of the Quartermaster and Commissary departments in an effort to root out corrupt supply officials. Exactly two weeks later, on 23 July, a committee appointed to regulate the staff departments recommended that the states be requisitioned for beef, pork, flour, rum, and forage and that the amount contributed to the army be credited toward their future tax quotas. The committee's recommendation marked the inception of the system of specific supplies. The plan, however, was not acted upon until 15 December, when Congress called on six states to furnish the army with grain or corn before 1 April 1780. And full implementation of the new system was delayed until 25 February 1780, while Congress calculated and wrangled over the amount of provisions due from each state.[19]

Anticipating the states' assumption of responsibility for feeding the army, Congress overhauled the Commissary Department in January 1780. Never totally comfortable with paying commissions to staff officers, Congress grasped the opportunity offered by the system of specific supplies to revert to paying department chiefs fixed salaries. Thus, in contrast to paying Jeremiah Wadsworth .5 percent on all money disbursed in his department, Congress granted the new Commissary General, Ephraim Blaine, who replaced Wadsworth on 13 January, a salary of $40,000 a year.[20] Blaine's deputies—Congress allowed him one assistant commissary for each state providing supplies—were to receive a 2 percent commission on goods they purchased or that were purchased under their supervision. Recognizing the fact of inflation yet anxious to prevent abuses and to hold down expenses, Congress ordered that commissions be restricted to that portion of the costs which did not exceed twenty times the price of similar commodities in 1774. In addition, Congress directed deputy commissaries to use part of their remuneration to pay their agents and to defray all expenses attending their purchases.[21] Most striking about Congress's reorganization of the Commissariat was its singular devotion to reducing public expenditures. The issue of whether the changes were conducive to supplying the army more effectively was hardly considered.

With the Commissary Department reorganized, Congress put the finishing touches on the system of specific supplies. In its final form, the new system required the states to collect and deliver provisions to various magazine sites designated by the commander in chief, according to specific quotas. Connecticut, for example, was to provide the army with 78,400 hundredweight of beef, 1,011 bushels of salt, 68,558 gallons of rum, and 500 tons of hay, while Pennsylvania was directed to collect 40,000 barrels of flour, 14,189 bushels of salt, 24,423 gallons of rum, 1,700 tons of hay, and 200,000 bushels of corn or short forage.

Congress also established standards of quality and set price ceilings. Pork "well fatted with corn or rice" was to be purchased at $7 per net hundredweight. Flour was to be "merchantable," the price not to exceed $4.50 a barrel. Likewise, West Indian rum was to be "good proof" and purchased at no more than $1.66 per gallon. In similar fashion, Congress designated and priced all of the provisions the states were to procure for the army. In addition, commissioners were assigned to inspect and approve the commodities collected before Congress would credit the states with their quota. As an incentive, states that provided more than their quota would be paid for the surplus in specie at 6 percent interest. Conversely, those that failed to meet their quotas were to be charged the deficiency at the same rate.[22]

Capping the first wave of congressional reform efforts in 1780 was a proposal advanced on 18 March to put the nation's finances in proper order. The plan was relatively simple and basically sound. Congress called upon the states to tax out of existence the "old" Continental currency, revalued at 40:1, at a rate of $15 million a month. As the "old" bills came in, Congress would destroy them and issue new currency at a 20:1 ratio, redeemable in six years at 5 percent interest per year. Thus for every $40 of "old" bills received, $2 of the new bills were released, six-tenths of which were reserved for the states, four-tenths to Congress. With its share of the new bills, Congress expected each state to pay its military personnel, defray government expenses, and purchase supplies for the army. Thus the success of the system of specific supplies hinged on the effectiveness of state taxation efforts.[23]

Although Congress was forced by financial necessity to turn to the states, it was convinced that the system of specific supplies was an improvement. Of course, a few delegates had reservations. New Jersey's Abraham Clark "dislike[d] the plan altogether," and New York's Ezra

L'Hommedieu feared that in practice the system would fail.[24] But congressmen with high expectations of the plan's success vastly outnumbered the naysayers. One benefit, according to the North Carolina delegation, was that the power of the states was "much better Established, much more simple and vigorous in its Operations relative to public Credit, and . . . much more relied on, than that of Congress." Hence the states were more competent than Congress to provide securities for appreciating Continental currency. Connecticut's delegates emphasized that the quota system was more equitable in apportioning the burden of supplying the army. In particular, it gave relief to states that, because the army was camped within their borders, had been made solely responsible for provisioning it.[25] Almost as an afterthought, congressmen pointed out that the new arrangement would provide the army with supplies on a regular and punctual basis.

The efficient supply of the army ought to have been the most compelling reason for shifting to the new plan, but few members of Congress gave it first priority.[26] Instead, the majority of congressmen stressed that the new system would save the public an immense amount of money. It would allow Congress to cut back on a considerable number of public officials, thus reducing the large amount of cash paid out in salaries. It would also permit the virtual elimination of the commission system and the return to fixed salaries for department chiefs. But most important, a cutback in the number of staff officers would bring a wholesale reduction in fraud and peculation.[27] Whether for reasons of efficiency, equity, or economy, congressmen were decidedly enthusiastic about the system of specific supplies. Writing to Governor Richard Caswell, the North Carolina delegation conveyed Congress's numerous grounds for approving the plan and also its infectious optimism: "In a word, Sir [it] will give us plenty of supplies, without incurring heavy public debts; without giving partial advantages; without causing partial burthens; without leaving us exposed to the abuses of peculation, or danger to our affairs from precarious subsistence of our army."[28]

In marked contrast to Congress's sanguine expectations, military officials in the field were far more skeptical and pessimistic about the new supply system. The consensus among staff officers was overwhelmingly negative. The plan, in their estimation, was "crude and undigested," "fundamentally wrong in its first principles," and would "infallibly be productive of great confusion and irregularity." All agreed it spelled the army's ruin. In an extended critique of the system of specific supplies, Quartermaster General Greene pointed out the plan's weaknesses. Congress, he wrote, had paid too little attention to the mechanics of the system: "There is no particular mode recommended to the different states for furnishing their proportion of supplies. . . . There is no plan of delivery, nor penalty on failure. . . . There is no plan for furnishing the deficiency of supplies that may be required from particular military movements, nor even for furnishing the . . . ordinary demands of service." In Greene's opinion, moreover, state provincialism would lead inevitably to the scheme's failure. Experience showed the states were partial to their own interests and often restricted the ways and means of supplying the army. Without a Continental agent at the head of each state supply system, Greene warned, the plan would fail because a state agent "will be too local in his views to accommodate his conduct to the demands of the Army."[29] Although Greene claimed he was not rejecting outright the system of specific supplies but only trying to suggest improvements, there is little doubt that he and other staff officers would have heartily agreed with one line officer's comment that "Congress have left it in the power of the States to starve the Army at pleasure."[30]

State response to the congressional resolve of 25 February bore out the worst fears of staff officers. From the outset, the controversy that enveloped the new plan delayed its full implementation. In matters for which cooperation between Continental administrators and state officials was most essential—the appointment and instruction of state agents—Commissary General Blaine reported that the New England states refused to act and had shunted the task back onto his shoulders.[31] In Connecticut, the only state for which the reasons for this lack of cooperation are clear, Governor Jonathan Trumbull defended the assembly's decision not to appoint an assistant commissary by endorsing its condemnation of Congress's tightfisted pay policy. Singling out Congress's recommendation that assistant commissaries be paid a 2 percent commission out of which they were expected to pay their deputies and defray all costs, Trumbull denounced the policy on the grounds that it was insufficient compensation for the work involved and an open invitation for sharpers to steal what they did not receive in pay. The congressional resolution, Trumbull noted, presented the state with two unpalatable choices. It could either offer inadequate pay, a prospect sure to attract only the dishonest, or it could incur an exorbitant and congressionally unauthorized expense by paying its agents generously. According to the governor, the assembly rejected both courses of action by refusing to appoint anyone.

In an effort to break the impasse, Trumbull urged Congress to increase the compensation for administrators, the better to entice trustworthy men, and lectured it on the evil consequences—"villainy, deception, and discontent in servants"—of its penny-pinching ways. Trumbull's strictures were a good case of the pot calling the kettle black, for if Connecticut had been less concerned about running into debt, it would have authorized the additional compensation for a state commissary, rather than urging Congress to assume the expense. In the aftermath, the New England states left it to Commissary General Blaine to appoint agents for Connecticut, Massachusetts, and Rhode Island.[32] The reluctance of these states to cooperate actively with the congressional resolution of 25 February was an early sign of the ultimate failure of the system of specific supplies. In its collapse lay the seeds of the Nationalist movement.

Although state compliance with Congress's plan to supply the army was far from adequate, the overall, initial response was promising. Aside from New England's uncooperative attitude, the other states promptly appointed commissarial agents, and by April 1780 most of the states had enacted some form of legislation to supply the army.[33] Although differing in minor details, the broad outlines of the various state supply systems were remarkably alike. Because of their similarity it is necessary to examine only one state organization—in this case New Jersey's—to demonstrate the states' response to the congressional resolutions of 14 December and 25 February.

On 25 December 1779, two weeks after Congress had called upon New Jersey to supply Washington's troops at Morristown, the state assembly appointed contractors in each of its thirteen counties to purchase provisions and a superintendent of purchases to oversee the supply operations. To facilitate the shipment of supplies, the legislature permitted contractors to impress wagons and boats upon securing a warrant from the local magistrate. As an incentive to perform their task, the assembly paid them £400 per year, plus a bounty based on the quantity of food they secured. For example, for every hundred bushels of wheat contractors purchased, they were to be paid an additional £20; for every ton of hay, £3. Thus when the New Jersey Assembly received Congress's 25 February resolution, its state supply system was already in place, and it merely had to divide its quota of supplies among the state's numerous counties.[34]

By the end of 1780, all of the states except Georgia and South Carolina, which had been overrun by the British, had set up similar supply systems. But it was one thing to pass laws and another to have them carried out. Almost from the first month of operation, it was evident to some observers that the states would fail to meet their assigned quotas. Such considerations prompted Quartermaster Greene to quip: "Perhaps this campaign is to be of the Marvelous kind. We are to . . . exist without support."[35] Two and one-half months later, on the evening of 25 May 1780, the Continental army ran out of miracles. Subjected to severely reduced meat rations for weeks, two regiments of the Connecticut line mutinied.[36] Fortunately, Continental officers prevailed upon the mutineers to return to the ranks. That hunger provoked them to such an extreme reaction is testimony to the failure of the states to supply the army with food. By August 1780, General Washington was denouncing the system of specific supplies as "the most uncertain, expensive, and injurious that could be devised."[37]

The scarcity of provisions continued through the fall. Commissary General Blaine reported in October 1780 that four of the army's principal magazines were destitute of flour, bread, beef, pork, fish, salt, and rum and that none of the others could furnish one day's supply. In addition, all the garrisons and posts in the Middle Department were without food, and supplies were forthcoming only from Massachusetts and New Hampshire.[38] Commenting on the wretched conditions his men struggled against in December 1780, Washington, like Greene, resorted to gallows humor. Writing to Gouverneur Morris, he observed that "it would be well for the Troops, if like Chameleons, they could live upon Air, or like the Bear, suck their paws for sustenance during the rigour of the approaching season."[39] It was obvious to Washington that the army should not place any confidence in the states. Unfortunately, Continental soldiers were not mythical creatures but mere mortals. During January 1781, the Continental army was wracked by two mutinies, which, had they spread, would have threatened the continuance of the army in the field. First, the Pennsylvania line, after seizing six artillery pieces, killing a captain, and wounding several officers, marched on Philadelphia to demand redress of their grievances. Three weeks later, on 19 January, the New Jersey line rose up and defied their officers. Both mutinies were quelled. Underlying and exacerbating the soldiers' discontent was the lack of pay, clothing, and food.[40]

WHY DID THE SYSTEM of specific supplies fail? A chief factor was Congress's poor planning, a perennial problem partly reflecting its usual lack of foresight and naive optimism. Three years before Congress proposed the system of specific supplies, General Washington had waspishly observed that Congress "think it is but to say Presto begone, and everything is done." Congress's blueprint for drawing supplies from the states attests to the continuing validity of Washington's gibe. The plan's most glaring failure was its omission of any instructions or funds for the transportation of the specific supplies beyond the state boundaries where they were purchased. Congress's assumption that the Quartermaster Department—whose responsibility it had been to secure the necessary transportation—would be reformed in the very near future and be capable of cooperating with state commissaries contributed to the uncertainty of shipping provisions. Congress guessed wrong, and the expected overhaul of the Quartermaster Department was delayed for four months; in the ensuing confusion, badly needed supplies rotted in state supply depositories. Congress did not identify the problem until May 1780, three months after its original resolve. And even then, its only solution was to throw the responsibility of providing transportation onto the shoulders of state executive authorities.[41]

Other congressional administrative oversights contributed to the failure of the system of specific supplies. Congress often seemed ignorant of basic facts concerning the abilities of the states to meet their quotas. For example, Congress called upon Connecticut for eight thousand barrels of flour, when according to Governor Jonathan Trumbull, "it is well known that this is not much of a wheat country."[42] Likewise, Pennsylvania, requested to forward bacon, rum, and salt, was unable to comply immediately because these items had to be imported from neighboring states.[43] In a similar vein, Congress called on the states to provide salted beef and pork after the animals had already been sent to market, thus forcing the states to purchase their quotas from engrossers. Referring to Congress's disdain for these agricultural facts of life, an exasperated Governor Trumbull asked President Samuel Huntington, "Is it impossible for Congress to make their Estimates and Requisitions on this Head in their proper Season? If it is not I think the Neglect is almost unpardonable."[44]

Congress's failure to keep itself informed of any special circumstances or internal matters that might prevent a state from meeting its assigned quota was just as serious a problem. Rhode Island's Governor William Greene instructed Congress that it was unable to meet its requisition of beef because a prolonged and severe drought had destroyed the state's cattle. Governor George Clinton patiently explained New York's inability to raise troops or supplies by reminding Congress that the British controlled its capital, New York City, and four counties; that the enemy was attacking the southern, western, and northern frontiers; and that because of a poor harvest and previous food requisitions by the army the state was incapable of providing its quota.[45] Thomas Jefferson, then governor of Virginia, ascribed his state's powerlessness to ship salted provisions northward to British warships "constantly cruising in our bay."[46] New Jersey and Pennsylvania pointedly informed Congress that having borne much of the brunt of supplying the army during the past two years, they were hard-pressed to meet the new demands.[47] The responses of the states make it clear that Congress was out of touch with its constituents.

A lack of communication between the states and Congress was partly responsible for Congress's ignorance about state capabilities. State legislatures felt no responsibility to keep even their own representatives informed of their activities. In January 1777, after repeated inquiries to which he received no reply, North Carolina Congressman William Hooper was forced to the extreme of asking his own legislature: "Am or am I not a delegate?" Members of Congress from New Hampshire, New York, Connecticut, and Virginia likewise fumed at being kept in the dark about civil and military matters occurring within their state.[48]

Congress fared no better. On several occasions state officials ignored formal requests for information concerning the system of specific supplies.[49] The problem became so serious that on 17 June 1780, Congress called on the states to inform it "with the utmost expedition, what measures they have taken" in compliance with congressional resolves. Most of the states replied.[50] But because of the initial indifference of state authorities, more than four months went by before Congress possessed the detailed information it needed to adjust state supply quotas. Moreover, once the states had complied with the 17 June resolve, they reverted to their old ways and made little effort to keep Congress informed of either financial or supply matters. Consequently, the information necessary to make informed administrative decisions was not at hand. Not surprisingly, in July 1781, the newly appointed superintendent of finance, Robert Morris, was forced to appeal to the states for information because he felt himself "fettered at every moment and embarrassed in every operation from my ignorance of our actual state and what is reasonably to be asked or expected."[51]

But if state officials were remiss in keeping Congress abreast of developments within their jurisdictions, Congress was equally at fault. Again, Congress's attitude of "Presto begone" was evident: it paid little attention to disseminating its resolves. The New York printer John Holt captured Congress's frame of mind: "They seem to conclude, that if published in their Journals, or in a Philadelphia newspaper, their proceedings would naturally be known all over the United States." Indeed, the problem was an old one. As early as August 1777, both state officials and staff officers complained of Congress's failure to keep them apprised of its measures. Deprived of "knowledge of the Acts of Congress," military officials made an effort to keep informed of the national legislature's activities by scanning the occasional newspaper that came their way. But as General Alexander McDougall noted, newspapers were easily lost, and as Quartermaster General Greene protested, this erratic method was not conducive to committing the resolves to memory.[52]

Congressional efforts to improve its lines of communication were slow and inefficient. In May 1779, New Hampshire Congressman William Whipple reported that the Journals of Congress for 1777 would be published "in a week or two." Two months later, Commissary General Jeremiah Wadsworth thanked his correspondent for "a Bundle of Journals" and then noted "there was none for the years 1777 or 1778"—a clear indication of Congress's continuing inefficiency. The result of Congress's failure to set up a formal and routinized communication system, in the words of

General McDougall, was that "in many instances the country and the army are total strangers to the law of either." Consequently and not surprisingly, the lack of communication hindered state efforts to supply the army. Governor Abner Nash of North Carolina deplored not receiving the 25 February resolve until 15 May, and other state officials also grumbled at not getting notices of congressional acts.[53] With the collapse of the nation's financial structure in 1780, the problem of communication worsened. From December 1780 to July 1781, the journals of the Continental Congress went unpublished for lack of money.[54]

Another circumstance responsible for the failure of the system of specific supplies was state legislatures' sluggish responses to congressional resolves. Both state and military authorities remarked upon the dilatory habits of state assemblies. "Experience has taught us," wrote Massachusetts revolutionary James Bowdoin to the president of Congress in September 1780, that "Assemblies . . . composed of a great number of Persons who must deliberate upon every measure . . . consequently must be very slow in the final Determinations for the Specific Article[s] that are wanted." Characteristically, Quartermaster General Greene raised this criticism to a universal maxim: "Political bodies are often too tardy in their measures for the emergencies of war." All critics agreed, however, that because of state legislatures' unhurried pace of complying with congressional directives, "the Army has been fed only from day to day and at some times entirely destitute."[55]

The slowness of gathering supplies was not, as Greene suggested, simply an inherent trait of large deliberative assemblies. Delays were more commonly a product of state provincialism. State legislatures placed their interests and their citizens' welfare (often one and the same) before the national interest as embodied in congressional resolves. The two worst offenders in this regard were Rhode Island and Delaware. Both states persevered in actions contrary to Congress's express orders. In August 1780, Governor William Greene of Rhode Island flatly refused to send food to the army, though called upon by Congress to do so. According to Greene, the state's first priority was to feed its own militia, which had been called out to repel an imminent British invasion.[56] The Delaware legislature similarly disregarded a congressional resolve by lifting its embargo on provisions in May 1780, thereby benefiting the state's merchants and draining scarce supplies away from its neighbors, particularly Pennsylvania. Worse, the assembly adjourned in November 1780 for two months although it had failed to furnish a fourth of its quota.[57]

Other states were not as flagrant as Rhode Island and Delaware in disregarding Congress's resolves, but the results were the same. This is not to say that the states made no efforts to forward supplies or that they were totally unsuccessful. Indeed, most agreed with the Maryland legislature that they had "complied in Substance with every Requisition of Congress. . . . We have constantly exerted ourselves for supporting the Common Cause."[58] And that support did allow the army to stay in the field and eventually win the war. But these facts should not obscure the way state and local authorities sabotaged their own efforts by accommodating the law to the special circumstances of their constituents. For example, when the Virginia Assembly passed a supplementary act to supply the army in October 1780, it carefully designed the statute, like the impressment laws, to minimize discomfort to its citizens and thus maximize delay to the army. Consequently, although the law was promulgated in October, the state legislature allowed the magistrates until February to hold court and apportion their county quotas among districts. Within ten days of the court, a majority of the inhabitants of the district were to assign individual contributions, "observing the rules of equality as near as can be." The inhabitant then had fifty days to furnish the goods. If after fifty days a district should fail to meet its quota, the statute directed the district receiver to give public notice for five days and then let to the lowest bidder the privilege of making up the deficiency, the cost to be borne by the district defaulters. Should the lowest bidder fail to produce the goods in thirty days, he would forfeit double their value.[59] Certainly the Virginia Assembly had provided for almost every contingency, but its stress on equalizing contributions, and the lengthy time intervals at each stage of the process, reveal its reluctance to coerce its citizens and virtually ensured that these supplies would never reach the army on time.

Although legalisms did not encumber other state supply systems to the same degree, the decentralized nature of their operations guaranteed similar consequences. The weakest link in these systems was their reliance on local officials—town selectmen and county magistrates and assessors—who had no realistic idea of the army's needs and who failed to cooperate with Continental agents. Commissary General Blaine criticized those states that, in setting up supply systems, passed over experienced military personnel and instead appointed "new persons . . . who are strangers to the Business, few of which have Spirit or perseverance to procure the Supplies."[60] Here Blaine touched upon an even more serious consequence of relying on local officials: many refused to pressure their neighbors. Whether from powerlessness, negligence, disaffection from the cause, or sympathy with inhabitants' economic distress—and these were not mutually exclusive categories—local officials did not execute their assigned roles in state supply systems. "The assessors have been very backward in making their assessment of cattle," one state official wrote Governor Clinton of New York in August 1780; "some have done nothing concerning it, and others so Indifferent that it puts me under great Difficulty."[61] In April 1781, Deputy Quartermaster Edward Carrington likewise complained of the behavior of local officials, "who fill their Offices without ever supposing it incumbent on them to discharge the duties thereof." Staff officers repeated similar criticism throughout the country.[62]

The final and most serious circumstance aggravating state supply of the army was the immense difficulty in acquiring provisions and transportation. State and local authorities now discovered at first hand what staff officers had been charging for the past year: supplies could not be purchased without money; engrossers and speculators were everywhere; and the French, with specie in hand, preempted state purchasers, especially in Maryland and Connecticut.[63]

At bottom, the problem was financial. State treasuries were empty, towns bankrupt, Continental currency worthless, and the marketplace glutted with Quartermaster and Commissary certificates. This last feature in particular was an almost insurmountable obstacle for state supply systems to overcome, for by early 1781 more than $93 million in certificates had been issued.[64] The plethora of certificates interfered with the production and purchase of supplies in several ways. First, Connecticut cattle-feeders, holding £2.4 million in certificates from Continental agents, were unable to purchase either lean cattle or the grain needed to fatten the beeves because sellers refused to accept the certificates and demanded specie. The result was a severe scarcity of beef for the army in 1781.[65] Second, because certificates could be used to pay the taxes demanded by the states, Congress's plan to put its financial house in order was fatally undermined. Instead of receiving "old" Continental currency, state treasuries were flooded with certificates. For example, out of a tax assessment of $500,000 on Dutchess County, New York, the state received only $30,-000 in currency, the remainder in certificates. Hence the states were prevented from remitting the "old" bills to Congress and did not receive the new ones. Consequently, state supply officials often lacked purchasing funds.[66]

Finally, and most obstructive of state supply efforts, inhabitants refused to part with their produce or wagons until the certificates in their possession were redeemed. Typical of the response received by state officials was Pennsylvania militia Colonel Joseph Hart's description of his attempt to procure transportation in August 1780: "Not a Man even of those who may have a horse to spare, but would [rather] give him away as to take the Certificates, and not a man Possessed of a Team but would rather lend it to a good Neighbor than hire it into the Continental Service for their promised pay."[67] State legislatures confronted the problem by conferring upon purchasing officials the power to impress. But citizens repeatedly resisted officials or evaded the half-hearted efforts to impress their goods. At every level of government—national, state, and local—the system of specific supplies failed.

THE INABILITY of national and state authorities to provision the army caused many soldiers to desert and generated serious mutinies among the troops of the New Jersey, Connecticut, and Pennsylvania lines. The lack of food, inadequate pay, and the harshest winter of the war combined to deter all but the hardiest and most committed revolutionaries from remaining with the army. In one year, from July 1779 to July 1780, Washington's army had shrunk from twenty-six thousand men to less than fifteen thousand.[68] As Continental currency continued to depreciate wildly, as states refused to cooperate with Congress, and as civilians rebelled against impressment, many revolutionaries concluded that Congress needed stronger powers to wage war successfully. The Nationalist movement of 1780–83 would be the result.

CHAPTER 8

THE NATIONALISTS

1780 – 1783

I will not pain your Excellency with further accounts of the wants and sufferings of this army; but I am not without great apprehension of its entire dissolution.
> —Nathanael Greene to George Washington,
> 28 December 1780

Unless the powers of Congress are made competent to all the purposes of War we are doing no more than wasting our time.
> —George Washington to William Fitzhugh,
> 25 March 1781

C O N G R E S S   W A S   S L O W to respond to the breakdown of the system of specific supplies. Outside of Congress, however, among military officers and state authorities, the specter of the Revolution's defeat set off a movement to strengthen Congress's powers. For the most part, the Nationalists' efforts to implement administrative reforms and confer a permanent revenue on Congress were not successful, defeated partly by their rigid determination to cut expenditures and partly by the constraints of the Articles of Confederation. The one bright spot during the Nationalist ascendancy was Robert Morris's success in provisioning the Continental army as it marched to Yorktown. Without Morris's financial connections, attention to detail, and superb administrative talents, the outcome of the battle, even of the war, might have been different.

C O N G R E S S   I N   I T S characteristic manner reacted slowly to the breakdown of the system of specific supplies. Exasperated delegates denounced their colleagues' indifference to the army's plight. "Were an angel from heaven to perch on the back of the President's Chair," grumbled Congressman John Mathews in March 1780, "and proclaim the immediate annihilation of the southern States, unless something vigorous, and effectual was done, and even point out the mode, I sincerely believe, as soon as he had taken his flight, and the surprise had subsided, they would just sink again into the same torpid State in which he found them." But Congress seemed impervious to sarcastic criticism. Referring to that body's preoccupation with "Trivial affairs," New Hampshire Congressman John Sullivan noted with resignation in November 1780 that "you might almost as Soon Teach the Streams to run back to their Sources as perswade Congress out of Their Ancient Trait."[1]

A fundamental inability to assess logistical problems compounded Congress's unhurried and haphazard management of the war. Congress's unwavering ideological predilection for ferreting out corruption and reducing public expenditures blinded it to the real problems of relying on the states to supply the army. Informed by General Washington on 3 April 1780 that the new supply system was "pernicious beyond description" and urged by Nathanael Greene "to send a committee of the best informed Members of their body to Head Quarters," Congress, ten days later, appointed Philip Schuyler of New York, John Mathews of South Carolina, and Nathaniel Peabody of New Hampshire to attend the army.[2]

Although Congress acted promptly, its monocular vision of the army's supply problems was evident in the instructions issued to the Committee at Headquarters. Congress directed the committee to confer with the commander in chief on methods to reduce the number of regiments, limit the number of officers' horses, retrench expenses in the Hospital Department, and curb abuses in the Quartermaster and Hide departments. In addition, Congress directed the committee to discharge superfluous medical officers, to abolish unnecessary posts, to stop the improper issuing of rations, to devise accounting methods to prevent fraud, and "to exercise every power which may be requisite to effect a reformation of abuses." True to its mandate, the committee's first action was to order the commissary general of issues to abolish the office of magazine keeper at Philadelphia and to fire the official in charge and his nineteen assistants. On the same day, 19 April 1780, the committee directed the quartermaster general or his deputy in Philadelphia to discharge twenty-four employees, including seventeen carpenters.[3] Both Congress's instructions to the Committee at Headquarters and the committee's initial handiwork reveal that as late as April 1780, most congressmen still believed that the army's logistical difficulties stemmed from corrupt and fraudulent military officials and that the solution lay in discharging military personnel, abolishing offices, and slashing expenses.

Within two weeks, the Committee at Headquarters set aside its preoccupation with reforming petty abuses. In that time it had acquired "Camp Education": firsthand experience of the army's tribulations. "Before we had an opportunity closely to view and examine into the real state of things," the committee wrote the president of Congress on 10 May, "we had no conception of the almost inextricable difficulties in which we found them involved." According to the committee, the army lacked camp equipage, forage, carriages, and hospital supplies. It did not possess a sufficient number of horses or boats to launch an offensive. The committee even doubted that it was capable of defensive maneuvers. The staff departments had neither money nor credit. Enlistments were down, deaths and desertions up. In camp, soldiers waited impatiently to be discharged, their pay five months in arrears. Hungry, without meat, the troops had been placed on half and quarter allowances for days. The commissaries were unable to predict when conditions would improve. In the committee's judgment, the system of specific supplies was the primary cause of the army's provision shortage. It warned Congress that "to Depend entirely on the States for *effectual* Supplies . . . would be hazarding too much."[4]

The committee dispatched John Mathews to Congress with its recommendations for correcting these problems. Its main proposal was to lodge "Dictatorial Powers" in Congress or a small group of men, authorizing them to impress everything from caulkers and carpenters to carriages and provisions, thus enabling the army to take the field and cooperate with the expected French fleet. Congress, however, conferred upon the committee the shadow rather than the substance of power. Congress granted it the authority to draw forth supplies for the army "as the exigency and nature of the service may require, and the Commander in Chief shall judge them necessary," but then directed the committee to call on state executive authorities to meet any future emergency. Congress's solution to the ineffectiveness of the states was to rely even more heavily on them.[5]

As a result of its zeal to ameliorate the army's ordeal, the Committee at Headquarters began losing the support of Congress. Repeatedly lashing out at the states' sluggish response to its appeals for supplies, the committee created a reservoir of ill feeling among state authorities, who in turn poured out their anger to members of Congress.[6] The committee added to its difficulties by agreeing with Nathanael Greene's criticisms of congressional reform of the Quartermaster Department. The new arrangement, conceived by Thomas Mifflin and Timothy Pickering, had been in the planning stages since January 1780, but objections by Washington and Greene caused it to be recommitted in April 1780. Referring to Congress's deliberations on the measure, Greene predicted that "as the members are generally unacquainted with the nature of the business, I am persuaded it will pass." Unveiled on 15 July 1780, the reorganization of the Quartermaster Department bore out the accuracy of Greene's remark. Still preoccupied with halting corruption and saving money, Congress failed to heed critics of the plan and instead implemented its cost-cutting ideas.[7]

The principal administrative innovation in Congress's reform of the Quartermaster Department was its reduction of staff personnel. By 1780, the quartermaster general commanded a small army. In addition to his 2 assistants, 28 deputy quartermasters general, and 109 assistant deputy quartermasters general, Greene oversaw the Wagon Department, with its wagonmaster general, 11 deputies, and numerous wagonmasters, wagoners, packhorse masters, and packhorse men; the boat division of the Quartermaster Department, with its masters of vessels, mates, and boatmen; and the Forage Department, headed by a commissary general of forage and staffed by his assistant, 25 deputies, 128 assistant deputy commissaries, and a host of lesser employees. All told, the Quartermaster Department engaged more than 3,000 men at a cost of $407,593 a month.[8] Under the new plan, Congress allowed the quartermaster general only one assistant and authorized the head of the department to appoint one deputy quartermaster for each army and one for each state. Significantly, the deputies had to be approved by both the Board of War and the state governors, thereby weakening the quartermaster's control of his appointees.

Congress's distrust of the staff departments and its desire to cut expenses were evident in other provisos. It permitted state deputy quartermasters to appoint as many storekeepers, contractors, clerks, conductors, artificers, and laborers as were necessary to carry on the public business, but any appointment exceeding two months' service required the quartermaster general's approval. The major cutbacks, however, occurred in the Forage and Wagon departments. Because Congress expected the states to provide forage, it ordered the quartermaster to appoint only one commissary general of forage to supply the main army, a deputy for each separate army, and all necessary lower-echelon officials. Issuing foragemasters and their assistants were eliminated. Likewise, Congress restricted the Wagon Department to one chief, a deputy, and essential assistants. To save money, it resolved that Wagon Department personnel be drawn from the line of the army, thus ending the employment of inefficient, wasteful civilian wagoners. Congress achieved further savings by revamping the pay system. Following the example of the Commissary Department, it abolished commissions and reintroduced salaries. Henceforth, both the quartermaster general and his assistant would receive $166 a month; deputy quartermasters general, $35.[9]

Congress's reform of the Quartermaster Department precipitated Nathanael Greene's resignation. Greene did not object to the reduction in pay for himself. Economic considerations had always played a secondary role in his involvement in the Revolution. But although he had no objections to fixed salaries per se—he even claimed he was in favor of them—he strongly believed that "men of interest and influence" would not undertake the burden of public service "without some very handsome consideration." In his letter of resignation, Greene declared that the elimination of key personnel and the drastic reduction in pay would make it physically impossible for him to run the department effectively. Specifically, Greene protested Congress's failure to provide positions for both of his assistants, a precondition of his having accepted the post in 1778. Moreover, Greene feared that the new pay schedule would drive a great many staff officers out of the service. "Systems without agents are useless things," he warned Congress, "and the probability of getting one should be taken into consideration in framing the other." Pouring oil on the fire, Greene taunted Congress: "Administration seem to think it far less important to the public interest to have this department well filled and properly arranged than it really is, and as they will find it by future experience."[10]

The extent to which the quartermaster general was culpable for the misdeeds of his men provided the basis for a dispute between Greene and Congress, which fueled Greene's angry resignation and undermined congressional support for the Committee at Headquarters. Congress, determined to eradicate fraud in the Quartermaster Department, flatly contended that Greene was accountable for the money expended by his deputies. Greene denied Congress's claim and declared it a "strange, new, and unexpected . . . doctrine." According to Greene, his responsibility was limited to showing the necessity of the appointment and the trustworthiness of the person designated. After these two provisions were met, Greene believed his responsibility ceased. To assert otherwise would deter all men from holding public office, or worse yet, encourage department chiefs to conceal fraud and misconduct.[11]

Congress disagreed. It insisted that it made no substantial difference who disbursed the money: the head of the department was accountable for all funds passing through his domain. Congress also reminded Greene that his deputies were supposed to be bonded, which, in effect, covered his liability. But in any case, Congress would not deviate from its principle that the superior was responsible for the actions of his subordinates. The only concession offered Greene was that each case would be investigated and allowance made "as justice may require."[12] Such assurances did not placate Greene, who, dissatisfied with the new arrangement for the Quartermaster Department, resigned on 26 July 1780.

Congress, in high dudgeon at Greene's effrontery in addressing it by the opprobrious term "Administration"—a term commonly associated with the iniquitous actions of the British ministry—accepted his resignation and barely refrained from booting him out of the army. On 5 August Congress appointed Timothy Pickering quartermaster general. The Committee at Headquarters, by agreeing with Greene in the dispute and, in effect, defying the authority of Congress, alienated whatever support it still may have retained. On 11 August, by a vote of ten to two, Congress dismissed the Committee at Headquarters.[13] Congress's reorganization of the Quartermaster Department, its acceptance of Greene's resignation, and its dismissal of the Committee at Headquarters demonstrate its stubborn reliance on the states to provide for the army. As Rhode Island's Congressman Ezekiel Cornell despairingly noted, Congress wished "to see their States without control (as the term is) free, sovereign, and independent. If anything appears difficult in regard to supply, etc., what can we do? Why, we can do nothing; the States must exert themselves; if they will not, they must suffer the consequences."[14]

Cornell's disgust at Congress's passivity presaged a widespread sentiment which began in August 1780 to gain adherents for increasing the powers of Congress. Forming the backdrop to the movement was the worsening state of Continental finances, the mutiny of the Connecticut line, and the inability of the states to comply with congressional tax requisitions or supply quotas. Between May and September 1780, three additional events immediately galvanized revolutionaries to advocate strengthening the authority of Congress. Disastrous military defeats in South Carolina, at Charleston on 12 May and at Camden on 16 August, dealt an almost mortal blow to the revolutionary war effort. At Charleston, General Benjamin Lincoln surrendered a force of more than thirty-three hundred men, the largest single loss of American soldiers during the revolutionary war. Three months later, at Camden, in the bloodiest battle of the war, the Americans suffered their worst defeat: the British killed more than a thousand Continental soldiers and decisively routed General Horatio Gates's army. Upon reassembling, only seven hundred soldiers of the original four-thousand-man army showed up. Finally, the treason of General Benedict Arnold dramatized the weakness of the Continental army and sent shock waves through the country.[15]

Rather than demoralizing Americans, these events awakened revolutionaries from the apathy they had slipped into during the past two years.[16] The loss of Charleston was especially electrifying, and according to one observer it had the effect of reviving "a spirit unknown since the year 1776, a spirit which is fast pervading the mass of the community."[17] The hoped-for revival of the *rage militaire* of 1775 never occurred, but among a significant number of revolutionaries, the very real possibility of losing the war provided the main impetus to advocating new solutions to winning the war.

The Nationalist movement of 1780–83 was a product of these supply failures and military reverses. Its dominant aim was to win the war, and its supporters believed the only way to do that was to strengthen the powers of Congress. Army officers and popularly elected state authorities were its major proponents. What these groups had in common and what compelled them to act when they did was either their firsthand acquaintance with the army's plight or knowledge of Congress's impotence in commanding the resources and cooperation of the states.[18]

As early as October 1779, Nathanael Greene, who as quartermaster general was painfully aware of the disruption of military operations resulting from Congress's inability to furnish his deputies with money, advocated a *"new plan of civil constitution,"* which permitted Congress at once to be more independent of the states and to exercise more control over them.[19] General Washington fully shared Greene's view, basing his opinion on the unreliability of the states in providing for the army. "One state will comply with a requisition of Congress," he wrote Virginia Congressman Joseph Jones on 31 May 1780, "another neglects to do it. A third executes it by halves, and all differ either in the manner, the matter, or so much in point of time, that we are always working up hill, and ever shall be." In the following months, Washington reiterated his dissatisfaction with state jealousies, stubbornness, and delays and repeatedly called for "an entire new plan" that would lodge ample powers in Congress "adequate to all the purposes of War." Without this crucial reform, Washington was convinced that "our Independence fails and each Assembly under its present Constitution will be annihilated, and we must once more return to the Government of Great Britain, and be made to kiss the rod preparing for our correction."[20]

The first step in achieving this goal was upgrading the quality of congressmen. Washington believed that the states must send their ablest and best men to Congress, men who understood the country's interests and the need to increase congressional powers. Other revolutionaries agreed with him. As early as the Valley Forge winter of 1777–78, Benjamin Rush and Alexander Hamilton criticized the absence of outstanding patriots in Congress and decried the lack of effective congressional leadership. A year later, in March 1779, similar thoughts about congressmen crossed Washington's mind, prompting him to ask, "Where are our men of abilities?"[21] The answer was that many revolutionaries preferred to serve at the state level as governors and legislators. It was extremely difficult to overcome their attraction to high state office, the traditional locus of power and distinction in colonial society. In addition, state service had the added appeal of being near the comforts of family and home. The high turnover rates in Congress suggest that this was no small enticement. Service in Congress proved to be arduous, tedious, inconvenient, and expensive. Its lack of power, loss of deference and prestige, and manifest ineffectiveness had made Congress by 1779 a distinctly unattractive place in which to serve one's country.[22]

The Nationalists hoped to attract superior individuals to Congress by replacing congressional executive boards with a single administrator at the head of each department. Boards needed to be abolished because they extinguished the passion that "topped all others in the eighteenth-century hierarchy of passions": the love of glory and fame.[23] It followed from this belief that "Men of the first pretensions" were reluctant to serve on boards because they would "be less co[n]spicuous, of less importance, have less opportunity of distinguishing themselves." But by allowing individuals to take charge of a department and by conferring "real trust and importance" on the office, gifted and enterprising men would be attracted to Congress and the management of the war greatly improved.[24] Seen from this perspective, the form the Nationalist program assumed was prompted not only by the desperate circumstances of the war but also by the desire to make Congress more appealing to men of ability and ambition.

The idea of restructuring congressional administrative boards was only one part of the most comprehensive plan put forth by any Nationalist in 1780. The plan was advanced, not surprisingly, by an army officer, Lieutenant Colonel Alexander Hamilton, who, having fought at the Battle of Long Island, wintered at Valley Forge, and witnessed the fruitless attempts to fight a war without sufficient men, money, or matériel, developed strong convictions about the changes needed at the national level. Though comprehensive, Hamilton's program was neither extreme nor atypical. In one form or another, most of the ideas he proposed were widely shared and would eventually be implemented by Congress. In a lengthy letter written in September 1780 to Congressman James Duane, Hamilton went quickly to the heart of the problem: "The fundamental defect is a want of power in Congress." Congressional powerlessness was a product of uncontrollable state sovereignty—the states, jealous of their independence, reserved to themselves the right to reject congressional resolves—and a timid and indecisive Congress, which lacked the means or energy to provide for the exigencies of the war. As a result, Congress was overly dependent on the states.[25]

To counteract the influence of the states, Hamilton called for a reversal of the balance of power within the Confederation by vesting Congress with "complete sovereignty," making it both more independent of the states and more efficient. Specifically, he proposed that Congress be granted a permanent revenue—for that government "which holds the purse strings absolutely, must rule"—by giving it the power to tax the states. In addition, Congress should appoint "great officers of state—A secretary for foreign affairs—A President of War—A President of Marine—A Financier"—to succeed congressional executive boards. With congressional revenue assured and its administrative apparatus centralized, Hamilton believed that the army could finally be built into a respectable fighting force. He recommended that Congress put the army on a more permanent footing and ensure its loyalty by making good on the depreciation of the soldiers' pay and by conferring half pay for life on officers. To provide the army with supplies—that being "the pivot of every thing else"—Hamilton proposed abolishing the state supply system. In its place, he called for "a foreign loan, heavy pecuniary taxes, a tax in kind, [and] a bank founded on public and private credit." He suggested two methods to carry this program into effect. The first was for Congress simply to assume the discretionary powers needed, which, according to Hamilton, it already possessed. But Hamilton was not optimistic about this strategy because he believed Congress would shrink from such a bold expedient. The second method, in which he had more confidence, was to call a convention of states, whose delegates would possess sufficient wisdom and power to implement the necessary changes in the balance of power between Congress and the states.[26]

That the movement to strengthen Congress should originate among army officers is readily understandable. They witnessed and daily felt the effects of the states' inability to provide for the army. They observed the damage caused by the refusal of the states to cooperate with Continental measures. And most important, they feared that the failure of the states to support the army would result in the Revolution's collapse. Yet it should be pointed out—if only because it is easy to overlook what is so often taken for granted—that Continental officers' first impulse during the discouraging months in late 1780 was to seek civilian solutions to military problems. In the flurry of rancorous letters Continental officers wrote to each other during 1780, in which they acidulously condemned the people's lack of virtue and the "supi[ne]ness & stupidity" of civil authorities, the most radical method they advanced to redress their grievances was simply to petition Congress. Significantly, they never contemplated a coup d'etat against the national government: the tradition of civilian primacy over the military continued inviolate.[27]

State governments were the second major group to advocate increasing the powers of Congress. This point needs to be underscored because it reveals that support of the Nationalist movement was widespread and popular. During the war, legislative bodies became even more representative of colonial society as artisans and ordinary farmers filled assembly halls and as backcountry areas gained seats in the legislature. Between 1774 and 1779, in New York, for example, the men who once dominated the streets and extralegal committees ruled the state's assembly and senate. Similarly in Pennsylvania by 1776, the old assembly leaders had been overthrown, their places taken by men of the mechanic or middle classes. Likewise in Connecticut, a political revolution occurred between 1779 and 1782 as citizens' anger with the way the state waged war resulted in an unprecedented rejection of incumbent officeholders.[28] That the Nationalist movement received popular support is surprising only if one views the Nationalists as a conservative, economically motivated group of aristocrats attempting to overturn the political rule of egalitarian radicals. Because the movement to strengthen the powers of Congress was primarily a response to the desperate military situation of 1780, these categories make little sense. New York's Governor George Clinton, for example, was at once the principal architect of Antifederalism in the Empire State and one of the staunchest advocates of Congress exercising implied powers. According to Clinton, if Congress did not have the requisite powers, "it ought to have them." Indeed, "these were powers that necessarily existed in Congress and we cannot suppose that they should want the Power of compelling the several States to their Duty and thereby enabling the Confederacy to expel the common Enemy." Inspiring every word of Clinton's analysis was his awareness of the British army camped in New York City, British-provoked Indian attacks on New York's western frontier, and widespread disaffection throughout the state.[29]

Other state governments threatened by British military power or unable to comply with congressional resolves shared Clinton's desire to strengthen Congress. They acted on this concern in two ways: by electing nationalist-minded men to Congress and by taking the lead in initiating conventions of states. As early as October 1779, New York and Virginia, two states most seriously menaced by British military operations, sent four Nationalists to Congress. The New York Assembly elected Philip Schuyler and Robert R. Livingston. Schuyler, an aristocratic, wealthy landlord, was a veteran of the Great War for the Empire and had been elected to the First Continental Congress. At the commencement of the war, he had the distinction of being appointed one of the four majors-general under Washington and had commanded the troops of the Northern Department until replaced in 1777 by Horatio Gates. Livingston, graduate of King's College (Columbia), member of the bar, and delegate to Congress in 1775–76, was politically conservative and had only reluctantly accepted America's decision for independence. Nevertheless, he remained a revolutionary and was active in state politics. From Virginia came Joseph Jones and James Madison, both strong Whigs, who in the Convention of 1776 were members of the committee that drafted the state's constitution and Declaration of Rights. These men joined two longstanding members of Congress who shared their Nationalist views, New York's James Duane and South Carolina's John Mathews.[30] Although these men were of different economic status, social background, and political persuasion, they could all agree on the need to increase the powers of Congress.

During most of 1780 the Nationalists were a distinct minority in Congress. But although they failed to persuade Congress to alter its dependence on the states, change its administrative procedures, or take a more active role in managing the war, the Nationalists did succeed in initiating new measures and advocating new ideas that eventually were implemented. It should be recalled, for example, that it was Philip Schuyler and John Mathews who in May 1780, as members of the Committee at Headquarters, advocated conferring "Dictatorial Powers" on Congress or the committee, thus placing the issue squarely before that body. In the same month, on a motion by James Duane, a committee was formed to take into consideration the reorganization of the Department of Foreign Affairs. Likewise, on 27 August, at the initiative of Robert R. Livingston and Joseph Jones, a committee of five was appointed to report a plan for the revision and new arrangement of the civil executive departments.[31]

The Nationalists received unexpected aid from the militant spokesman of states' rights, North Carolina's Thomas Burke. Fearing the impending British attack on Charleston, Burke proposed in March 1780 a resolution calling on the states "to pass laws enabling Congress to levy an impost of one percent on all exports and imports." Burke's motion went down to quick defeat, overwhelmed by localist opposition. But on 22 August Livingston raised the issue again. In a series of resolutions, he called upon the states to levy a 2.5 percent tax on exports, the money collected to be used for the payment of the foreign debt and to procure additional credit. His second motion requested the states to assess a 5 percent duty on captured enemy vessels and cargoes, the funds to be used to support the navy. These proposals were better received than Burke's earlier resolution: a committee was formed to consider them.[32]

Five weeks later, on 30 September, the Nationalists achieved a measure of success in the reorganization of the Hospital Department. With little fanfare Congress centralized the department by conferring upon the director-general the "superintendence and direction of all the hospitals." In sharp contrast to earlier congressional reorganizations of the Hospital Department, the chain of command and the various duties of the medical personnel were clear. Still evident in these instructions, however, was Congress's continuing effort to cut back on public expenditures and ferret out dishonest staff officers, a concern no doubt motivated by the court-martial proceedings against the head of the Hospital Department, Dr. William Shippen, Jr., accused of speculation and profiteering.[33]

On this issue Nationalists and their localist opponents were in perfect agreement, although they probably reached their positions by different routes. Nationalists such as James Duane and Robert R. Livingston viewed waste and extravagance as undermining the financial integrity of the new nation, while localists such as Samuel Adams and James Lovell interpreted fraud and profligacy as a sign that the body politic lacked virtue, a symptom of a diseased republic. But whatever the underlying reason, both Nationalists and localists agreed that waste and corruption had no place in revolutionary America. Thus Congress instructed the director-general to "pay particular attention to the conduct of the several officers in the hospital department, and arrest, suspend, and bring to trial all delinquents." In the absence of the director-general, chief hospital physicians were similarly enjoined to guard against abuses and authorized to suspend and confine individuals guilty of "negligence and ill-behavior." Congress now expected doctors to be both healers and constables. Congress also broadened its conflict-of-interest proviso to include not only members of the Quartermaster and Commissary departments but also medical personnel, who were explicitly prohibited from engaging in trade while employed by the public.[34]

But what was good for the financial and moral health of the country was not necessarily good for the army. On 15 July, General Washington had sent Dr. John Cochran to Philadelphia to lay before Congress the Shippen court-martial and to discuss all the problems under which the Hospital Department labored. But the Medical Committee ignored his warnings of personnel shortages and rejected his plea for an increase in the number of physicians.[35] Convinced, in the words of one medical officer, that "surgeons and villains are synonymous terms," the committee instead reduced the number of medical officers.[36] Nationalist Ezekiel Cornell was pleased to inform the governor of Rhode Island that the new system eliminated more than fifty surgeons, "by which means I am sure much money will be saved, and I trust the sick will be better taken care of."[37] Cornell did not explain how the latter proposition followed from the former. But from the standpoint of the wounded soldier, frugality was a poor substitute for expert medical attention. In wartime, less is not always more.

The Nationalists in Congress had little success relieving the distress of the army in 1780. Their resolutions were easily defeated, and those that were referred to committee became bogged down in Congress's institutional inertia. In its one administrative achievement, the reorganization of the Hospital Department, the cure proved worse than the disease. The ineffectiveness of the national government became increasingly evident.

With the army unable to keep men in the field for lack of food and clothing and Congress standing by helplessly, several New England states decided in the summer of 1780 that more drastic measures were required if the war were to be won. To express their views, they met in a series of conventions. The first, composed of delegates from New Hampshire, Connecticut, and Massachusetts, met in Boston from 3 to 9 August 1780 to promote measures for strengthening the war effort. This convention passed thirteen resolutions, most of which exhorted the other states to redouble their efforts to comply with congressional resolves regarding the collection of taxes and the provision of supplies and recruits to the army. The twelfth resolution, however, sounded an entirely new note: it called on the states to "invest their Delegates in Congress with powers competent for the government and direction of . . . national affairs" and urged that all matters concerning the nation as a whole "be under the superintendency and direction of one supreme head." In effect, these New England states were asking Congress to assume sufficient power to coerce all the states into doing their duty with respect to the army. Upon adjourning on 9 August, the delegates called for another convention to be held at Hartford in early November and invited New York and Rhode Island to attend.[38]

Upon receiving the report of the Boston Convention and noting its contents "with Pleasure," Governor Clinton laid it before the New York Assembly. The assembly fully shared Clinton's assessment of the "defects in the present System, and the Necessity of a supreme and coercive Power in the Government of these States" and on 26 September voted to send commissioners to Hartford. "Unless Congress [was] authorized to direct

uncontrollably the Operations of War, and enabled to enforce a Compliance with their Requisitions," the assembly asserted, "the Common Force
can never be properly united." Two weeks later, on 10 October, it spelled
out exactly what it meant by enforcing a compliance. Should any state fail
to provide its quota of men, money, provisions, or other supplies, the
assembly wrote its congressional delegates, Congress must "direct the
Commander-in-Chief, without delay, to march the Army . . . into such
state; and by a Military Force, compel it to furnish its deficiency."[39] As in
other state assemblies, New York's justification for this unprecedented and
radical action was the fear of the Revolution's imminent collapse and the
urgent need for concerted action to prevent it. Rhode Island likewise
agreed to send delegates.

The Hartford Convention, which met from 11 to 22 November, was in
many respects similar to its predecessor: its delegates again urged the states
to execute promptly every congressional resolve relating to the army's
support. They went beyond the Boston Convention's resolves, however,
by calling for Congress to levy taxes upon "specific Articles, or duties or
imposts." Even more far-reaching, and a measure of the states' desperation
over the future of the Revolution, was their recommendation that Congress confer upon General Washington the power "to induce the several
States to a punctual compliance with the requisitions which have been or
may be made by Congress for supplies for the year 1780 and 1781." In effect,
the Hartford commissioners asked Congress to make George Washington
a military dictator. Finally, in a cover letter to the president of Congress,
the commissioners endorsed the idea of centralizing congressional executive boards and recommended the appointment of a man of "Talents,
abilities, and integrity" to manage the nation's finances.[40]

In other ways, the states demonstrated the depth of their commitment
to winning the war. While state commissioners sat in conventions, state
legislatures gave bite to their proposals by sending an additional contin-
gent of Nationalists to Congress to put them into effect. Significantly,
most of the new congressmen had served in the Continental army. From
New Hampshire came General John Sullivan, a lawyer who had fought in
every major engagement of the war, had commanded the Newport expedition of 1778, and had laid waste to the Seneca lands in western Pennsylvania
and New York in 1779. The Rhode Island legislature elected Generals
Ezekiel Cornell and James Mitchell Varnum, both experienced soldiers,
who had participated in the siege of Boston and the Battle of Long Island.
Cornell, a self-educated mechanic, had served as deputy adjutant general
and distinguished himself at the Battle of Rhode Island in August 1778.
Varnum, a lawyer admitted to the Rhode Island bar in 1771, had been with
Washington at Valley Forge and was later made commander of the Depart-

ment of Rhode Island. Also returned to Congress was John Witherspoon, the Presbyterian clergyman who emigrated to America in 1768 to become president of the College of New Jersey (Princeton). Witherspoon was elected to Congress in 1776 and was an enthusiastic signer of the Declaration of Independence. During his three-year tenure, he served on more than one hundred committees and was a staunch advocate of centralizing the civil executive departments.[41]

The Nationalists had been given a mandate. How they would implement it remained to be seen. Before Robert Morris took de facto command of the movement in May 1781, the Nationalists acknowledged no leader. They were an abrasive, individualistic group united less by their economic status or social position than by their contempt for Congress's impotent and lethargic management of the war and by their conviction that its powers had to be strengthened if the war was to be won. Almost as soon as they entered Congress, they began criticizing it. According to Ezekiel Cornell, Congress never accomplished anything because most of its time was "taken up in disputes about diction, commas, colons, consonants, vowels, etc." John Sullivan likewise complained bitterly that Congress had become "a Body without power and the States the Several Component parts of a Monster with Thirteen heads."[42]

Although they agreed that Congress's powers needed to be increased, the Nationalists were not of one mind about the best means to achieve their goals. Rather, as might be expected of a heterogeneous group thrown together to solve a problem during a crisis of unprecedented magnitude, the Nationalists advocated different measures at different times and disagreed among themselves. In the fall of 1780, the most common solution proposed was to call a convention of states that would vest Congress with authority to coerce "those States which Refuse to comply with reasonable requisitions." This plan was especially popular with army officers in and out of Congress who saw it as a quick, forceful, and legal method to secure their ultimate end, the success of the Revolution.[43] The Hartford Convention's resolves, presented to Congress on 12 December, in great measure fulfilled these Nationalist goals, but a good many in Congress, including other Nationalists, shrank from the use of military force, even when sanctioned by civil authority. "Few persons have a higher opinion of or confidence in Gen. Washington than myself or a greater desire of having vigorous executive powers put into the hands of persons at the head of our affairs either in the military or civil department," John Witherspoon declared to the governor of New Jersey on 16 December, "yet that resolution is of such a nature that I should never give my voice for it unless you or my constituents should specifically direct it, perhaps *even not then*."[44] Revolutionaries' fear of concentrating power in the hands of the military was too strong to be easily overcome even in an emergency.

With the rejection of resolves that would have authorized Congress to use force against the states, Nationalists' efforts to strengthen Congress focused on centralizing the civil executive departments and securing a permanent revenue for Congress. In the aftermath of the mutiny of the Pennsylvania line on 1 January 1781, and with reports circulating that the mutineers were heading for Philadelphia, a renewed sense of urgency pervaded Congress. In the following weeks, measures that had languished in committee for months or had been easily voted down earlier were brought before Congress and approved. To handle foreign policy matters, Congress established the position of secretary for foreign affairs on 10 January 1781. On 3 February an amendment to the as yet unratified Articles of Confederation proposed by John Witherspoon and seconded by Thomas Burke was approved, vesting Congress with the power to levy a duty of 5 percent ad valorem on imports and prize goods. Four days later, Congress approved a plan, prepared primarily by James Duane, for creating the posts of secretary at war, secretary of marine, and superintendent of finance. With these reforms, the Nationalists hoped to achieve two of their foremost goals: the efficient administration of the army and the establishment of an effective power for Congress to tax the states.[45]

The Nationalists were unanimously in favor of abandoning congressional boards but were less united on the question of the impost. Reflecting their tactical differences, their individualism, and the absence of a strong party leader, prominent Nationalists such as James Madison, John Sullivan, Joseph Jones, and John Witherspoon voted against the impost.[46] Defections from the Nationalists' ranks were compensated for by unexpected support from localists such as Virginia's Theodorick Bland and Massachusetts's James Lovell, men who usually opposed any resolve that even hinted at diminishing state power.[47] Localists' support of Nationalist measures is testimony to the widespread fear that the Revolution might indeed fail.

Although broad-based, the congressional consensus was fragile because localists remained apprehensive about concentrating power in the hands of individuals. Hence the question of who would head up the new civil executive posts led inevitably to temporizing as the two factions wrangled over nominations. An extreme example of this tendency was Congress's lengthy delay in filling the position of secretary at war. General John Sullivan was a strong candidate for the post, but the opposition of Samuel Adams was sufficient to defer a final decision until 30 October 1781. On that date Congress settled upon Major-General Benjamin Lincoln, but he did not arrive in Philadelphia until 20 November and did not have the Department of War fully functioning until sometime in January 1782, nearly three months after the victory at Yorktown.[48] Robert R. Livingston's election to the office of secretary for foreign affairs was likewise postponed until 10 August 1781 because of the antagonism of Virginia's Arthur Lee, who disliked Livingston's pro-French attitude and feared his readiness to negotiate away the New England fisheries. Lee imagined that Livingston's nomination was part of a conspiracy against liberty, citing as evidence the preponderance of New Yorkers nominated to head the civil executive departments. Good Whigs had to be on their guard, he warned Samuel Adams, for the "plot is deep, the times are favorable to it, & we may be fettered before we are aware."[49]

Similar delays, though not as extensive, characterized the appointment of officials to the other two top administrative posts. On 27 February, General Alexander McDougall was nominated for the position of secretary of marine, but he declined to serve when Congress refused to meet his conditions. A victim of congressional inertia, the office remained vacant until 7 September, when Congress authorized the superintendent of finance to perform as acting agent of the marine.[50] Robert Morris was offered the post of superintendent of finance on 20 February but also attached conditions to accepting office, and again Congress delayed making a decision. Morris had demanded that he be permitted to continue his mercantile activities while holding public office and be allowed to appoint and dismiss all public officials handling public expenditures or public property. Both of Morris's stipulations, but especially the power to dismiss all public officials, were opposed by the localists. After nearly three months, however, the Nationalists overcame their opponents' fears that Morris would abuse his power, and Congress agreed to his demands.[51] "Desperate Diseases require peculiar remedies" was how one congressman defended such ideological inconsistency.[52]

Even if one lays all the blame on the localists for preventing nominees from taking office promptly, it is evident from the Nationalists' reorganization of Congress's top managerial posts that they were every bit as deficient in administrative expertise as their predecessors. A surprising lack of boldness and a reliance on previous administrative practices characterized the Nationalists' reform of the civil executive departments. Most striking was the similarity that the powers and responsibilities of the new department chiefs bore to those of the congressional boards they were replacing: their functions were still mostly clerical. Thus the secretary at war was not authorized to direct military strategy but, like the Board of War before him, was empowered only to keep military records, communicate congressional orders and resolves to the army, and report to the

Department of Finance estimates of the army's manpower, supply, and pay needs. The power of directing the war remained divided between the secretary at war, the Department of Finance, the Congress, the commander in chief, and the states. Similarly, the Nationalists envisioned the new secretary for foreign affairs not as the architect of America's foreign policy but as Congress's amanuensis, a mere recorder and transmitter of congressional foreign policy initiatives.[53]

The Nationalists likewise never spelled out exactly how any of these reforms would alleviate the army's logistical problems. The impost is a good example of their administrative myopia. Because the impost passed Congress in the form of an amendment to the as yet unratified Articles of Confederation, it needed the unanimous consent of the states. No one in Congress, least of all the Nationalists, should have expected prompt action by the states. Moreover, even if the tax were quickly approved by the states, it would yield only about $500,000 to $700,000: "A triffle when compared with our wants," observed John Mathews.[54] Thus there was a curious split between the ideological importance of vesting Congress with the power to tax the states, which was great, and the actual effect such a measure would have on reducing the army's distress, which was small.

The disjunction between broad objectives and specific means was especially noticeable in the new position of superintendent of finance, a post that would figure prominently in facilitating the army's march to Yorktown. In the congressional instructions outlining the office's responsibilities, the only mention made of logistical matters was the general statement that the superintendent of finance would "direct and control all persons employed in procuring supplies for the public service." But the bulk of the financier's duties, like those of the Board of Treasury, consisted in monetary matters involving revenues, expenditures, the public debt, and the settlement of accounts.[55] These were important issues, but restoring the nation's fiscal health was a long-term project, and it is difficult to see how the Nationalists thought it would immediately help the army. Thus in practice, the Nationalists' prescription for winning the war was just as ineffective and visionary as their adversaries' program of relying on the states. The only difference was the Nationalists' powerful faith in the capacity of individual genius to surmount administrative difficulties and provide the leadership necessary to win the war. Necessity, Robert Morris, and the passage of time would prove their faith well founded.

A leading member of Philadelphia's mercantile community and an active opponent of British revenue measures in the early stages of the Revolution, Robert Morris was appointed by the Pennsylvania Assembly in 1775 to the Council of Safety and later that year to the Continental Congress. During the next three years, Morris involved himself strenuously in congressional administrative work, serving on both the important Secret Committee of Trade and the Committee of Secret Correspondence. Morris's work on the Secret Committee of Trade involved securing war matériel such as gunpowder and clothing from overseas. He also continued to carry on his extensive commercial enterprises in the firm of Willing and Morris. Inevitably and unavoidably, his public and private activities became intertwined, and in 1779 Morris was charged with using public funds for his personal advantage. Subsequent investigation by a congressional committee failed to substantiate the charges, but Morris's reputation was blackened. Between 1778 and early 1781 Morris avoided public service, preferring to devote his time to the pursuit of wealth. By February 1781, when Morris was called upon to assume the office of superintendent of finance, he had become the most prominent and influential merchant in America.[56]

Morris took office with no intention of assisting the army with its logistical problems. In his letter of acceptance written on 14 May, Morris informed the president of Congress of his immediate plans. These included securing office space, recruiting assistants, becoming familiar with the nation's financial problems, devising solutions to them, and dissolving his private business affairs. These time-consuming tasks coupled with the lateness in preparing for the campaign of 1781 convinced Morris that he would be of little assistance to the war effort in the immediate future. He suggested that Congress carry on the management of the war "according to the present Arrangements" and warned President Huntington that in order to succeed in his new position he would need time. Should he be forced to turn his attention to immediate problems, he would be "inevitably involved in a Labyrinth of Confusion from which no human Efforts can ever afterwards extricate me."[57] A month later, in June 1781, Morris was still proclaiming his unwillingness to become involved in the day-to-day exigencies of war administration. When, on 16 October, General William Heath complained that his troops at West Point were without food, he was told his men would have to look to the states for specific supplies. Morris told him point-blank: "I by no means hold myself responsible for feeding the Army during the present Campaign."[58]

If Morris did not intend to intervene personally in army supply problems, neither did his plans for reviving the nation's financial health promise any immediate relief for Washington's troops. Aside from proposing the establishment of a national bank three days after accepting office, Morris had no specific blueprint for rescuing the country from bankruptcy.[59] Rather, at the outset, he aimed to accomplish two basic objectives: first, to raise revenues—which he acknowledged was Congress's responsibility—and second, to expend the funds in the most frugal and honest manner. This last goal he believed to be "the most Essential part of the duty of the Superintendent of Finance. He must ever have it in View to reduce the Expenditures as nearly as possible to what in Reason and Justice they ought to be."[60]

This point cannot be overemphasized. For at the heart of every financial measure Morris would eventually propose was the belief that the country had been brought to financial ruin by waste, extravagance, and the lack of systematic administration. These practices, he believed, had prolonged the war by destroying public credit and undermining widespread support for the Revolution. Thus all of Morris's subsequent actions were designed to restore public credit and revive popular support for the war. "If I can regain for the United States the Confidence of Individuals so as they will trust their property and exertions in the hands of Government," Morris wrote the governor of Virginia, "our Independence and Success are certain but without that confidence we are nothing."[61] Morris understood that within the weak framework of the Articles of Confederation, "the people must be wooed and won to do their duty." By slashing expenditures, eliminating wasteful practices, and introducing order and regularity into the army's administrative procedures, Morris hoped to convince the people that America's government merited their support.[62]

The same ends—the attraction of new sources of revenue, the restoration of the public credit, and the revival of the people's confidence in the Revolution—were behind Morris's plans to establish a national bank and a mint, to reorganize the Treasury, to issue "Morris notes," and, most important, to fund the Confederation's debts.[63] Since the virtue of the people could no longer be counted on, Morris planned to use economic self-interest to promote the public good. As he explained his proposal for a national bank, "One very strong Motive [was] to unite the several States more closely together in one general Money Connection, and indissolubly to attach many powerful Individuals to the cause of our Country, by the strong Principle of Self-Love, and the immediate Sense of private Interest."[64]

Although Morris rarely spoke directly of increasing the powers of the national government, his condemnation of the states' failure to comply with congressional resolves left no doubt as to his position. The fault lay with state legislators, "Characters too full of Local attachments and Views to permit sufficient attention to the general interest."[65] Only the national government was capable of viewing the entire situation and legislating for the public good. And if Congress was accountable for prosecuting the war, it had to possess the means, an adequate revenue, and the power to tax. In pursuit of these goals, Morris directed much of his energy after Yorktown to cajoling and threatening the states to meet their congressional tax and supply quotas and to ratify the impost.[66]

Above all else, Morris's financial program was designed to win the war. To be sure, Morris, the consummate economic technocrat, needed no higher justification for implementing his financial reforms. They were an end in themselves, a positive and necessary purgative to a financially ill nation. But for Morris, raising revenue and restoring public credit served a purpose far beyond that of simply enabling Congress to meet current expenses and provide for the public debt. A financially revitalized America would have the effect on England of a psychological Yorktown. In Morris's vision of winning the war, there was no need for planning military strategy, for fighting battles, or for paying soldiers. Once Great Britain perceived America's fiscal resolve—the tangible sign of a people determined to fight for their liberty—it would quickly sue for peace.

In a circular letter written in October 1781, Morris laid out the logic connecting the nation's financial integrity to winning the war. Working backward from the effect to the cause, Morris told the state governors he was "thoroughly convinced that the Enemy must ask Peace, whenever we are in a Condition vigorously to prosecute the War; and that we shall be in that Condition, whenever our Affairs are reduced to order and our Credit restored; and that for these Purposes, nothing more is necessary than a proper System of Taxation." Conversely, all that kept England in the war—its one hope—was for "the Derangement of our Finances" to continue. Should the states ratify the impost and put the national government in possession of an adequate revenue "that Hope must cease."[67] Morris was convinced that England would capitulate rather than continue fighting against a united and solvent America. Although Morris's financial policies resulted in making America safe for public creditors and also laid the groundwork for America's economic expansion in the 1780s, they were not primarily designed with those ends in mind. Their origins stemmed from the frustrations of the war and Morris's genuine desire to see America "independent, Really and Truly independent, Independent of our Enemies, of our Friends, of all but the Omnipotent."[68]

Ironically, Morris spent the better part of his first four months in office intervening in and directing the Continental army's logistical operations. He was forced into this role by the continuing failure of the states to meet their quotas of specific supplies. By 8 May 1781, the lack of beef and flour had reduced the army to such desperate straits that the commander in chief wrote Congress that "if there is not a very great and sudden change of measures it will be next to impossible to keep the Army together." Two days later, Washington sent Major-General William Heath to the New

England states to secure supplies. Washington bluntly told Heath that on the success of his mission "the very existence of the Army depends." For unless the army received an immediate supply of food, "the Garrison of Fort Schuyler must inevitably, that of West Point may probably *fall*, and the whole Army be disbanded."[69]

The financier's decision to become involved in supplying the army stemmed directly from Congress's reaction to Washington's plea for help. On 28 May, it referred to a committee a resolution by Virginia's Meriwether Smith conferring upon Washington the power to impress all provisions not furnished by the states under the system of specific supplies. This congressional committee met with Morris. He was utterly opposed to the use of military force against civilians and assured the committee that he would provide for the army. The next day, he wrote Philip Schuyler and Thomas Lowrey asking them to send one thousand barrels of flour to the army, and he pledged his own personal credit in hard money to ensure compliance. Morris's business associates succeeded in providing the army with the flour, and Congress never acted upon Smith's impressment resolve.[70]

Morris became further entangled in army supply matters when on 25 June the Pennsylvania Assembly placed funds at his disposal and empowered him to procure the state's quota of specific supplies. Morris accepted his post as agent of Pennsylvania with a hearty dislike of the state supply system. He believed that "taxing in specifics [was] expensive to the people, cumbersome to the Government and generally inadequate to the Object."[71] To augment state supplies, Morris introduced a system of contracts to feed the army. The first contract, calling for sealed bids for supplying the army with rations, was advertised in several newspapers on 30 June 1781. A ration was to consist of one pound of bread, one pound of beef or three-quarters of a pound of pork, and one gill of rum. Future contracts called for the addition of one quart of salt, two quarts of vinegar, eight pounds of soap, and three pounds of candles to every one hundred rations. The lowest bidder would be awarded the contract. The states were still expected to meet their specific supply quotas, but any provisions collected were to be sold, the money to be forwarded to the Treasury. The state would be credited for meeting its quota of specific supplies or a proportion thereof, and Morris would use the money to pay the contractors.[72]

After six weeks as the "Financier Elect," as he called himself, Morris finally took the oath of office as superintendent of finance on 27 June. Consistent with his intention of familiarizing himself with the nation's problems, Morris had planned to consult with Washington, but the task of organizing and administering the Office of Finance prevented him from leaving Philadelphia. At last, on 7 August, in the company of Richard

Peters, a member of the Board of War, Morris journeyed to army head-quarters at Dobbs Ferry, New York, where for a week (11–18 August), he held high-level discussions with the commander in chief. With a dedication to frugality that would have brought smiles to the faces of Samuel Adams and Richard Henry Lee, Morris proposed eliminating posts, cutting back soldiers' pay, economizing on hospital expenses, reducing the number of regiments, abolishing franking privileges for officers, and curtailing the expenditures for military stores, provisions, and forage. These proposals were temporarily shelved, however, when on the afternoon of 14 August, Washington learned that a French fleet of twenty-nine warships carrying three thousand men was sailing for Chesapeake Bay and would be arriving in mid-October. Washington immediately recognized the possibility of trapping the British with the aid of French sea power and countered Morris's program of retrenchments by asking for increased logistical support.[73]

Morris complied with Washington's request, and for the next month, while keeping creditors at bay and fending off insistent requests for money from staff officers, he plunged into the complexities of transporting and supplying the army on its four-hundred-mile march from the Hudson to the York. Morris ultimately succeeded in this last major logistical operation of the war and deserves a large portion of the credit for the victory at Yorktown. The most important factor in his administrative success was his ability to command money and credit combined with a knowledge of the army's need and the responsibility for coordinating the activities of the staff departments. In short, success was largely the result of centralizing planning, direction, and responsibility in the person of Robert Morris.

Morris was particularly well-suited to oversee the army's logistical operations. His commercial knowledge, his mercantile connections, his ability to pay, and especially his caution and attention to detail help explain why he was successful where others had failed. For example, he rarely relied on only one agent to carry out his orders and always followed up his requests to make sure they had been carried out. Thus, upon arriving back in Philadelphia after his talks with Washington, Morris immediately wrote Matthew Ridley, a Baltimore merchant and close friend, asking him to purchase three thousand barrels of flour and forward them to Head of Elk, a major supply depot in Maryland. Morris likewise called upon Commissary General Ephraim Blaine to erect a small magazine of provisions there from the specific supplies collected from Delaware and Maryland. In addition, to ensure compliance, Morris sent letters to the governors of the states urging them to cooperate with Blaine.[74] The same backup system and close scrutiny of the progress of matters was evident in Morris's efforts to secure transportation. At the same time that he engaged Ridley to purchase flour, Morris asked him to hire boats. Morris similarly called on several other Baltimore merchants to aid him in obtaining vessels. Finally, Morris ordered Donaldson Yeates, quartermaster for Maryland and Delaware, to prepare a sufficient number of boats to transport six to seven thousand men from Head of Elk to Virginia. All of these agents were informed of the others' activities and advised to work together. By staying in close touch with his agents, Morris was able to intervene quickly if problems developed. When state governments, for example, appeared to be faltering in their efforts to supply food, Morris fired off letters exhorting them to do their duty.[75]

Most important, throughout this crucial period—from approximately 21 August, when Morris left army headquarters, to 6 September, when the Continental army arrived at Head of Elk—Morris juggled loans from France and funds given him by Pennsylvania and used his own fortune and personal credit to ensure that the army's transportation and provisions would be paid for promptly and in hard money. He was successful: the Continentals sailed down the Chesapeake on 18 September and eleven days later began the siege of Yorktown.[76]

After the victory at Yorktown, Morris pushed forward with his long-range plans to restore public credit. But although he focused on the intricacies of high finance, Morris remained deeply involved in logistical matters. All of his plans to cut back on military expenditures were now given full rein. In carrying out his program, Morris had the complete cooperation of top staff officers. Timothy Pickering, whose first concern as quartermaster general was to suggest eliminating the assistant quartermaster general and who considered "the want of public credit . . . a greater calamity than the war itself," was particularly amenable to Morris's cost-cutting ideas. Together they enthusiastically shut down various posts used for collecting state supplies.[77]

Cushioned by French loans, Morris also began in December 1781 to extend to the entire army the system of contracts he used to supply Pennsylvania's military posts. This was Morris's single most important innovation in supplying the army, but he would have been the first to admit that he was only following traditional practice. Morris was critical of Congress's failure to adopt the European contract system from the very beginning of the war. "The experience of Other Countries could not satisfy America," he noted with exasperation. "We must have it of our own acquiring, we have at length bought it, but the purchase ha[s] nearly been our ruin." But Morris was not attracted to the contract system simply because it was conventional. He was convinced it was "the cheapest, most certain, and consequently the best, mode of obtaining those articles, which are necessary for the subsistence, covering, cloathing, and moving of an

Army." It was the cheapest because sealed, competitive bidding would keep the price per ration down to a minimum while allowing him to eliminate transportation and personnel costs, shut down expensive military posts, and save on paying for wastage and spoilage. It was the most certain because the contractors were sure to provide a sufficient number of good rations. If they failed to supply an adequate amount, they would deprive themselves of a portion of the profits. Likewise, if they supplied bad rations, "the Contractors will suffer the loss of it when condemned, so that they are bound in Interest to take care that the Beef put up be of a good quality."[78] As with the Bank of North America, Morris sought to harness economic self-interest to the public good.

But for all of Morris's attention to the army, he never lost sight of the means he believed would bring an end to the war—the collection of tax revenues, the prudent expenditure of government funds, and the restoration of public credit. All else was subordinated to these goals. His commitment not to allow "any Consideration to divert me from that Line which Reason points out as my Duty to walk in" boded ill for the troops. If push came to shove, the soldiers would be sacrificed for the greater good: the revival of public credit. Thus Morris stubbornly expected the states to continue to meet congressional tax and supply requisitions. He would not bail them out, believing that their reasons—"that each has done [the] most, and that the people are not able to pay taxes"—were pretexts for "Langour and Inexertion." As a result of Morris's fiscal triage, the contract system was not extended to the Southern Army until the middle of 1782. Consequently, throughout much of 1782, Greene's army suffered and almost disbanded because it was forced to rely on state supplies and impressment. When Greene complained, Morris turned aside his requests for aid and blithely consoled his friend: "You, therefore my Dear Sir must continue your Exertions with, or without Men, Provisions, Cloathing or pay, in hopes that all Things will come right at last."[79]

The army in the North fared no better. Despite Morris's reforms, it continued to suffer from shortages of military equipment and food. One major problem was the quartermaster general's negligence. Although Pickering preached economy, he had neither the temperament nor the skills to oversee the department. Much of his time was spent in Philadelphia or nearby at his home, out of touch with the army. Washington, who was acting under the assumption that the British would renew the fighting when the campaigning season opened in the spring of 1782, complained bitterly to the secretary at war that he was left totally in the dark about Quartermaster Department matters. He had not seen Pickering for the past three months and during that time had heard from him by letter only twice. "For any good, or even knowledge I derive from this Gentleman, in his office," Washington observed, "I might almost as well act without a Qr. Mr. Genl." As a result of Pickering's dereliction, Washington warned, he had no idea when the army would be able to take the field or even whether it could.[80]

The failure of the contract system added to Washington's anger and the army's distress. Morris had been overly optimistic in trusting to economic self-interest to solve the army's supply problems. In the hands of grasping merchants, a contract, even with arbitration clauses written into it, was a frail reed to lean upon: the agreement's stipulations could be shoddily complied with or simply ignored. This was the experience of the troops fed by "Mr. Comfort Sands, wrongly named so," whose firm was awarded the contracts for West Point and the Moving Army.[81] Sands, a New York merchant, whose putative maxim in trade was "that no poor person can be honest," did everything in his power to grow prosperous at the expense of the army.[82] Disputes between Sands and the army arose as early as March 1782, and by May the complaints were legion, if not exactly novel. For it was the same litany heard throughout the war: spoiled flour, rotten meat, bad rum, and adulterated whiskey. Adding insult to injury, the soldiers were made to walk upward of three miles from camp to where the food was issued, a spot chosen to suit the contractor's convenience.[83] On 25 May, Washington exploded at Sands's continued neglect of the army: "Why Sir are the Troops without Provisions? Why are the deposits which have so often, and so long ago been required by General Heath, and pressed by myself, neglected? Why do you so pertinaciously adhere to all those parts of the Contracts as are promotive of your own Interest and convenience . . . and at the same time disregard the most essential claims of the public; thereby hazarding the dissolution of the Army and risking the loss of the most important Post in America?"[84] Washington also supplied the answer to his questions. It was Sands's "thirst of Gain" which caused him to cut corners, to avoid necessary expenses, and to interpret every dispute in his own favor.[85]

Washington was essentially correct. Sands was arrogant to army officers, punctilious to a fault, and mendacious in negotiations. But he and the other contractors did have some legitimate complaints. Unruly soldiers broke into supply magazines, and an army constantly on the move was inherently difficult to supply. In addition, the contractors feared bringing supplies so near the front without a guarantee of indemnification for loss or damages.[86]

A much more serious problem arose during the summer of 1782 as a result of Morris's inability to meet his obligations to the contractors. Financial setbacks deprived Morris of the revenue he had counted on to pay the contractors, and he was forced to offer them long-term Morris notes. The contractors claimed that Morris's lack of punctuality was responsible for their failure to keep the army well supplied. Perhaps looking for a way out of the unprofitable business, the contractors alleged that they had immediate debts due, and they would not accept Morris notes redeemable in January and February 1783. Instead, they demanded full indemnification and prompt settlement of their accounts, one-half in specie and three times that amount in notes. If Morris failed to comply by 1 October, the contractors threatened to abrogate their agreements.[87]

Morris refused their terms. He was motivated by several factors. By canceling the contract with Sands he could put an end to the army's complaints and also please Washington, who had lost all confidence in the contractor. Above all else, however, was the issue of public credit. Morris would no more go against his pledge to restore public credit to meet the contractors' terms than he would to aid Greene's army. Again, at the heart of his refusal were considerations of war and peace: his decision to cancel the contract with Sands was predicated upon his belief that "the loss of our credit (slender as it is) might have some influence on the negotiations for peace."[88]

In Morris's estimation, he was left with only two choices: he could find a contractor who would accept long-term credit, or he could allow the troops "to subsist themselves by military collection." Morris avoided the prospect of impressment by entering into a contract with the firm of Wadsworth and Carter, which extended him the necessary credit but at a cost of one-third more per ration than Comfort Sands and Company.[89] The extra expense did not please Morris, and he admitted it was a bad bargain. But he had no alternative: "In a situation where only bad things can be done, to adopt the least pernicious is all which can be expected."[90]

In the following months, although the army grew to nearly fourteen thousand men by late 1782, its logistical problems disappeared, mainly as a result of the ensuing peace that brought stability and regularity to administrative affairs.[91] Few soldiers now complained of a lack of supplies. On 5 February 1783, Washington wrote, "I have . . . the satisfaction of seeing the troops better covered, better clothed, and better fed than they have ever been in any former Winter Quarters."[92] After seven and a half years, Washington finally had an army ready to fight. Five weeks later, Congress received the provisional peace treaty from Paris.

THE NATIONALIST MOVEMENT of 1780–83, initiated by army officers and popularly elected state legislatures, was a reaction to economic chaos and military defeat. Both these groups had experienced at first hand the consequences of Congress's inefficient administration of the war and the defects of relying on weak and obstructive state governments to provide men and supplies for the army. What is surprising is not that the Nationalists emerged in 1780 but that they were supported by their philosophical opponents, the localists, who had been adamantly opposed to increasing the powers of Congress. Localist participation in the Nationalist coalition is a true measure of the magnitude of the economic and military crisis. At stake was the fate of the Revolution.

Once in power, however, Nationalist administrative theory and practice had much in common with earlier congressional management of the war. In particular, the Nationalists, like the localists, distrusted the military, abhorred fraud and extravagance, and passionately believed in the need to reduce public expenditures drastically. Their commitment to these republican virtues ensured that their direction of the war would be as ineffective as former attempts had been. Only Robert Morris's ability—combined with French military aid—prevented the Nationalists' administrative inefficiency from endangering American victory at Yorktown. Nor did the Nationalists succeed in their effort to increase the powers of Congress. Their strongest measure, the impost, went down to defeat by the refusal of a single state, Rhode Island, to ratify it.[93] But although they were administratively inept, the Nationalists achieved their ultimate goal: not the restoration of aristocratic rule, or the enrichment of public creditors, but Independence.

CONCLUSION

ON THE EVE of the American Revolution, colonists lived in a political world as broad as the British Empire and as narrow as the nearby tavern. It was a political world in which British officials were few, provincial authorities distant, and local magistrates familiar. Power was diffused and decentralized throughout the various levels of the colonial political structure, and colonists tended to approach politics from a localist perspective. Eighteenth-century Americans also lived in a deferential society, albeit one that was beginning to crumble. Given the reality of religious toleration, the absence of a legal aristocracy, and the abundance of land and economic opportunity, colonial America was a relatively fluid society in which it was difficult to maintain rigid distinctions of class. Nevertheless, notions of hierarchy and deference persisted in the political world of the eighteenth century, and the electorate regularly voted the "better sort" into office. Finally, Real Whig ideology, with its conspiratorial fear of power, suspicion of corruption, hatred of standing armies, and idealization of republican virtue, helped form the assumptions and expectations through which Americans interpreted their political world.

After war broke out in 1775, Congress proceeded to administer the Continental army along the same principles that shaped colonial American politics. Inexperience in military matters and the belief that Americans would quickly win the war undoubtedly influenced the way Congress initially organized and structured logistical operations. But Congress's stubborn insistence on dividing authority and relying on the states to supply the army suggests that deeper patterns of political thought and practice—the fear of concentrated power and a localist world view—guided congressional decisions.

The realities of fighting a war, however, began to change the way many revolutionaries understood power. The ineffectiveness of the administrative structure became increasingly evident as military defeat followed defeat and as reports mounted of ill-clad, poorly equipped, and hungry soldiers. The disastrous effects of decentralization were keenly felt by officers in the field such as George Washington and Nathanael Greene, who frequently complained to Congress of the army's distress.

Congress had the good sense to follow the advice of officers in the field rather than relying on its "paper schemes." In 1778 it centralized authority in the Quartermaster and Commissary departments and began to pay staff officers on a commission basis. But these efforts at reform were bound to fail because of the strength of America's tradition of virtual self-government, localism, and republican ideals. No matter how much power Congress delegated to staff department chiefs, staff officers had to work with, not above or around, state and local officials. They needed the cooperation of these authorities to ensure that supplies passing through the states were not stopped, to exempt staff personnel from militia duty, and especially to assist in civil impressment.

State and local authorities, however, had their own set of priorities that had been shaped by political practices in the colonial era. They believed that their primary responsibility was to protect the citizens of their state, county, or town. They feared the army intensely and went to great lengths to uphold the primacy of the civil power over the military. As a result, they were fundamentally committed to defending their own territory from British attack and to equalizing the burdens of the war among the inhabitants, in defiance of national priorities. The consequences of state and local provincialism were constant disruption of logistical operations as staff officers struggled against state interference with provision shipments, the drafting of military supply officers into state militias, and magistrates' refusal to cooperate with them during civil impressment. Repeatedly, state and local authorities subordinated the needs of the army to the sanctity of private property and the liberties of their constituents.

Congressional reform of the administration of the Continental army was also thwarted by other aspects of American political culture. Americans' belief in conspiracies, fear of corruption, and adherence to the Puritan/republican ideals of economy and frugality consistently undermined Congress's tentative efforts to centralize logistical operations. At bottom, the excesses of the printing press and the consequent depreciation of the currency after 1778–79 caused most of the army's supply problems. But congressmen responded to this economic emergency in ways that only exacerbated logistical difficulties. They blamed staff officers for the economic chaos and denounced them as corrupt, thus undercutting their ability to function, and proceeded to cut staff personnel and economize on all facets of supply services in the middle of the war. Finally, Congress disregarded all previous experience of state inefficiency and, with the system of specific supplies, turned back the responsibliity for feeding the army to state legislatures. Thus Congress continued its tendency to explain complex events as a series of conspiracies and to assume that continental problems could best be solved by decentralizing power and trusting local officials.

The ensuing failure of the states to supply the Continental army adequately, combined with military defeats at Charleston and Camden in May and August 1780, gave birth to the Nationalist movement to strengthen the powers of Congress. It should be emphasized that before 1780 few demands for increasing Congress's powers had emanated from Continental army officers or popularly elected state legislatures. The Nationalist movement was solely a response to congressional and state administrative inefficiency and military defeat, the consequences of which, its adherents feared, would be the destruction of the army and the loss of the war. But though experience had taught the Nationalists not to fear professional armies and central power excessively, their adherence to republican ideals led them to continue the process of reducing costs and personnel in the staff departments and to confer the shadow rather than the substance of power on the newly created executive positions. The victory at Yorktown revealed a familiar pattern: men with firsthand experience of the war—in this case, George Washington—sought to persuade congressional authorities—in the person of Robert Morris—to alter their ideological preconceptions and support the army with money and supplies. There is more than a grain of truth in the statement that Americans won the War of Independence in spite of, rather than because of, their political ideals.

Yet the political legacy of military victory was ambiguous if not paradoxical. For many Americans the defeat of the British at Yorktown erased from their memories the army's difficulties in obtaining supplies, the militia's unreliability, and Congress's inability to collect or levy taxes under the Articles of Confederation. For these revolutionaries America's triumph only confirmed their localist perspective and their fear of standing armies, aristocratic privilege, and strong central government. The goals and rhetoric of the Shaysites and Antifederalists, for example, suggest the strength and persistence of America's prerevolutionary political culture in the postwar era.

But if older attitudes and behavior remained, there were also some new features in the political landscape beyond the severance of the imperial connection and the creation of a new nation. This was especially true in the realm of political theory. The implications of Real Whig ideology and the experience of state constitution-making forced Americans to articulate in theory what they only dimly perceived before the Revolution: ultimate sovereignty lay in the people, who were free to parcel it out to various branches of government. These notions laid the foundation for the American federal system. Moreover, the disruption of the revolutionary war increased antiauthoritarian tendencies among the American people, accelerating the decline in deference and resulting in the election of middle-class state legislators. Appeals to the wisdom or influence of the "better sort" would continue in the postwar period but only among a small group of Americans and with far less effect than before the Revolution.

Most importantly, the experience of the war changed many Americans' attitudes toward two institutions they had strongly opposed before the conflict with England: professional armies and strong central government. Few colonists favored either concept before the conflict with England. But the near fatal consequences of waging war under a weak central government and the difficulties of securing the cooperation of thirteen sovereign states during wartime convinced many Americans of the limitations of eighteenth-century political culture. During the Confederation period, the debility of Congress—as manifested by its inability to alleviate the commercial depression, to conduct foreign relations effectively, or to mediate conflicts between the states—reinforced these Americans' belief in the need for a powerful central government. Proposals to increase the powers of Congress thus continued to emanate from such men as George Washington, Nathanael Greene, Jeremiah Wadsworth, Robert Morris, and Alexander Hamilton.[1] A realization of unfulfilled opportunity haunted many Nationalists. As Robert Morris wrote on 24 August 1782, "A firm, wise, manly system of federal government is what I once wished, what I now hope, what I dare not expect, but what I will not despair of."[2] Morris thus spoke of the future. Many of those who would attend the Philadelphia Convention in 1787, and many of those who would vote to ratify the Constitution, would look to the past and recall the lessons of the war.

APPENDIX

A Statistical Portrait of Staff Officers

This Appendix tabulates data from a sample of 27 of the approximately 133 staff officers who handled public funds during the war. The sample is small because I could find biographical information on only these twenty-seven men. As a rule, staff officers did not leave extensive personal correspondence. Most of them, it appears, came from humble or middle-class origins, served their country briefly, and receded into the obscurity from which they sprang. Usually, biographical information about staff officers can be found only because of the prominence they achieved in some other field of endeavor. Nathanael Greene was a successful general; Jeremiah Wadsworth a Connecticut congressman; Peter Colt and Royal Flint, Yale graduates. The sample is thus weighted toward the more prosperous, better-educated, and famous—those who left their mark upon the world. It is not a random sample, but it is the best I could do without investing extraordinary time on the project. I feel reasonably confident about concluding that the average staff officer was a native-born merchant about thirty-seven years old and most likely from the Middle colonies.

Information has been found and tabulated on the following individuals: William Aylett, Owen Biddle, Clement Biddle, Mark Bird, Ephraim Blaine, Alexander Blaine, Henry Champion, Peter Colt, Jacob Cuyler, Royal Flint, Benjamin Flower, Robert Forsyth, Jonathan Gostelowe, Nathanael Greene, Udny Hay, Robert Lettis Hooper, Jr., Hugh Hughes, Nathaniel Irish, Morgan Lewis, Thomas Mifflin, Stephen Moylan, Charles Pettit, Timothy Pickering, Charles Stewart, Joseph Trumbull, Jeremiah Wadsworth, and Jacob Weiss.[1]

TABLE A. I.
Nativity of Staff Officers

	Number	Percent
Native-born	18	66.6
Foreign-born	2*	7.4
No data available	7	25.9

*Both from Ireland.

TABLE A. 2.
Prerevolutionary Residence of Staff Officers

	Number	Percent
New England	7	25.9
Middle colonies	17	63.0
South	2	7.4
No data available	1	3.7

TABLE A. 3.
Age at First Appointment to Staff Department

Age Distribution	Number	Percent
20–29 years	6	22.2
30–39	12	44.4
40–49	5	18.5
50–59	3	11.1
No data available	1	3.7
Median age	35 years	
Mean age	37	

TABLE A. 4.
Occupation of Staff Officers

	Number	Percent
Merchant	13	48.1
Manufacturer	2	7.4
Artisan	3	11.1
Lawyer	1	3.7
Seaman	1	3.7
Schoolteacher	1	3.7
No data available	6	22.2

TABLE A. 5.
Highest Level of Education Attained by Staff Officers

		Number	Percent
Classical education		4	14.8
College education		7	25.9
Harvard	2		
Yale	3		
Princeton	1		
College of Philadelphia	1		
No data available		16	59.3

NOTES

Freeman, *GW*	Douglas Southall Freeman, *George Washington: A Biography.* 7 vols. New York, 1945–57.
Furman Letters	*The Letters of Moore Furman: Deputy Quartermaster General of New Jersey in the Revolution*, ed. Anne de B. MacIlvaine et al. New York, 1912.
Furman Papers	Moore Furman Papers, New Jersey State Archives, Military Records Revolutionary War, Box 15, New Jersey State Library, Trenton.
Gates Papers	Horatio Gates Papers, New-York Historical Society, New York City.
Greene Letters	Nathanael Greene Letters, New Jersey Historical Society, Newark.
Greene Papers, APS	Nathanael Greene Papers, American Philosophical Society, Philadelphia, microfilm.
Greene Papers, WCL	Nathanael Greene Papers, William L. Clements Library, University of Michigan, Ann Arbor.
Greene Papers	*The Papers of General Nathanael Greene*, ed. Richard K. Showman et al. 2 vols. to date. Chapel Hill, 1979–.
GW	George Washington
GW Papers	Presidential Papers Microfilm, Papers of George Washington, Series 4, Library of Congress, Washington, D.C.
GW Writings	*The Writings of George Washington from the Original Manuscript Sources, 1745–1799*, ed. John C. Fitzpatrick. 39 vols. Washington, D.C., 1931–44.
Hamilton Papers	*The Papers of Alexander Hamilton*, ed. Harold C. Syrett, Jacob E. Cooke, et al. 26 vols. New York, 1961–79.
Heath Papers	*The Heath Papers, Collections of the Massachusetts Historical Society*, ser. 5, vol. 4; ser. 7, vols. 4–5. Boston, 1878–1905.
Hening, *Statutes*	*The Statutes at Large: Being a Collection of All the Laws of Virginia*, ed. William Waller Hening. 13 vols. Richmond, 1809–23.
HSP	Historical Society of Pennsylvania, Philadelphia.
Hughes Ltrbks.	Hugh Hughes Letterbooks, New-York Historical Society, New York City.
Hughes Papers	Hugh Hughes Papers, Library of Congress, Washington, D.C.
JCC	Worthington C. Ford et al., eds., *Journals of the Continental Congress, 1774–1789*. 34 vols. Washington, D.C., 1904–37.
Jefferson Papers	*The Papers of Thomas Jefferson*, ed. Julian P. Boyd et al. 20 vols. to date. Princeton, 1950–.
JPCNY	*Journals of the Provincial Congress, Provincial Convention, Committee of Safety and Council of Safety of the State of New York, 1775–1776–1777.* 2 vols. Albany, 1842.
LC	Library of Congress, Washington, D.C.
LDC	Paul H. Smith, ed., *Letters of Delegates to Congress, 1774–1789*. 8 vols. to date. Washington, D.C., 1976–.
Lee Papers	*The Lee Papers, Collections of the New-York Historical Society*, vols. 4–7. New York, 1872–75.
Lewis Letters	Joseph Lewis Letters, Morristown National Historical Park, Morristown, N.J.
LMCC	Edmund C. Burnett, ed., *Letters of Members of the Continental Congress.* 8 vols. Washington, D.C., 1921–36.
Md. Arch.	*Archives of Maryland*, ed. William Hand Browne et al. 72 vols. to date. Baltimore, 1883–.
Misc. MS	Miscellaneous Manuscripts.
Morris Papers	*The Papers of Robert Morris, 1781–1784*, ed. E. James Ferguson et al. 5 vols. to date. Pittsburgh, 1973–.

N.C. Recs.	*The State Records of North Carolina*, ed. Walter Clark. 16 vols. Winston and Goldsboro, 1895–1925.
NG	Nathanael Greene
N.J. Arch.	*Archives of the State of New Jersey: Documents Relating to the Revolutionary History of the State of New Jersey*, ed. William S. Stryker et al. 2d ser., 5 vols. Trenton, 1901–7.
N.J. Assembly Acts	*Acts of the General Assembly of the State of New Jersey*. Burlington and Trenton, 1777–83.
N.J. Gaz.	*New Jersey Gazette* (Trenton).
NJHS	New Jersey Historical Society, Newark.
NYHS	New-York Historical Society, New York City.
N.Y. Journ.	*The New York Journal; or, the General Advertiser.*
Pa. Arch.	*Pennsylvania Archives*, ed. Samuel Hazard et al. 138 vols. Philadelphia and Harrisburg, 1852–1935.
Pa. Col. Recs.	*Pennsylvania Colonial Records: Minutes of the Supreme Executive Council of Pennsylvania*. 16 vols. Harrisburg, 1852–53.
Pa. Packet	*Dunlap's Pennsylvania Packet, or, the General Advertiser* (Philadelphia).
Pa. Statutes	*The Statutes at Large of Pennsylvania from 1682 to 1801*, ed. James T. Mitchell and Henry Flanders. 17 vols. Harrisburg, 1896–1915.
PCC	Papers of the Continental Congress, 1774–89 (M-247), National Archives, Washington, D.C., microfilm.
Pickering Papers	Timothy Pickering Papers, Library of Congress, Washington, D.C., microfilm (originals owned by the Massachusetts Historical Society, Boston).
Reed Papers	Joseph Reed Papers, New-York Historical Society, New York City.
RG 93	War Department Collection of Revolutionary War Records, Record Group 93, National Archives, Washington, D.C., microfilm.
RH Lee Letters	*The Letters of Richard Henry Lee*, ed. James Curtis Ballagh. 2 vols. New York, 1911–14.
R.I. Acts	*Acts and Resolves of Rhode Island*. Newport, 1755–84.
Risch, *QM Support*	Erna Risch, *Quartermaster Support of the Army: A History of the Corps, 1775–1939*. Washington, D.C., 1962.
RM	Robert Morris
Rodney Letters	*Letters to and from Caesar Rodney, 1756–1784*, ed. George Herbert Ryden. Philadelphia, 1933.
Stewart Papers, LC	Charles Stewart Papers, Library of Congress, Washington, D.C., microfilm
Stewart Papers, NYSHA	Charles Stewart Papers, New York State Historical Association, Cooperstown.
Sullivan Papers	*Letters and Papers of Major-General John Sullivan*, ed. Otis G. Hammond. New Hampshire Historical Society, *Collections*, vols. 13–15. Concord, N.H., 1930–39.
Trumbull Coll.	Governor Joseph Trumbull Collection, Connecticut State Library, Hartford.
Trumbull Papers	*The Trumbull Papers, Collections of the Massachusetts Historical Society*, ser. 5, vols. 9–10; ser. 7, vols. 2–3. Boston, 1885–1902.
Va. Gaz.	*Virginia Gazette* (Williamsburg).
VCSP	*Calendar of Virginia State Papers and Other State Manuscripts*, ed. William P. Palmer. 11 vols. Richmond, 1875–93.
Wadsworth Family Coll.	Wadsworth Family Collection, Box 1, Yale University Library, New Haven, Conn.

Abbreviations

Wadsworth Letters	Jeremiah Wadsworth Letters, Wadsworth Atheneum, Hartford (stored at the Connecticut Historical Society).
Wadsworth Papers	Jeremiah Wadsworth Papers, Connecticut Historical Society, Hartford.
YUL	Yale University Library, New Haven, Conn.

Preface

1. Higginbotham, *War of American Independence*; Royster, *Revolutionary People at War*; Royster, *Light-Horse Harry Lee*; Shy, *Toward Lexington*; Shy, *People Numerous and Armed*.

Prologue

1. Robert Levers to Timothy Matlack, 8 Dec. 1777, *Pa. Arch.*, 1st ser., 6:77–78; Council to delegates in Congress, 7 Feb. 1778, ibid., 242–43; President Wharton to Thomas McKean, 15 Feb. 1778, ibid., 266–68; Coleman, *Thomas McKean*, 225; Brunhouse, *Counter-Revolution in Pennsylvania*, 48–49; Mintz, *Gouverneur Morris*, 95–96; Hart, "Colonel Robert Lettis Hooper," 74.

2. NG to McKean, 3 June 1778, Thomas McKean Papers, 1, HSP; Coleman, *Thomas McKean*, 225.

3. McKean to NG, 9 June 1778, Thomas McKean Papers, 1, HSP; Brunhouse, *Counter-Revolution in Pennsylvania*, 49.

4. Greene, "Changing Interpretations of Early American Politics," 172. Although they offer conflicting interpretations, the following works are essential to understanding eighteenth-century colonial politics: Bailyn, *Origins of American Politics*; Greene, "Growth of Political Stability"; Greene, "Changing Interpretations of Early American Politics"; Murrin, "Review Essay."; Murrin, "Colonial Political Development."

5. The same problems would bedevil the American way of war down through the twentieth century. See, for example, Linderman, *Mirror of War*, chap. 3; Kennedy, *Over Here*, chap. 2. Despite its oversimplified historical framework, Huntington, *Soldier and the State*, remains the most penetrating book on the nature of American civil-military relations.

6. Barrow, *Trade and Empire*, 112–13; Andrews, *Colonial Background of the American Revolution*, 43, 75–79; Labaree, *Royal Government in America*, 37–73, 172–217; Wickwire, *British Subministers*, chap. 1; Katz, *Newcastle's New York*, chap. 1; Murrin, "Great Inversion," 380–86.

7. Bailyn et al., *Great Republic*, 131. For the English patronage system and the appointment of governors, see Katz, *Newcastle's New York*, chaps. 2–3; Sheridan, *Lewis Morris*.

8. Labaree, *Royal Government in America*, chaps. 5–9; Bailyn, *Origins of American Politics*, chaps. 2–3; Greene, "Changing Interpretations of Early American Politics," 159–77.

9. Greene, "Growth of Political Stability," 28; Dinkin, *Voting in Provincial America*, 6.

10. Ferguson, "County Court in Virginia," 14–15; Bockelman, "Local Government in Colonial Pennsylvania," 220–21; Reed and Palermo, "Justices of the Peace in Early Delaware," 230–32; Ekirch, *"Poor Carolina,"* 52; Cook, *Fathers of the Towns*, 152. In Rhode Island and Connecticut justices of the peace were elected by the assembly (ibid., 154). For the high social status of magistrates, see ibid., 145, 152, 153, 155, 159; Sydnor, *Gentlemen Freeholders*, chap. 5. Colonial New York and backcountry North Carolina magistrates appear to be an exception to this statement. See Bonomi, "Local Government in Colonial New York," 37; Greenberg, *Crime and Law Enforcement*, 174–77, 186; Ekirch, *"Poor Carolina,"* 168–74.

11. Breen, "Persistent Localism," 3–28; Zuckerman, *Peaceable Kingdoms*, chaps. 3–4.

12. Benton, *Warning Out in New England*; Zuckerman, *Peaceable Kingdoms*, 112–13; Gewehr, *Great Awakening in Virginia*, 54–58, 122–28. For the continuing importance of localism in American political culture, see Keller, *Affairs of State*.

13. Labaree, *Royal Government in America*, chaps. 5–9; Greene, "Role of the Lower Houses of Assembly," 96, 100–101; Pencak, *War, Politics, and Revolution*, chaps. 4–6; Ward, "*Unite or Die*," 31, 33, 38, 74.

14. Rogers, *Empire and Liberty*, chaps. 4–5.

15. William Shirley to Thomas Robinson, 24 Dec. 1754, Lincoln, ed., *Correspondence of William Shirley*, 2:112; Andrews, *Colonial Period of American History*, 4:413–15. For the Albany Congress, see Newbold, *Albany Congress*; Gipson, *British Empire*, vol. 5, chaps. 4–5; Rogers, *Empire and Liberty*, chap. 2.

16. Greene, *All Men Are Created Equal*, 12–23; Dinkin, *Voting in Provincial America*, 28–33.

17. Dinkin, *Voting in Provincial America*, 49; Speck, *Stability and Strife*, 16. Historians have hotly debated the extent of colonial suffrage and its meaning. For the historiography of the issue, see Brown, "Controversy over the Franchise," 212–41.

18. Pole, "Historians and the Problem of Early American Democracy," 626–46; Bailyn, *Origins of American Politics*, 19–23.

19. Buel, "Democracy and the American Revolution," 135–36, 141, 145; Labaree, *Conservatism in Early American History*, 104–6; Dinkin, *Voting in Provincial America*, 5–6; Greene, "Changing Interpretations of Early American Politics," 173.

20. Main, "Government by the People," 397; Dinkin, *Voting in Provincial America*, 59–61; Greene, "Growth of Political Stability," 48; Murrin, "Colonial Political Development," 63–65.

21. Bailyn, *Ideological Origins*, 165–73; Buel, "Democracy and the American Revolution," 143–44; Pocock, "Classical Theory of Deference," 516–23. Petitioning was another influential and effective way citizens shaped legislators' actions. See Bailey, *Popular Influence upon Public Policy*, 166–69. For the increasingly oligarchical nature of colonial society, see Greene, "Legislative Turnover in British America," 442–63; Daniels, *Connecticut Town*, 131–32, 165–67; Martin, *Men in Rebellion*, 108–19; Purvis, "'High-Born, Long-Recorded Families,'" 592–615, esp. 608–9; Murrin, "Colonial Political Development," 65–66.

22. Papers of the Proceedings of the Justices of the Peace in Monmouth County, 4 Feb. 1779, PCC, reel 192, item 173, 3:41; Buel, "Democracy and the American Revolution," 136, 142; Bailey, *Popular Influence upon Public Policy*, 54, 166–69; Dinkin, *Voting in Provincial America*, 69–71; Greene, "Society, Ideology, and Politics," 28–29, 33–34. North Carolina's political officials appear to be an exception to this generalization. See Ekirch, "*Poor Carolina*," 168–74.

23. Bailyn, *Ideological Origins*, 173; Morgan and Morgan, *Stamp Act Crisis*, chaps. 6–7.

24. Unless otherwise noted, this and the following five paragraphs are heavily indebted to Bailyn, *Origins of American Politics*, chap. 1; Bailyn, *Ideological Origins*, chap. 2; Schwoerer, "*No Standing Armies!*"; Cress, *Citizens in Arms*, 16–25; and Wood, *Creation of the American Republic*, chap. 2. These works should be supplemented by Pocock, *Machiavellian Moment*, chaps. 12–15; Banning, *Jeffersonian Persuasion*, chaps. 1–2; Bonwick, *English Radicals*, chap. 1; Colbourn, *Lamp of Experience*, 9–16; Murrin, "Great Inversion," 385–86.

25. Jacobson, ed., *English Libertarian Heritage*, 226–27.

26. Cited in Banning, *Jeffersonian Persuasion*, 54 n. 29.

27. Bailyn, *Origins of American Politics*, 38–39.

28. Middlekauff, *Glorious Cause*, chaps. 4–11; Jensen, *Founding of a Nation*, chaps. 4–17.

29. Jensen, ed., *English Historical Documents*, 779–85; Ammerman, *In the Common Cause*, chap. 1.

30. Wood, *Creation of the American Republic*, 47. In the past decade, republicanism has become a growth industry in studies of the American Revolution. For a review of the literature, see Shalhope, "Toward a Republican Synthesis," and "Republicanism and Early

American Historiography." My discussion of republicanism relies heavily upon Wood, *Creation of the American Republic*, chap. 3, which remains the best account.

31. Banning, *Jeffersonian Persuasion*, 47. See also Peck, "British Case," 35–49. The problem of corruption in American political life has only recently received the attention it deserves. A start has been made with the wide-ranging essays in Eisenstadt, ed., *Before Watergate*.

32. John Adams to Mercy Otis Warren, 8 Jan. 1776, *Warren-Adams Letters*, 72:202.

Chapter 1

1. GW to John Augustine Washington, 18 Dec. 1776, *GW Writings*, 6:398; Higginbotham, *War of American Independence*, 115; Wallace, *Appeal to Arms*, 86.

2. Freeman, *GW*, 4:364–67. See also Weigley, *American Way of War*, 3–5.

3. Mackesy, *War for America*, 12–18; Bowler, *Logistics and the Failure of the British Army*, chap. 1; Baker, *Government and Contractors*, chap. 1. Mackesy and Bowler criticize British administration for its lack of overall direction of war policy and the confusion in logistical support. Baker is less critical and sees a definite improvement in the efficiency of the British supply system after 1776.

4. They were Eliphalet Dyer (Conn.), Roger Sherman (Conn.), Oliver Wolcott (Conn.), George Clinton (New York), and Robert Treat Paine (Mass.), who was a chaplain on the Crown Point expedition of 1755. This biographical information is derived from the *DAB*. I have not included George Washington because he was in Congress less than six weeks before setting out to take command of the Continental army.

5. *JCC*, 5:636; Hawke, *Benjamin Rush*, 166.

6. Adams, Notes of Debates, 23 Sept. 1775, *JCC*, 3:471. Sutlers were civilian storekeepers who accompanied an army and sold liquor, provisions, and other supplies to the troops. Adams to Warren, 23 July 1775, *LDC*, 1:652. The inexperience of Congress is also noted by Bowler, "Logistics and Operations," 56.

7. Adams to Warren, 23, 26 July 1775, *LDC*, 1:652, 667.

8. For a fuller discussion, see Risch, *QM Support*, 2.

9. Adams to William Tudor, 26 July 1775, *LDC*, 1:667; Adams to Warren, 26 July 1775, ibid., 668.

10. Rakove, *Beginnings of National Politics*, chap. 4; Royster, *Revolutionary People at War*, 49; Applegate, "Medical Administrators," 1; Bush, *Revolutionary Enigma*, 34; Weigley, *American Way of War*, 7; Freeman, *GW*, 4:365; Brown, *Medical Department*, 17.

11. Paine to Philip Schuyler, 2 Apr. 1776, *LDC*, 3:477; Samuel Adams to Warren, 4 Nov. 1775, ibid., 2:298. For the shortage of gunpowder, see Stephenson, "Supply of Gunpowder in 1776," 273; Freeman, *GW*, 3:510–15; Nuxoll, "Munitions Merchants," 8.

12. Nuxoll, "Munitions Merchants," 27–28, 35; Stephenson, "Supply of Gunpowder in 1776," 277.

13. *JCC*, 4:169, 171; John Adams to Warren, 27 June 1775, *LDC*, 1:545, 546 n. 1. Instructions for making saltpeter appeared in the *Pennsylvania Journal*, 26 July 1775; *Boston-Gazette*, 11 Sept., 23 Oct., 11 Dec. 1775, 22 Jan. 1776; *Va. Gaz.*, supplement, 16 Feb. 1776. The four basic ingredients in gunpowder are saltpeter, sulphur, charcoal, and water. For a description of the process, see Salay, "Production of Gunpowder," 424–25.

14. Committee of Congress to the Maryland Convention, 28 Mar. 1776, *LDC*, 3:455; *JCC*, 2:219, 85, 3:247–48, 4:170–71; Nuxoll, "Munitions Merchants," 14–17; Stephenson, "Supply of Gunpowder in 1776," 277. For the difficulties of making saltpeter from newspaper instructions, see Reynolds, "Ammunition Supply," 57–58. Salay estimates that America produced

only 34.6 percent of the gunpowder used during the first two years of the war ("Production of Gunpowder," 441).

15. Nuxoll, "Munitions Merchants," 37; *JCC*, 7:241, 9:799. For the Medical Committee, see ibid., 2:250, 4:188, 5:622, 633, 7:34; Applegate, "Hospital Department," 297; Griffenhagen, "Drug Supplies," 112. The Medical Committee was abolished in May 1781 and its duties assumed by the Board of War.

16. *JCC*, 3:260, 317–18, 349, 360, 4:159, 118, 304, 333.

17. Ibid., 4:106, 6:983. Mease alone was called upon to purchase tents, camp kettles, canteens, blankets, shoes, hats, and stockings (ibid., 4:390, 5:719, 751, 823, 6:983, 998, 1015). For Lowrey, see ibid., 4:17, 106, 150, 197. For orders to Mease and Blaine, see ibid., 5:751, 4:296–97, 7:213. See also ibid., 5:523, 706.

18. Ibid., 4:191, 3:418, 419; John Hancock to Schuyler, 11 Oct. 1775, *LDC*, 2:162. Congress left most of the work of supplying the troops in the Northern Department in the hands of General Schuyler. See Johnson, *Commissariat*, 117–18. For sutlers and the contract with Bates, see *JCC*, 4:158, 5:443.

19. *JCC*, 2:110, 265, 306–7, 3:399, 408, 442, 4:160, 5:466–67, 479, 706, 763, 836–37, 6:1001, 1043, 7:26–27; Hancock to Jonathan Trumbull, Sr., 27 June 1775, *LDC*, 1:547; President of Congress to New Jersey Assembly, 2 Oct. 1776, *LMCC*, 2:112; Hancock to New York Provincial Congress, 10 Nov. 1775, *LDC*, 2:326; see also *JCC*, 2:274–75, 6:897.

20. *JCC*, 15:1431–42; Robinson, "Treasury Administration," 130.

21. Staff officers, by definition, were support troops as opposed to line officers, who were combat soldiers. Staff positions in the Continental army included the quartermaster general, commissary general, director-general of the Hospital Department, adjutant general, paymaster general, commissary general of musters, chief of engineers, commissary of artillery stores, judge advocate general, and inspector general (Boatner, *Encyclopedia of the American Revolution*, 1048–50). This study concentrates on the supply and medical corps.

22. *JCC*, 3:338, 4:303, 6:988. Congress also directed quartermasters to purchase supplies from individuals (ibid., 5:821–22).

23. Ibid., 2:94, 190–91, 186; Eliphalet Dyer to Joseph Trumbull, 21 July 1775, *LDC*, 1:642; Hancock to GW, 24 July 1775, ibid., 662; Risch, *QM Support*, 3–4; Rossman, *Mifflin*, 46–47. Congress appointed Donald Campbell deputy quartermaster for the Northern Department on 17 July 1775 (*JCC*, 2:186). Trumbull was also recommended by GW (GW to president of Congress, 10 July 1775, *GW Writings*, 3:325; Trumbull, "Joseph Trumbull," 26).

24. On Church's role in the formation of the Hospital Department, see Gibson, *Dr. Bodo Otto*, 86.

25. *JCC*, 2:209–11 (quotation on 210), 249; Brown, *Medical Department*, 7–8; Bell, *Morgan*, 178; Cash, *Medical Men at the Siege of Boston*, 69–70; Duncan, *Medical Men in the American Revolution*, 60–61, 84.

26. Regimental surgeons were appointed by provincial assemblies and sometimes by the colonel of the regiment (Cash, *Medical Men at the Siege of Boston*, 48–51; Bell, *Morgan*, 184).

27. Estes, "'A Disagreeable and Dangerous Employment,'" 278, 281; Officers' petition against Dr. Church, n.d., *Sullivan Papers*, 1:84–87; French, *Gage's Informers*, 173–77; Cash, *Medical Men at the Siege of Boston*, 136; Applegate, "Medical Administrators," 3.

28. Cash, *Medical Men at the Siege of Boston*, 136; Applegate, "Medical Administrators," 3; GW, General Orders, 7 Sept. 1775, *GW Writings*, 3:481; Court of Inquiry Held in General Sullivan's Brigade, 9 Sept. 1775, GW Papers, reel 34. Another court of inquiry held in General Heath's brigade found that "the conduct of the Director-General Justly merits approbation and applause" (French, *Gage's Informers*, 181–82, quotation on 182).

29. *JCC*, 3:297; Brown, *Medical Department*, 8–10; Bell, *Morgan*, 178. For Church's treason, see Cash, *Medical Men at the Siege of Boston*, chap. 9; French, *Gage's Informers*, chap. 5.

234

Notes to Pages 27–32

30. Bell, *Morgan*, 185–87, 192; Applegate, "Medical Administrators," 3–4; Cash, *Medical Men at the Siege of Boston*, 74–75; Morgan, *Vindication*, 69–70.

31. *JCC*, 5:568, 569, 6:837; Bell, *Morgan*, 196–97, quotation on 197.

32. Morgan to president of Congress, 18 June 1776, PCC, reel 51, item 41, 6:3; William Finnie to [Congress], 17 Aug. 1776, ibid., reel 95, item 78, 9:31–32; William Aylett to John Adams, 3 Oct. 1776, ibid., reel 90, item 78, 1:23–24. See also Joseph Trumbull to president of Congress, 15 June 1777, *LMCC*, 2:393 n. 3.

33. Risch, *QM Support*, 6–7; Johnson, *Commissariat*, 28. For a list of employees in the Commissary Department on 20 January 1776, see *JCC*, 4:386–87.

34. Cash, *Medical Men at the Siege of Boston*, 133; Morgan, *Vindication*, xxii, 2; Gibson, *Dr. Bodo Otto*, 95, 97; Bell, *Morgan*, 191; *JCC*, 5:568. See also ibid., 857–58.

35. Risch, *QM Support*, 5; Lossing, *Philip Schuyler*, 1:478–79.

36. RM to Horatio Gates, 27 Oct. 1776, *LMCC*, 2:136; John Adams's Memorandum of Measures to be Pursued in Congress [9–23 Feb. 1776], *LDC*, 3:218; *JCC*, 5:434–35; 7:241; 9:799; Ward, *Department of War*, 2; Sanders, *Executive Departments*, 9; Risch, *QM Support*, 5. For the high hopes entertained for the Department of War, see president of Congress to GW, 14 June 1776, *LMCC*, 1:488.

37. Quoted in Ward, *Department of War*, 2. At the other extreme, epitomizing Congress's decentralized war administration, was Thomas McKean's membership on no less than thirty-three committees and chairmanship of five more during one period of the war (Sanders, *Executive Departments*, 4 n. 3).

38. Rakove, *Beginnings of National Politics*, 218; Bowler, "Logistics and Operations," 57. For a perceptive discussion of legislators' ambivalent attitude toward service in Congress, see Rakove, *Beginnings of National Politics*, chap. 10.

39. Harrison to GW, 21 July 1775, *LDC*, 1:645; Rakove, *Beginnings of National Politics*, 201–3; Adams, *Diary and Autobiography*, 3:381.

40. Ferguson, *Power of the Purse*, 30; *JCC*, 2:209, 94, 220, 3:269; Richard Smith's Diary, 26 Jan. [1776], *LDC*, 3:157; Morgan, "Puritan Ethic," 88–138. The commission also applied to the quartermaster in the Northern Department. See Richard Smith's Diary, 23 Sept. [1775], *LDC*, 2:49.

41. Joseph Trumbull to Jeremiah Wadsworth, 17 May 1777, *LMCC*, 2:364 n. 2; Johnson, *Commissariat*, 71–72; Joseph Trumbull to president of Congress, 9 June 1776, Force, ed., *American Archives*, 4th ser., 6:790–91. For the traditional nature of commissions in merchant activities, see Harrington, *New York Merchant*, 71, 88–89; Martin, *Merchants and Trade*, 118–19, 122–23. For the lucrativeness of wartime mercantile activities, see Chapter 6, n. 2.

42. Petition of the surgeons, apothecary, and mates to Congress, 20 June 1776, PCC, reel 49, item 41, 3:167; Trumbull to Hancock, 30 June 1777, ibid., reel 103, item 78, 22:245–46; Joseph Trumbull to the Continental Congress, 18 May 1776, ibid., reel 56, item 42, 7:326; Morgan, *Vindication*, 40.

43. Ferguson, *Power of the Purse*, 30–31; Nettels, *Emergence of a National Economy*, 24.

44. *JCC*, 4:387; 5:570. Nurses' wages were raised to $1 per week in October 1776 (ibid., 6:858).

45. Ibid., 7:245, 359, 8:465. Deputy directors-general were paid $5 a day and six rations; deputy commissaries' salaries were raised to $5 a day plus four rations; deputy quartermasters' wages were increased to $75 per month (ibid., 7:245, 163).

46. For continuing complaints of low wages, see GW to president of Congress, 18 April 1777, *GW Writings*, 7:436; Joseph Trumbull to Charles Stewart, 30 June 1777, PCC, reel 103, item 78, 22:241.

Chapter 2

1. Lee to GW, 20 Nov. 1777, *RH Lee Letters*, 1:352; Richard Smith's Diary [19 Mar. 1776], *LDC*, 3:412. See also Samuel Chase to John Sullivan, 24 Dec. 1776, *LMCC*, 2:186; Samuel Adams to John Adams, 9 Jan. 1777, ibid., 210; Rakove, *Beginnings of National Politics*, 199–201; Ward, *Department of War*, 3.

2. *JCC*, 6:1041–42, 9:962–63, quotation on 6:1041; *LMCC*, 2:210 n. 7. See also Sanders, *Executive Departments*, 11; Ward, *Department of War*, 4.

3. Ward, *Department of War*, 5; Rakove, *Beginnings of National Politics*, 201. For similar delays in the appointment of a new Board of Treasury, see Sanders, *Executive Departments*, 65–66; Robinson, "Treasury Administration," 204–8, 222.

4. Engagement of Members to Meet Punctually, 12 Apr. 1778, *LMCC*, 3:165; Carroll to the governor of Maryland, 21 Apr. 1778, ibid., 181. Complaints by its members of Congress's unproductive proceedings were common. See John Mathews to Thomas Bee, 22 Sept. 1778, ibid., 420–21; Josiah Bartlett to William Whipple, 27 July 1778, ibid., 351; Lee to James Jay, 3 Nov. 1778, ibid., 478. See also Rakove, *Beginnings of National Politics*, 201–2, quotation on 203.

5. Adams to James Warren, 6 Apr. 1777, *LMCC*, 2:318.

6. *JCC*, 6:1041, 7:221–23, 323, 8:487, 9:1023–26. GW appointed James Mease clothier general on 10 January 1777 (Commission to James Mease, 10 Jan. 1777, GW Papers, reel 39). Christopher Ludwig was elected superintendent of bakers on 3 May 1777 (*JCC*, 7:323). George Ewing was elected commissary of hides, 5 August 1777 (ibid., 8:607). Joseph Ward was elected commissary general of musters on 10 April 1777 (ibid., 7:252). General Thomas Conway was elected inspector-general on 13 December 1777 (ibid., 8:1026).

7. Rossman, *Mifflin*, 83; Risch, *QM Support*, 24–25; GW to president of Congress, 26 Jan., 14 Feb. 1777, *GW Writings*, 7:65, 149; GW to Alexander McDougall, 7 May 1777, ibid., 8:25; *JCC*, 7:267; Johnson, *Commissariat*, 70; Elbridge Gerry to Joseph Trumbull, 19 Apr. 1777, *LMCC*, 2:335; Roger Sherman to governor of Connecticut, 14 May 1777, ibid., 361–62; New York delegates to the New York Council of Safety, 19 June 1777, ibid., 381.

8. *JCC*, 7:161–64, 231–37, 244–45, 253. One of the leading authorities of the Continental army's Hospital Department contends that Congress's reorganization of 1777 provided the "necessary centralization" that the department had previously lacked (Applegate, "Medical Administrators," 1). As evidence, Applegate cites the extensive duties of the director-general (pp. 1–2). But the director-general's responsibilities were just as broad in 1775–76 as after the reorganization. Contrary to Applegate's interpretation, the main purpose of Congress's reform was not to increase the director-general's duties but to add new positions and specify areas of responsibility. The Hospital Department remained in the same ambiguous position as before: a director-general ostensibly in charge of officials, who, because they were appointed by Congress, felt they could do as they pleased. For the new director-general's problems with his subordinates, see Bell, "Court Martial of Dr. William Shippen," 222.

9. *JCC*, 7:355, 359, 8:434; Joseph Trumbull to Jonathan Trumbull, 14 May 1777, *LMCC*, 2:361 n. 3; New York delegates to the New York Council of Safety, 19 June 1777, ibid., 381.

10. Revealing more about modern distaste for lengthy regulations than about eighteenth-century American attitudes toward them, historians have wrongly criticized the excessive detail of Congress's reorganization of the Commissariat. For examples, see Burnett, *Continental Congress*, 273–74; Destler, *Connecticut*, 31; Risch, *QM Support*, 27; Johnson, *Commissariat*, 72. The problems afflicting the Commissariat did not stem from the complexity or length of the regulations, nor did most commissaries object to the new regulations because they were too complicated or burdensome.

11. *JCC*, 7:236–37, 355–58, 8:435–37, 440–45. The commissary general of issues was also

required to see that his deputies received a book to record all transactions (ibid., 435). For the Hospital Department, see ibid., 7:236–37.

12. Ibid., 8:434–35, 9:766–67.

13. Joseph Trumbull to Jeremiah Wadsworth, 17 May 1777, *LMCC*, 2:364 n. 2. See also Joseph Trumbull to John Hancock, 15 June 1777, to GW, 19 July 1777, Trumbull Coll.; Trumbull to Hancock, 7 Sept. 1776, PCC, reel 103, item 78, 22:117.

14. Joseph Trumbull to GW, 19 July 1777, Trumbull Coll.; Trumbull to Wadsworth, 8 July 1777, Wadsworth Letters. Trumbull claimed he would not resign if Congress appointed men he designated; "otherwise No consideration will Induce me to take any part in the matter" (Trumbull to Wadsworth, 6 June 1777, Wadsworth Family Coll.).

15. *JCC*, 8:607; Bodle and Thibaut, *Valley Forge*, 2:46–48, 74, 77, 80. On supplying the army at Valley Forge, this massive work supersedes all others.

16. Aylett to Trumbull, 22 June 1777, PCC, reel 103, item 78, 22:282; *JCC*, 8:498, 517, 601, 617, 627, 629–30, 640.

17. Seven deputy commissaries to Joseph Trumbull, 1 July 1777, Trumbull Coll.; Charles Stewart to president of Congress, 10 July 1777, PCC, reel 102, item 78, 20:127–28. See also Trumbull to GW, 9 July 1777, ibid., reel 167, item 152, 4:335. According to Trumbull, the "Insolence and Abuse" deputies suffered at the hands of arrogant officers contributed to their discontent (Trumbull to Wadsworth, 6 June 1777, Wadsworth Family Coll.).

18. William Buchanan to the Board of War, 7 Jan. 1778, PCC, reel 91, item 78, 2:333–34; Hughes to Horatio Gates, 24 Aug. 1777, Gates Papers; Colt to Hancock, 4 Oct. 1777, PCC, reel 93, item 78, 5:415.

19. Bodle and Thibaut, *Valley Forge*, 2:46–48, 74, 77, 80; Bill, *Valley Forge*, 105; Trussell, *Birthplace of an Army*, 33.

20. Thomas Wharton to the Pennsylvania delegates in Congress, 20 Dec. 1777, *Pa. Arch.*, 1st ser., 6:116; GW to the Committee of Congress with the Army, 29 Jan. 1778, *GW Writings*, 10:393; Bodle and Thibaut, *Valley Forge*, 2:107–8, 465–66.

21. The wagonmaster general, Joseph Thornburgh, also resigned in October 1777. Congress acted with unusual speed in replacing him with James Thompson a month later. See Bowler, "Logistics and Operations," 59, 176 n. 18.

22. Bodle and Thibaut, *Valley Forge*, 2:240; Johnson, *Commissariat*, 95–96; Risch, *QM Support*, 36–37; Timothy Pickering to Alexander Scammell, 17 Feb. 1778, in Pickering and Upham, *Pickering*, 1:206–7. Although Congress belatedly accepted Mifflin's resignation on 8 November 1777, it passed a resolution asking him to continue in office until a new quartermaster general was appointed (*JCC*, 9:882). Mifflin refused and delegated his authority to his assistant, Henry Lutterloh (Risch, *QM Support*, 37). Only Mifflin's biographer believes that he resigned in good faith, that is, that Mifflin was genuinely ill and that he honestly thought his assistants were capable of fulfilling his duties in his absence. But even Rossman acknowledges that "it was a bad time for the quartermaster-general to quit his post" (*Mifflin*, 94–95).

23. Stewart to Hancock, 14 Aug. 1777, PCC, reel 102, item 78, 20:143; *JCC*, 9:768.

24. For a more detailed examination of these logistical problems, see Chapter 3. Cf. Trussell, *Birthplace of an Army*, 34–35, who seriously underestimates the importance of leadership and experience in carrying out successful supply operations.

25. *JCC*, 9:905; Hatch, *Administration*, 90–91; Johnson, *Commissariat*, 88–89, 98–99. Johnson notes that of all the methods tried, state purchasing commissioners were the most successful in providing the army with food and impressment was the least successful (92–93, 101).

26. *JCC*, 10:39–41. Committee members eventually included Joseph Reed, Nathaniel Folsom, John Harvie, and Gouverneur Morris (*LMCC*, 3:61 n. 2). For a detailed account of the

committee's reports back to Congress concerning the reform of the quartermaster general's department, see *Greene Papers*, 2:308n–11n.

27. Committee of Congress at Camp to president of Congress, 12, 25 Feb. 1778, PCC, reel 40, item 33, pp. 125, 188.

28. Committee of Congress at Camp to president of Congress, 25 Feb. 1778, ibid., pp. 189, 187, 188. The committee was reacting to a plan submitted by Mifflin and approved by Congress on 5 February 1778, which called for further decentralization. (*JCC*, 10:102–3, 126–27; Risch, *QM Support*, 38, 40).

29. Committee of Congress at Camp to president of Congress, 25 Feb. 1778, PCC, reel 40, item 33, pp. 189, 190–91, 193, quotations on 193.

30. Committee of Congress at Camp to president of Congress, 29 Jan., 12 Feb., 1778, ibid., 75–76, 126; Trussell, *Birthplace of an Army*, 40.

31. Brown to president of the Medical Committee, 20 Jan. 1778, PCC, reel 91, item 78, 2:367, 363; Rush to William Duer, 8 Dec. 1777, Rush, *Letters*, 1:172–73. Rush's quotation is from Hawke, *Benjamin Rush*, 209.

32. The phrase is from Rush's letter to Duer, 8 Dec. 1777, Rush, *Letters*, 1:171. Rush frequently expressed admiration of the British system. See Rush to John Adams, 21 Oct. 1777, ibid., 160–61; Rush to NG, 2 Dec. 1777, ibid., 168–69. Characteristically, Rush exaggerated the superior organization of the British army's Medical Department. For the administrative problems besetting the British system, see Cantlie, *Army Medical Department*, 1:65, 107, 120, 125, 131.

33. Rush to Duer, 8 Dec. 1777, Rush, *Letters*, 1:172; Brown to president of the Medical Committee, 20 Jan. 1778, PCC, reel 91, item 78, 2:363.

34. Brown to president of the Medical Committee, 20 Jan. 1778, PCC, reel 91, item 78, 2:363. Rush's attitude was inconsistent. To John Adams he wrote, "The fault is both in the establishment and in the Director-General" (Rush to Adams, 21 Oct. 1777, Rush, *Letters*, 1:161). Three weeks later, he denied he was suggesting "anything to the prejudice of the present director-general of our hospitals" and admitted that the job was too extensive for even the most competent medical man (Rush to Duer, 8 Dec. 1777, ibid., 173). Five days later, Rush reversed himself and blamed the maladministration of the Hospital Department on Director-General William Shippen (Rush to Duer, 13 Dec. 1777, ibid., 175–76). Rush's most recent biographer is unable to explain his sudden change of opinion (Hawke, *Benjamin Rush*, 212–13).

35. Laurens to Francis Dana, 1 Mar. 1778, LMCC, 3:102–3; Trussell, *Birthplace of an Army*, 41; Bill, *Valley Forge*, 102–3; Ellery to William Churchill Houston, 13 Feb. 1778, LMCC, 3:84. See also Abraham Clark to Lord Stirling, 15 Jan. 1778, ibid., 39; Eliphalet Dyer to Joseph Trumbull, 8 Feb. 1778, ibid., 78; Ellery to governor of Rhode Island, 1 Mar. 1778, ibid., 103; Laurens to Dana, 1 Mar. 1778, ibid., 102–3.

36. *JCC*, 10:128–30; Applegate, "Hospital Department," 298. See also James Lovell to Langdon, 8 Feb. 1778, LMCC, 3:77. Congress followed Dr. Brown's suggestion and ordered the deputy-directors to appoint a purveyor of hospital stores and a purveyor of medicines, though they were not designated as such (*JCC*, 10:129).

37. Folsom to Bartlett, 2 Jan. 1778, LMCC, 3:4. For similar assessments, see Clark to Stirling, 15 Jan. 1778, ibid., 39; Gerry to Samuel Adams, 7 Feb. 1778, ibid., 76; Dyer to William Williams, 17 Feb. 1778, ibid., 88; Lee to GW, 20 Nov. 1777, *RH Lee Letters*, 1:352; Pickering to Scammell, 17 Feb. 1778, Pickering and Upham, *Pickering*, 1:206; Daniel Roberdeau to Wharton, 30 Dec. 1777, *Pa. Arch.*, 1st ser., 6:147.

38. Gerry to Samuel Adams, 7 Feb. 1778, LMCC, 3:76. Modern historians have not been so charitable. See Bodle and Thibaut, *Valley Forge*, 2:46–48, 87–88.

39. *JCC*, 10:210, 328, 345, quotation on 345. Buchanan saved Congress the embarrassment of firing him by conveniently resigning on 29 March 1778 (Johnson, *Commissariat*, 109). Greene, Pettit, and Cox agreed to split the commission equally, each receiving one-third of 1 percent (NG to Joseph Reed, 9 Mar. 1778, *Greene Papers*, 2:307).

40. NG to John Davis, 23 Mar. 1778, *Greene Papers*, 2:320, 321 n. 3; NG to Moore Furman, 25 Apr. 1778, ibid., 354. In one case, NG offered Owen Biddle an extra .75 percent commission on purchases to be paid by the states and the commissary general of forage. See Terms Proposed for Owen Biddle, 1 Apr. 1779, Society Miscellaneous Collection, Box 15B, HSP.

41. *JCC*, 10:327. Ironically, Joseph Trumbull received the commissions he so desired only after he was dead (ibid., 13:395–401). Dyer to Wadsworth, 10 Mar. 1778, Wadsworth Papers, Box 126.

42. Lovell to Samuel Adams, 19 Apr. [1778], *LMCC*, 3:175.

43. For their identification as radicals, see Henderson, *Party Politics*, 103–6, 112, 165. For evidence of their attitudes toward the reforms of 1778, see letters cited in n. 37 above.

44. Support for this view of Congress can be found in a recent study, which persuasively challenges the Progressive historians' interpretation that Congress was divided into radical and conservative factions, distinguished by ideological or sectional differences. This revisionist interpretation stresses the similar assumptions congressmen shared toward resistance and the critical role that military considerations and institutional constraints played in shaping their decisions. See Rakove, *Beginnings of National Politics*. The classic Progressive study of the Continental Congress during the war is Jensen, *Articles of Confederation*. Other historians have qualified, extended, and enlarged Jensen's seminal work. See Ferguson, *Power of the Purse*; Henderson, *Party Politics*.

45. GW to Wadsworth, 22 Nov. 1779, *GW Writings*, 17:163; GW to president of Congress, 15 Dec. 1779, ibid., 272; GW, circular to governors of the Middle states, 16 Dec. 1779, ibid., 273; Risch, *QM Support*, 56–57.

Chapter 3

1. President of Congress to governor of Rhode Island, 3 Jan. 1778, *LMCC*, 3:11. See also Caesar Rodney to John Dickinson, 17 Apr. 1779, *Rodney Letters*, 299; *New-England Chronicle* (Boston), 26 Mar. 1778; William Heath to GW, 22 Mar. 1778, GW Papers, reel 48. Laurens would later join those delegates who blamed corrupt staff officers for the army's logistical problems. See Chapter 5 at n. 35.

2. A General Return of Provisions and Stores Issued in Camp . . . for the Month of December 1777, PCC, reel 199, item 192, p. 519; A General Return of Provisions and Stores Issued . . . January 1778, ibid., 517; A General Return of Provisions and Stores Issued . . . February 1778, ibid., 425.

3. General Return of Forage Issued under the Direction of Owen Biddle Assistant Forage Master General for the Year 1778, 12 May 1779, Greene Papers, APS, reel 2, 11:68. Biddle noted that four of his assistants had failed to file returns, hence the number should be even higher. For the number of horses, see State of Horses in Winter Quarters from 1 December 1778 to 1 May 1779, 24 Nov. 177[9], ibid., reel 2, 10:21.

4. Estimate of Stores for an Army of Twenty-Five thousand Men as far as Concerns the Quartermaster General's Department, 6 Mar. 1781, PCC, reel 46, item 39, 3:431–40. See also Appendix II: Items Handled by Quartermaster Department, *Greene Papers*, 2:554–57. "Iron mongery" included such items as scythes, sickles, cutting knives, grindstones, spikes, nails, bar iron, glue, padlocks, and crowbars (PCC, reel 46, item 39, 3:436).

5. For the ineffectiveness of the British blockade for the first three years of the war, see

Gruber, *Howe Brothers*, 80–81, 103–4, 136, 139–40, 159, 204. British naval weakness is also evident in General Clinton's persistent worry that his supply ships were in danger of being intercepted by American privateers or the French fleet. See Bowler, *Logistics and the Failure of the British Army*, 98.

6. Bush, *Revolutionary Enigma*, 31–32.

7. Higginbotham, *War of American Independence*, 304; McBride, "Virginia War Effort," 34. For a small sampling of these common problems, see GW to president of Congress, 15 Apr. 1776, *GW Writings*, 4:480; Clement Biddle to GW, 5 Mar. 1778, GW Papers, reel 47; James Gamble to Charles Stewart, 3 Mar. 1780, Stewart Papers, NYSHA; William Pendergast to NG, 23 Jan. 1781, Greene Papers, WCL; Timothy Pickering to Colonel Neil, 14 Oct. 1780, RG 93, reel 25, vol. 122.

8. John Fitch to Joseph Strang, 18 Dec. 1779, John Fitch Papers, CSL; Freeman, *GW*, 5:133. Sudden thunderstorms at harvest time also seriously damaged crops. See Rodney to GW, 27 Jan. 1779, *Rodney Letters*, 293; Bradford, "Hunger Menaces the Revolution," 5; GW, General Orders, 11 Nov. 1779, *GW Writings*, 17:92–93.

9. Destler, *Connecticut*, 37. See also GW to the magistrates of New Jersey, 8 Jan. 1780, *GW Writings*, 17:363; GW to William Buchanan, 28 Dec. 1777, ibid., 10:217; George Gipson to GW, 19 Mar. 1778, GW Papers, reel 34; Bill, *Valley Forge*, 105; Owen Biddle circular, 15 Sept. 1778, Biddle Ltrbks. The importance of the weather is conveyed on almost every page of Joslin, "Journal," 299–369. Heavy snowfall could be a blessing in disguise for it permitted the use of sleighs to transport supplies. See, for example, John Patton to Rodney, 17 Jan. 1780, *Rodney Letters*, 333–34.

10. Luttwak, *Dictionary of Modern War*, 123.

11. NG to John Jay, 15 Apr. 1779, Greene Papers, WCL. See also Royal Flint to Jacob Cuyler, 10 Sept. 1778, Wadsworth Papers, Letterbook: 1778; Peter Colt to George Clinton, 27 Feb. 1779, *Clinton Papers*, 4:589–90.

12. Gar Rooback to Charles Lee, 1 Mar. 1776, *Lee Papers*, 4:342.

13. NG to Mr. Johnson, 14 June 1779, Greene Papers, APS, reel 1, 6:67; Charles Young to GW, 21 July 1778, GW Papers, reel 50; Thomas Posey to NG, 16 Mar. 1782, Misc. MS (NG), NYHS; Mathew Ramsey to NG, 29 Jan. 1781, Greene Papers, WCL; GW to Nicholas Cooke, 2 Nov. 1775, *GW Writings*, 4:62. The phrase "ruinous punctillio" is in John Pryor to William Davies, 15 July 1781, *VCSP*, 2:220. The simple formula is in E. Bowen to Pickering, 6 Oct. 1780, Rhode Island, "Revolutionary Correspondence," 274.

14. Royster, *Revolutionary People at War*, 79–96; Heath to GW, 16 Jan. 1781, GW Papers, reel 74. For Hutchinson, see Bailyn, *Ideological Origins*, 220–22.

15. James Mease to GW, 22 July 1777, GW Papers, reel 42. For Sullivan's defense of his action, see Sullivan to GW, 11 July 1777, *Sullivan Papers*, 1:414. For other instances of interference by Continental officers, see GW to Mease, 13 June 1777, *GW Writings*, 8:237; GW to Israel Putnam, 11 Nov. 1777, ibid., 10:41; Richard Peters to GW, 3 Aug. 1777, GW Papers, reel 43; Board of War to GW, 13 Oct. 1779, ibid., reel 61; Henry Lutterloh to Pickering, 8 Feb. 1781, Pickering Papers, reel 39; Buchanan to Stewart, 8 Oct. 1777, Stewart Papers, NYSHA; Timothy Pickering to GW, 14 Jan. 1781, RG 93, reel 25, vol. 123. Militia officers also stopped supplies destined for the Continental army. See, for example, Andrew Craigie to Jonathan Potts, 4 Apr. 1778, Jonathan Potts Papers, 4:437, HSP; Thomas Nelson to Colonel Barbour, 19 Sept. 1781, *VCSP*, 2:463.

16. *R. I. Acts*, May 1775, 9–10; Feb. 1776, 274; Oct. 1778, 36; *Conn. St. Recs.*, 1:466–67; *Pa. Statutes*, 9:181–85, 189–91; *N.C. Recs.*, 10:337, 355; Hening, *Statutes*, 9:375–77; New York, *Laws*, 1:24–25, 91–92, 114–16; *N.J. Assembly Acts*, Nov.–Dec. 1777, chap. 1, pp. 3–7.

17. Pickering to GW, 17 Mar. 1777, GW Papers, reel 40; R. Allison to Jeremiah Wadsworth, 13 Aug. 1778, Wadsworth Papers, Box 126; William Kennon to Charles Lee, 7 Dec. 1776, *Lee*

Papers, 5:333–34; Crittenden, *Commerce of North Carolina*, 147–48; Bond, *State Government in Maryland*, 48; Johnson, *Commissariat*, 155, 157.

18. Memorial of Officers of the Pennsylvania Battalions, 4 June 1778, *Pa. Arch.*, 2d ser., 3:202. Ironically, Pennsylvania was not one of the states that sent clothing to its own troops. See Pennsylvania Council to Anthony Wayne, 12 Dec. 1777, ibid., 1st ser., 6:87. Virginia supplied its soldiers directly. When supplies were accidentally sent to a Continental deputy quartermaster instead of to Virginia's state agent, consternation and denunciation resulted (James Wood to GW, 12 Nov. 1778, GW Papers, reel 54).

19. James Livingston to GW, 22 Jan. 1777, GW Papers, reel 39; Mease to GW, 6, 21 June 1777, ibid., reel 42; GW to president of Congress, 26 Jan. 1777, *GW Writings*, 7:63–64; JCC, 7:473, 8:472–73; Stewart to Samuel Gray, 17 Feb. 1778, Stewart Papers, LC.

20. For the problems of recruitment, see Royster, *Revolutionary People at War*, 62–69, 131–36, 267–70; Sellers, "Common Soldier," 156–58; Lender, "Enlisted Line," chap. 3.

21. Blaine to president of Congress, 15 Aug. 1780, PCC, reel 82, item 165, 1:328. Blaine replaced Jeremiah Wadsworth as commissary general of purchases on 2 December 1779 (JCC, 15:1342–43). Flower to Wharton, 2 May 1778, *Pa. Arch.*, 1st ser., 6:405–6. For similar complaints, see George Rice to Thomas Jefferson, 24 Mar. 1781, *Jefferson Papers*, 5:237; William Rippey to John Davis, 12 June 1778, Davis Papers, reel 79; Cuyler to Clinton, 19 May 1780, *Clinton Papers*, 5:726–27; Gustavus Risberg to Stewart, 22 Oct. 1779, Stewart Papers, NYSHA; Peter T. Curtenius to Clinton, 22 Sept. 1778, *Clinton Papers*, 4:71. Curtenius was a state agent.

22. Hening, *Statutes*, 10:177, 425; Massachusetts, *Acts and Resolves*, 5:729; Clinton to the mayor and corporation of Albany, 2 June 1778, *Clinton Papers*, 3:388; Pennsylvania Council to GW, 13 Apr. 1778, *Pa. Arch.*, 1st ser., 6:416. The final sentence in the paragraph is a paraphrase of an idea expressed about Congress by Cunliffe, "Congressional Leadership," 48.

23. NG to GW, 18 Feb. 1778, GW Papers, reel 47; GW to the Committee of Congress with the Army, 29 Jan. 1778, *GW Writings*, 10:393; Owen Biddle to Archibald Dick, 26 Feb. 1780, Biddle Ltrbks.; George Weedon to the Marquis de Lafayette, 4 June 1781, Maryland, *Papers Relating to the Maryland Line*, 148; James Abeel to Charles Pettit, 15 Nov. 1778, Abeel Ltrbk. Complaints about the lack of forage were legion. According to one authority, "In the more than 2,500 letters that have survived from Nathanael Greene's two and a half years as quartermaster, no refrain is sounded oftener than the want of forage—with the possible exception of the want of money" (*Greene Papers*, 2:319n).

24. Stewart to Wadsworth, 20 June 1779, Wadsworth Papers, Box 128; Thomas Posey to NG, 16 Mar. 1782, Greene Papers, WCL; Graeff, "Henry Vanderslice," 68–69; Higginbotham, *War of American Independence*, 304; Stewart to Sullivan, 24 July 1779, Brophy and Tripp, eds., "Supplies for General Sullivan," pt. 3, 49; Van Dusen, "Trade of Revolutionary Connecticut," 270–71. For Maryland's action, see Johnson, *Commissariat*, 104; NG to Thomas Polk, 14 Apr. 1781, Greene Papers, WCL; NG to William Richardson Davie, 14 Apr. 1781, ibid.; Greene, *Nathanael Greene*, 3:42; Wallace, *Appeal to Arms*, 214.

25. NG to GW, 24 Feb. 1779, PCC, reel 175, item 155, 1:112; Entries of 4 May 1777, 28 Apr. 1778, Joslin, "Journal," 310, 355; See also Graeff, "Henry Vanderslice," 67–73; Van Dusen, "Trade of Revolutionary Connecticut," 271–72.

26. James Thompson to NG, 24 Feb. 1779, Greene Papers, APS, reel 1, 4:100; Entries of 5 May, 8 Nov. 1777, Joslin, "Journal," 310, 333; NG to GW, 24 Feb. 1779, PCC, reel 175, item 155, 1:112; JCC, 11:467; Thomas Chase to NG, 12 Oct. 1779, Greene Papers, APS, reel 1, 3:25.

27. As reported by William Sharp to Capt. Brady, 1 June 1779, Davis Papers, reel 81. See also Moore Furman to NG, 7 May 1779, *Furman Letters*, 3.

28. T. Wederstrandt to Blaine, 28 Apr. 1780, Blaine Papers, reel 1. For other examples of staff officers' inability to retain wagoners for lack of money, see Joseph Lewis to NG, 3 Mar. 1780, Lewis Letters; NG to GW, 19 Apr. 1779, GW Papers, reel 57; David Greer to Davis, 22 Mar.

1780, Davis Papers, reel 82; John Mitchell to NG, 2 Jan. 1780, PCC, reel 193, item 173, 5:217; Furman to Thomas Durie, 29 Mar. 1780, *Furman Letters*, 60.

29. Williams to Wadsworth, 20 Apr. 1778, Wadsworth Papers, Box 126. See also Petition application of William Burnett, Dann, ed., *Revolution Remembered*, 373.

30. Stewart to Wadsworth, 20 June 1779, Wadsworth Papers, Box 128; John Chaloner and John White to Mitchell, 1 Apr. 1779, C and W Ltrbks.; John Burrowes to GW, 3 Feb. 1779, GW Papers, reel 55; Davis to David Williamson, 22 May 1779, Davis Papers, reel 81; Thompson to NG, 24 Feb. 1779, Greene Papers, APS, reel 1, 4:100; Royster, "'Nature of Treason,'" 177; Gates to GW, 19 Apr. 1777, GW Papers, reel 41; Gates to Jonathan Trumbull, 21 May 1777, *Trumbull Papers*, 2:50; Committee of Congress at Camp to president of Congress, 12 Feb. 1778, PCC, reel 40, item 33, p. 125; Blaine to GW, 28 Feb. 1778, GW Papers, reel 47; James Young to Lutterloh, 3 Mar. 1778, PCC, reel 199, item 192, p. 393 (Young was Pennsylvania's wagonmaster general); GW to George Measam, 10 Mar. 1779, *GW Writings*, 14:217; GW, Orders and Instructions to John Parke, 13 Apr. 1776, ibid., 3:466; Samuel H. Parsons to Clinton, 16 Mar. 1778, *Clinton Papers*, 3:49–51.

31. *JCC*, 14:572. Deputy issuing commissaries were paid $200 per month (ibid., 571); Memorial to John Fitch from assistant commissaries, 4 Oct. 1779, Brophy and Tripp, "Supplies for General Sullivan," pt. 3, 72–73; Risch, *QM Support*, 54.

32. The Memorial of sundry Carpenters and Wheel Wrights engaged in Public employment in Fishkill, 6 Jan. 1779, PCC, reel 192, item 173, 1:83–84; NG to Lewis, 10, 20 Feb. 1779, ibid., reel 193, item 173, 4:98, 139–40, quotation on 140; NG to Udny Hay, 20 Feb. 1779, ibid., 144.

33. NG to Hay, 7, 9 Nov. 1779, ibid., reel 192, item 173, 2:99–101, 113–14; Furman to [Greene?], 8 Nov. 1779, *Furman Papers*, 34. For other examples, see Greer to Davis, 20 May 1780, Davis Papers, reel 82; Assistant deputy quartermasters to Hay, 5 Oct. 1779, Greene Papers, APS, reel 1, 3:54; Samuel Gray to Stewart, 30 Apr. 1780, Samuel Gray Papers, CHS; Fitch to Stewart, 17 Dec. 1778, Stewart Papers, NYSHA. For the same problem in the Hospital Department, see Resolutions of the Surgeons and Mates to Congress, 2 May 1780, Peter Turner Papers, LC.

34. GW to president of Congress, 15 Dec. 1777, *GW Writings*, 10:159; William Duer to GW, 2 Mar. 1777, GW Papers, reel 40; Leiby, *War in the Hackensack Valley*, 48; Wadsworth to Connecticut delegates at Congress, 27 May 1778, Wadsworth Papers, Box 126; Henry Champion to GW, 28 Feb. 1778, GW Papers, reel 47; Destler, "Henry Champion," 58–59; Scott, "Price Control in New England," 464, 472; Johnson, *Commissariat*, 104–5, 134; *JCC*, 11:569–70; Gipson to GW, 22 Feb. 1778, GW Papers, reel 47; Main, *Sovereign States*, 237; Morris, "Labor and Mercantilism in the Revolutionary Era," 103; Handlin and Handlin, "Revolutionary Economic Policy in Massachusetts," 15; Burke to governor of North Carolina, 10 [16?] Feb. 1777, *LMCC*, 2:258. Burke voted for price controls hoping to discourage northern speculators.

35. *R.I. Acts*, Aug. 1777, p. 14; *Conn. St. Recs.*, 1:104–5; *Pa. Statutes*, 9:297–99, 414–17; New York, *Laws*, 1:112; Biddle to Furman, 23 Sept. 1778, Biddle Ltrbks. For additional evidence of farmers holding back their crops or selling them for high prices, see Lee to the Board of War, 27 Apr. 1776, *Lee Papers*, 5:244–45; Buchanan to Henry Laurens, 21 Nov. 1777, PCC, reel 91, item 78, 2:301; Pettit to GW, 10 Sept. 1778, ibid., reel 99, item 192, pp. 225–26; Sullivan to Jeremiah Powell, 17 Oct. 1778, *Sullivan Papers*, 2:392–93; Gipson to GW, 22 Feb. 1778, GW Papers, reel 47; GW to NG, 22 Sept. 1778, *GW Writings*, 12:479; Hooper to Jacob Morgan and Philip Marsteller, 22 Sept. 1778, Biddle Corr., folder 5; Samuel Townsend to Clinton, 7 June 1779, *Clinton Papers*, 5:47–48; Lewis to Furman, 31 Jan. 1780, Lewis Letters; Cuyler to Wadsworth, 20 July 1778, Wadsworth Papers, Box 126; Flint to Clement Biddle, 27 Nov. 1779, *Furman Letters*, 47; *Pa. Statutes*, 9:373; Jensen, "American Revolution and American Agriculture," 114.

36. Francis Wade to GW, 29 Jan. 1777, GW Papers, reel 39; *R.I. Acts*, Dec. 1778, 14; Adam

Jamison to NG, 15 Dec. 1780, Greene Papers, WCL; Hughes to Walter Pynchon, 20 Feb. 1782, Hughes Ltrbks., 11; William Churchill Houston to Philip Schuyler, 13 May 1780, *LMCC*, 5:137; NG to president of Congress, 14 July 1779, PCC, reel 175, item 155, 1:148. See also *N.J. Gaz.*, 3 Aug. 1780, in *N.J. Arch.*, 2d ser., 4:572–73; John Mihelm to Stewart, Nov. 1777, Stewart Papers, NYSHA; Abeel to NG, 23 May 1779, Greene Papers, APS, reel 1, 5:68; *N.J. Gaz.*, 28 June 1779, in *N.J. Arch.*, 2d ser., 3:511; GW to Heath, 14 Sept. 1778, *GW Writings*, 12:446–47.

37. Richard Claiborne to NG, 18 May 1779, Greene Papers, APS, reel 1, 5:18; Furman to Stephen Lowrey, 29 Aug. 1779, *Furman Letters*, 15; Hughes to GW, 3 Feb. 1777, GW Papers, reel 39; Joseph Pettingill, John Wiley, and Seth Dress to GW, 20 Dec. 1777, ibid., reel 46; William Smallwood to GW, 27 Feb. 1778, ibid., reel 47; John Keese to Hughes, 13 Sept. 1781, Hughes Ltrbks., 15; Chaloner and White to Blaine, 12 Aug. 1778, C and W Ltrbks.; GW to Mease, 23 June, 18 July 1777, *GW Writings*, 8:292, 432; James Hamilton to Stewart; 3 Oct. 1778, Stewart Papers, NYSHA; NG to Nicholas Cooke, 4 July 1775, *Greene Papers*, 1:94; Royster, "'Nature of Treason,'" 177. The Continental officer is quoted in Freeman, *GW*, 4:580.

38. GW, General Orders, 4 Aug. 1775, 21 June 1776, 5 Sept. 1782, *GW Writings*, 3:385, 5:165, 25:131; GW to Daniel Morgan, 12 Nov. 1778, ibid., 13:250; GW to William Livingston, 3 Mar. 1779, ibid., 14:185; Royster, *Revolutionary People at War*, 59; Martin, *Private Yankee Doodle*, 52; Entries of 19 May, 18 June 1776, Henshaw, "Orderly Books," 133, 157; Lauber, ed., *Orderly Books of the Fourth and Second New York Regiments*, 309; Supreme Executive Council of Pennsylvania to Congress, 3 Nov. 1777, *Pa. Arch.*, 1st ser., 5:739; Risch, *Supplying Washington's Army*, 344–45; GW, General Orders, 4 Aug. 1775, 21 May 1776, 7 Aug. 1778, 25 Aug. 1780, 5 Sept. 1782, *GW Writings*, 3:385, 5:72–73, 12:289, 19:439, 25:131; *R.I. Acts*, Dec. 1777, 16; New Jersey Committee of Safety, 23 Apr. 1776, *N.J. Arch.*, 2d ser., 1:91–92.

39. GW to Peter Scull, 19 Mar. 1778, *GW Writings*, 11:109. Congress ratified Steuben's appointment in August 1778 (*JCC*, 11:882); Chase, "Baron von Steuben," 126, 129–30, 171.

40. See, for example, Lauber, ed., *Orderly Books of the Fourth and Second New York Regiments*, 261. Steuben always had difficulty in filling the key posts of deputy and brigade inspector (Chase, "Baron von Steuben," 259). For examples of the continuing lack of discipline among the troops, see GW, General Orders, 16 Feb., 25 Aug. 1780, *GW Writings*, 18:16, 19:439; GW to Lord Stirling, 5 Mar. 1780, ibid., 18:71; GW to James Clinton, 28 Oct. 1780, ibid., 20:260; Freeman, *GW*, 5:150, 154–55. For a more positive evaluation of Steuben's effect on the discipline of soldiers, see Royster, *Revolutionary People at War*, 222, 239; Palmer, *General von Steuben*, 198. For Steuben's return to drilling Continental soldiers, see Chase, "Baron von Steuben," 265–67; Peters, "Letter to John Montgomery [1784]," 680.

41. Charges against Mr. Ebenezer Clarke, Issuing Commissary to General Poor's Brigade, 23 Feb. 1779, John Fitch Papers, CSL; Alexander McDougall to Heath, 14 Nov. 1780, *Heath Papers*, 5:132; GW, General Orders, 11 Jan. 1778, *GW Writings*, 10:289; Martin, *Private Yankee Doodle*, 31; John Erskine to NG, 11 Feb. 1779, Greene Papers, APS, reel 1, 4:19; Gipson to GW, 8 Mar. 1778, GW Papers, reel 47.

42. GW, General Orders, 20 Nov. 1775, *GW Writings*, 4:103; GW to Robert Morris, 27 Jan. 1777, ibid., 7:68; NG to William Greene, 7 Mar. 1778, *Greene Papers*, 2:302. For an extended discussion of the militia's theft and waste of public stores, see Jameson, "Equipment for the Militia," 121–30.

43. Joseph Reed to Thomas Wharton, 30 Oct. 1778, quoted in Reed, *Joseph Reed*, 1:333; Weedon to [Col. Grayson, probably], 22 May 1781, Maryland, *Papers Relating to the Maryland Line*, 145; GW, General Orders, 18 June 1776, *GW Writings*, 5:156; *JCC*, 7:151.

44. GW to the Board of War, 1 June 1779, to Livingston, 21 Nov. 1776, *GW Writings*, 15:200, 6:302; Freeman, *GW*, 4:529; Ward, *War of the Revolution*, 2:492; Richard Henry Lee to [Arthur Lee], 20 Apr. 1777, *RH Lee Letters*, 1:281; Cometti, "Depredations in Virginia," 144–

45; Leiby, *War in the Hackensack Valley*, 68; Heath, *Memoirs*, 79; Martin, *Private Yankee Doodle*, 36. See also GW to president of Congress, 16 Sept. 1776, *GW Writings*, 6:59; Entry of 16 Sept. 1777, "Timothy Pickering's Journal," Pickering and Upham, *Timothy Pickering*, 1:161.

45. Lewis Morris to Pettit, 9 Sept. 1778, GW Papers, reel 51; Charles Carroll to GW, 27 Sept. 1777, ibid., reel 44; Lauber, ed., *Orderly Books of the Fourth and Second New York Regiments*, 140; Jefferson to Edward Stevens, 4 Aug. 1780, *Jefferson Papers*, 3:529–30; Davies to Jefferson, 25 Jan. 1781, ibid., 4:446; George Muter to Jefferson, 1 Feb. 1781, ibid., 496; Bolton, *Private Soldier*, 101, 103; Freeman, *GW*, 4:579; Nichols, ed., "Doughboy of 1780," 462.

46. Wolcott to governor of Connecticut, 18 Dec. 1780, *LMCC*, 5:491; Nettels, *National Economy*, 25; Ferguson, *Power of the Purse*, 32. Figures have been computed from the table in Bezanson, *Prices and Inflation*, 321. A hundredweight equals 112 pounds.

47. Ferguson, *Power of the Purse*, 46, 51; Harlow, "Revolutionary Finance," 61.

48. Robinson, "Treasury Administration," 216, 222; Pettit to NG, 5–7 Nov. 1779, Greene Papers, APS, reel 2, 9:96.

49. Robinson, "Treasury Administration," 231.

50. Pettit to president of Congress, 17 Nov. 1779, PCC, reel 199, item 192, pp. 257–58; Chaloner and White to [Wadsworth?], 17 May 1779, Wadsworth Papers, Box 128; Pettit to NG, 17 Mar. 1780, Greene Papers, WCL.

51. Abeel to John Cox, 22 Aug., 30 Dec. 1778, Abeel Ltrbk.; Pettit to NG, 1 Oct. 1778, Greene Papers, WCL; Hooper to Blaine, 25 Dec. 1779, Blaine Papers; Flint to Wadsworth, 7 Nov. 1779, GW Papers, reel 62; NG to GW, 24 Dec. 1779, ibid., reel 63; Wadsworth to GW, 3 Jan. 1780, ibid.; Udny Hay to Pettit, 11 Nov. 1779, PCC, reel 199, item 192, p. 271; Archibald Steel to Pettit, 5 Nov. 1779, ibid., 273; Hooper to NG, 27 Feb. 1780, ibid., 286; Mitchell to NG, 2 Jan. 1780, ibid., reel 193, item 173, 5:217; Furman to Pettit, 4 Nov. 1779, ibid., 275; Davis to Owen Biddle, 11 Jan. 1780, Davis Papers, reel 81; Rippey to Davis, 22 Sept. 1779, ibid.; Greer to Davis, 10 Apr. 1780, ibid., reel 82; Abraham Smith to Davis, 25 Dec. 1780, ibid., reel 83; Owen Biddle to Pettit, 3 Feb., 23 June, 28 July 1780, Biddle Ltrbks.; Nicholas Quackenbush to Hughes, 6 Nov. 1780, Hughes Ltrbks., 8; Pickering to Pettit, 12 Nov. 1780, RG 93, reel 25, vol. 123; James Reed to Flint, 19 Oct. 1778, Wadsworth Papers, Box 127; Colt to Wadsworth, 2 Jan. 1779, ibid.; Lewis to NG, 11 Nov. 1779, Greene Papers, APS, reel 2, 9:72; Nehemiah Hubbard to NG, 20 Oct. 1779, ibid., reel 1, 3:81.

52. Ferguson, *Power of the Purse*, 57; *Pa. Packet*, 15 April 1778; *JCC*, 8:752–53; Council of Safety, 22 May 1778, *Pa. Col. Recs.*, 11:496. In 1780 states permitted Quartermaster and Commissary certificates to be used to pay taxes (Ferguson, *Power of the Purse*, 64–65).

53. Reed to Flint, 19 Oct. 1778, Wadsworth Papers, Box 127; Moore to NG, 25 Dec. 1780, Greene Papers, WCL; Hay to George Clinton, 28 Jan. 1780, PCC, reel 93, item 173, 5:123. Six months later Hay reported he had contracted "a Loan upon my own Credit which has already brought me in ten thousand dollars" (Hay to NG, 14 July 1780, ibid., reel 175, item 155, 1:335). It is unclear whether this loan was from the New York legislature or from a private lender. The latter seems more likely.

54. Duncan to Biddle, 3 Jan. 1780, Biddle Corr., folder 7. For additional evidence of staff officers using their own money, borrowing funds, or doing both to secure supplies for the army, see William Smith to Owen Biddle, 24 June 1780, ibid., folder 17; Wadsworth to Chaloner, 11 Mar. 1780, Misc. MS (Letters to John Chaloner, 1780–90), NYHS; Furman to NG, 9 June 1779, *Furman Letters*, 8; Abeel to NG, 27 Dec. 1778, Abeel Ltrbk.; Hubbard to NG, 20 Oct. 1779, Greene Papers, APS, reel 1, 3:81; Lewis to NG, 11 Nov. 1779, ibid., reel 2, 9:72; Hay to Greene, 14 July 1780, PCC, reel 175, item 155, 1:335; Rippey to Davis, 29 May 1778, Davis Papers, reel 79; Francis Cluggage to Davis, 24 Sept. 1778, ibid.; David Kennedy to Davis, 16 June 1779, ibid., reel 81; Thomas Smith to Davis, 11 May 1780, ibid., reel 82; Wade to Mitchell, 29 Apr. 1780, ibid.; Davis to Pettit, 28 June 1780, ibid.; Greer to Davis [Jan. 1781],

ibid., reel 83; Owen Biddle to Pettit, 13 June 1780, Biddle Ltrbks.; Polk to NG, 14 Jan. 1781, Greene Papers, WCL; Moore to NG, 25 Dec. 1780, ibid.; Henry Glenn to Quackenbush, 17 July 1781, Hughes Ltrbks., 8; Walter Pynchon to Hughes, 16 Feb. 1782, ibid.; Pickering to Hughes, 4 Nov. 1782, RG 93, reel 25, vol. 123; Hughes to Pickering, 2 Dec. 1782, Hughes Papers; Owen Biddle to Steel, 3 Mar. 1780, Biddle, "Owen Biddle," 319. The only evidence Ferguson, *Power of the Purse*, 72, provides for his contention that merchants were expected to make loans to the government is a citation to Edward Channing, *A History of the United States*, 6 vols. (New York, 1905–1925), 4:114n. Channing, however, is discussing the 1790s, not the revolutionary period. Moreover, Channing's discussion centers on indebtedness of high public officials to the government and does not mention merchants.

55. Biddle to Pettit, 27 Nov. 1779, Biddle Ltrbks.; Biddle to GW, 9 Dec. 1779, Clement Biddle Papers, HSP; Pension application of Epaphroditus Champion, Dann, ed., *Revolution Remembered*, 369. For references that indicate staff officers' widespread use of credit to support the army, see n. 56. Destler, *Connecticut*, 41; for Champion, see ibid., 43. For Bostwick, see Owen Biddle to Clement Biddle [Aug. 1780], Biddle Ltrbks.

56. Duncan to Davis, 25 Oct. 1781, Davis Papers, reel 83. For additional expressions of the breakdown of credit, see Wade to Mitchell, 29 Apr. 1780, ibid., reel 82; Cox and Pettit to president of Congress, 3 July 1779, PCC, reel 98, item 78, 5:362; Steel to Clement Biddle, 5 Nov. 1779, ibid., reel 199, item 192, p. 265; Hay to Pettit, 11 Nov. 1779, ibid., 271; Hooper to Pettit, 28 Feb. 1780, ibid., reel 175, item 155, 1:228; Owen Biddle to Pettit, 6 Mar. 1780, Biddle Ltrbks.; Miller and Tracy to Wadsworth, 14 July 1778, Wadsworth Papers, Box 126; Blaine to Major Forsyth, 6 May 1780, Blaine Papers, reel 2; W. Pickering to Richard Claiborne, 1 July 1781, *VCSP*, 2:194–95; James Madison to Jefferson, 27 Mar. 1780, Madison, *Papers*, 2:6.

57. Steel to Pettit, 5 Nov. 1779, PCC, reel 199, item 192, p. 273; Davis to NG, 25 Jan. 1780, GW Papers, reel 63; Heath to GW, 26 Jan. 1780, ibid.; Owen Biddle to Pettit, 24, 29 Feb. 1780, Biddle Ltrbks.; Colt to Chaloner and White, 17 June 1779, C and W Ltrbks. For other complaints about the lack of cash and consequent lost opportunities to purchase goods, Owen Biddle to Clement Biddle, 14 Oct. 1779, Biddle Ltrbks.; Furman to Pettit, 28 Feb. 1780, PCC, reel 199, item 192, p. 275; Pettit to president of Congress, 2 Mar. 1780, ibid., 290; Chaloner and White to Board of Treasury, 10 Apr. 1779, C and W Coll., Box 8, folder 2; NG to Cox, 28 Nov. 1779, PCC, reel 192, item 173, 2:49. For contractors' refusal to honor their agreements, see NG to GW, 11 May 1780, GW Papers, reel 66; Greer to Davis, 22 Mar. 1780, Davis Papers, reel 82.

58. Greer to Davis, 29 Mar. 1779, Davis Papers, reel 80.

59. Thomas Chase to NG, 7 Dec. 1779, Greene Papers, APS, reel 2, 8:14. See also NG to president of Congress, 12 Dec. 1779, PCC, reel 175, item 155, 1:189; Furman to Cox and Pettit, 29 June 1779, ibid., reel 93, item 78, 5:367; Hay to Pettit, 11 Nov. 1779, ibid., reel 199, item 192, p. 271; Colt to Wadsworth, 16 June 1779, Wadsworth Papers, Box 128; Heath to GW, 26 Jan. 1780, GW Papers, reel 63; Hay to Robert Howe, 14 May 1780, ibid., reel 66; Pickering to President Reed, 12 Nov. 1780, RG 93, reel 25, vol. 123.

60. The best study of the logistical problems besetting the Continental army at Morristown is Bradford, "Hunger Menaces the Revolution." Risch, *QM Support*, 56, writes: "With the supply departments all but paralyzed [the army's] sufferings exceeded those endured by the soldiers at Valley Forge."

61. Wade and Lively, *Glorious Cause*, 52; Norton, *Liberty's Daughters*, 178–88; Kerber, *Women of the Republic*, 99–105; *Pennsylvania Gazette*, 21 June 1780; *JCC*, 17:549–50; Smith, *James Wilson*, 142–45.

62. Edward Stevens to Jefferson, 27 Aug. 1780, *Jefferson Papers*, 3:564; William Smallwood to GW, 7 Jan. 1779, GW Papers, reel 55; Wade and Lively, *Glorious Cause*, 41, 42, 53; Laurens, *Army Correspondence*, 124–25.

63. GW, General Orders, 16 Aug. 1776, 14 May 1779, *GW Writings*, 5:441, 15:67–68; Entry of 3 Nov. 1775, Fogg, *Orderly Book*, 7; Entry of 12 Oct. 1777, Muhlenberg, "Orderly Book," 75; Martin, *Yankee Doodle*, 23. For the plundering of inhabitants, see GW to president of Congress, 5 Jan. 1780, to the magistrates of New Jersey, 8 Jan. 1780, *GW Writings*, 17:357–58, 363; Lauber, ed., *Orderly Books of the Fourth and Second New York Regiments*, 38–39, 56, 114–15.

64. Entry of 30 Dec. 1776, Heath, *Memoirs*, 95; Ward, *War of the Revolution*, 2:539; Wildes, *Anthony Wayne*, 196; Richard Henry Lee to Charles Lee [25 March 1776], *LDC*, 3:439. For privateering, see Risch, *Supplying Washington's Army*, 25, 286; Bowler, *Logistics and the Failure of the British Army*, 95–97; Morgan, "American Privateering," 86.

Chapter 4

1. Risch, *QM Support*, 29–34, 36–37, 40–46. The phrase "gross confusion" is from 37; Johnson, *Commissariat*, 92; Hatch, *Administration*, 98–103.

2. Bezanson, *Prices and Inflation*, 86–87; Nettels, *National Economy*, 25; Ferguson, *Power of the Purse*, 27, 32; Main, *Sovereign States*, 235; Morris, "Labor and Mercantilism," 92–115.

3. Depositions accusing Shippen appeared in the *Pa. Packet*, 9 Sept. 1780. For background on the incident, see Bell, "Court Martial of Dr. William Shippen"; Robert R. Livingston to George Clinton, 23 Sept. 1778, *Clinton Papers*, 4:76; Pennsylvania Council to Colonel Lutterloh, 10 Mar. 1778, *Pa. Arch.*, 1st ser., 6:171.

4. Council of Safety to Representatives of the Freemen of the Commonwealth of Pennsylvania, 24 Dec. 1777, *Pa. Col. Recs.*, 11:390. See also Council of Safety to Clement Biddle, 5 Nov. 1777, *Pa. Arch.*, 1st ser., 5:745; Hening, *Statutes*, 10:496; *Pa. Statutes*, 9:384.

5. Shy, *Toward Lexington*, 168. For English antimilitary attitudes, see above, Prologue; also Schwoerer, "*No Standing Armies!*" For colonial antimilitary attitudes, see Rogers, *Empire and Liberty*, chap. 5; Cress, *Citizens in Arms*, 1–34; Higginbotham, *War of American Independence*, 205–7.

6. Massachusetts, *Journals of Each Provincial Congress*, 150; *Conn. St. Recs.*, 1:17–18. Other states set up similar systems. See *R.I. Acts*, Dec. 1778, 16–17; New York, *Laws*, 1:55–60; Massachusetts, *Acts and Resolves*, 20:392; *Del. Assembly Acts*, 3d sess., 20 Oct. 1778, 13–14; *N.C. Recs.*, 24:3–4, 194–95, 382; *N.J. Assembly Acts*, 1st sess., chap. 59, pp. 124–26.

7. NG to the Committee of Congress, 24 July 1780, PCC, reel 175, item 155, 1:348; *Providence Gazette*, 16 Jan. 1779; *R.I. Acts*, Dec. 1778, 16–17; Justices of Sussex County, New Jersey, 13 Jan. 1780, Wadsworth Papers, Box 130.

8. *Providence Gazette*, 16 Jan. 1779. See also Clinton to Alexander McDougall, 15 Dec. 1778, *Clinton Papers*, 4:388; Maryland Council, 4 May 1778, 12 May 1778, 28 July 1778, *Md. Arch.*, 21:66, 78, 167.

9. New York, *Laws*, 1:58. For additional examples of state efforts to equalize the burden of impressment, see *Pa. Statutes*, 9:181; *N.J. Assembly Acts*, 25 Nov.–12 Dec. 1777, 3; *Del. Assembly Acts*, 3d sess., 20 Oct. 1778, 15; Virginia Council to Mr. Browne, 19 Jan. 1781, *Jefferson Papers*, 4:405–6; Governor Nelson to Charles Carter and James Tutt, 21 Sept. 1781, *VCSP*, 2:474; Rhode Island, *Records*, 8:357; North Carolina Board of War to Robert Burton, 7 Oct. 1780, *N.C. Recs.*, 14:409; President of the Convention to the Committee of Albany, 15 Jan. 1777, *JPCNY*, 2:479.

10. *R.I. Acts*, Dec. 1778, 10. See also *Conn. St. Recs.*, 1:421–22; *N.J. Assembly Acts*, 25 Nov.–12 Dec. 1777, 3; Philadelphia Council of Safety to GW, 20 Dec. 1776, GW Papers, reel 39.

11. *Pa. Statutes*, 9:183; *Del. Assembly Acts*, 3d sess., 20 Oct. 1778, 15; *N.J. Assembly Acts*, 1st sess., 27 Oct. 1776–11 Oct. 1777, 126; Thomas Jefferson to Richard Claiborne and Granville Smith, 24 Mar. 1781, *Jefferson Papers*, 5:225.

12. *Pa. Statutes*, 9:181–82. In 1781 Virginia introduced a similar scheme for providing wagons to the army (Virginia Council to Browne, 19 Jan. 1781, *VCSP*, 1:447–48).

13. Cometti, "Impressment," 102; Brunhouse, *Counter-Revolution in Pennsylvania*, 48; *Pa. Statutes*, 9:384–87.

14. President Wharton to GW, 15 Jan. 1778, *Pa. Arch.*, 1st ser., 6:180. For a sampling of state authorities' complaints, see Massachusetts Council to John Sullivan, 21 Oct. 1778, *Sullivan Papers*, 2:398–99; William Livingston to GW, 16 Feb. 1778, Sparks, ed., *Correspondence of the Revolution*, 2:75–76; Clinton to Udny Hay, 26 May 1779, *Clinton Papers*, 4:849; Jefferson to Baron von Steuben, 10 Mar. 1781, *Jefferson Papers*, 5:120; Governor Rutledge to Colonel Horry, 27 Oct. 1781, Gibbes, ed., *Documentary History of the American Revolution*, 2:198; Abner Nash to the North Carolina Assembly, 28 Jan. 1781, *N.C. Recs.*, 17:717–18.

15. For the relationship between impressment and the increase in disaffection, see Jonathan Bayard Smith to Joseph Reed, 21 Feb. 1778, *LMCC*, 3:94. For the problem of establishing political legitimacy in New York, see Countryman, "Consolidating Power in Revolutionary America." For the constitutional problems in Pennsylvania, see Brunhouse, *Counter-Revolution in Pennsylvania*.

16. Supreme Executive Council to president of Congress, 17 Sept. 1777, *Pa. Arch.*, 1st ser., 5:630.

17. *JCC*, 3:323–24. This power was subsequently renewed and augmented (ibid., 9:1013–15).

18. GW to Timothy Pickering, 24 Apr. 1781, *GW Writings*, 21:498. For a small but representative sampling of GW's persistent aversion to impressment, see GW to David Forman, 24 Nov. 1776, ibid., 6:307; GW to Israel Putnam, 3 Feb. 1777, ibid., 7:97; GW to George Measam, 28 Oct. 1778, ibid., 13:172; GW to Clement Biddle, 29 May 1779, ibid., 15:178; GW to Henry Lee, 24 Aug. 1780, ibid., 19:432; GW to the magistrates of Orange, Ulster, Dutchess, and Westchester counties, 30 Mar. 1781, ibid., 21:391.

19. GW to Hugh Hughes, 25 Apr. 1781, ibid., 21:500. See also GW to James Mease, 15 Oct. 1777, ibid., 9:375; GW to William Irvine, 4 Jan. 1780, ibid., 17:348.

20. GW to Forman, 24 Nov. 1776, ibid., 6:307; GW to Carpenter Wharton, 20 Dec. 1776, ibid., 409; GW to Mease, 15 Oct. 1777, ibid., 9:375; GW, Powers to Officers to Collect Clothing, etc., Nov. 1777, ibid., 10:124–25; GW to the Officers Ordered to Remove Provisions from the Country Near the Enemy, [15?] Dec. 1777, ibid., 163; GW to Clement Biddle, 20 Nov. 1778, ibid., 13:296; GW to Irvine, 4 Jan. 1780, ibid., 17:348; GW, Impress Warrant to Clement Biddle, 11 July 1780, ibid., 19:159; GW to Clement Biddle, 29 May 1779, ibid., 15:178; GW, Instructions to Officers to Collect Provisions, 8 Jan. 1780, ibid., 17:361–62.

21. GW, Instructions to Officers to Collect Provisions, 8 Jan. 1780, ibid., 361. See also GW to Edward Hand, 28 Feb. 1779, ibid., 14:163; GW, Impress Warrant to Hugh Hughes, 24 Apr. 1781, ibid., 21:499; GW, Impress Warrant to Timothy Pickering, 5 Nov. 1781, ibid., 23:335.

22. GW to Livingston, 15 June 1781, ibid., 22:223; GW to president of Congress, 5 Jan. 1779, ibid., 10:267. See also GW, Circular to the States, 27 Aug. 1780, ibid., 19:450.

23. GW to Clinton, 3 Nov. 1779, ibid., 17:67. For the persistence of the problem of plundering, see GW, General Orders, 19 Sept. 1776, 25 Dec. 1777, 30 June 1778, ibid., 72, 10:205–6, 12:132; GW to Benjamin Tallmadge, 2 Nov. 1779, ibid., 17:62; GW to NG, 26 Aug. 1780, ibid., 18:446.

24. GW, General Orders, 5 July 1775, ibid., 3:312; GW, Circular to the States, 27 Aug. 1780, ibid., 19:450. See also GW, General Orders, 1 Jan. 1777, ibid., 6:466; GW to president of Congress, 11 Nov. 1777, 5 Jan. 1778, ibid., 10:37, 267; GW to Putnam, 28 Nov. 1777, ibid., 119; GW to Lutterloh, 20 Dec. 1777, ibid., 179; GW to Pickering, 24 Apr. 1781, ibid., 21:498.

25. GW to Alexander Hamilton, 22 Sept. 1777, ibid., 9:250. See also GW to Measam, 28 Oct. 1778, ibid., 13:172; GW to Jonathan Mifflin, 1 Oct. 1777, ibid., 9:292; GW to Clement Biddle, 29 May 1779, ibid., 15:178.

26. Daniel Brodhead to Samuel Brady, 21 Sept. 1780, *Pa. Arch.*, 1st ser., 8:566; Samuel H. Parsons to Jonathan Trumbull, 2 Nov. 1777, *Trumbull Papers*, 2:183–84; William Heath to William Shepard, 10 Jan. 1780, *Heath Papers*, 5:7; Sullivan to Jabez Bowen, 9 Jan. 1779, *Sullivan Papers*, 2:488; Lord Stirling to NG, 4 Jan. 1779, Reed Papers; NG, General Orders for the Southern Army, 28 Oct. 1782, BV-War-Orderly Books (Nathanael Greene), NYHS; Robert Lawson to Jefferson, 28 Jan. 1781, *Jefferson Papers*, 4:460; James Hendricks to William Davis, 8 Oct. 1781, *VCSP*, 2:531; Instructions to General Nixon from Major-General Charles Lee, 22 Nov. 1776, *Lee Papers*, 2:302; Copy of the Proceedings of a Division General Court Martial, 2 Mar. 1779, PCC, reel 192, item 173, 1:6–7.

27. Flint to Colt, 15 Oct. 1778, Wadsworth Papers, Box 151, Letterbook B. For staff officers' preference for civil impressment over military force, see William Buchanan to Thomas Wharton, 24 Nov. 1777, *Pa. Arch.*, 1st ser., 6:34; Thomas Richardson to Ephraim Blaine, Jan. 1778, Blaine Papers, reel 1; Pickering to Council of New Jersey, 20 Oct. 1780, RG 93, reel 25, vol. 122; Hay to Clinton, 24 June 1778, *Clinton Papers*, 3:487. For evidence of staff officers' dislike of impressment in any form, see John Mitchell to Jacob Morgan, Jr., 21 June 1780, *Pa. Arch.*, 6th ser., 14:219; Pickering to Charles Pettit, 1 Dec. 1780, Pickering Papers, reel 33; John Campbell to Hughes, 25 Feb. 1781, Hughes Ltrbks., 5; Jacob Cuyler to Clinton, 16 June 1778, *Clinton Papers*, 3:461–62; Mitchell to John Davis, 20 May 1779, Davis Papers, reel 81.

28. NG to Nicholas Cooke, July 1777, Rhode Island, "Revolutionary Correspondence," 194. For similar expressions, see Parsons to Trumbull, 2 Nov. 1777, *Trumbull Papers*, 2:184; Brodhead to Brady, 21 Sept. 1780, *Pa. Arch.*, 1st ser., 8:566.

29. NG to GW, 27 May 1779, GW Papers, reel 59. See also Claiborne to Jefferson, 7 Mar. 1781, *Jefferson Papers*, 5:82–83; Pickering to Pettit, 1 Dec. 1780, Pickering Papers, reel 33; Hay to Clinton, 29 June 1778, *Clinton Papers*, 3:497–98; Hay to William Hall, 27 Jan. 1780, PCC, reel 193, item 173, 5:115; James Burnside, Circular Letter to the Inhabitants of Morris County, 8 Dec. 1778, Burnside Ltrbk.; Evans, *Thomas Nelson*, 108.

30. NG to the Committee of Congress, 24 July 1780, PCC, reel 175, item 155, p. 348; NG to GW, 27 May 1779, GW Papers, reel 59. On the difficulty of keeping a mobile army adequately fed, see Johnson, *Commissariat*, 80, 137–38.

31. Sullivan to governor of Rhode Island, 5 Jan. 1779, Rhode Island, *Records*, 8:522–23. Sullivan published a variation of his letter to Governor Cooke in the *Providence Gazette*, 9 Jan. 1779, under the pseudonym "A Freeman" (*R.I. Acts*, Jan. 1779, 2).

32. New York, *Laws*, 1:58–59, 135, 264–65; *Pa. Statutes*, 9:183; *R.I. Acts*, Dec. 1778, 17; Cometti, "Impressment," 104. In New York, justices of the peace were to be fined £50 for failure to cooperate with staff officers (New York, *Laws*, 1:94).

33. Maryland Council to delegates in Congress, 26 March 1779, *Md. Arch.*, 21:328; Journal of the House of Delegates, 25 Nov. 1777, Virginia, *Official Letters of the Governors of Virginia*, 1:205. Pennsylvania made no distinction in who was to seize concealed goods without the owner's permission. It directed its state commissioners to apply to a justice of the peace for a warrant (*Pa. Statutes*, 9:190).

34. Clinton to Benedict Arnold, 24 Aug. 1780, GW Papers, reel 69. See also Clinton to Stirling, 29 Oct. 1781, *Clinton Papers*, 7:456. For other examples of state authorities' legalism, see Massachusetts Council to Sullivan, 21 Oct. 1778. For the dubious distinction between "a marching army and one in quarters," see *Sullivan Papers*, 2:398–99. See also Jefferson to Steuben, 10 Mar. 1781, *Jefferson Papers*, 5:120; Pennsylvania Council to NG, Apr. 1778, *Pa. Col. Recs.*, 11:467.

35. Pennsylvania Council to GW, 13 Apr. 1778, *Pa. Arch.*, 1st ser., 6:416.

36. *R.I. Acts*, Dec. 1778, 17. New York likewise suspended its impressment law only "in cases of an incursion of the enemy" (New York, *Laws*, 1:59).

37. Supreme Executive Council to president of Congress, 17 Sept. 1777, *Pa. Arch.*, 1st ser.,

5:630; Eckenrode, *Revolution in Virginia*, 213–14; Peterson, *Thomas Jefferson*, 208–9. For Virginia's impressment regulations, see above at n. 11.

38. *R.I. Acts*, Jan. 1779, 9; *Pa. Statutes*, 9:189–91; Jefferson to NG, 1 Apr. 1781, *Jefferson Papers*, 5:313–14. Cf. ibid., 6:37n.

39. NG to Jefferson [28 Apr. 1781], *Jefferson Papers*, 5:568, 569. See also Pickering to Andrew Coldilough or Alexander Turner, 1 Dec. 1780, RG 93, reel 25, vol. 123; Sullivan to governor of Rhode Island, 5 Jan. 1779, Rhode Island, *Records*, 8:523; A Return of Horses Impressed by Thomas Hamilton, 3 May 1781, Peter Force Collection, Thomas Hamilton Papers, LC, microfilm, reel 41.

40. Hay to Clinton, 1 Oct. 1778, *Clinton Papers*, 4:129.

41. Bogart to John Bancker, 6 Mar. 1779, Greene Papers, APS, reel 2, 11:80. See also Burnside to Moore Furman, 27 Nov. 1778, Burnside Ltrbk.; Pickering to David Humphreys, 22 Jan. 1781, GW Papers, reel 74; W. Keese to Hughes, 19 Mar. 1781, Hughes Ltrbks., 19; Stewart to Jeremiah Wadsworth, 20 June 1779, Wadsworth Papers, Box 128.

42. Hay to GW, 21 Sept. 1778, GW Papers, reel 52; Jas. Greene, Jr., to Governor Caswell, 14 Feb. 1778, *N.C. Recs.*, 13:47; Wolfe to Hughes, 9 Dec. 1781, Hughes Ltrbks., 10; Andrew Taylor to Clinton, 8 May 1778, *Clinton Papers*, 3:283.

43. NG to president of Congress, 12 Dec. 1779, PCC, reel 193, item 173, 4:249. See also Morgan Lewis to Clinton, 17 June 1780, *Clinton Papers*, 5:844; Lemuel Trescott to Campbell, 4 Jan. 1782, Hughes Ltrbks., 5.

44. *N.J. Assembly Acts*, 1st sess., chap. 59, p. 124. For the historical background, see Pargellis, *Lord Loudoun in North America*, chap. 7; Jensen, *Founding of a Nation*, 211–14. Cf. Shy, *Toward Lexington*, 250–59.

45. NG to GW, 21 Dec. 1779, PCC, reel 193, item 173, 4:346.

46. James Fallon to Clinton, 3 Jan. 1779, *Clinton Papers*, 4:462; Hay to the supervisors, assessors, and justices of the peace, June 1780, ibid., 848; NG to Joseph Lewis, 3 Sept. 1779, PCC, reel 192, item 173, 2:181; Joseph Lewis to Furman, 15 Jan. 1780, Lewis Letters. Magisterial cooperation was particularly valuable in supplying the troops with food at Morristown in 1780. See Bradford, "Hunger Menaces the Revolution," 21–22; Lundin, *Cockpit of the Revolution*, 421–22.

47. For additional complaints of magistrates' unresponsiveness, see Taylor to Clinton, 8 May 1778, *Clinton Papers*, 3:283; Hay to Clinton, 14 Feb. 1779, ibid., 4:566–67; Hughes to Lutterloh, 20 Feb. 1781, Hughes Ltrbks., 1; Wolfe to Hughes, 9 Dec. 1781, ibid., 10; Hughes to Pickering, 8 May 1781, GW Papers, reel 77; Hay to NG, 10 Feb. 1779, Greene Papers, APS, reel 1, 4:63; NG to Pettit, 14 Feb. 1779, ibid., reel 2, 11:7; NG to Henry Hollingsworth, 16 Feb. 1779, PCC, reel 193, item 173, 4:133; NG to the Committee of Congress, 24 July 1780, ibid., reel 175, item 155, 1:347–49; Richard Platt to Humphreys, 29 Mar. 1781, GW Papers, reel 76; Biddle to GW, 11 July 1780, ibid., reel 68; James Brown to NG, 4 Jan. 1781, Greene Papers, WCL; Joseph Lewis to James Gamble, 24 Mar. 1780, Lewis Letters; Lewis to NG, 26 Apr. 1780, ibid.; John Neilson to Pickering, 21 Nov. 1780, RG 93 (M859), Misc. Numbered Records (Manuscript File), reel 80.

48. Hay to the justices of the peace, 23 Jan. 1780, PCC, reel 193, item 173, 5:118.

49. Justices of the peace for Ulster to Uriah Mitchell, 30 Nov. 1781, Hughes Ltrbks., 4.

50. NG to president of Congress, 20 Feb. 1779, PCC, reel 175, item 155, 1:91.

51. The phrase is from Papers of the Proceedings of the Justices of the Peace in Monmouth County, 4 Feb. 1779, ibid., reel 192, item 173, 3:41.

52. Van Harlingen to NG, 18 May 1779, Greene Papers, APS, reel 1, 5:41. Personal economic considerations were undoubtedly a factor. In 1776–77, van Harlingen sustained £626.9.11 in property losses from British attacks (McLachlan, *Princetonians*, 333). These losses coupled with the fact that three of the barns requested were owned by van Harlingen certainly had

something to do with his refusal, but one did not have to be economically self-interested to dislike the military. The uncooperative attitude of justices was common. See Clement Biddle to GW, 11 July 1780, GW Papers, reel 68; Daniel Marsh to GW, 26 Aug. 1780, ibid., reel 70; Brown to NG, 4 Jan. 1781, Greene Papers, WCL; NG to president of Congress, 12 Dec. 1779, PCC, reel 193, item 173, 4:249; NG to John Cox, 28 Nov. 1778, ibid., reel 192, item 173, 2:48; David Rhea to Clement Biddle, 12 Feb. 1779, ibid., 3:37–38.

53. NG to Hay, 16 Feb. 1779, PCC, reel 193, item 173, 4:130.

54. Biddle to GW, 11 July 1780, GW Papers, reel 68; NG to president of Congress, 12 Dec. 1779, PCC, reel 193, item 173, 4:249, 251. For other accounts of magistrates arresting or suing staff officers over impressment, see Hay to NG, 10 Feb. 1779, Greene Papers, APS, reel 1, 4:63; Brown to NG, 4 Jan. 1781, Greene Papers, WCL; NG to Cox, 28 Nov. 1779, PCC, reel 192, item 173, 2:48.

55. Hay to Clinton, 27 May 1778, *Clinton Papers*, 3:369–70. See also Henry Remsen to Robert Yates, 7 Sept. 1776, *JPCNY*, 2:225–26; Pickering to Philip Marsteller, 12 Nov. 1780, RG 93, reel 25, vol. 123.

56. See, for example, Andrew Taylor to the chairman, N. Burgh, 13 Jan. 1778, *Clinton Papers*, 2:672–73; Andrew Bostwick to Clinton, 26 July 1778, ibid., 3:586–87; Hay to Clinton, 23 Apr. 1778, ibid., 4:750.

57. Owen Biddle to Francis Wade, 16 Nov. 1778, Biddle Ltrbks.

58. Duncan to Blaine, 5 May 1781, Blaine Papers, reel 1. For additional complaints, see Col. Wederstrandt to Blaine, 27 Dec. 1779, ibid.; John Chaloner and John White to Blaine, 18 Apr. 1779, C and W Ltrbks.; Owen Biddle to Philip Marsteller, 17 Nov. 1779, Biddle Ltrbks.; Richardson to Owen Biddle, 7 Jan. 1780, Biddle Corr., folder 7; Colt to Wadsworth, 2 Jan. 1779, Wadsworth Papers, Box 127; Cuyler to Wadsworth, 29 Sept. 1780, ibid., Box 131; Blaine to Robert Morris, 19 Feb. 1782, *Morris Papers*, 4:268.

59. NG to president of Congress, 12 Dec. 1779, PCC, reel 175, item 155, 1:190; Owen Biddle to Pettit, 17, 29 Feb. 1780, Biddle Ltrbks.; Clement Biddle to Owen Biddle, 10 Mar. 1780, Biddle Corr., folder 11; Blaine to the Board of Treasury, 24 May 1780, Blaine Papers, reel 2; Blaine to president of Congress, 20 July 1782, ibid.; Wederstrandt to Blaine, 8 Mar. 1783, ibid.; Abraham Smith to Davis, 16 Nov. 1781, Davis Papers, reel 83; Walter Pynchon to Hughes, 16 Feb. 1782, Hughes Ltrbks., 11; Pickering to Nicholas Quackenbush, 2, 27 Dec. 1782, Hughes Papers; Pickering to president of Congress, 25 Feb. 1782, Pickering Papers, reel 34.

60. NG to president of Congress, 16 Feb. 1780, PCC, reel 175, item 155, 1:209.

61. Pynchon to Hughes, 16 Feb. 1782, Hughes Ltrbks., 11; Wadsworth to Chaloner, 11 Mar. 1780, Wadsworth Papers, Box 151, Letterbook I; Patton to Davis, 28 Dec. 1781, Davis Papers, reel 83; Pickering to president of Congress, 30 March 1781, Pickering Papers, reel 33.

62. Pickering to Quackenbush, 22 Jan. 1782, Hughes Ltrbks., 8; Copies of Writs vs N. Quackenbush, ADQM at Albany, Jan. 1782, PCC, reel 199, item 192, p. 99.

63. Pickering to president of Congress, 25 Feb. 1782, Pickering Papers, reel 34; *JCC*, 22:138–39; *Pa. Statutes*, 11:11–14.

64. Pickering to GW, 18 Jan. 1783, Pickering Papers, reel 34; New York, *Laws*, 1:559–60; Pickering and Upham, *Timothy Pickering*, 1:397–99; Clarfield, *Timothy Pickering*, 78.

65. See, for example, Wederstrandt to Blaine, 8 Mar. 1783, Blaine Papers, reel 2; Hughes to Pickering, 27 Dec. 1782, Hughes Papers.

66. Clement Biddle to Thomas Mitchell, 20 Nov. 1778, Washington-Biddle Collection, 1, HSP; Joseph Lewis to Furman, 5 Feb. 1780, Lewis Letters; Hay to Clinton, 28 June 1780, *Clinton Papers*, 5:891.

67. The phrase is from Jeremy Belknap, *History of New Hampshire* (Philadelphia, 1784; Boston, 1791–92), quoted in Adams, *First American Constitutions*, 27.

68. NG to GW, Nov. 1780, quoted in Greene, *Nathanael Greene*, 3:61.

69. Gerth and Mills, eds., *From Max Weber*, chap. 9.

70. GW to Irvine, 4 Jan. 1780, *GW Writings*, 17:348. See also Joseph Lewis to Jonathan Dickinson, 21 Mar. 1780, Lewis Letters.

71. Flint to Cuyler, 10 Sept. 1778, Wadsworth Papers, Box 151, Letterbook: 1778; NG to William R. Davie, 10 Dec. 1780, quoted in Greene, *Nathanael Greene*, 3:75–76. For staff officers' extensive reliance on influence, see Colt to Clinton, 27 Feb. 1779, *Clinton Papers*, 4:589–90; George Morgan to Wadsworth, 29 Apr. 1779, Wadsworth Papers, Box 128; Furman to NG, 9 June 1779, Furman Letters, 8; Owen Biddle to Marsteller, 17 June 1779, Biddle Ltrbks.; Joseph Lewis to Nathaniel Ayers, 21 Mar. 1780, Lewis Letters; Hay to NG, 7 Aug. 1780, GW Papers, reel 69; Hollingsworth to NG, 4 Feb. 1779, Greene Papers, APS, reel 1, 1:19; NG to Furman, 9 Dec. 1779, PCC, reel 193, item 173, 4:204; NG to Colonel Chase, 13 Dec. 1779, ibid., 263.

72. Hay to Clinton, 18 June 1780, *Clinton Papers*, 5:847; Hay to the Inhabitants on both Sides of the Hudson, 14 June 1780, ibid., 848–51.

73. Hay to the supervisors, assessors, and justices of the peace, June 1780, ibid., 848, 851; Taylor to Hay, 20 June 1780, ibid., 869; Hay to Clinton, 21 June 1780, ibid., 868. For additional examples of the use of this informal supply system, see Burnside, Circular Letter to the Justices of the Peace, Morristown, 18 Oct. 1778, Burnside Ltrbk.; Burnside to Furman, 12 Oct. 1778, ibid.; Joseph Lewis to Justice John Carle, 1 Jan. 1780, Lewis Letters; Hay to William Heath, 9 Dec. 1779, *Heath Papers*, 4:332–33; NG to president of Congress, 19 Sept. 1779, PCC, reel 175, item 155, 1:181; Edward Carrington to Thomas Nelson, 7 Sept. 1781, *VCSP*, 2:401.

74. Glen to Quackenbush, 17 July 1781, Hughes Ltrbks., 8 (see also Wolfe to Hughes, 15 Apr. 1781, ibid.; Hughes to Clinton, 1 Dec. 1780, *Clinton Papers*, 6:454); Reed to Blaine, [7–8] Aug. 1780, *Pa. Arch.*, 1st ser., 8:494 (see also Brodhead to President Reed, 17 Oct. 1780, ibid., 589); H. Peckwell to Keese, 4 Mar. 1781, Hughes Ltrbks., 5. For similar reports, see NG to president of Congress, 3 Apr. 1780, PCC, reel 175, item 155, 1:222–23; Robert Howe to GW, 1 May 1780, GW Papers, reel 66; Hughes to Pickering, 8 May 1781, ibid., reel 77; Joseph Lewis to NG, 26 Apr. 1780, Lewis Letters; Pickering to Lt. Strubing, 3 Jan. 1781, RG 93, reel 25, vol. 123.

75. For the war in the South, see Alden, *South in the Revolution*, chaps. 13–16; Ward, *War of the Revolution*, 2:655–896; Weigley, *Partisan War*.

76. Claiborne to Steuben, 18 May 1781, *Jefferson Papers*, 5:667n. For additional examples, see NG to Pickering, 4 April 1781, Greene Papers, WCL; Virginia, *Journals of the Council*, 2:390; David Jameson to Nelson, 18 Sept. 1781, Virginia, *Official Letters of the Governors of Virginia*, 3:57.

77. Claiborne to William Davies, 30 July 1781, *VCSP*, 2:271. See also Thomas Anderson to Davies, 1 Oct. 1781, ibid., 513.

78. Presly Thornton to the governor, 19 Aug. 1781, ibid., 346. See also Richard Henry Lee to GW, 17 Sept. 1781, Sparks, ed., *Correspondence of the Revolution*, 3:409; Fries, ed., *Records of Moravians*, 4:1542; Robert Burton to Thomas Burke, 11 Aug. 1781, *N.C. Recs.*, 15:603.

79. Peyton to Davies, 14 Sept. 1781, *VCSP*, 2:429. See also A. Bohannan to Davies, 9 Aug. 1781, ibid., 308; Bourne Price to Davies, 10 Aug. 1781, ibid., 310. For a report of Pennsylvanians destroying their wagons to avoid impressment, see Reed to GW, 15 July 1780, Sparks, ed., *Correspondence of the Revolution*, 3:22. Other historians have also attributed the breakdown of deference to the effects of the war. See, for example, Hoffman, "'Disaffected' in the Revolutionary South"; Shy, "American Revolution," 154; Shy, "Legacy of the American Revolutionary War," 57–58.

80. Blaine to RM, 2 July 1781, *Morris Papers*, 1:216; Cometti, "Depredations in Virginia," 145. See also McBride, "Virginia War Effort," 161, 196, 275.

Chapter 5

1. Kaplan, "Rank and Status," 325; Bolton, *Private Soldier*, 129.
2. Laurens to Henry Laurens, 26 Nov. 1777, Laurens, *Army Correspondence*, 83. For similar sentiments, see GW to the Board of War, 27 Nov. 1777, *GW Writings*, 10:116; *N.J. Gaz.*, 24 Dec. 1777; *JCC*, 8:609; Kapp, *John Kalb*, 132.
3. Mathews to GW, 15 Sept. 1780, Sparks, ed., *Correspondence of the Revolution*, 3:88.
4. *N.Y. Journ.*, 1 Feb. 1779; *N.J. Gaz.*, 24 Dec. 1777, 7 Apr. 1779. See also *Providence Gazette*, 10 March 1779; *Va. Gaz.*, 13 Nov. 1779, 5 Feb. 1780; *Independent Chronicle* (Boston), 26 Mar. 1778, 26 Oct. 1780.
5. Biddle to Moore Furman, 23 Sept. 1778, Biddle Ltrbks. Criticism of the Hospital Department is quoted in Gibson, *Dr. Bodo Otto*, 274.
6. Tench Tilghman to GW, 19 Feb. 1778, GW Papers, reel 47; *N.J. Gaz.*, 24 Dec. 1777; *Providence Gazette*, 11 Sept. 1779.
7. Livingston to GW, 2 Mar. 1778, quoted in Sedgwick, *William Livingston*, 264; *JCC*, 10:139–40, 242. See also Macmillan, *War Governors*, 214–15.
8. *JCC*, 6:858, 859, 880, 7:355–59, 8:487–89. For the increase in staff personnel, see Chapter 2.
9. See Chapter 3 at n. 16. The increase in the number of public officials occurred throughout the states. Ronald Hoffman notes that in Maryland "between 1776 and 1778 some 913 new positions were established at the county level to enforce the various administrative programs adopted by the legislature" (*Spirit of Dissension*, 223). See also the long list of state commissaries in Van Dusen, "Trade of Revolutionary Connecticut," 277–78; Flick, *Revolution in New York*, 181.
10. *Providence Gazette*, 11 Sept., 23 Oct. 1779, 26 Feb. 1780.
11. NG to John Cox, 20 July 1779, Greene Letters; A Return of Officers by Deputy Quartermaster Morgan Lewis, 12 Feb. 1779, Greene Papers, APS, reel 2, 10:82. Quartermaster camps ranged in size from thirty-five to two hundred men. By 1778 there were three thousand employees in the department (Thayer, *Nathanael Greene*, 228).
12. Lewis to NG, 12 Mar. 1780, Lewis Letters.
13. NG to the Board of War, 25 July 1779, PCC, reel 193, item 173, pp. 32–33.
14. Royster, "Continental Army," 415–19; Royster, "'Nature of Treason,'" 173–75; Lundin, *Cockpit of the Revolution*, 403–7.
15. *N.J. Gaz.*, 17 Mar. 1779.
16. Ferguson, *Power of the Purse*, 30.
17. *Pa. Packet*, 27 Mar. 1779; *N.J. Gaz.*, 17 Mar., 7 Apr., 26 May 1779; *Boston-Gazette*, 6 Apr. 1778; Harlow, "Economic Conditions in Massachusetts during the Revolution," 167–79.
18. For a small sampling, see *N.J. Gaz.*, 17 Mar. 1779; George Clinton to Gouverneur Morris, 18 Dec. 1778, *Clinton Papers*, 4:404–5; Daniel of St. Thomas Jenifer to [?], 26 May 1779, *LMCC*, 4:235–36.
19. *Pa. Packet*, 3 July 1779. See also *N.J. Gaz.*, 26 May 1779; *N.Y. Journ.*, 1 Feb. 1779; *Va. Gaz.*, 5 Feb. 1780.
20. Fitch to NG, 12 Apr. 1779, John Fitch Papers, CSL; *N.Y. Journ.*, 1 Feb. 1779.
21. *N.J. Gaz.*, 26 May 1776. For additional sources, see Carp, "Supplying the Revolution," chap. 5, n. 31.
22. *Va. Gaz.*, 5 Feb. 1780; *N.J. Gaz.*, 10 Mar., 7 Apr. 1779. The logic was common. See, for example, *Va. Gaz.*, 5 Feb. 1780; Henry Laurens, Notes of Proceedings [17 May 1779], *LMCC*, 4:215.
23. Bezanson, *Prices and Inflation*, 12, 13, 82–83. Prices rose throughout the country. See Gray, *History of Agriculture*, 2:587–88; Russell, *Long Deep Furrow*, 224; Cometti, "Inflation in Revolutionary Maryland."

24. Blaine to John Patton, 25 Aug. 1777, Society Collection, Case 19, Box 14, HSP. For similar instructions, see Furman to Daniel Marsh, 16 Aug. 1779, *Furman Letters*, 12–13; Biddle to Robert Hooper, 17 Aug. 1778, Biddle Ltrbks.; John Chaloner and John White to Azariah Dunham, 29 Sept. 1778, C and W Ltrbks.; Bezanson, *Prices and Inflation*, 89; Johnson, *Commissariat*, 83, 94.

25. Furman to Jacob Tagart, 13 Oct. 1779, *Furman Letters*, 23. For compliance, see Henry Hollingsworth to Biddle, 12 Feb. 1780, Biddle Corr., folder 9.

26. Biddle to Jacob Morgan, 24 Sept. 1778, Biddle Ltrbks.; Biddle to William Finnie, 3 Aug. 1779, ibid.; Chaloner and White to Jeremiah Wadsworth, 20 Apr. 1779, C and W Ltrbks.; Peter Colt to Royal Flint, 5 Oct. 1778, Wadsworth Papers, Box 127; Destler, *Connecticut*, 19, 23; Johnson, *Commissariat*, 94.

27. Jacob Cuyler to Wadsworth, 20 July 1778, Wadsworth Papers, Box 126; Furman to Clement Biddle, 27 Nov. 1779, *Furman Letters*, 41; Furman to [NG?], 18 Oct. 1779, ibid., 25; Owen Biddle to Morgan, 23 Jan. 1779, Biddle Ltrbks.

28. Burnside to Charles Stewart, 15 Nov. 1778, Burnside Ltrbk. See also GW to NG, 22 Sept. 1778, *GW Writings*, 16:79; Furman to Clement Biddle, 27 Nov. 1779, *Furman Letters*, 41; Furman to Samuel Flanaghan, 13 Oct. 1779, ibid., 18; Owen Biddle to Furman, 23 Sept. 1778, Biddle Ltrbks.; Joseph Lewis to Furman, 31 Jan. 1780, Lewis Letters; Bezanson, *Prices and Inflation*, 116.

29. Owen Biddle to Finnie, 28 Oct. 1778, Biddle Ltrbks.; Mitchell to James Sutter, 31 May 1781, *Pa. Arch.*, 6th ser., 14:209. For other examples, see NG to Nehemiah Hubbard, 17 Sept. 1779, Ely Collection, NJHS; Chaloner and White to Gouverneur Morris, 29 May 1779, C and W Ltrbks.; Owen Biddle to Cornelius Sheriff, 24 Sept. 1778, Biddle Ltrbks. Anticipating price rises, some staff officers devised schemes to prevent them. See, for example, Colt to Flint, 5 Oct. 1778, Wadsworth Papers, Box 127; Owen Biddle to Thomas Richardson, 25 Oct. 1779, Biddle Ltrbks.; Buel, *Dear Liberty*, 151.

30. Owen Biddle to John Davis, 25 Sept. 1778, Biddle Ltrbks.; Furman to Clement Biddle, 27 Nov. 1779, *Furman Letters*, 41; Clement Biddle to Hubbard, 17 Oct. 1778, Clement Biddle Papers, HSP; Wadsworth to Cuyler, 2 Oct. 1779, Wadsworth Papers, Box 151, Letterbook G.

31. Furman to Clement Biddle, 27 Nov. 1779, *Furman Letters*, 41.

32. Wadsworth to Blaine, 18 July 1779, Wadsworth Papers, Box 151, Letterbook E; Wadsworth to Blaine, 30 June 1779, ibid. For other examples of staff officers' hard-nosed attitude toward fraud and corruption, see Owen Biddle to Henry Archer, 5 Jan. 1780, Biddle Ltrbks.; Chaloner and White to John Ladd Howell, 21 Dec. 1778, C and W Ltrbks.; Flint to Jonathan Childs and Isaac Tickner, 10 Dec. 1779, Wadsworth Papers, Box 151, Letterbook F; Fitch to Stewart, 3 Oct. 1779, Stewart Papers, NYSHA.

33. NG to William Greene, 11 Sept. 1778, Rhode Island, "Revolutionary Correspondence," 217–18, quotation on 217. See also NG to GW, 16 Sept. 1778, Sparks, ed., *Correspondence of the Revolution*, 2:206.

34. Pettit to GW, 10 Sept. 1778, PCC, reel 199, item 192, pp. 225-26; Owen Biddle to Morgan, 23 Dec. 1779, Biddle Ltrbks.; *JCC*, 14:809.

35. Wadsworth to Blaine, 5 Oct. 1778, Wadsworth Papers. For Wadsworth's strenuous objections to Connecticut's regulating act, see Wadsworth to John Hancock, 22 May 1778, Wadsworth Papers, Box 151, Letterbook A; Wadsworth to Samuel Huntington and Oliver Wolcott, 27 May 1778, ibid.

36. NG to Morgan Lewis, 15 Dec. 1779, PCC, reel 193, item 173, 4:280; NG to Furman, 11 July 1779, ibid., reel 192, item 173, 2:70; Johnson, *Commissariat*, 104–5, 134–35.

37. *JCC*, 7:267. Subsequent investigation by the Committee of Congress to Camp found these charges to be groundless. See Bodle and Thibaut, *Valley Forge*, 1:214, 2:159, 239.

38. Pettit to NG, 13 May 1779, Greene Papers, APS, reel 1, 7:90; George Morgan to

Wadsworth, 29 Apr. 1779, Wadsworth Papers, Box 128; Flint to Cuyler, 28 Aug. 1778, ibid., Box 151, Letterbook: 1778; Calhoun to David Greer and Davis, 13 Nov. 1778, Davis Papers, reel 80; Owen Biddle to Francis Wade, 30 July 1779, Biddle Ltrbks.; Chaloner and White to Patrick Ewing, 8 Aug. 1778, C and W Ltrbks.; Timothy Pickering to Jabez Hatch, 8 Nov. 1780, RG 93, reel 25, vol. 123.

39. Bezanson, *Prices and Inflation*, 19–20, 59–60, 88; Gray, *History of Agriculture*, 582; Destler, *Connecticut*, 35; Main, *Sovereign States*, 233.

40. Buel, "Time," 135.

41. GW to the Massachusetts legislature, 29 Aug. 1775, *GW Writings*, 3:455; *JCC*, 4:404, 397–98; Destler, *Connecticut*, 24. Monopolizing the wheat crop seems to have been a fairly common practice in New York. See Harrington, *New York Merchant*, 78. For other examples of speculative practices, see *JCC*, 6:906, 915–16, 1014; Force, ed., *American Archives*, 4th ser., 5:85–86.

42. Owen Biddle to Furman, 23 Sept. 1778, Biddle Ltrbks.; Flint to Tilghman, 8 Nov. 1778, GW Papers, reel 54; Johnson, *Commissariat*, 143, 144, 151; Hoffman, *Spirit of Dissension*, 244–45.

43. Colt to Wadsworth, 26 Oct. 1778, Conn. Arch., ser. 1, vol. 13, Doc. 48. For similar complaints, see Samuel McClellan to Colt, 5 Nov. 1778, Wadsworth Papers, Box 129; James Watson to Wadsworth, 7 May 1779, ibid., Box 128; Chaloner and White to Blaine, 18 Apr. 1779, C and W Ltrbks.; Colt to Clinton, 9 Nov. 1778, *Clinton Papers*, 4:258. The denunciation of speculators was widespread. For a sampling, see GW to Joseph Reed, 12 Dec. 1778, *GW Writings*, 13:383; *JCC*, 9:1071–72, 12:974–75, 14:650.

44. *Conn. St. Recs.*, 2:266–67, quotation on 266; Hening, *Statutes*, 9:382–84; *N.J. Assembly Acts*, 1st sitting, 4th sess., Oct.–Dec. 1779, 23–25; *N.C. Recs.*, 13:18, 19, 29, 47–48; South Carolina, *Statutes at Large*, 4:395-96, 402-3; *Pa. Statutes*, 9:177–80, 326–28, 421–32; *R.I. Acts*, Dec. 1776, 30–38, May 1777, 17–29; New York, *Laws*, 1:92–94.

45. Wadsworth to Clinton, 28 Feb. 1779, Wadsworth Papers, Box 127.

46. *JCC*, 10:71–72. See also Royster, *Revolutionary People at War*, 47–48; Colt to Wadsworth, 26 Oct. 1778, Conn. Arch., ser. 1, vol. 13, Doc. 48. For similar problems, see Chaloner and White to Ewing, 23 Oct. 1778, C and W Ltrbks.; Flint to Wadsworth, 22 Jan. 1779, Wadsworth Papers, Box 151, Letterbook D; Council of Maryland to the Chevalier de La Luzerne, 24 Jan. 1780, *Md. Arch.*, 43:66.

47. Colt to Clinton, 9 Nov. 1778, *Clinton Papers*, 4:258; Destler, *Connecticut*, 35; Johnson, *Commissariat*, 148; Ward, *War of the Revolution*, 2:587–93.

48. Kennett, *French Forces in America*, 71–72, 74, 133, 138; Stinchcombe, *French Alliance*, 37; Bezanson, *Prices and Inflation*, 135; Van Dusen, *Connecticut*, 159; Bond, *State Government in Maryland*, 91; Buel, *Dear Liberty*, 241–42. French gold was particularly disruptive in the South. See Jason Hendricks to Col. Davis, 21 Sept. 1781, *VCSP*, 2:476; Richard Claiborne to David Jamison, 25 Sept. 1781, ibid., 496.

49. Quoted in Stillé, *Anthony Wayne*, 157; Wildes, *Anthony Wayne*, 146, 153. See also Hollingsworth to Owen Biddle, 10 Feb. 1780, Biddle Corr., folder 9; Lossing, *Philip Schuyler*, 1:436–37.

50. Sullivan to GW, 29 Nov. 1778, Wadsworth Papers, Box 127; Sullivan to Colt, 10 Nov. 1778, *Sullivan Papers*, 2:428; Sullivan to GW, 20 Nov. 1778, ibid., 438–40; McClellan to Colt, 5 Nov. 1778, Wadsworth Papers, Box 129; GW to Sullivan, 18 Nov. 1778, *GW Writings*, 13:277–78; Whittemore, *General of the Revolution*, 112–15. For Colt's complaint, see Colt to Sullivan, 6 Nov. 1778, *Sullivan Papers*, 2:423–25. Colt vigorously denied Sullivan's charges of negligence. Colt claimed that Sullivan did not keep him regularly informed of daily food expenditures or the low state of his magazines. In addition, the Commissary Department was short of provisions because of the urgent demand for flour by the French fleet at Boston, a British

excursion into New Jersey that interrupted supplies coming from Pennsylvania, and French agents and "private Jobbers" outbidding staff officers for flour in New York. Colt also claimed that as soon as the matter was brought to his attention, he made every effort to supply Sullivan. See Colt to Sullivan, 9 Nov. 1778, *Sullivan Papers*, 4:257–58. Staff officers stood little chance in confrontations with Continental line officers. A court of inquiry found the commissaries responsible for the shortage of food and declared that their negligence proceeded from a fondness for their private interest. Nothing more was done. Sullivan's biographer notes, however, that the court of inquiry was "certainly not an impartial body" (Whittemore, *General of the Revolution*, 114–15).

51. Nuxoll, "Munitions Merchants," 96–97.

52. Johnson, *Commissariat*, 100–103; *JCC*, 10:176–77; Memorial of [Pennsylvania] Council and Assembly to Congress, 6 Mar. 1778, *Pa. Arch.*, 1st ser., 6:333–36. For Hooper's problems with Pennsylvania, see *JCC*, 13:453n–454n; Brunhouse, *Counter-Revolution in Pennsylvania*, 47–48; Mintz, *Gouverneur Morris*, 95–96. For competition between state and army purchasers, see R. Allison to Wadsworth, 13 Aug. 1778, Wadsworth Papers, Box 126; William Kennon to Charles Lee, 7 Dec. 1776, *Lee Papers*, 2:333–34; Johnson, *Commissariat*, 155, 157; Crittenden, *Commerce of North Carolina*, 147–48; Bond, *State Government in Maryland*, 48.

53. Dashiell quoted in Hoffman, *Spirit of Dissension*, 230–31. See also *JCC*, 13:59. For trading with the enemy, see Leiby, *War in the Hackensack Valley*, 109–11; Buel, "Time," 140–43; East, *Business Enterprise*, 180–88; Calhoon, *Loyalists in Revolutionary America*, 326–27; Van Dusen, "Trade of Revolutionary Connecticut," 359–62.

54. Rodney to John Dickinson, 17 Apr. 1779, *Rodney Letters*, 299.

55. Benjamin Rush to John Morgan [? June 1779], Rush, *Letters*, 1:225–26.

56. Jason Craik to Jonathan Potts, 4 Mar. 1780, Potts Papers, LC; Richard Henry Lee to William Shippen, 18 Apr. 1779, *RH Lee Letters*, 2:45–46; *Providence Gazette*, 11 Sept. 1779.

57. Clinton to Gouverneur Morris, 18 Dec. 1778, *Clinton Papers*, 4:404–5; Clinton to Wadsworth, 4 Jan. 1779, Wadsworth Papers, Box 127.

58. New York, *Laws*, 1:117; president of Congress to GW, 20 Nov. 1778, Sparks, ed., *Correspondence of the Revolution*, 2:236; Ferguson, *Power of the Purse*, 70.

59. Owen Biddle to Wade, 26 Oct. 1778, Biddle Ltrbks. For additional examples of staff officers not condoning corruption, see Flint to Childs and Tickner, 10 Dec. 1779, Wadsworth Papers, Box 151, Letterbook H; Wadsworth to Blaine, 27 Oct. 1779, ibid., Letterbook G; Pettit to Davis, 3 Sept. 1779, Davis Papers, reel 81; Chaloner and White to Mathew Thomas and John Irwin, 15 Sept. 1778, C and W Ltrbks.; NG to Uriah Mitchell, 20 July 1779, Etting Coll., 3:12.

60. Wadsworth to Clinton, 28 Feb. 1779, Wadsworth Papers, Box 127. See also Wadsworth to Clinton, 28 Feb. 1779, Dreer Coll., 5:86. Wadsworth's activities as commissary general of purchases have been misrepresented by East, *Business Enterprise*, 86. East claims that Wadsworth "indirectly admitted . . . that he was carrying on private trade in cattle and other things." There is no evidence to support this charge. In the letter East quotes, Wadsworth vehemently denied the charge. East was probably misled because Wadsworth summarizes his accuser's charges at the beginning of the letter only to deny them later. See Wadsworth to Stephen Keyes, 6 Apr. 1779, Wadsworth Papers, Box 151, Letterbook E. For the demands of other staff officers to be investigated, see Hay to Horatio Gates, 4 Feb. 1779, Gates Papers; Colt to Wadsworth, 28 Aug. 1779, Wadsworth Papers, Box 129; Hooper to Wadsworth, 23 Aug. 1779, ibid.; *Pa. Gaz.*, 20 Aug. 1778; *New York Packet*, 4, 23 Jan. 1781.

61. *N.Y. Journ.*, 8 Feb., 15 Mar. 1779. Hay's call for an investigation appeared in the 8 February issue. The quotation is from the 15 March issue. NG identified Hay as " Q U A R - T E R M A S T E R" (NG to Wadsworth, 25 Mar. 1779, Wadsworth Papers). I am indebted to Richard K. Showman for this information.

62. *Va. Gaz.*, 11 Dec. 1779; *N.J. Gaz.*, 21 Apr., 2 June 1779.

63. *N.J. Gaz.*, 26 May 1779.

64. *Va. Gaz.*, 5 Feb. 1780.

65. *N.J. Gaz.*, 10 Nov. 1779. For the initial accusation, see ibid., 12 May 1779.

66. Committee for Hanover Precinct, 12 Aug. 1779, Wadsworth Papers, Box 129.

67. *Pa. Gaz.*, 25 Aug. 1779. This is the only public defense of staff officers that I have found that did not originate from within their own ranks. Of course, it is possible that the author was a member of one of the staff departments, despite his denial.

68. *N.J. Arch.*, 2d ser., 3:431, 639; *Boston-Gazette*, 15 May 1780; *N.J. Gaz.*, 15 May 1779; *Va. Gaz.*, 13 Nov. 1779.

69. *JCC*, 10:39–40, 139–40, 356–57, 249, 11:591–92, 813.

70. Ibid., 11:787–88, 12:1083; John Fell Diary [22–26 Jan., 15, 16 Feb. 1779], *LMCC*, 4:44, 71; William Paca to the Pennsylvania Council, 9 Mar. 1779, ibid., 93–94; *JCC*, 13:453n–454n.

71. See, for example, Burnett, *Continental Congress*, chap. 19; Ferguson, *Power of the Purse*, 81–94; Rakove, *Beginnings of National Politics*, 249–74.

72. See the excellent discussion in Rakove, *Beginnings of National Politics*, 270–73. Ferguson, *Power of the Purse*, 104, has his chronology backward. He states that the Deane-Lee controversy reached its climax in a "disturbed era of scandal" involving the staff departments. But the events he describes—corruption in the Hospital Department, the 9 July resolution, the reorganization of the staff departments, and the problems with Wadsworth's and Greene's accounts (pp. 99–102)—occurred after the Deane-Lee affair was over.

73. Lee to Shippen, 18 Apr. 1779, *LMCC*, 4:163; Bell, *John Morgan*, 226. Privately, many congressmen were keenly aware that Congress's excessive currency emissions were responsible for the depreciation. See, for example, Samuel Adams to John Winthrop, 6 Feb. 1779, Adams, *Writings*, 4:121; James Duane to Clinton, 3 Jan. 1779, *LMCC*, 4:2; William Whipple to Josiah Bartlett, 3 Jan. 1779, ibid., 5. Publicly, however, they defended the necessity of issuing large amounts of paper currency and blamed the depreciation on speculators and "the misconduct of inferior officers in the public service" (*JCC*, 14:649–50).

74. *JCC*, 13:492, 14:519.

75. Ibid., 14:812–13.

76. Ibid., 813–14. Ferguson, *Power of the Purse*, 105, mistakenly claims that the first conflict of interest law was enacted in 1789. Out of twenty-nine votes cast, only Virginia's Meriwether Smith voted against the measure. Not surprisingly, Smith was under attack at the time by the Virginia Assembly for mixing private with public business (Henderson, *Party Politics*, 205). The statute was reenacted in March 1780 and was extended in September 1780 to include personnel in the Hospital Department (*JCC*, 16:302, 18:876–77).

77. *JCC*, 14:812, 650. Cf. Rakove, *Beginnings of National Politics*, 211.

78. Macmillan, *War Governors*, 214 n. 86, exaggerates the responsiveness of state executives to the congressional resolution of 9 February 1778 by citing the actions of Delaware's President Caesar Rodney and South Carolina's Governor Rawlins Lowndes. She is mistaken in citing Rodney's action because it was in response to the 9 July 1779 resolution, not the one in 1778. See Rodney to James Booth, 20 July 1779, *Rodney Letters*, 310. And as Macmillan notes, Congress had to remind Lowndes that he already had authority under the 9 February 1778 resolution to discipline the errant quartermaster. Lowndes's request for authority reveals that he was unaware of Congress's resolution and was acting independently. See also Henry Laurens to William Moultrie, 18 May [1778], *LMCC*, 3:253. For responses of other states, see Supreme Executive Council, Minutes, 21 June 1779, *Pa. Col. Recs.*, 12:27; Report of a Committee of Council [to Investigate Abuses in the Staff Departments, Massachusetts], 6 Jan. 1779, Greene Papers, APS, reel 2, 11:85; Jonathan Trumbull to the Committee of Congress, 10 Dec. 1778, *Trumbull Papers*, 2:320–21.

79. New York, *Laws*, 1:117–18; *Del. Assembly Acts*, 3d sess., 13.

80. *N.J. Assembly Acts*, 2d sitting, 3d sess., May–June 1779, 70–83, quotation on 71. This was perhaps the first "windfall profits" tax in American history. NG to Pettit, 29 July 1779, Greene Papers, APS, reel 2, 11:4; NG to Jay, 24 June 1779, ibid., reel 1, 6:96.

81. NG to John Jay, 24 June 1779, Greene Papers, APS, reel 1, 6:96; Thayer, *Nathanael Greene*, 265; John Fell Diary, 1 July 1779, *LMCC*, 4:292–93; *JCC*, 14:808. A week earlier a congressional committee had issued an even less sympathetic report (ibid., 779–80). When by August, New Jersey authorities had given no sign they would act in accordance with the committee's recommendation, Pettit and Cox tendered their resignations. A congressional committee reconsidered the problem and reversed the earlier committee's findings. The new committee concluded that Pettit and Cox's grievance was "well founded." Consequently, their resignations were refused and a promise made to them that they would both be indemnified for any tax New Jersey assessed. As a result, both assistant quartermasters were persuaded to remain at their posts (*JCC*, 14:930–33; Pettit to president of Congress, 20 Oct. 1779, PCC, reel 199, item 192, pp. 253–54). In the following year, New Jersey refrained from singling out staff officers for purposes of taxation. See *N.J. Assembly Acts*, 1st sitting, 4th sess., Oct.–Dec. 1779, 3–15.

82. *JCC*, 13:453n–454n.

83. Reed to delegates in Congress, 15 July 1779, *Pa. Arch.*, 1st ser., 7:557; Livingston, Proclamation, 25 Aug. 1779, *N.J. Arch.*, 2d ser., 3:567–70. Connecticut authorities issued a similar proclamation (Governor and Committee of Safety of Connecticut, 11 Sept. 1779, *Conn. St. Recs.*, 2:395–96). See also Rodney to Booth, 20 July 1779, *Rodney Letters*, 310; *Conn. St. Recs.*, 2:473–77. Connecticut later ordered five staff officers to appear in person before the state committee charged with investigating corruption in the staff departments. See Connecticut General Assembly to Hubbard, Colt, Henry Champion, Elizah Hubbard, and George Starr, 30 Mar. 1780, GW Papers, reel 65.

84. Hay to Gates, 11 Aug. 1779, Gates Papers. For similar responses, see NG to Pettit, 29 July 1779, Greene Papers, APS, reel 2, 11:4; NG to Clinton, 27 July 1779, PCC, reel 192, item 173, 2:25; Hay to the assistant deputy quartermasters, 24 July 1779, Fisher Papers, reel 1; Assistant deputy quartermasters to Hay, 24 July 1779, Wadsworth Papers, Box 128; Colt to Wadsworth, 29 July 1779, C and W Ltrbks.; Banks to Furman, 24 July 1779, Furman Papers.

85. NG to Clinton, 27 July 1779, PCC, reel 192, item 173, 2:25; NG to Jay, 28 July 1779, ibid., 157–58.

86. Colt to Wadsworth, 29 July 1779, Wadsworth Papers, Box 128; Hubbard to Wadsworth, 20 July 1779, ibid.; NG to Hubbard, 21 July 1779, Greene Papers, WCL; NG to Cox, 20 July 1779, Greene Letters, NJHS; NG to Jay, 28 July 1779, PCC, reel 192, item 173, 2:157.

87. NG to Jay, 28 July 1779, PCC, reel 192, item 173, 2:157–58, 172–73; NG to Moses Hazen, 29 July 1779, ibid., 93–94; NG to Hay, 26 July 1779, ibid., 87; NG to Ephraim Bowen, 12 Sept. 1779, ibid., reel 193, item 173, 4:45; NG to Hubbard, 11 Apr. 1780, Greene Papers, WCL; Colt to Wadsworth, 6 Aug. 1779, Wadsworth Papers, Box 129.

88. Pettit to Davis, 3 Sept. 1779, Davis Papers, reel 81; Hugh Hughes to Nicholas Quackenbush, 7 Nov. 1780, Hughes Ltrbks., 8; NG to Furman, 11 July 1779, PCC, reel 192, item 173, 2:70.

89. NG to Mitchell, 20 July 1779, Etting Coll.

90. Pickering to Hughes, 31 Aug. 1780, Hughes Papers; Pickering to Aaron Forman, 20 Oct. 1780, Pickering Papers, reel 5; Pickering to W. Davies, 19 Oct. 1780, RG 93, reel 25, vol. 122. For an informative discussion of Pickering's opposition to aristocracy, see McLean, "Timothy Pickering," 145–46.

91. Hughes to David Wolfe, 4 Mar. 1781, Hughes Ltrbks., 10. See also Davis to Daniel Brodhead, 25 Sept. 1780, Davis Papers, reel 82.

92. Conn. Arch., vol. 19, Doc. 257.

93. Macmillan, *War Governors*, 214n. For staff officers accused of fraud or corruption and subsequently cleared, see *JCC*, 9:1093, 10:230–31, 11:741, 831–33, 14:724; Ferguson, *Power of the Purse*, 98, 99. For the results of other investigations, see Pennsylvania Supreme Executive Council, 21 June 1779, *Pa. Col. Recs.*, 12:27; Trumbull to the Committee of Congress, 10 Dec. 1778, *Trumbull Papers*, 2:320–21; Report of Committee of Council [to Investigate Abuses in the Staff Department, Massachusetts], 6 Jan. 1779, Greene Papers, APS, reel 2, 11:85; Johnson, *Commissariat*, 157. I have not included minor figures who held office for only a short time. Lists of officeholders are conveniently located in Thian, *Legislative History of the General Staff*, 140, 238, 361.

94. For Hay, see New York, *Laws*, 1:117. For Hughes, see *Greene Papers*, 2:329n. For Champion, see *Conn. St. Recs.*, 2:531.

95. Wood, "Conspiracy and the Paranoid Style," quotations on 417, 421.

96. Morgan, "Puritan Ethic," 91–92, 95, 98–100. These ideas and values complemented and reinforced important aspects of republican ideology. For a fresh and insightful discussion of luxury and commerce in republican ideology, see McCoy, *Elusive Republic*, chaps. 1–3.

97. Quoted in Thayer, "Army Contractors," 32. For the illegal wartime activities of merchants, see White, *Beekmans of New York*, 163, 224–29, 282–83; Weaver, *Jonathan Trumbull*, 40, 78–79; Hedges, *Browns of Providence Plantations*, vol. 1, chap. 3; Leach, *Arms for Empire*, 269–70.

98. Harrington, *New York Merchant*, 57, 65; Baxter, *House of Hancock*, 62; White, *Beekmans of New York*, 265 and chap. 8; Ferguson, *Power of the Purse*, 71.

99. Freeman, *GW*, 5:505–9; Thayer, *Nathanael Greene*, 229–38.

100. See Proceedings of a Court of Inquiry held at Morristown, 21 Sept. 1779, BV-War of the Revolution, NYHS. For the distinction between private and public, see Davis to Thomas Smith, 27 Apr. 1780, Davis Papers, reel 82. NG's statement that "I make a standing rule Never to make up of the Public money for any private purposes whatever" has stood up to the scrutiny of modern scholars. See Thayer, *Nathanael Greene*, 232; Freeman, *GW*, 5:505–9, Appendix V-2. No staff officer ever justified the use of public money for private purposes.

101. Charges against Mr. Ebenezer Clarke, Issuing Commissary to General Poor's Brigade, 23 Feb. 1779, Fitch Papers; Alexander McDougall to William Heath, 14 Nov. 1780, *Heath Papers*, 3:132; GW, General Orders, 11 Jan. 1778, *GW Writings*, 10:289; Rhode Island, *Records*, 8:378–79; Johnson, *Commissariat*, 47. The confusion over the two groups of soldiers was helped along by brigade quartermasters, who were frequently assigned the duties of deputy quartermasters without special appointment. See NG to General Putnam, 10 Feb. 1779, PCC, reel 193, item 173, 4:85.

102. Wadsworth to Clinton, 28 Feb. 1779, Wadsworth Papers, Box 127. Governor Clinton often attested to Wadsworth's trustworthiness and reliability. See, for example, Clinton to Gouverneur Morris, 18 Dec. 1778, *Clinton Papers*, 4:404.

103. Wade to Rodney, 14 Sept. 1779, *Rodney Letters*, 318–20, esp. 320. For Morgan, see Applegate, "Medical Administrators," 5.

104. Shippen to Lee, 22 June 1779, *LMCC*, 4:282; *Pa. Packet*, 3 July 1779.

105. Whipple to Bartlett, 21 May 1779, Bartlett, *Papers*, 255.

106. Morgan, "Puritan Ethic," 97–98, 109–10; Wood, *Creation of the American Republic*, 65–70, 412–25; Pocock, *Machiavellian Moment*, chaps. 14–15.

107. Quoted in Rakove, *Beginnings of National Politics*, 204.

108. Wood, "Rhetoric and Reality in the American Revolution," 31.

109. Rakove, *Beginnings of National Politics*, 209; Risch, *QM Support*, 54–55.

110. For an example of a similar psychological reaction, see Royster, "'Nature of Treason,'" 163–93.

111. Chaloner and White to Wadsworth, 16 Mar. 1780, Wadsworth Papers, Box 130. See also George Morton to Blaine, 23 Mar. 1780, Blaine Papers, reel 2; Joseph Lewis to Peter Thinnan, 17 Sept. 1780, Lewis Letters; John Cochran to Abraham Clark, 28 Feb. 1781, Cochran, *Surgeon to Washington*, 98–99.

112. Salaried workers, such as Quartermaster Department clerks, tried to collect wages owed them, but it is unclear whether they ever received their due. See Records of Accounts of the Commissioner for Settling the Accounts of the Quartermaster Department, May 1786–Mar. and Apr. 1790, RG 93, reel 24, vol. 101.

113. Udny Hay, Accounts, 1776–78, 23 May 1788, PCC, reel 48, item 41, 4:262–63; Report of the Board of Treasury on the Memorial of Donald Campbell, 30 July 1787, ibid., reel 151, item 138, 1:170–71; Thayer, *Nathanael Greene*, 232. Neither of Thayer's two sources supports his contention that NG made $170,000. In fact, it is highly unlikely that NG received any pay for his public service. Congress refused to honor staff officers' claims without documentation, and NG was never able to account for $86 million disbursed to his deputies.

114. NG to GW, 21 May 1780, PCC, reel 46, item 39, 1:209. See also Pickering to Samuel Miles, 12 June 1781, RG 93, reel 26, vol. 127.

115. Furman to Jacob Tagart, 27 Apr. 1780, Moore Furman Papers, Box 15, NJSL; Ferguson, *Power of the Purse*, 188; NG to John Davis, 7 May 1780, Davis Papers, reel 82; Stewart to Samuel Gray, 12 July 1779, Stewart Papers, LC.

116. List of Accounts . . . of the Commissary Department, 17 Sept. 1788, PCC, reel 155, item 143, pp. 131–33; List of Accounts . . . of the Quartermaster Department, 17 Sept. 1788, ibid., 141–43. By 1790, more than four hundred accounts remained unsettled in the staff departments. By the mid-1790s the number had declined to three hundred (Ferguson, *Power of the Purse*, 191, 192).

117. *N.J. Gaz.*, 25 Oct. 1780; Morgan Lewis to NG, 4 Feb. 1780, Greene Papers, APS, reel 1, 1:173; John Davis to Pettit, 12 Feb. 1780, Davis Papers, reel 81.

118. Morgan Lewis to NG, 4 Feb. 1780, Greene Papers, APS, reel 1, 1:173; Wade to Owen Biddle, 28 Feb. 1780, Biddle Corr., folder 10; Hollingsworth to Owen Biddle, ibid., folder 9; William Milan to Wade, 26 Feb. 1780, Greene Papers, APS, reel 1, 3:63; Davis to Pettit, 12 Feb. 1780, Davis Papers, reel 81; Owen Biddle to Pettit, 10 May 1780, Biddle Ltrbks.

119. Blaine to Joseph Hugg, Jonathan Hugg, Jonathan Patton, and John Howell, 9 July 1780, Blaine Papers, reel 2; Blaine, Circular Letter, 2 Nov. 1780, ibid.; Blaine to RM, 19 Feb. 1782, ibid.; Memorial of Ephraim Blaine to Congress, 20 Apr. 1787, PCC, reel 48, item 41, 1:443–44. For Blaine's admonitions to his deputies, see Blaine to Howell, 6 Mar. 1782, Simon Gratz Autograph Collection, Case B, Box 17, HSP; Blaine to Thomas Huggins, 21 July 1783, Blaine Papers, reel 2; Blaine to Robert Dodd, 2 Aug. 1783, ibid.; Blaine to Col. Miller, 1 Aug. 1783, ibid.; Report of the Board of Treasury on the Memorial of Ephraim Blaine, 9 Feb. 1788, PCC, reel 151, item 138, 1:126–30.

120. Blaine to president of Congress, 9 Apr. 1781, PCC, reel 182, item 165, 1:397; Robert Howe to Clinton, 21 Apr. 1780, *Clinton Papers*, 5:647–48; John Ingram to NG, 20 Dec. 1780, Greene Papers, WCL; Mary Aylett to Wadsworth, 23 May 1780, C and W Coll., Box 9, folder 29.

121. *Boston-Gazette*, 5 May 1777; W. Nichols to Davis, 26 June 1778, Davis Papers, reel 79; Pettit to NG, 26 Feb. 1779, Greene Papers, APS, reel 1, 2:35; Pettit to Duane, 17 Feb. 1781, PCC, reel 41, item 34, p. 205; Pettit to John Gibson, 16 May 1780, Greene Papers, WCL.

122. Hughes to Pickering, 12 Jan. 1783, Hughes Papers; Thomas Pratt to Stewart, 28 May 1779, Stewart Papers, NYSHA; Hay to Hughes, 11 Dec. 1780, Hughes Ltrbks., 19; Pickering to Miles, 30 Nov. 1780, RG 93, reel 25, vol. 123; Cochran to Clark, 30 Apr. 1781, Cochran, *Surgeon to Washington*, 112.

123. Miles to Davis, 30 July 1781, Davis Papers, reel 83; Blaine to RM, 20 Mar. 1782, Blaine Papers, reel 2; Fitch to Stewart, 3 Oct. 1779, Stewart Papers, NYSHA; James Gray to Samuel Huntington, 17 Apr. 1780, PCC, reel 46, item 39, 2:108; Chaloner and White to Anthony

Broderick, 30 Sept. 1778, C and W Ltrbks.; Furman to M. Williamson, 13 Sept. 1779, *Furman Letters*, 16.

124. Hay to Pettit, 1 May 1781, PCC, reel 199, item 192, p. 351; Hughes to Pickering, 13 Jan. 1784, Hughes Papers; Furman to Josiah Hornblower, 15 May 1781, *Furman Letters*, 64–65.

125. Wood, *Creation of the American Republic*, 413–25.

126. Johnson, "Internal Financial Reform," 33–34. I am indebted to James H. Kettner for bringing this article to my attention.

127. Board of Treasury, Circular, 3 May 1780, PCC, reel 147, item 136, 4:479, 487. The deadline was later extended to 1 August (ibid., 485).

128. Chaloner and White to Robert Forsyth, 25 Jan. 1780, C and W Ltrbks.

129. Pettit to Cox, 1 Dec. 1779, Greene Papers, APS, reel 2, 9:1.

130. Gibson to Pettit, 9 May 1780, Biddle Corr., folder 16; Pettit to NG, 10 May 1780, PCC, reel 46, item 39, 1:100.

131. RM to the commissioners for settling accounts in the several departments, 19 Sept. 1782, quoted in Ferguson, *Power of the Purse*, 189; *JCC*, 22:102–4, 204, 425, 23:645–46, 24:402.

132. Burrall to RM, 4 Nov. 1783, PCC, reel 150, item 137, 3:275; *JCC*, 31:736–37, 34:260–62; Burrall to Blaine, 8 Dec. 1786, Blaine Papers, reel 2; Blaine to Robert Buchanan, 2 Aug. 1783, ibid.; Thomas Jones et al. to president of Congress, 23 Oct. 1783, PCC, reel 150, item 137, 3:279–81, 283–85. Cf. Ferguson, *Power of the Purse*, 190.

133. For examples of the legalistic attitude of the Board of Treasury, see Report of the Board of Treasury on the Memorial of Patrick Bennet, 24 May 1786, PCC, reel 151, item 138, 1:107–8; Report of the Board of Treasury on the Memorial of William Betts et al., 25 Jan. 1788, ibid., 111–14; Report of the Board of Treasury on the Memorial of E. Blaine, 9 Feb. 1788, ibid., 126–30; Report of the Board of Treasury on the Memorial of David Reynolds, 9 May 1786, ibid., 289–90; Report of the Board of Treasury on the Memorial of Weston Clark, 19 Apr. 1786, ibid., 245–46; *JCC*, 31:676–77.

134. Holstein, *Swedish Holsteins in America*, 82; Hughes, *Memorial*, 1–44 (quotation by Hughes on 2; quotation by Pickering on 44).

135. See Chapter 8, at n. 12; Thomas Mifflin to Henry Laurens, 25 May 1778, PCC, reel 179, item 161, 1:36–37; Report of the Board of Treasury on the Memorial of E. Blaine, 9 Feb. 1788, ibid., reel 151, item 138, 1:126–30.

Chapter 6

1. See Appendix.

2. For the lucrativeness of wartime mercantile activities, see Nash, *Urban Crucible*, 56–57, 168–69; Baxter, *House of Hancock*, 103–6, 141; White, *Beekmans of New York*, 361–62; Harrington, *New York Merchant*, 300–312.

3. Dalton to Trumbull, 3 Aug. 1775, Trumbull Coll.; Dyer to Trumbull, 25 Sept., 26 Dec. 1775, ibid.; Trumbull to president of Congress, 9 June 1776, Force, ed., *American Archives*, 4th ser., 6:790–91; Trumbull to Jeremiah Wadsworth, 17 May 1777, *LMCC*, 2:364 n. 2.

4. Rossman, *Thomas Mifflin*, 52, 94, 159; Richard Henry Lee to GW, 20 Nov. 1777, *RH Lee Letters*, 1:349–50; Timothy Pickering to Roger Sherman, 5 Aug. 1780, Pickering Papers, reel 5; McLean, "Timothy Pickering," 124; Wadsworth to Elbridge Gerry, 13 Aug. 1778, Wadsworth Papers, Box 126; Wadsworth to John Chaloner and John White, 27 Sept. 1779, ibid., Box 151, Letterbook F; NG to president of Congress, 16 Apr. 1780, PCC, reel 175, item 155, 1:129; NG to GW, 21 July 1778, Sparks, ed., *Correspondence of the Revolution*, 2:165; GW to NG, 3 Sept. 1779, *GW Writings*, 16:224–25; Greene, *Nathanael Greene*, 2:47, 156–57; Wells, "Resignation of Nathanael Greene," 42, 43, 48.

5. NG to the Board of War, 28 July 1779, PCC, reel 193, item 173, 4:38–39. Wadsworth

expressed identical sentiments: "I unwillingly in a bad time entered into office and shall cheerfully quit it" (Wadsworth to Horatio Gates, 1 July 1778, Gates Papers). In this respect, the attitude of staff officers in the Hospital Department was exceptional. The office of director-general was eagerly sought after, and no director-general ever voluntarily resigned. The history of the position was marked by intrigue, jealousy, and ambition. At issue, however, was prestige, not money. See Gibson, *Dr. Bodo Otto*, chap. 11 and pp. 89, 200. Nevertheless, see a letter by Richard Henry Lee referring to William Shippen, Jr.'s reluctance to accept the office of director-general (ibid., 225).

6. Memorial of Colonel [Lewis] Nicola Relative to the Barracks, 20 May 1780, *Pa. Arch.*, 2d ser., 3:404. For an insightful discussion of the way revolutionaries merged public and private interest, see Maier, *Old Revolutionaries*, 51–100.

7. Olney to NG, 30 Aug. 1780, Greene Papers, WCL.

8. McPherson to Blaine, 9 Apr. 1779, Blaine Papers, reel 1. For other examples of revolutionaries eager to secure office, see Jonathan Worth to Blaine, 27 Dec. 1779, ibid.; Barrister Carroll to council, 19 Feb. 1776, *Md. Arch.*, 11:172. Requests for positions in the staff departments were common, especially during the first three years of the war, and are scattered throughout the Wadsworth Papers, Box 126; the Trumbull Coll.; and the Davis Papers, reels 79 and 82; Flint to Wadsworth, 20 Feb. 1779, Wadsworth Papers, Box 151, Letterbook D.

9. Bailyn, *Ideological Origins*, 95.

10. NG to James Duane, 16 Apr. 1779, quoted in Johnson, *Nathanael Greene*, 1:139–40; Thayer, *Nathanael Greene*, 226–27; Tracy to Wadsworth, 22 Mar. 1778, Wadsworth Papers, Box 126. For other examples, see Pickering to Hugh Hughes, 31 Aug. 1780, Hughes Papers; Samuel Huntington to Pickering, 5 Aug. 1780, Pickering Papers, reel 39.

11. Keese to Hughes, 10 Nov. 1781, Hughes Ltrbks., 15; Moylan to GW, 18 Feb. 1781, GW Papers, reel 75. See also Jacob Morgan, Jr., to President Wharton, 4 Apr. 1778, *Pa. Arch.*, 1st ser., 6:399.

12. NG to the Committee of Congress, 6 May 1780, PCC, reel 175, item 173, 1:249–50.

13. Wadsworth to Chaloner and White, 27 Sept. 1779, Wadsworth Papers, Box 151, Letterbook F; NG to Wadsworth, 12 Aug. 1780, Knollenberg Collection, Box 4, YUL; NG to Wadsworth, 2 Apr. 1780, Greene Papers, General Correspondence, vol. 1, LC.

14. For additional expressions of serious disenchantment with public service, see Udny Hay to NG, 26 Jan. 1780, PCC, reel 193, item 173, 5:109–10; John Mitchell to NG, 7 Jan. 1780, ibid., 217; Olney to NG, 30 Aug. 1780, Greene Papers, WCL; Clement Biddle to Owen Biddle, 14 Feb. 1780, Biddle Corr., folder 10; Joseph Lewis to Moore Furman, 31 Jan., 28 Mar., 27 Sept. 1780, Lewis Letters; Furman to William Williamson, 8 Mar. 1780, *Furman Letters*, 58; Thomas Jones to Charles Stewart, 18 Feb. 1778, Stewart Papers, NYSHA.

15. For Blaine's threats to resign, see Blaine to Mr. Buchanan, 20 Jan. 1778, Blaine Papers, reel 2; Blaine to John Davis, 3 Feb. 1778, Davis Papers, reel 79; Blaine to president of Congress, 31 Dec. 1780, PCC, reel 182, item 165, 1:335. Biographical material on Blaine can be found in Blaine, comp. and ed., *Blaine Family*. One is constantly surprised to run across names of staff officers still serving the public, though they had announced their resignations years before.

16. NG to Hughes, 16 Apr. 1778, *Greene Papers*, 2:343; NG to Hughes, 31 Mar. 1778, Hughes Ltrbks., 1; Hughes to NG, 8 Apr. 1778, ibid. See also John Cochran to George Campbell, 26 Mar. 1781, Cochran, *Surgeon to Washington*, 108–9; Blaine to president of Congress, 12 Jan. 1780, PCC, reel 182, item 165, 1:315.

17. Hughes to NG, 23 Apr. 1778, *Greene Papers*, 2:352. Hughes was also concerned about losing his rank of colonel as a result of the congressional reorganization (ibid., 353 n. 1).

18. NG to John Jay, 28 July 1779, PCC, reel 192, item 173, 2:172–73.

19. Biddle to Finnie, 10 Nov. 1778, Biddle Ltrbks.; Blaine to Forsyth, 27 May 1780, Blaine

Papers, reel 2; NG to James Abeel, 5 June 1779, Misc. MS (Nathanael Greene), NYHS. For additional examples, see Owen Biddle to Francis Wade and Henry Hollingsworth, 23 Sept. 1778, Biddle Ltrbks.; Andrew Bostwick to Clement Biddle, 8 July 1778, ibid.; Chaloner and White, circular, 18 Sept. 1778, C and W Ltrbks.; Pickering to Samuel Miles, 9 Nov. 1780, RG 93, reel 25, vol. 123; Mitchell to William Smith [June 1780], *Pa. Arch.*, 6th ser., 14:209; Lewis to Constant Cooper, 16 Feb. 1780, Lewis Letters.

20. NG to Lewis, 12 June 1779, Greene Papers, APS, reel 1, 6:84; NG to Abeel, 12 June 1779, ibid., 52; NG to Davis, 9 May 1778, *Greene Papers*, 2:386; Thomas Smith to Davis, 11 Oct. 1778, Davis Papers, reel 79.

21. Morton to Isaac Carty, 9 Mar. 1780, Blaine Papers, reel 2.

22. Assistant deputy quartermasters to Hay, 5 Oct. 1779, Greene Papers, APS, reel 1, 3:54; Hay to assistant deputy quartermasters, 6 Oct. 1779, ibid., 55; assistant deputy quartermasters to Hay, 8 Oct. 1779, ibid., 56. See also Samuel Hodgdon to Pickering, 1 Aug. 1779, RG 93, reel 33, vol. 111.

23. NG to Reed, 29 June 1780, Reed Papers; Wadsworth to Henry Champion, 8 June 1778, Wadsworth Papers, Box 151, Letterbook A. For similar expressions of concern for the army, see Wadsworth to Champion, 20 Dec. 1780, ibid., Letterbook I; Flint to Blaine, 24 Jan. 1779, ibid., Letterbook D; Blaine to Davis, 21 Oct. 1778, Davis Papers, reel 80; Blaine to president of Congress, 15 Aug. 1780, PCC, reel 182, item 165, 1:327–28; NG to Reed, 10, 20 May 1780, Reed Papers; Lewis to James Gamble, 24 Mar. 1780, Lewis Letters; John Meals to NG, 2 Feb. 1782, Greene Papers, WCL; Circular letter from Owen Biddle to the purchasing commissaries of forage, 15 Sept. 1778, Biddle Ltrbks.; Flint to Anthony Wayne, 16 Dec. 1779, Wayne Papers, HSP, 9:85; Furman to NG, 11 Jan. 1780, Dreer Coll.; Stewart to Furman, 17 Oct. 1778, Burnside Ltrbk.; Gamble to Stewart, 3 Mar. 1780, Stewart Papers, NYSHA; Pickering to Samuel Osgood and Oliver Philips, 22 Oct. 1780, RG 93, reel 25, vol. 122; Furman to NG, 9 June 1779, *Furman Letters*, 9; Finnie to Nicholas Long, 26 Mar. 1778, *N.C. Recs.*, 13:388.

24. Freeman, *GW*, 4:71; Chaloner and White to Flint, 18 June 1779, C and W Ltrbks. For additional examples, see Chaloner and White to Flint, 27 Apr. 1779, ibid.; Flint to Champion, 5 Apr. 1779, Wadsworth Papers, Box 151, Letterbook E; Lewis to Furman, 27 Jan. 1780, Lewis Letters; Lewis to Daniel Marsh, 20 Jan. 1780, ibid.; Furman to Samuel Gray, 9 Feb. 1780, *Furman Letters*, 57. It is also obvious that staff officers were frequently unsuccessful in keeping Washington well supplied. For Washington's humorous description of his meager table fare, see GW to Cochran, 16 Aug. 1779, *GW Writings*, 16:116–17.

25. Blaine to Buchanan, 18 Feb. 1778, Blaine Papers, reel 2; Flint to Chaloner and White, 26 Apr. 1779, Wadsworth Papers, Box 151, Letterbook E; Wadsworth to Blaine, 27 June 1779, ibid.; Morton to Wadsworth, 29 Apr. 1779, ibid., Box 128; Stewart to Blaine, 23 Dec. 1777, Blaine Papers, reel 1; Blaine to John Patton, 3 Nov. 1777, Society Collection, Case 19, Box 14, HSP; Chaloner to Wadsworth, 17 May 1778, *Clinton Papers*, 2:797; Pickering to GW, 28 Oct. 1780, Pickering and Upham, *Timothy Pickering*, 1:263–65.

26. Blaine to Hollingsworth and Thomas Huggins [14–18 May 1778], Blaine Papers, reel 2; Chaloner and White to the Board of Treasury, 25 Mar. 1779, C and W Ltrbks. For additional examples of the use of GW's name to ensure compliance with orders, see Chaloner to Wadsworth, 7 May 1778, Wadsworth Papers, Box 126; Flint to Blaine, 2 Mar. 1779, ibid., Box 151, Letterbook D; Lewis to Marsh, 27 Feb. 1780, Lewis Letters; Jacob Weiss to Colonel Kreider, 14 Feb. 1781, Boyer, ed., "Letterbook of Jacob Weiss," 117; Owen Biddle to Solomon Maxwell, 24 July 1779, Biddle Ltrbks.; Thomas Richardson to Owen Biddle, 10 June 1780, Biddle Corr., folder 17; Hughes to Gates, 24 Aug. 1777, Gates Papers; George Morgan to Chaloner and White, 25 Mar. 1779, C and W Coll., Box 7, folder 8; Furman to Samuel Flanaghan, 13 Oct. 1779, *Furman Letters*, 19.

27. Nehemiah Hubbard to NG, 5 Sept. 1780, Greene Papers, WCL. For almost identical

wording, see Davis to NG, 7 Sept. 1780, Davis Papers, reel 82. Similar expressions of Washington's character were nearly universal. For the best discussion of this phenomenon, see Royster, "Continental Army," 386–99, 555–62.

28. Wadsworth to Blaine, 24 Nov. 1779, Wadsworth Papers, Box 151, Letterbook G. For Washington's effect on resignations, see Blaine to GW, 10 Apr. 1780, GW Papers, reel 65; Clement Biddle to Owen Biddle, Mar. 1780, Biddle Corr., folder 12; John Fitch to William Heath, 3 Jan. 1780, Fitch Papers; GW to Henry Emanuel Lutterloh, 17 Mar. 1778, *GW Writings*, 11:102. For one commissary's positive response to GW's refusal to grant him a leave of absence, see Flint to Wadsworth, 14 Apr. 1779, Wadsworth Papers, Box 128.

29. East, *Business Enterprise*, 97, 103–4, 153.

30. Davis to Patton, 28 July 1779, Davis Papers, reel 81.

31. NG to Davis, 9 July 1780, Davis Papers, reel 82; Hay to assistant deputy quartermasters, 24 July 1779, Fisher Papers, reel 1; William Shippen to Henry Laurens, 18 Jan. 1778, PCC, reel 102, item 78, 20:171–72; Owen Biddle to Clement Biddle, 3 May 1780, ibid., reel 175, item 155, 1:257; Blaine to Reed, 12 Apr. 1781, Blaine Papers, reel 2; Furman to James Caldwell, 31 Dec. 1779, *Furman Letters*, 50.

32. Bodo Otto to Shippen, 18 June 1779, Gibson, *Dr. Bodo Otto*, 244–45.

33. Colt to Wadsworth, 27 July 1779, Wadsworth Papers, Box 128. For additional examples of subordinates' loyalty to their superiors, see Mitchell to NG, 27 Nov. 1779, Greene Papers, APS, reel 2, 9:81; Smith to Davis, 11 May 1780, Davis Papers, reel 82; Lewis to Furman, 6 Aug. 1780, Lewis Letters; assistant deputy quartermasters to Hay, 24 July 1779, Fisher Papers, reel 1; Keese to Hughes, 12 Sept. 1780, Hughes Papers; Robert Dill to Stewart, 10 Mar. 1780, Stewart Papers, NYSHA; Jones to Stewart, 23 Feb. 1779, ibid.

34. East, *Business Enterprise*, 86–87, chaps. 11, 14; Sakolski, *Great American Land Bubble*, 44–46.

35. NG to Hubbard, 4 Dec. 1778, Greene Papers, General Correspondence, vol. 1, LC.

36. For professionalism, see Haber, "Professions and Higher Education," 240–41.

37. *Va. Gaz.*, 11 Dec. 1779.

38. For the British background, see James, "English Politics and the Concept of Honor." For the deferential nature of colonial society, see the Prologue at n. 19. The importance of the concept of reputation has generally been overlooked in secondary works of colonial politics and society. Suggestive on the issue is Persons, *Decline of American Gentility*, chap. 2. For the importance of credit, see Bailyn, *New England Merchants*, 34–35; Price, *Capital and Credit*.

39. Wadsworth to NG, 2 Apr. 1780, Wadsworth Letters; Kennett, *French Forces in America*, 73–74; *Conn. St. Recs.*, 3:2, 169, 231, 305. See also East, *Business Enterprise*, 84.

40. Adair, "Fame and the Founding Fathers," 24.

41. NG to McDougall, 28 Mar. 1778, *Greene Papers*, 2:326; NG to GW, 24 Apr. 1779, quoted in Greene, *Nathanael Greene*, 2:506; NG to Duane, 16 Apr. 1779, PCC, reel 175, item 155, 1:128. Thayer, *Nathanael Greene*, mistakenly identifies the recipient of the letter as William Duer. According to Mifflin's biographer, Mifflin also quit as quartermaster general "the better to achieve his ambitions for military glory" (Rossman, "Thomas Mifflin," 14).

42. NG to Charles Pettit, 2 Jan. 1780, Lewis Letters. Pettit was of the same mind (Pettit to president of Congress, 9 Aug. 1780, Reed Papers).

43. Mitchell to Pettit, 15 Nov. 1779, PCC, reel 199, item 192, p. 261. See also Owen Biddle to Pettit, 10 May 1780, Biddle Ltrbks.; Bostwick to Clement Biddle, 8 July 1780, ibid.

44. Chaloner to Buchanan, 27 Feb. 1778, Blaine Papers, reel 2. See also Sherman to Trumbull, 2 Apr. 1777, *LMCC*, 2:315; Owen Biddle to Philip Marsteller, 19 May 1779, Biddle Ltrbks.

45. Biddle to Archibald Steel, 3 Mar. 1780, Biddle Ltrbks. See also Owen Biddle to Pettit, 6 Mar. 1780, PCC, reel 199, item 192, p. 327; Chaloner and White to Cornelius Cox, 15 Nov. 1778, C and W Ltrbks.; Furman to NG, 9 May 1780, *Furman Letters*, 63.

46. Flint to Jonathan Childs and Isaac Tickner, 10 Dec. 1779, Wadsworth Papers, Box 151, Letterbook H. See also Wadsworth to Blaine, 18 July 1779, ibid., Letterbook E.

47. John Armstrong to Davis, 23 June 1779, Davis Papers, reel 81.

48. Stewart to Gray, 12 July 1779, Stewart Papers, LC. See also Anthony Butler to Davis, 1 Apr. 1778, Davis Papers, reel 79; Butler to Hughes, 5 Mar. 1779, Hughes Ltrbks., 1; Owen Biddle, circular, 24 Dec. 1779, Biddle Ltrbks.

49. Blaine to Azariah Dunham, 7 Jan. 1778, Blaine Papers, reel 2. See also Mitchell to NG, 2 Jan. 1780, PCC, reel 193, item 173, 5:217; George Ross to NG, 7 Nov. 1779, ibid., reel 175, item 155, 1:175; Owen Biddle to Pettit, 6 Mar. 1780, ibid., reel 199, item 192, p. 27.

50. Blaine to Dr. Uston, 16 Dec. 1777, Blaine Papers, reel 2. See also Abeel to Jacob Morgan, 22 Aug. 1778, Abeel Ltrbk. For staff officers' fears that military defeat might be blamed on the staff departments, see Stewart to Gray, 9 Mar. 1778, Stewart Papers, LC; Flint to Blaine, 25 July 1778, Wadsworth Papers, Box 151, Letterbook: 1778; Wadsworth to Blaine, 29 July 1779, C and W Ltrbks.; Mitchell to Davis, 27 Sept. 1778, Davis Papers, reel 79.

51. Wadsworth to Blaine, 13 July 1779, Wadsworth Papers, Box 151, Letterbook D. See also Abeel to John Morgan, 22 Aug. 1778, Abeel Ltrbk.; Pickering to the deputy quartermasters of the different states, 16 Dec. 1780, RG 93, reel 25, vol. 123; Cochran to Thomas Waring, 28 Feb. 1781, Cochran, *Surgeon to Washington*, 97.

52. Hooper to NG, 15 May 1779, Greene Papers, APS, reel 2, 7:101.

53. Resolutions of the surgeons and mates to Congress, 2 May 1780, Dr. Peter Turner Papers, LC.

54. Duncan to Blaine, 5 May 1781, Blaine Papers, reel 1. See also Colt to Wadsworth, 13 Feb. 1779, Wadsworth Papers, Box 127; Mitchell to Pettit, 15 Nov. 1779, PCC, reel 199, item 192, pp. 261–62.

55. NG to president of Congress, 16 Feb. 1779, GW Papers, reel 64.

56. Hubbard to Wadsworth, 2 Aug. 1779, Wadsworth Papers, Box 128. For staff officers' reaction to Congress's 9 July resolution, see Chapter 5 at n. 85 and 86.

57. NG to Pettit, 24 July 1779, Greene Papers, APS, reel 2, 11:5.

58. Hughes to NG, 3 May 1778, Hughes Ltrbks., 1. NG clearly understood this line of reasoning. He recommended a similar course of action to the foragemaster, Clement Biddle, who was contemplating resigning in 1779. NG advised him, "You must not think of quitting even if you resign; but must offer your Services as a Volunteer for some time to come" (NG to Biddle, 28 July 1779, Nathanael Greene Papers, Duke University Library, Durham, N.C. I am indebted to Charles Royster for this reference).

59. Hughes, *Memorial*, 8.

60. Destler, "Colonel Henry Champion," 61. For examples of similar behavior, see GW to Flint, 26 Mar. 1780, *GW Writings*, 18:158; Hooper to NG, 2 Jan. 1780, PCC, reel 193, item 173, 5:217; Furman to John Cox and Pettit, 29 June 1779, ibid., reel 93, item 78, 5:369.

Chapter 7

1. This summary rests on the following sources: Freeman, *GW*, vol. 5, chaps. 7–9; Ward, *War of the Revolution*, vol. 2, chaps. 49–50, 55; Wallace, *Appeal to Arms*, chaps. 18–19.

2. Entry of 1 Jan. 1780, Thacher, *Military Journal*, 185; Bradford, "Hunger Menaces the Revolution," 2; Ward, *War of the Revolution*, 2:612; Freeman, *GW*, 5:143.

3. Entry of 20 Jan. 1780, Washington, *Diaries*, 3:343. For the weather during January, see ibid., 342–44.

4. Ward, *War of the Revolution*, 2:613. For the weather during March, see Washington,

Diaries, 3:347–49. On 31 March, GW noted it was "snowing more or less all day & generally pretty fast" (ibid., 349).

5. Royal Flint to Henry Champion, 27 Dec. 1779, Wadsworth Papers, Box 151, Letterbook H. See also Bradford, "Hunger Menaces the Revolution," 6.

6. GW, circular to the governors of the Middle states, 16 Dec. 1779, *GW Writings*, 17:273, 274; Bradford, "Hunger Menaces the Revolution," 6.

7. Patten quoted in Ward, *War of the Revolution*, 2:613; Risch, *QM Support*, 57; Bradford, "Hunger Menaces the Revolution," 12–13.

8. Bradford, "Hunger Menaces the Revolution," 2–6, 15–18, 21; GW to the magistrates of New Jersey, 8 Jan. 1780, *GW Writings*, 17:362–65; Freeman, *GW*, 5:145.

9. *JCC*, 14:561–62, 519.

10. NG to the Board of War, 25 July 1779, PCC, reel 193, item 173, 4:35, 31. See also NG to president of Congress, 27 July 1778, ibid., reel 175, item 155, 1:72; NG to John Cox, 20 July 1779, Ely Coll.; Timothy Pickering to president of Congress, 22 May 1781, RG 93, reel 26, vol. 127.

11. *JCC*, 15:1412; Sherman to governor of Connecticut, 28 Dec. 1779, *LMCC*, 4:550; President of Congress to NG, 29 Dec. 1779, ibid.; *JCC*, 15:1412.

12. Hay to William Heath, 28 Jan. 1780, *Heath Papers*, 5:26; Pettit to NG, 1 Jan. 1780, PCC, reel 193, item 173, 5:247. NG shared Pettit's fears. See NG to Alexander Hamilton, 4 Jan. 1780, *Hamilton Papers*, 2:253.

13. Pettit to president of Congress, 10 Jan. 1780, PCC, reel 193, item 173, 5:261; Robert Hooper to NG, 3 Feb. 1780, ibid., 173–74; Owen Biddle to Clement Biddle, 11 May 1780, Biddle Ltrbks.

14. GW to president of Congress, 5 Jan. 1780, *GW Writings*, 17:355–56; *JCC*, 16:455.

15. *JCC*, 16:47, 76.

16. Elbridge Gerry to James Warren, 25 Jan. 1780, *LMCC*, 5:515. Although it was proposed to send a committee to headquarters in January, Congress did not dispatch one until April 1780. See Chapter 8 at n. 2. The phrase "the evil of a numerous Staff department" is from the North Carolina delegates to governor of North Carolina, 29 Feb. 1780, *LMCC*, 5:57.

17. William Floyd to governor of New York [28 Jan. 1780], ibid., 19.

18. *JCC*, 11:545–46, 812–13, 13:353–56; Risch, *QM Support*, 49–50, 62. For Mease, see Chastellux, *Travels in North America*, 1:176–77.

19. *JCC*, 14:727–28, 812–13, 872–80, 1377–78, 16:44–46, 17:196–201; Johnson, *Commissariat*, 161–64.

20. Congress appointed Ephraim Blaine commissary general on 2 December 1779, but he did not accept office until 13 January 1780 (*JCC*, 15:1343, 16:47). Risch, *QM Support*, 59, mistakenly calls Blaine's $40,000 salary "generous" and contrasts it with the subsequent reduction in the commissary general's pay to $2,124 ordered in November 1780. In fact, the reverse is true. The $40,000 figure represents Blaine's salary in "old" Continental bills, whereas the $2,124 figure represents his salary in "new" currency issued under Congress's 18 March resolve (*JCC*, 16:262–67). Thus at Congress's revaluation ratio of 40:1, Blaine's $40,000 salary is equivalent to $83.33 specie dollars a month. Consequently, Blaine's pay of $2,124 or $177 a month actually represents a doubling of his salary.

21. *JCC*, 16:5.

22. Ibid., 196–201.

23. Ibid., 262–67. See also Ferguson, *Power of the Purse*, 51; Ver Steeg, *Robert Morris*, 25–46.

24. Clark to the Speaker of the New Jersey Assembly, 17 Feb. 1780, *LMCC*, 5:40; L'Hommedieu to governor of New York, 22 Feb. 1780, ibid., 45; Rakove, *Beginnings of National Politics*, 276–77.

25. North Carolina delegates to governor of North Carolina, 15 July 1779, *LMCC*, 4:318; Connecticut delegates to governor of Connecticut, 20 Mar. 1780, ibid., 5:84. The North

Carolina delegation shared Connecticut's concern. See North Carolina delegates to governor of North Carolina, 29 Feb. 1780, ibid., 57.

26. Only the Connecticut and North Carolina delegations mentioned this consideration. See the sources above in n. 25.

27. For the belief in the great savings the system of specific supplies would have on public expenditures, see president of Congress to Jonathan Trumbull, 13 Dec. 1779, *LMCC*, 4:535 n. 3; president of Congress to governor of New Jersey, 14 Dec. 1779, ibid., 535; William Ellery to governor of Rhode Island, 14 Dec. 1779, ibid., 535–36; Allen Jones to governor of North Carolina, 23 Dec. 1779, ibid., 548–49; John Armstrong to Horatio Gates, 16 Feb. 1780, ibid., 5:38; president of Congress to the several states, 20 Feb. 1780, ibid., 52; *JCC*, 16:386–87.

28. North Carolina delegates to governor of North Carolina, 29 Feb. 1780, *LMCC*, 5:57. Cf. Rakove, *Beginnings of National Politics*, 276–77.

29. Clement Biddle to Owen Biddle, 12 Mar. 1780, Biddle Corr., folder 12; Remarks on the Resolution of Congress of the 25th February 1780 . . . by Nathanael Greene [Mar. 1780?], GW Papers, reel 65; Hay to NG, 9 Feb. 1780, Greene Papers, APS, reel 1, 1:30. See also Hooper to Owen Biddle, 12 Mar. 1780, Biddle Corr., folder 12; NG to GW, Sparks, ed., *Correspondence of the Revolution*, 2:371–72.

30. J. Burnett to Jeremiah Wadsworth, 18 Mar. 1780, Wadsworth Papers, Box 130.

31. Johnson, *Commissariat*, 165.

32. Trumbull to the delegates from Connecticut, 10 March 1780, *Trumbull Papers*, 3:17–18, quotation on 18; Destler, *Connecticut*, 42; Buel, *Dear Liberty*, 222; Johnson, *Commissariat*, 165.

33. *Pa. Statutes*, 9:437–40, 10:176–82, 214–18; Hening, *Statutes*, 10:233–37, 338–43; *Conn. St. Recs.*, 2:521–26, 3:15, 31–32; New York, *Laws*, 1:200–202, 266–75, 292–94; *R.I. Acts*, Mar. 1780, 5, July 1780, 19–21, Sept. 1780, 14; *N.J. Assembly Acts*, 26 Feb.–Mar. 1780, chap. 17, pp. 41–47, chap. 33, pp. 69–73; House Journal, 22 Jan. 1779, *N.C. Recs.*, 13:642–43, 24:345; Massachusetts, *Acts and Laws*, 205–10; New Hampshire, *Documents*, 8:864–86; Bond, *State Government in Maryland*, 48–49.

34. *N.J. Assembly Acts*, 26 Feb.–Mar. 1780, chap. 17, pp. 41–47, chap. 33, pp. 67–73.

35. NG to Wadsworth, 2 Mar. 1780, Knollenberg Collection, YUL.

36. GW to Champion, 26 May 1780, *GW Writings*, 18:424; GW to the Board of War, 27 May 1780, ibid., 427–28; Van Doren, *Mutiny in January*, 22–23.

37. GW to president of Congress, 20 Aug. 1780, *GW Writings*, 19:403.

38. Ephraim Blaine to president of Congress, 17 Oct. 1780, Blaine Papers, reel 1. Blaine was more optimistic a month later. See Johnson, *Commissariat*, 175.

39. GW to Morris, 10 Dec. 1780, *GW Writings*, 20:459.

40. For details of the Pennsylvania line's mutiny, see Van Doren, *Mutiny in January*. For the outbreak of the mutiny of the New Jersey line, see Israel Shreve to GW, 20 Jan. 1780, *GW Writings*, 21:124n; GW, circular to the New England states and New York, 22 Jan. 1781, ibid., 129–30.

41. GW to RM, 2 Mar. 1777, *GW Writings*, 7:225; Committee at Headquarters to the several states, 25 May 1780, *LMCC*, 5:167; Connecticut delegates to governor of Connecticut, 1 Sept. 1780, ibid.; Burnett, *Continental Congress*, 451.

42. Trumbull to Samuel Huntington, 10 July 1780, *Trumbull Papers*, 3:60. See also Trumbull to Huntington, 10 July 1780, ibid., 63; Fowler, "Breakdown of Congressional Authority," 79.

43. Statement of Joseph Reed to Congress, 30 July 1780, *Pa. Arch.*, 1st ser., 8:466.

44. Trumbull to Huntington, 27 Nov. 1788, PCC, reel 80, item 66, 2:119; Van Dusen, "Trade of Revolutionary Connecticut," 293–94.

45. Greene to president of Congress, 8 July 1780, Staples, *Rhode Island in the Continental Congress*, 204–5; Clinton to Huntington, 9 Mar. 1780, PCC, reel 81, item 67, 2:238–39; Clinton to Huntington, 8 July 1780, ibid., 287; Committee at Headquarters to the states of

Delaware, Pennsylvania, Maryland, and Virginia, 10 July 1780, *LMCC*, 5:255; Spaulding, *His Excellency George Clinton*, 118.

46. Jefferson to the Committee of Congress at Headquarters, 2 July 1780, *Jefferson Papers*, 3:476. Maryland was also prevented from supplying the army because of British warships in its bay. See Council of Maryland to the delegates in Congress, 28 July 1780, *Md. Arch.*, 43:238; Council of Maryland to Jefferson, 28 Aug. 1780, ibid., 269.

47. Address of the New Jersey legislature to Congress, 15 Mar. 1780, PCC, reel 82, item 68, p. 525; Statement of Joseph Reed to Congress, 30 July 1780, *Pa. Arch.*, 1st ser., 8:458–68.

48. Pavlovsky, "'Between Hawk and Buzzard,'" 353–54, quotation on 353.

49. Committee at Headquarters to GW, 30 June 1780, GW Papers, reel 67; Committee at Headquarters to president of Pennsylvania, 13 July 1780, ibid., 263; Committee at Headquarters to state of New Hampshire, 13 July 1780, ibid.; Timothy Pickering to Colonel N. Hubbard, 2 Nov. 1780, RG 93, reel 25, vol. 123; Risch, *QM Support*, 64.

50. *JCC*, 17:525, 540, quotation on 525. For state authorities' replies, see Jefferson to Huntington, 27 July 1780, *Jefferson Papers*, 3:508–12; Representation of the Conduct of the State of Maryland to president of Congress, 11 Aug. 1780, PCC, reel 84, item 70, pp. 419–27; Statement of Joseph Reed to Congress, 30 July 1780, *Pa. Arch.*, 1st ser., 8:458–68; Trumbull to Huntington, 10 July 1780, *Trumbull Papers*, 3:58–61; William Greene to president of Congress, 8 July 1780, Staples, *Rhode Island in the Continental Congress*, 204–5.

51. RM, circular to the governors of the states, 25 July 1781, *Morris Papers*, 1:382.

52. Holt to George Clinton, 15 Apr. 1780, *Clinton Papers*, 5:622; Report of a committee of Congress, 5 Aug. 1777, *JCC*, 8:609; Rakove, *Beginnings of National Politics*, 130; Alexander McDougall to Reed, 25 Mar. 1779, quoted in Reed, *Joseph Reed*, 2:58–59; NG to Henry Laurens, 1 June 1778, PCC, reel 199, item 192, p. 6.

53. Whipple to Meshech Weare, 18 May 1779, *LMCC*, 4:211n; Wadsworth to John Chaloner and John White, 26 July 1779, C and W Coll., Box 8, folder 19; McDougall to Reed, 25 Mar. 1779, quoted in Reed, *Joseph Reed*, 2:58–59; Abner Nash to president of Congress, 18 July 1780, PCC, reel 86, item 72, p. 88; Fowler, "Breakdown of Congressional Authority," 75–76. See also Thomas Sim Lee to Maryland delegates, 10 Feb. 1780, PCC, reel 84, item 70, p. 343; Council of Maryland to delegates in Congress, 22 Sept. 1780, *Md. Arch.*, 43:299–300; John Rutledge to the delegates of South Carolina, 12 Oct. 1780, Rutledge, "Letters," 141.

54. Connecticut delegates to governor of Connecticut, 12 July 1781, *LMCC*, 6:142. It is possible that the *Journals* continued unpublished beyond July 1781. Although it is not clear when publication began again, it is evident that Congress was still having trouble communicating with the states as late as 1782. See, for example, Col. Davies to governor of Virginia, 19 Jan. 1782, *VCSP*, 3:36.

55. Bowdoin to Huntington, 30 Sept. 1780, PCC, reel 79, item 65, 1:456; NG to Trumbull, 7 May 1780, *Trumbull Papers*, 3:37.

56. Governor Greene also cited the need to provision the French fleet (William Greene to the Committee of Cooperation of Congress, 22 Aug. 1780, Staples, *Rhode Island in the Continental Congress*, 308–9).

57. Blaine to president of Congress, 12 Nov. 1780, Blaine Papers, reel 2; Blaine to Caesar Rodney, 20 Nov. 1780, ibid.; Reed to president of Congress [17–18] Nov. 1780, *Pa. Arch.*, 1st ser., 8:609. Under congressional prodding, Delaware authorities reinstituted their embargo a month later (June 1780) but declared it would remain in effect only until 20 October 1780. See *Rodney Letters*, 346.

58. Representation of the Conduct of the State of Maryland to president of Congress, 11 Aug. 1780, PCC, reel 84, item 70, p. 424. For similar expressions, see the Resolve of the General Assembly of Connecticut, 29 Nov. 1780, ibid., reel 80, item 66, 2:117; Statement of Joseph Reed to Congress, 30 July 1780, *Pa. Arch.*, 1st ser., 8:458–68; Spaulding, *His Excellency George Clinton*, 118.

59. Hening, *Statutes*, 10:338–43, quotation on 340.

60. Blaine to GW, 15 Aug. 1780, GW Papers, reel 69. For local officials' lack of cooperation, see Blaine to GW, 19 July 1780, ibid., reel 68; Champion to GW, 25 May 1780, ibid., reel 66; James Wilkinson to the Board of War, 24 May 1781, Blaine Papers, reel 2; Blaine to the governor and council at Trenton [N.J.], 22 Nov. 1780, ibid.; Francis Wade to Owen Biddle, 23 Feb. 1780, Biddle Corr., folder 10.

61. D. Wynkoop to Clinton, 16 Aug. 1780, *Clinton Papers*, 6:132.

62. Carrington to William Davies, 16 Apr. 1781, *VCSP*, 2:47. For other examples, see Richard Claiborne to the Hon. Speaker of the [Virginia] Assembly, 18 June 1781, ibid., 171; Robert Forsyth to Davies, 4 Aug. 1781, ibid., 293; Charles Russell to Claiborne, 2 Sept. 1781, ibid., 378; James Monell to Clinton, 14 Aug. 1780, *Clinton Papers*, 6:132; New York, *Assembly Journal*, 9 Sept. 1780, N.Y., A.1b, reel 4, unit 1; Blaine to GW, 14 May 1781, GW Papers, reel 77; Blaine to the Board of War, 24 May 1781, Blaine Papers, reel 2; Johnson, *Commissariat*, 189; Ver Steeg, *Robert Morris*, 100; Van Dusen, "Trade of Revolutionary Connecticut," 292–93.

63. For state officials' inability to purchase goods, see *Conn. St. Recs.*, 3:158. For speculators, see above Chapter 5 at n. 45. For the French, see Blaine to GW, 19 July 1780, GW Papers, reel 68; Buel, *Dear Liberty*, 241–42.

64. Ferguson, *Power of the Purse*, 63. Ferguson notes that this figure does not include certificates issued in the Carolinas and Georgia.

65. Destler, *Connecticut*, 45.

66. Pierre Van Cortlandt to the New York delegates, 1 July 1780, PCC, reel 81, item 67, 2:279. See also Ferguson, *Power of the Purse*, 64–65; Rakove, *Beginnings of National Politics*, 277; Fowler, "Breakdown of Congressional Authority," 72–73, 88.

67. Hart to Reed, 14 Aug. 1780, *Pa. Arch.*, 1st ser., 8:504. For additional evidence of inhabitants' reluctance to accept certificates, see John Hayes, Jr., to Reed, 12 June 1780, ibid., 317–18; Peter White to Rodney, 12 Aug. 1780, *Rodney Letters*, 366; Address of the New Jersey legislature to Congress, 15 Mar. 1780, PCC, reel 82, item 68, p. 525; Reed to GW, Reed, *Joseph Reed*, 2:235; Hay to GW, 18 Sept. 1780, GW Papers, reel 71; Trumbull to president of Congress, 8 June 1780, *Trumbull Papers*, 3:50–53; Johnson, *Commissariat*, 196; Fowler, "Breakdown of Congressional Authority," 65, 72, 98.

68. Lesser, ed., *Sinews of Independence*, 125, 173.

Chapter 8

1. Mathews to Horatio Gates, 4 Mar. 1780, *LMCC*, 5:71–72; Pavlovsky, "'Between Hawk and Buzzard,'" 356; Sullivan to GW, 26 Nov. 1780, *Sullivan Papers*, 3:223.

2. *JCC*, 16:362; GW to president of Congress, 3 Apr. 1780, *GW Writings*, 18:209; Philip Schuyler to Alexander Hamilton, 8 Apr. 1780, *LMCC*, 5:110; NG quotation from Burnett, *Continental Congress*, 446–47. I have relied heavily upon chap. 24 of Burnett for details of the Committee at Headquarters' activities.

3. *JCC*, 16:354–57, quotation on 356. See also *LMCC*, 5:140 n. 3; Committee at Headquarters to commissary general of issues, 19 Apr. 1780, ibid., 5:120–21; Committee at Headquarters to quartermaster general, 19 Apr. 1780, ibid., 121.

4. Committee at Headquarters to president of Congress, 10 May 1780, *LMCC*, 5:134. The phrase "Camp Education" is from James Lovell to Elbridge Gerry, 5 Sept. 1780, ibid., 362. Committee at Headquarters, Minute, 15 May 1780, ibid., 142; Committee at Headquarters to the several states, 25 May 1780, ibid., 165–66.

5. Committee at Headquarters, Minute, 14 May 1780, ibid., 140–41; Burnett, *Continental Congress*, 447–48; *JCC*, 17:438–49, quotation on 438.

6. On 13 July 1780, Congress rebuked the committee for its impolitic remarks to Pennsylvania's President Joseph Reed. See Fowler, "Breakdown of Congressional Authority," 85–88; Burnett, *Continental Congress*, 451–52.

7. Background on the reform of the Quartermaster Department is in Clarfield, *Timothy Pickering and the American Republic*, 63–65. For NG's comment, see NG to GW, 3 Apr. 1780, GW Papers, reel 65.

8. Risch, *QM Support*, 60–61.

9. *JCC*, 17:615–35. Pettit joked to NG that in light of his munificent new salary, he should consider his "fortune as made" (Pettit to NG, 2 July 1780, quoted in Greene, *Nathanael Greene*, 2:298).

10. NG to Committee at Headquarters, 14 July 1780, PCC, reel 175, item 155, 1:340; NG to president of Congress, 26 July 1780, Nathanael Greene Papers, General Correspondence, vol. 1, LC; NG to Joseph Reed, 29 Aug. 1780, Reed, *Joseph Reed*, 241–43.

11. NG to president of Congress, 19 June 1780, PCC, reel 175, item 155, 1:303–5, quotation on 303. See also Wells, "Inquiry into the Resignation of Nathanael Greene," 44–45.

12. *JCC*, 17:656–58, quotation on 658.

13. Greene, *Nathanael Greene*, 2:320–24, esp. 324; Burnett, *Continental Congress*, 463–64; *JCC*, 17:720. For the Committee at Headquarters' approval of NG's position, see the Committee at Headquarters to NG, 16 July 1780, Reed Papers.

14. Ezekiel Cornell to NG [21 July 1780], *LMCC*, 5:281.

15. For good accounts of the battles of Charleston and Camden, see Ward, *War of the Revolution*, vol. 2, chaps. 61, 65. The figures for soldiers captured, killed, and wounded are from Peckham, ed., *Toll of Independence*, 70, 74. On the reaction to Arnold, see Royster, "'Nature of Treason,'" 163–93.

16. Royster, *Revolutionary People at War*, 284–86.

17. William Houston to John Jay, 10 July 1780, Jay, *Correspondence*, 1:380n. See also Patterson, "From Revolution to Constitution," 70–71. For the strong effect on Congress, see Henderson, *Party Politics*, 247, 253–54.

18. Historians have generally agreed that the Nationalist movement of 1780–83 emerged during the nadir of the revolutionary war and was committed to increasing the powers of the Continental Congress. Although noting the serious military reversals the Continental army suffered in 1780 and the near collapse of the nation's financial structure during this period, some scholars have located the emergence of the movement in 1781 and the origins and motivations of the Nationalists in the realm of economic self-interest and political conservatism rather than wartime experiences or revolutionary patriotism. This interpretation portrays the Nationalists as a coalition of reactionary interest groups attempting to roll back the democratic gains of the Revolution; or it pictures them trying to protect their investments; or it sees them grasping for government back pay and pensions. Whatever the motivation, though, the Nationalists appear as little more than loyalists in revolutionary clothing who exploited the army's defeats and the nation's economic distress in an attempt to restore aristocratic rule and to gain financial advantage. The most important studies of this historical school include Jensen, "Idea of a National Government"; Jensen, *The New Nation*; Ferguson, "Nationalists of 1781–1783," esp. 242–43; Ferguson, *Power of the Purse*, chap. 6, esp. 110, 114. See also Henderson, *Party Politics*, chaps. 10–12. For a denial of the existence of a Nationalist party, see Rakove, *Beginnings of National Politics*, 323–24.

19. NG to [?], 29 Oct. 1779, quoted in Johnson, *Nathanael Greene*, 1:144. See also NG to GW, 21 May 1780, PCC, reel 46, item 39, 1:209; NG to Robert L. Hooper, 11 Jan. 1780, ibid., reel 193, item 173, 5:161.

20. GW to Jones, 31 May 1780, *GW Writings*, 18:453; GW to George Mason, 22 Oct. 1780, ibid., 20:242; GW to John Parke Custis, 28 Feb. 1781, ibid., 21:320. GW never tired of voicing his belief in the need to strengthen Congress's powers. For a sample, see GW to James

Duane, 4 Oct. 1780, ibid., 117; GW to Robert R. Livingston, 31 Jan. 1781, ibid., 21:164. See also Bradley, "Political Thinking of George Washington," 473–74.

21. GW to Custis, 28 Feb. 1781, 21:320; GW to Mason, 27 March 1779, *GW Writings*, 14:301. For Rush and Hamilton, see Benjamin Rush to Patrick Henry, 12 Jan. 1778, Rush, *Letters*, 1:182; Hamilton to George Clinton, 13 Feb. 1778, *Hamilton Papers*, 1:427.

22. Rakove, *Beginnings of National Politics*, chap. 10; Pavlovsky, "'Between Hawk and Buzzard,'" 349–64. In New Hampshire, even state government was viewed as a hardship. See Daniell, *Experiment in Republicanism*, 126.

23. Stourzh, *Alexander Hamilton*, 106.

24. Hamilton to Duane [3 Sept. 1780], *Hamilton Papers*, 2:405. For a penetrating discussion of the role of fame in Hamilton's conception of human nature, see Stourzh, *Alexander Hamilton*, 99–106.

25. Hamilton to Duane [3 Sept. 1780], *Hamilton Papers*, 2:401.

26. Ibid., 404–8, 411, quotations on 407, 404, 408, 411. Hamilton quickly qualified the meaning of the phrase "complete sovereignty" by adding, "except as to that part of internal politics, which relates to the rights of property and life among individuals and to raising money by internal taxes" (ibid., 407–8). It is important to note that in enumerating the areas over which Congress should have complete sovereignty, Hamilton gave first place to the war effort. Commercial matters were secondary. See also Hamilton to Isaac Sears [12 Oct. 1780], ibid., 472–73.

27. For a perceptive and more detailed treatment of this theme, see Kohn, "American Generals of the Revolution," 104–23. For Continental officers' growing disenchantment with American society, see Royster, *Revolutionary People at War*, 311–20. For several insightful accounts of how inadequate support of the army created Nationalist sentiment among Continental officers, see Royster, *Light-Horse Harry Lee*, chap. 3; Champagne, *Alexander McDougall*, 169–70; McLean, "Timothy Pickering," 133, 138–41.

28. Main, "Government by the People"; Countryman, *People in Revolution*, chap. 8; Ryerson, *Revolution Is Now Begun*, chap. 8; Buel, *Dear Liberty*, 207–8.

29. Clinton to president of Congress, 5 Feb. 1781, PCC, reel 81, item 67, 2:358; Spaulding, *His Excellency George Clinton*, 119–20. For Clinton's Antifederalism, see Main, *Antifederalists*, chap. 13. For the British in New York, see Countryman, "Consolidating Power in Revolutionary America."

30. *DAB*, s.v. "Jones, Joseph," "Livingston, Robert R.," "Madison, James," "Schuyler, Philip." Schuyler's activities in Congress can be followed in Bush, *Revolutionary Enigma*. For Livingston, see Dangerfield, *Robert R. Livingston*. For Madison, see Brant, *James Madison*, vol. 2.

31. *JCC*, 17:428, 791.

32. Ibid., 16:261; 17:758–59; Watterson, "Thomas Burke, Paradoxical Patriot," 676; Douglass, "Thomas Burke, Disillusioned Democrat," 173.

33. *JCC*, 18:878–88, 646, 648; Gibson, *Dr. Bodo Otto*, 264–65; Bell, "Court Martial of Dr. William Shippen, Jr.," 234. The trial was replayed in the Philadelphia newspapers. The charges and countercharges began appearing in the *Pa. Packet* on 2 September 1780. Shippen resigned in January 1781 (*JCC*, 19:15).

34. *JCC*, 18:881–82, 885, quotation on 881.

35. Cochran, *Surgeon to Washington*, 62.

36. Quoted in Gibson, *Dr. Bodo Otto*, 261. An unintended consequence of the new hospital system was to precipitate the resignation of many veteran medical officers who were affronted by Congress's creation of the egalitarian rank of "Hospital Physician and Surgeon." The result was a serious shortage of physicians in the Middle Department (Cochran, *Surgeon to Washington*, 64).

37. Cornell to governor of Rhode Island, 10 Oct. 1780, *LMCC*, 5:416.

38. The proceedings of the Boston Convention can be found in *Conn. St. Recs.*, 3:559–64. The most comprehensive account of the Boston Convention is in Crosskey and Jeffrey, *Politics and the Constitution*, 3:136.

39. Clinton to New York Assembly, 7 Sept. 1780, New York, *Assembly Journ.*, N.Y., A.1b, reel 4, unit 1; Address of the New York Assembly to George Clinton, 9 Sept. 1780, ibid.; Resolutions of the New York Assembly, 10 Oct. 1780, *LMCC*, 5:445 n. 6.

40. The Hartford Convention's proceedings can be found in *Conn. St. Recs.*, 3:564–74, quotations on 571, 573.

41. *DAB*, s.v. "Cornell, Ezekiel," "Sullivan, John," "Varnum, James Mitchell," "Witherspoon, John." Sullivan's activities in Congress are related in Whittemore, *General of the Revolution*, chaps. 10–11. For Witherspoon, see Collins, *President Witherspoon*, vol. 2, chap. 1. A fourth general, Alexander McDougall, was elected to Congress from New York but served only thirty-seven days, from 17 January to 2 March 1781. His brief congressional career is discussed in Champagne, *Alexander McDougall*, 170–72.

42. Cornell to NG [21 July 1780], *LMCC*, 5:281; Sullivan to president of New Hampshire, 2 Oct. 1780, ibid., 397.

43. Sullivan to president of New Hampshire, 2 Oct. 1780, ibid., 398. Other officers included Philip Schuyler, Alexander Hamilton, and NG (Burnett, *Continental Congress*, 487–88).

44. Witherspoon to governor of New Jersey, 16 Dec. 1780, *LMCC*, 5:487. See also Duane to governor of New York, 14 Nov. 1780, ibid., 445. The issue of using military force against the states was raised again in March 1781 by a congressional committee composed of Madison, Duane, and James Mitchell Varnum. The committee's report, which favored using force, was deferred until May and overwhelmingly rejected in August 1781 (*JCC*, 19:236, 20:469–71, 773; Rakove, *Beginnings of National Politics*, 289–91).

45. *JCC*, 19:43, 102–3, 105–6, 110–13, 126–28; Burnett, *Continental Congress*, 490–91; Alexander, *Revolutionary Conservative*, 144–45. The clearest summary of the complicated history of the impost is the editor's note in *Morris Papers*, 1:395–97.

46. Madison's about-face was pragmatic. He thought the measure too strong and expected it would be voted down by the states (Brant, *James Madison*, 2:211–12). For an insightful analysis of Madison's inconsistent Nationalism, see Banning, "James Madison." Sullivan's biographer suggests that his contradictory behavior might be explained either by his not wanting to alienate his state's commercial interests or by his dislike of Thomas Burke, with whom he almost fought a duel in 1777 (Whittemore, *General of the Revolution*, 164). I have been unable to discover why Witherspoon or Jones voted against the impost. Witherspoon may have believed the amended version too weak.

47. *JCC*, 19:111–12; Henderson, *Party Politics*, 273–75.

48. The genesis of the office of the secretary at war is fully covered in Ward, *Department of War*, 7–11. For Adams's objections to Sullivan, see Sullivan to GW, 6 Mar. 1781, *LMCC*, 6:11–12; Wells, *Samuel Adams*, 3:128–30; Sanders, *Executive Departments*, 98–99.

49. Quoted in Sanders, *Executive Departments*, 110. See also Dangerfield, *Robert R. Livingston*, 140.

50. McDougall insisted on serving in the army during the summer and being allowed to retain his rank and pay while holding the secretaryship (Champagne, *Alexander McDougall*, 171–72; Ver Steeg, *Robert Morris*, 71–72).

51. RM to president of Congress, 13 Mar. 1781, *Morris Papers*, 1:18; Ver Steeg, *Robert Morris*, 60–61.

52. Houston to Thomas McKean, 31 Mar. 1781, *LMCC*, 6:41.

53. Ward, *Department of War*, 13; Dangerfield, *Robert R. Livingston*, 144.

54. Quoted in Burnett, *Continental Congress*, 481.

55. *JCC*, 19:126. RM was not authorized to purchase or sell specific supplies until June 1781 (ibid., 180, 20:598).

56. The best study of RM is Ver Steeg, *Robert Morris*. See also Ferguson, *Power of the Purse*, chaps. 6–8.

57. RM to president of Congress, 14 May 1781, *Morris Papers*, 1:62–63, quotation on 63; RM to GW, 29 Mar. 1781, ibid., 97.

58. RM to Heath, 16 Oct. 1781, ibid., 3:64; RM to president of Congress, 30 June 1780, ibid., 1:205–6; Johnson, "Robert Morris," 8.

59. Ver Steeg, *Robert Morris*, 72–73; Henderson, *Party Politics*, 291.

60. RM to a committee of Congress, 26 Mar. 1781, *Morris Papers*, 1:22, 24. For additional examples of RM's insistence on frugality and retrenchment, see RM to Schuyler, 29 May 1781, ibid., 92; RM to GW, 29 May 1781, ibid., 95; RM to Jay, 4 July 1781, ibid., 222–23; RM, Diary, 21 Aug. 1781, ibid., 2:79; RM to GW, 26 Jan. 1782, ibid., 4:119.

61. RM to governor of Virginia, 15 Jan. 1782, *Morris Papers*, 4:46–47; RM to GW, 29 May 1781, ibid., 1:97.

62. RM to Benjamin Franklin, 27 Sept. 1782, Wharton, ed., *Revolutionary Diplomatic Correspondence*, 5:774. See also RM to president of Congress, 21 Sept. 1781, *Morris Papers*, 2:323; RM to NG, 24 Apr. 1782, ibid., 327.

63. Ver Steeg, *Robert Morris*, chaps. 4–5; Ferguson, *Power of the Purse*, chap. 7. "Morris notes" were warrants drawn on the Office of Finance and backed by Morris's personal credit. They were issued in denominations of $20, $50, and $80 (Ver Steeg, *Robert Morris*, 87).

64. RM to Jay, 13 July 1781, *Morris Papers*, 1:287; Ver Steeg, *Robert Morris*, 67–68. The role of merchants and public creditors in the origins of the Nationalist movement has been vastly overemphasized. What is most striking about this earlier period is the lack of support the Nationalists' financial program received from the very economic interests it was purportedly designed to serve. Thus, for example, the mercantile community demonstrated a remarkable lack of interest in subscribing to the Bank of North America. On this point, see *Morris Papers*, 1:315 n. 3; NG to RM, 18 Aug. 1781, ibid., 2:69; editor's note, ibid., 3:121 n. 1; Ver Steeg, *Robert Morris*, 84. In addition, rather than pleasing public creditors, RM's financial program was initially denounced by them. Public creditors' hostility was directed at RM's recommendation to halt the practice of giving loan office certificates in lieu of the interest due them and at his proposal in June 1782 to stop further payment of interest on loan office certificates in bills of exchange on France. For the adverse reaction of public creditors to Morris's program, see RM to Donaldson Yeates, 28 Dec. 1781, *Morris Papers*, 3:460; RM, circular to the governors of Massachusetts, Rhode Island, and Maryland, 3 Jan. 1782, ibid., 482; editor's note, ibid., 5:398n. For the order stopping interest payments in loan office certificates see RM, circular to the Continental loan officers, 13 Oct. 1781, ibid., 3:50–51; editor's note, ibid., 5:397n–399n.

65. RM to NG, 24 Apr. 1782, *Morris Papers*, 5:50. See also RM, circular to the governors of the states, 16 May 1782, ibid., 190–92; RM to NG, 22 Jan. 1783, Sanders, *Executive Departments*, 139. For a detailed discussion by Morris of his belief that the national government was better able to act in the public interest, see RM to the Speaker of the Pennsylvania Assembly, 13 Feb. 1782, *Morris Papers*, 4:227–29. Rakove, *Beginnings of National Politics*, 307, is essentially correct in stating that RM's program "was not a model for leviathan." But he is mistaken in drawing from that premise the conclusion that RM did not want to change the balance of power in favor of Congress.

66. RM, circular to the governors of Massachusetts, Rhode Island, and Maryland, 3 Jan. 1782, *Morris Papers*, 3:481–82.

67. RM, circular to the governors of the states, 19 Oct. 1781, *Morris Papers*, 3:88; RM to the governors of Massachusetts, Rhode Island, and Maryland, 3 Jan. 1782, ibid., 482. See also RM to Lovell, 10 July 1781, Wharton, ed., *Revolutionary Diplomatic Correspondence*, 5:604; RM to president of Congress, 29 July 1782, ibid., 624; RM to the governors of the states, 21 Oct. 1782, ibid., 828.

68. RM, circular to the governors of the states, 9 Feb. 1782, *Morris Papers*, 4:196. For

variations on this theme, see RM, circular to the governors of the states, 9 Mar. 1782, ibid., 375–76; RM to Nathaniel Appleton, 13 Mar. 1782, ibid., 402; RM to [George] Olney, 1 June 1782, Wharton, ed., *Revolutionary Diplomatic Correspondence*, 5:468. Cf. Jensen, "Idea of a National Government," 366–67; Rakove, *Beginnings of National Politics*, 303–5.

69. GW to president of Congress, 8 May 1781, *GW Writings*, 22:60; GW to Heath, 9 May 1781, ibid., 63–64, quotation on 64; GW, circular to the New England states, 10 May 1781, ibid., 68.

70. RM to GW, 29 May 1781, *Morris Papers*, 1:94–95, 95 n. 1; RM to Thomas Lowrey, 29 May 1781, ibid., 90–91; RM to Schuyler, 29 May 1781, ibid., 92–93; Ver Steeg, *Robert Morris*, 73; Johnson, "Robert Morris," 9.

71. RM to Oliver Phelps, 30 Mar. 1782, *Morris Papers*, 4:484; Ver Steeg, *Robert Morris*, 106.

72. Advertisement for Philadelphia Contract Proposals, 30 June 1781, *Morris Papers*, 1:207. The simplicity of the system was belied in practice. For the bureaucratic "ordeal facing successful bidders," see ibid., 4:157–58 n. 3. For RM's plan to sell specific supplies, see RM to GW, 5 July 1781, ibid., 1:237; RM to GW, 23 July 1781, ibid., 372.

73. RM, Diary, 21 Aug. 1781, ibid., 2:75–76. See also RM and Richard Peters to GW, 13 Aug. 1781, ibid., 50–53; Ver Steeg, *Robert Morris*, 74; Freeman, *GW*, 5:309; Johnston, *Yorktown Campaign*, 83. The best description of the background to RM's meeting with GW is the editor's note in ibid., 2:73–74. The phrase "Financier Elect" is found in RM to GW, 15 June 1781, *Morris Papers*, 1:153.

74. RM to Matthew Ridley, 21 Aug. 1781, *Morris Papers*, 2:85; RM to commissary general of purchases, 24 Aug. 1781, ibid., 102; RM to president of Delaware, 26 Aug. 1781, ibid., 107; RM to governor of Maryland, 26 Aug. 1781, ibid., 108.

75. RM to Ridley, 21 Aug. 1781, *Morris Papers*, 2:85; RM, circular to Stephen Steward and Son, Jonathan Hudson, David Stewart, and Samuel Smith, 28 Aug. 1781, ibid., 123; RM to Donaldson Yeates, 28 Aug. 1781, ibid., 147–48; RM to president of Delaware, 1 Sept. 1781, ibid., 176. Even with all of RM's efforts there was still a shortage of vessels (Freeman, *GW*, 5:323–24).

76. On the sources of RM's funds, see RM to president of Congress, 18 Oct. 1781, *Morris Papers*, 3:80; Ver Steeg, *Robert Morris*, 76–77; Ferguson, *Power of the Purse*, 126–30. For a detailed account of the preparations for the siege at Yorktown, see Johnston, *Yorktown Campaign*, chaps. 4–5.

77. RM, Diary, 8 Dec. 1781, *Morris Papers*, 3:353–54. For Pickering's suggestion to abolish the assistant quartermaster general's position, see Timothy Pickering to president of Congress, 24 March 1781, Pickering Papers, reel 33. The quotation is from Pickering to president of Congress, 3 March 1781, ibid.

78. RM to Phelps, 30 March 1782, *Morris Papers*, 4:482–83; RM to Heath, 22 Dec. 1781, ibid., 3:428. See also RM to Heath, 13 Nov. 1781, ibid., 179; Ver Steeg, *Robert Morris*, 106–7.

79. RM to GW, 26 Jan. 1782, *Morris Papers*, 4:119; RM to NG, 24 Apr. 1782, ibid., 5:50. For RM's refusal to supply the southern troops by contract, see RM to NG, 19 Dec. 1781, ibid., 4:406–9, 410 n. 4. For the poor condition of NG's army, see Thayer, *Nathanael Greene*, 396–97; Johnson, *Nathanael Greene*, 2:315–17.

80. GW to Benjamin Lincoln, 15 May 1782, *GW Writings*, 24:255–56. See also GW to Pickering, 15 May 1782, ibid., 257–58. GW's dissatisfaction with Pickering's performance was of long standing. See Clarfield, *Timothy Pickering*, 66. Pickering gave the lack of money as his excuse for not coming to camp (Pickering to GW, 29 May 1782, *GW Writings*, 24:258n).

81. The Moving Army consisted of fighting troops not assigned to a specific post. For the contracts, see Contract with Comfort Sands and Company [6 Dec. 1781], *Morris Papers*, 3:342–47; Contract for the Moving Army [6 Apr. 1782], ibid., 4:525–30. The two contracts were later merged. The intricate business partnerships between RM, Comfort Sands, and

other merchants are skillfully untangled in ibid., 4:497 n. 8, 530n–531n; Ver Steeg, *Robert Morris*, 142–51. The quotation is from John Campbell to Hugh Hughes, 20 Apr. 1782, Hughes Ltrbks., 5.

82. D. Carthy to William Duer, 2 July 1787, William Duer Papers, 2:27, NYHS.

83. Heath to Benjamin Lincoln, 27 Mar. 1782, GW Papers, reel 83. For typical examples of the complaints, see Heath to Comfort Sands, 1 Mar. 1782, ibid.; Proceedings of a Meeting of a Board of Officers respecting the Issues of Provisions under Contract, 29 Apr. 1782, ibid. See also *Morris Papers*, 5:212n–213n; Ver Steeg, *Robert Morris*, 142–43, 146. Sands denied all wrongdoing. For his defense, see Sands and Company to David Humphreys and Jonathan Trumbull, Jr., 11 May 1782, GW Papers, reel 84; Sands and Company to the Committee of Field Officers of the Army, 14 May 1782, ibid., reel 85.

84. GW to Sands, 25 May 1782, *GW Writings*, 24:285. Of the hundreds of people GW dealt with during the war, no one angered him more than Sands. See esp. GW to Sands, 25 May 1782, ibid., 282–84.

85. GW to the superintendent of finance, 16 June, 14 Sept. 1782, 8 Jan. 1783, *GW Writings*, 24:349, 25:124, 26:20.

86. For a sample of negative assessments of Sands's character, see Herman Swift to Heath, 26 Mar. 1782, GW Papers, reel 83; Minutes of Conversation of Colonel Humphreys and Jonathan Trumbull, Jr., with Mr. Sands, 6 May 1782, ibid., reel 84; Ver Steeg, *Robert Morris*, 147.

87. RM to GW, 29 Aug. 1782, Wharton, ed., *Revolutionary Diplomatic Correspondence*, 5:676; RM to president of Congress, 21 Oct. 1782, ibid., 823; Sands and Company to Heath, 28 July 1782, GW Papers, reel 86; Sands to RM, 11 Sept. 1782, ibid.; Ver Steeg, *Robert Morris*, 147–50.

88. RM to president of Congress, 21 Oct. 1782, Wharton, ed., *Revolutionary Diplomatic Correspondence*, 5:824–25, quotation on 825.

89. RM to the governors of the states, 21 Oct. 1782, ibid., 826; RM to president of Congress, ibid., 21 Oct. 1782, 824; Ver Steeg, *Robert Morris*, 150.

90. RM to president of Congress, 21 Oct. 1782, Wharton, ed., *Revolutionary Diplomatic Correspondence*, 5:825.

91. Lesser, ed., *Sinews of Independence*, 240.

92. GW to Heath, 5 Feb. 1783, *GW Writings*, 26:97.

93. Polishook, *Rhode Island and the Union*, chap. 3; Ver Steeg, *Robert Morris*, 129–31; Ferguson, *Power of the Purse*, 152–54.

Conclusion

1. GW to Hamilton, 31 Mar. 1781, *GW Writings*, 26:224; NG to [Edward] Carrington, 24 Jan. 1782, Nathanael Greene Papers, Letterbooks (1 Jan.–8 Apr. 1782), LC; Jeremiah Wadsworth to NG, 12 Dec. 1782, Wadsworth Letters; "The Continentalist No. 6" [4 July 1782], *Hamilton Papers*, 3:99–106; RM to Hamilton, 28 Aug. 1782, Wharton, ed., *Revolutionary Diplomatic Correspondence*, 5:674.

2. RM to Hamilton, 28 Aug. 1782, Wharton, ed., *Revolutionary Diplomatic Correspondence*, 5:674.

Appendix

1. *DAB*; Dexter, *Biographical Sketches of the Graduates of Yale College*; Sibley and Shipton, *Biographical Sketches of Those Who Attended Harvard College*; Blaine, *Blaine Family*; Holstein, *Swedish Holsteins in America*, 70–83; Griffin, *Stephen Moylan*; Bodle and Thibaut, *Valley Forge*, 2:352–53, 581 n. 7; *Morris Papers*, 1:89 n. 2, 178, 218, 261 n. 6, 9; *Greene Papers*, 1:329n, 2:371–72n; Rossman, *Thomas Mifflin*; Thayer, *Nathanael Greene*; Aylett, "Correspondence," 1:87; Biddle, "Owen Biddle"; Destler, "Colonel Henry Champion"; Hart, "Colonel Robert Lettis Hooper"; Brophy and Tripp, eds., "Supplies for General Sullivan," pt. 1, 245–56; Boyer, ed., "Letterbook of Jacob Weiss," 22–136.

BIBLIOGRAPHY

Primary Sources

MANUSCRIPT COLLECTIONS

American Philosophical Society Library, Philadelphia
  Nathanael Greene Papers
William L. Clements Library, University of Michigan, Ann Arbor
  Nathanael Greene Papers
Connecticut Historical Society, Hartford
  Samuel Gray Papers
  Joseph Trumbull Papers
  Jeremiah Wadsworth Papers
  Jeremiah Wadsworth Letters (Wadsworth Atheneum, Hartford)
Connecticut State Library, Hartford
  Connecticut Archives, Revolutionary War
  John Fitch Papers
  Governor Joseph Trumbull Collection
Duke University Library, Durham, North Carolina
  Nathanael Greene Papers
Friends Historical Society, Swarthmore College, Swarthmore, Pennsylvania
  Biddle Manuscripts, Owen Biddle Letterbooks
  Biddle Manuscripts, Correspondence
Historical Society of Pennsylvania, Philadelphia
  Clement Biddle Papers
  James Burnside Letterbook
  Chaloner and White Letterbooks
  Chaloner and White Collection
  Ferdinand J. Dreer Collection
  Etting Collection
  Simon Gratz Autograph Collection
  Thomas McKean Papers
  Jonathan Potts Papers
  Society Collection
  Society Miscellaneous Collection

Washington-Biddle Collection
    Anthony Wayne Papers
Library of Congress, Washington, D.C.
    Ephraim Blaine Papers
    Peter Force Collection:
        John Davis Papers
        John Fisher Papers
        Thomas Hamilton Papers
        Charles Stewart Papers
    Nathanael Greene Papers, General Correspondence
    Nathanael Greene Papers, Letterbooks
    Hugh Hughes Papers
    Jonathan Potts Papers
    Dr. Peter Turner Papers
    Papers of George Washington, Presidential Papers Microfilm, Series 4
Massachusetts Historical Society, Boston
    Timothy Pickering Papers (Microfilm copy in Library of Congress)
Morristown National Historical Park, Morristown, New Jersey
    Joseph Lewis Letters
National Archives, Washington, D.C.
    Papers of the Continental Congress, 1774–89 (M-247):
        Reel 40: Reports of the Committees of Conference with the Commander in Chief at
            Cambridge, 1775, and Valley Forge, 1778–79
        Reel 41: Report on the public debt in 1781 and estimate of expenses, with related papers,
            1779–80
        Reel 46: Letters and other Records of the Committee to Headquarters, 1780
        Reels 48–52: Memorials Addressed to Congress, 1775–88
        Reels 53–56: Petitions Addressed to Congress, 1775–89
        Reel 80: Connecticut State Papers, 1775–89
        Reel 81: New York State Papers, 1775–88
        Reel 84: Maryland and Delaware State Papers, 1775–89
        Reels 90–104: [Miscellaneous] Letters Addressed to Congress, 1775–89
        Reel 175: Letters from Maj. Gen. Nathanael Greene, 1775–86
        Reel 182: Letters from Colonels, 1775–83
        Reel 192–93: Letters of Nathanael Greene with Various Papers Relating to the Quarter-
            master's Department, 1778–80
        Reel 199: Letters and Papers Relative to the Quartermaster's Department, 1777–84
    War Department Collection of Revolutionary War Records, Record Group 93:
        Letters Sent by Timothy Pickering, Quartermaster General
        Records of Accounts of the Commissioner for Settling the Accounts of the Quarter-
            master Department, May 1786–March 1789 and April 1790
        Miscellaneous Numbered Records (The Manuscript File)
        Letters Sent by Samuel Hodgdon, Richard Frothingham, and Benjamin Flower, 19 July
            1778–24 May 1784
New Jersey Historical Society, Newark
    James Abeel Letterbook
    Ely Collection
    Nathanael Greene Letters
    Nathanael Greene Papers
New Jersey State Library, Trenton
    Moore Furman Papers

New-York Historical Society, New York City
  BV-War of the Revolution
  William Duer Papers
  Horatio Gates Papers
  Hugh Hughes Letterbooks
  Alexander McDougall Papers
  Miscellaneous Manuscripts:
    Letters to John Chaloner, 1780–90
    Nathanael Greene
  Joseph Reed Papers
New York State Historical Association, Cooperstown
  Charles Stewart Papers
Yale University Library, New Haven, Connecticut
  Knollenberg Collection
  Wadsworth Family Collection

NEWSPAPERS

Boston-Gazette, and Country Journal
Dunlap's Pennsylvania Packet, or, the General Advertiser (Philadelphia)
Independent Chronicle. And the Universal Advertiser (Boston)
New-England Chronicle (Boston)
New Jersey Gazette (Trenton)
New-York Journal; or, the General Advertiser
New York Packet. And the American Advertiser
Pennsylvania Gazette (Philadelphia)
Pennsylvania Journal; and the Weekly Advertiser (Philadelphia)
Providence Gazette; and Country Journal (R.I.)
Virginia Gazette (Williamsburg)

PUBLISHED SOURCES

Adams, John. *Diary and Autobiography of John Adams*. Edited by L. H. Butterfield et al. 4 vols. Cambridge, Mass., 1961.
Adams, Samuel. *The Writings of Samuel Adams*. Edited by Harry Alonzo Cushing. 4 vols. New York, 1904–8.
Aylett, William. "Correspondence of Col. William Aylett, Commissary General of Virginia." *Tyler's Quarterly Historical and Genealogical Magazine* 1 (1920): 87–110, 142–61.
Bartlett, Josiah. *The Papers of Josiah Bartlett*. Edited by Frank C. Mevers. Hanover, N.H., 1979.
Boyer, Melville J., ed. "The Letterbook of Jacob Weiss, Deputy Quartermaster General of the Revolution." *Lehigh County Historical Society Proceedings* 21 (1956): 5–136.
Brophy, Marion, and Wendell Tripp, eds. "Supplies for General Sullivan: The Correspondence of Colonel Charles Stewart, May–September, 1779." *New York History* 60 (1979): pts. 1 and 2, 245–81, 439–67; 61 (1980): pt. 3, 43–80.
Burnett, Edmund C., ed. *Letters of Members of the Continental Congress*. 8 vols. Washington, D.C., 1921–36.
Chastellux, Marquis de. *Travels in North America in the Years 1780, 1781 and 1782*. Translated and edited by Howard C. Rice. 2 vols. Chapel Hill, 1963.

Clinton, George. *The Public Papers of George Clinton, First Governor of New York, 1777–1795, 1801–1804.* Edited by Hugh Hastings. 10 vols. New York, 1899–1914.

Cochran, John. *Surgeon to Washington: Dr. John Cochran 1730–1807.* Edited by Morris Saffron. New York, 1977.

Connecticut. *The Public Records of the State of Connecticut.* Edited by Charles J. Hoadly and Leonard W. Labaree. 11 vols. Hartford, 1894–.

Dann, John C., ed. *The Revolution Remembered: Eyewitness Accounts of the War for Independence.* Chicago, 1980.

Delaware. *Acts of the General Assembly of the Delaware State.* Wilmington, 1775–83.

Fogg, Jeremiah. *Orderly Book Kept by Jeremiah Fogg.* Edited by Albert A. Folsom. Exeter, N.H., 1903.

Force, Peter, ed. *American Archives.* . . . 9 vols. Washington, D.C., 1839–53.

Ford, Worthington C., et al., eds. *Journals of the Continental Congress, 1774–1789.* 34 vols. Washington, D.C., 1904–37.

Fries, Adelaide L., ed. *Records of Moravians in North Carolina.* 11 vols. Raleigh, N.C., 1922–69.

Furman, Moore. *The Letters of Moore Furman: Deputy Quarter-Master General of New Jersey in the Revolution.* Edited by Anne deB. MacIlvaine et al. New York, 1912.

Gibbes, R. W., ed. *Documentary History of the American Revolution.* 3 vols. New York, 1853–57, and Columbia, S.C., 1853.

Greene, Nathanael. *The Papers of General Nathanael Greene.* Edited by Richard K. Showman et al. 2 vols. to date. Chapel Hill, 1979–.

Hamilton, Alexander. *The Papers of Alexander Hamilton.* Edited by Harold C. Syrett, Jacob E. Cooke et al. 26 vols. New York, 1961–79.

Heath, William. *The Heath Papers. Collections of the Massachusetts Historical Society.* Ser. 5, vol. 4; Ser. 7, vols. 4–5. Boston, 1878–1905.

————. *Memoirs of Major-General William Heath.* Edited by William Abbatt. New York, 1901.

Henshaw, William. "The Orderly Books of Colonel William Henshaw, October 1, 1775, through October 3, 1776." *Proceedings of the American Antiquarian Society* 57 (1947): 17–234.

Hughes, Hugh. *The Memorial and Documents in the Case of Hugh Hughes.* . . . Washington City [D.C.], 1802.

Jacobson, David L., ed. *The English Libertarian Heritage from the Writings of John Trenchard and Thomas Gordon in The Independent Whig and Cato's Letters.* Indianapolis, 1965.

Jay, John. *The Correspondence and Public Papers of John Jay.* Edited by Henry P. Johnston. 4 vols. New York, 1890–93.

Jefferson, Thomas. *The Papers of Thomas Jefferson.* Edited by Julian P. Boyd et al. 20 vols. to date. Princeton, 1950–.

Jensen, Merrill, ed. *English Historical Documents,* Vol. 9: *American Colonial Documents to 1776.* New York, 1955.

Joslin, Joseph, Jr. "Journal of Joseph Joslin, Jr., of South Killingly, a teamster in Western Connecticut, 1777–1778." *Collections of the Connecticut Historical Society.* Vol. 7. Hartford, 1899.

Lauber, Almon W., ed. *Orderly Books of the Fourth New York Regiment, 1778–1780 [and] the Second New York Regiment, 1780–1783.* Albany, 1932.

Laurens, John. *The Army Correspondence of Colonel John Laurens in the Years 1777–1778.* Edited by William Gilmore Simms. New York, 1867.

Lee, Charles. *The Lee Papers. Collections of the New-York Historical Society.* Vols. 4–7. New York, 1872–75.

Lee, Richard Henry. *The Letters of Richard Henry Lee*. Edited by James Curtis Ballagh. 2 vols. New York, 1911–14.

Lincoln, Charles Henry, ed. *The Correspondence of William Shirley: Governor of Massachusetts and Military Commander in America, 1731–1760*. 2 vols. New York, 1921.

Madison, James. *The Papers of James Madison*. Edited by William T. Hutchinson, William M. E. Rachal et al. 13 vols. to date. Chicago and Charlottesville, 1962–.

Martin, Joseph Plumb. *Private Yankee Doodle: Being A Narrative of Some of the Adventures, Dangers and Sufferings of a Revolutionary Soldier*. Edited by George F. Scheer. 1830, rpt. Boston, 1962.

Maryland. *Archives of Maryland*. Edited by William Hand Browne et al. 72 vols. to date. Baltimore, 1883–.

———. *Papers Relating Chiefly to the Maryland Line during the Revolution*. Edited by Thomas Balch. Philadelphia, 1857.

Massachusetts. *Acts and Resolves, Public and Private, of the Province of Massachusetts Bay*. 21 vols. Boston, 1869–1922.

———. *Acts and Laws of the Commonwealth of Massachusetts [1780–1805]*. Boston, 1890–98.

———. *The Journals of Each Provincial Congress of Massachusetts in 1774 and 1775*. Edited by William Lincoln. Boston, 1838.

Morgan, John. *A Vindication of His Public Character in the Station of Director-General of the Military Hospitals and Physician in Chief to the American Army*. Boston, 1777.

Morris, Robert. *The Papers of Robert Morris, 1781–1784*. Edited by E. James Ferguson et al. 5 vols. to date. Pittsburgh, 1973–.

Muhlenberg, John Peter Gabriel. "Orderly Book of General John Peter Gabriel Muhlenberg, March 26–December 20, 1777." *Pennsylvania Magazine of History and Biography* 35 (1911): 59–89, 156–87, 290–303.

New Hampshire. *Documents and Records Relating to the State of New Hampshire*. Edited by Nathaniel Bouton et al. 40 vols. Concord, N.H., 1867–1941.

New Jersey. *Acts of the General Assembly of the State of New Jersey*. Burlington and Trenton, 1777–83.

———. *Documents Relating to the Revolutionary History of New Jersey. Archives of the State of New Jersey*. 2d Series. Edited by William S. Stryker et al. 5 vols. Trenton, 1901–17.

———. *Selections from the Correspondence of the Executive of New Jersey, from 1776 to 1786*. Newark, 1848.

New York. *Journals of the Provincial Congress, Provincial Convention, Committee of Safety and Council of Safety of the State of New York 1775–1776–1777*. 2 vols. Albany, 1842.

———. *Laws of the State of New York*. 5 vols. Albany, 1886.

———. *New York [State] Assembly Journal*. Poughkeepsie, N.Y., 1777–83.

Nicholas, James R., ed. "The Doughboy of 1780: Pages from a Revolutionary Diary." *Atlantic Monthly* 124 (1924): 459–63.

North Carolina. *The State Records of North Carolina*. Edited by Walter Clark. 16 vols. Winston and Goldsboro, 1895–1925.

Pennsylvania. *Pennsylvania Archives*. Edited by Samuel Hazard et al. 138 vols. Philadelphia and Harrisburg, 1852–1935.

———. *Pennsylvania Colonial Records: Minutes of the Supreme Executive Council of Pennsylvania*. 16 vols. Harrisburg, 1852–53.

———. *The Statutes at Large of Pennsylvania from 1682 to 1801*. Edited by James T. Mitchell and Henry Flanders. 17 vols. Harrisburg, 1896–1915.

Peters, Richard. "Letter to John Montgomery [1784]." *Magazine of Western History* 4 (1886): 680.

Rhode Island. *Acts and Resolves of Rhode Island*. Newport, R.I., 1755–84.

————. *Records of the State of Rhode Island and Providence Plantations in New England, 1632–1792*. Edited by John Russell Bartlett. 10 vols. Providence, 1856–65.

————. "Revolutionary Correspondence from 1775 to 1782." *Collections of the Rhode Island Historical Society* 6 (1867): 107–300.

Rodney, Caesar. *Letters to and from Caesar Rodney, 1756–1784*. Edited by George Herbert Ryden. Philadelphia, 1933.

Rush, Benjamin. *Letters of Benjamin Rush*. Edited by L. H. Butterfield. 2 vols. Princeton, 1951.

Rutledge, John. "Letters of John Rutledge." *South Carolina Historical and Genealogical Magazine* 17–18 (1916–17): 131–46, 42–69, 155–67.

Smith, Paul H., ed. *Letters of Delegates to Congress, 1774–1789*. 8 vols. to date. Washington, D.C., 1976–.

South Carolina. *The Statutes at Large of South Carolina*. Edited by Thomas Cooper and D. J. McCord. 10 vols. Columbia, S.C., 1836–41.

Sparks, Jared, ed. *Correspondence of the American Revolution*. 4 vols. Boston, 1853.

Staples, William R. [ed.]. *Rhode Island in the Continental Congress*. Providence, 1870.

Sullivan, John. *Letters and Papers of Major-General John Sullivan*. Edited by Otis G. Hammond. *Collections of the New Hampshire Historical Society*. Vols. 13–15. Concord, N.H., 1930–39.

Thacher, James. *A Military Journal during the American Revolutionary War*. Boston, 1823.

Trumbull, Jonathan. *The Trumbull Papers. Collections of the Massachusetts Historical Society*. Ser. 5, vols. 9–10; Ser. 7, vols. 2–3. Boston, 1885–1902.

Virginia. *Calendar of Virginia State Papers and Other State Manuscripts*. Edited by William P. Palmer. 11 vols. Richmond, 1875–93.

————. *Journals of the Council of the State of Virginia*. Edited by H. R. McIlwaine and Wilmer Hill. 3 vols. Richmond, 1939–52.

————. *Official Letters of the Governors of Virginia, 1776–1783*. Edited by H. R. McIlwaine. 3 vols. Richmond, 1926–29.

————. *The Statutes at Large: Being a Collection of All the Laws of Virginia*. Edited by William Waller Hening. 13 vols. Richmond, 1809–23.

Wade, Herbert T., and Robert A. Lively. *This Glorious Cause: The Adventures of Two Company Officers in Washington's Army*. Princeton, 1958.

Warren-Adams Letters: Being Chiefly a Correspondence among John Adams, Samuel Adams, and James Warren. Collections of the Massachusetts Historical Society. Vols. 72–73. Boston, 1917–25.

Washington, George. *The Diaries of George Washington*. Edited by Donald Jackson et al. 4 vols. Charlottesville, 1976–78.

————. *The Writings of George Washington from the Original Manuscript Sources, 1745–1799*. Edited by John C. Fitzpatrick. 39 vols. Washington, D.C., 1931–44.

Wharton, Francis, ed. *The Revolutionary Diplomatic Correspondence of the American Revolution*. 6 vols. Washington, D.C., 1889.

Secondary Sources

REFERENCE WORKS

Boatner, Mark Mayo, III. *Encyclopedia of the American Revolution*. Bicentennial edition. New York, 1975.

Dexter, Franklin B. *Biographical Sketches of the Graduates of Yale College with Annals of the College History*. 6 vols. New York, 1885–1912.

Johnson, Allen, Dumas Malone, et al., eds. *Dictionary of American Biography*. 20 vols. New York, 1928–37. Supplements 1–6. New York, 1944–80.
Lesser, Charles H., ed. *The Sinews of Independence: Monthly Strength Reports of the Continental Army*. Chicago, 1976.
Luttwak, Edward. *A Dictionary of Modern War*. New York, 1971.
McLachlan, James. *Princetonians, 1748–1768: A Biographical Dictionary*. Princeton, 1976.
Peckham, Howard H., ed. *The Toll of Independence: Engagements and Battle Casualties of the American Revolution*. Chicago, 1974.
Sibley, John Langdon, and Clifford K. Shipton. *Biographical Sketches of Those Who Attended Harvard College*. 17 vols. Cambridge and Boston, 1873–1975.
Thian, Raphael P. *Legislative History of the General Staff of the Army of the United States, 1775–1901*. Washington, D.C., 1901.

BOOKS

Adams, Willi Paul. *The First American Constitutions: Republican Ideology and the Making of the State Constitutions in the Revolutionary Era*. Chapel Hill, 1980.
Alden, John Richard. *The South in the Revolution, 1763–1789*. Baton Rouge, 1957.
Alexander, Edward P. *A Revolutionary Conservative: James Duane of New York*. New York, 1938.
Ammerman, David. *In the Common Cause: American Response to the Coercive Acts*. Charlottesville, 1974.
Andrews, Charles M. *The Colonial Background of the American Revolution*. Rev. ed. New Haven, 1931.
_____. *The Colonial Period of American History*. 4 vols. New Haven, 1934–38.
Bailey, Raymond C. *Popular Influence upon Public Policy: Petitioning in Eighteenth-Century Virginia*. Westport, Conn., 1979.
Bailyn, Bernard. *The Ideological Origins of the American Revolution*. Cambridge, Mass., 1967.
_____. *The New England Merchants in the Seventeenth Century*. Cambridge, Mass., 1955.
_____. *The Origins of American Politics*. New York, 1967.
_____, et al. *The Great Republic: A History of the American People*. 1st ed. Boston, 1977.
Baker, Norman. *Government and Contractors: The British Treasury and War Supplies, 1775–1783*. London, 1971.
Banning, Lance. *The Jeffersonian Persuasion: Evolution of a Party Ideology*. Ithaca, N.Y., 1978.
Barrow, Thomas C. *Trade and Empire: The British Customs Service in Colonial America, 1660–1775*. Cambridge, Mass., 1967.
Baxter, W. T. *The House of Hancock: Business in Boston, 1724–1775*. Cambridge, Mass., 1945.
Bell, Whitfield J., Jr. *John Morgan: Continental Doctor*. Philadelphia, 1965.
Benton, Josiah Henry. *Warning Out in New England*. Boston, 1911.
Bezanson, Anne. *Prices and Inflation during the American Revolution: Pennsylvania, 1770–1790*. Philadelphia, 1951.
Bill, Alfred Hoyt. *Valley Forge: The Making of an Army*. New York, 1952.
Blaine, John Ewing. *The Blaine Family: James Blaine, Emigrant, and His Children*. Cincinnati, 1920.
Bodle, Wayne K., and Jacqueline Thibaut. *Valley Forge Historical Research Report*. 3 vols. Valley Forge, 1980.
Bolton, Charles K. *The Private Soldier under Washington*. New York, 1902.
Bond, Beverly. *State Government in Maryland, 1777–1781*. Johns Hopkins Studies in Historical and Political Science, no. 23. Baltimore, 1905.
Bonwick, Colin. *English Radicals and the American Revolution*. Chapel Hill, 1977.

Bowler, R. Arthur. *Logistics and the Failure of the British Army in America, 1775–1783.* Princeton, 1975.

Brant, Irving. *James Madison.* 6 vols. New York, 1941–61.

Brown, Harvey E. *The Medical Department of the United States Army from 1775 to 1783.* Washington, D.C., 1873.

Brunhouse, Robert L. *The Counter-Revolution in Pennsylvania, 1776–1790.* Philadelphia, 1942.

Buel, Richard, Jr. *Dear Liberty: Connecticut's Mobilization for the Revolutionary War.* Middletown, Conn., 1980.

Burnett, Edmund Cody. *The Continental Congress.* New York, 1941.

Busch, Noel F. *Winter Quarters: George Washington and the Continental Army at Valley Forge.* New York, 1974.

Bush, Martin H. *Revolutionary Enigma: A Reappraisal of General Philip Schuyler of New York.* Port Washington, N.Y., 1969.

Calhoon, Robert McCluer. *The Loyalists in Revolutionary America, 1760–1781.* New York, 1973.

Cantlie, Neil. *A History of the Army Medical Department.* 2 vols. Edinburgh and London, 1974.

Cash, Philip. *Medical Men at the Siege of Boston, April 1775–April 1776. Memoirs of the American Philosophical Society.* Vol. 98. Philadelphia, 1973.

Champagne, Roger J. *Alexander McDougall and the American Revolution in New York.* Schenectady, N.Y., 1975.

Chester, Sir Norman. *The English Administrative System, 1780–1870.* Oxford, 1981.

Clarfield, Gerard H. *Timothy Pickering and the American Republic.* Pittsburgh, 1980.

Colbourn, H. Trevor. *The Lamp of Experience: Whig History and the Intellectual Origins of the American Revolution.* Chapel Hill, 1965.

Coleman, John M. *Thomas McKean: Forgotten Leader of the Revolution.* Rockaway, N.J., 1975.

Collier, Christopher. *Roger Sherman's Connecticut: Yankee Politics and the American Revolution.* Middletown, Conn., 1971.

Collins, Varnum Lansing. *President Witherspoon: A Biography.* 2 vols. Princeton, 1925.

Cook, Edward M. *The Fathers of the Towns: Leadership and Community Structure in Eighteenth-Century New England.* Baltimore, 1976.

Countryman, Edward. *A People in Revolution: The American Revolution and Political Society in New York, 1760–1790.* Baltimore, 1981.

Cress, Lawrence Delbert. *Citizens in Arms: The Army and Militia in American Society to the War of 1812.* Chapel Hill, 1982.

Crittenden, Charles Christopher. *The Commerce of North Carolina, 1763–1789.* New Haven, 1936.

Crosskey, William Winslow, and William Jeffrey, Jr. *Politics and the Constitution in the History of the United States.* 3 vols. Chicago, 1953–80.

Dangerfield, George. *Chancellor Robert R. Livingston of New York, 1746–1813.* New York, 1969.

Daniell, Jere R. *Experiment in Republicanism: New Hampshire Politics and the American Revolution, 1741–1794.* Cambridge, Mass., 1970.

Daniels, Bruce C. *The Connecticut Town: Growth and Development, 1635–1790.* Middletown, Conn., 1979.

Delaplaine, Edward S. *The Life of Thomas Johnson.* New York, 1927.

Destler, Chester M. *Connecticut: The Provisions State.* Connecticut Bicentennial Series, no. 5. Chester, Conn., 1973.

Dinkin, Robert J. *Voting in Provincial America: A Study of the Thirteen Colonies, 1689–1776.* Contributions in American History, No. 64. Westport, Conn., 1977.

Duncan, Louis C. *Medical Men in the American Revolution, 1775–1783.* Army Medical Bulletin, No. 25. Carlisle Barracks, Pa., 1931.

East, Robert A. *Business Enterprise in the American Revolutionary Era*. New York, 1938.

Eckenrode, H. J. *The Revolution in Virginia*. Boston, 1916.

Eisenstadt, Abraham S., et al., eds. *Before Watergate: Problems of Corruption in American Society*. Studies on Society in Change, No. 4. New York, 1979.

Ekirch, A. Roger. *"Poor Carolina": Politics and Society in Colonial North Carolina, 1729–1776*. Chapel Hill, 1981.

Evans, Emory G. *Thomas Nelson of Yorktown: Revolutionary Virginian*. Charlottesville, 1975.

Ferguson, E. James. *The Power of the Purse: A History of American Public Finance, 1776–1790*. Chapel Hill, 1961.

Flick, Alexander C. *The American Revolution in New York*. New York, 1926.

Freeman, Douglas Southall. *George Washington: A Biography*. 7 vols. New York, 1948–57.

French, Allen. *General Gage's Informers*. Ann Arbor, 1932.

Gerth, H. H., and C. Wright Mills. *From Max Weber: Essays in Sociology*. New York, 1946.

Gewehr, Wesley M. *The Great Awakening in Virginia, 1740–1790*. Durham, N.C., 1930.

Gibson, James E. *Dr. Bodo Otto and the Medical Background of the American Revolution*. Springfield, Ill., 1937.

Gipson, Lawrence Henry. *The British Empire before the American Revolution*. 15 vols. New York, 1936–70.

Gray, Lewis Cecil. *History of Agriculture in the Southern United States to 1860*. 2 vols. Washington, D.C., 1933.

Greenberg, Douglas. *Crime and Law Enforcement in the Colony of New York, 1691–1776*. Ithaca, N.Y., 1976.

Greene, George Washington. *The Life of Nathanael Greene.* . . . 3 vols. New York, 1867–71.

Greene, Jack P. *All Men Are Created Equal: Some Reflections on the Character of the American Revolution*. Oxford, 1976.

Griffin, Martin I. J. *Stephen Moylan.* . . . Philadelphia, 1909.

Gruber, Ira D. *The Howe Brothers and the American Revolution*. Chapel Hill, 1972.

Harrington, Virginia. *The New York Merchant on the Eve of the Revolution*. New York, 1953.

Hatch, Louis C. *The Administration of the American Revolutionary Army*. New York, 1904.

Hawke, David Freeman. *Benjamin Rush: Revolutionary Gadfly*. New York, 1971.

Hedges, James B. *The Browns of Providence Plantations*. 2 vols. Cambridge, Mass., 1952.

Henderson, H. James. *Party Politics in the Continental Congress*. New York, 1974.

Higginbotham, Don. *The War of American Independence: Military Attitudes, Policies, and Practice, 1763–1789*. New York, 1971.

Hoffman, Ronald. *A Spirit of Dissension: Economics, Politics, and the Revolution in Maryland*. Baltimore, 1973.

Holstein, Anna M. *Swedish Holsteins in America from 1644 to 1892*. Norristown, Pa., 1892.

Huntington, Samuel P. *The Soldier and the State: The Theory and Practice of Civil-Military Relations*. Cambridge, Mass., 1957.

Jensen, Merrill. *The Articles of Confederation: An Interpretation of the Social-Constitutional History of the American Revolution*. Madison, Wis., 1941.

————. *The Founding of a Nation: A History of the American Revolution, 1763–1776*. New York, 1968.

————. *The New Nation: A History of the United States during the Confederation, 1781–1789*. New York, 1950.

Johnson, Victor Leroy. *The Administration of the American Commissariat during the Revolutionary War*. Philadelphia, 1941.

Johnson, William. *Sketches of the Life and Correspondence of Nathanael Greene.* . . . 2 vols. Charleston, S.C., 1822.

Johnston, Henry P. *The Yorktown Campaign and the Surrender of Cornwallis*. New York, 1881.

Kapp, Friedrich. *The Life of John Kalb*. New York, 1884.

Katz, Stanley Nider. *Newcastle's New York: Anglo-American Politics, 1732–1753*. Cambridge, Mass., 1968.

Keller, Morton. *Affairs of State: Public Life in Late Nineteenth-Century America*. Cambridge, Mass., 1977.

Kennedy, David M. *Over Here: The First World War and American Society*. New York, 1980.

Kennett, Lee. *The French Forces in America, 1780–1783*. Westport, Conn., 1977.

Kerber, Linda K. *Women of the Republic: Intellect and Ideology in Revolutionary America*. Chapel Hill, 1980.

Labaree, Leonard Woods. *Conservatism in Early American History*. 1948; rpt. Ithaca, N.Y., 1967.

———. *Royal Government in America: A Study of the British Colonial System before 1783*. New Haven, 1930.

Leach, Douglas Edward. *Arms for Empire: A Military History of the British Colonies in North America*. New York, 1973.

Leiby, Adrian C. *The Revolutionary War in the Hackensack Valley: The Jersey Dutch and the Neutral Ground, 1775–1783*. New Brunswick, N.J., 1962.

Linderman, Gerald F. *The Mirror of War: American Society and the Spanish American War*. Ann Arbor, 1974.

Lossing, Benson J. *The Life and Times of Philip Schuyler*. 2 vols. New York, 1860.

Lundin, Leonard. *Cockpit of the Revolution: The War for Independence in New Jersey*. Princeton, 1940.

McCoy, Drew R. *The Elusive Republic: Political Economy in Jeffersonian America*. Chapel Hill, 1980.

Mackesy, Piers. *The War for America, 1775–1783*. Cambridge, Mass., 1964.

Macmillan, Margaret Burnham. *The War Governors in the American Revolution*. New York, 1943.

Maier, Pauline. *The Old Revolutionaries: Political Lives in the Age of Samuel Adams*. New York, 1980.

Main, Jackson Turner. *The Antifederalists: Critics of the Constitution, 1781–1788*. Chapel Hill, 1961.

———. *The Sovereign States, 1775–1783*. New York, 1973.

Martin, James Kirby. *Men in Rebellion: Higher Governmental Leaders and the Coming of the American Revolution*. New Brunswick, N.J., 1973.

Martin, Margaret E. *Merchants and Trade of the Connecticut River Valley, 1750–1820*. Smith College Studies in History, Vol. 24. Northampton, Mass., 1938.

Middlekauff, Robert. *The Glorious Cause: The American Revolution, 1763–1789*. New York, 1982.

Mintz, Max M. *Gouverneur Morris and the American Revolution*. Norman, Okla., 1970.

Mitchell, Broadus. *Alexander Hamilton: The Revolutionary Years*. New York, 1970.

Morgan, Edmund S., and Helen M. Morgan. *The Stamp Act Crisis: Prologue to Revolution*. Chapel Hill, 1953.

Nash, Gary B. *The Urban Crucible: Social Change, Political Consciousness, and the Origins of the American Revolution*. Cambridge, Mass., 1979.

Nettels, Curtis P. *The Emergence of a National Economy, 1775–1815*. New York, 1962.

Newbold, Robert C. *The Albany Congress and Plan of Union in the Colonies*. New York, 1955.

Norton, Mary Beth. *Liberty's Daughters: The Revolutionary Experience of American Women, 1750–1800*. Boston, 1980.

Palmer, John McAuley. *General von Steuben*. New Haven, 1937.

Pargellis, Stanley McCrory. *Lord Loudoun in North America*. New Haven, 1933.

Pencak, William. *War, Politics, and Revolution in Provincial Massachusetts*. Boston, 1981.

Persons, Stow. *The Decline of American Gentility*. New York, 1973.

Peterson, Merrill D. *Thomas Jefferson and the New Nation*. New York, 1970.

Pickering, Octavius, and Charles W. Upham. *The Life of Timothy Pickering*. 4 vols. Boston, 1867–73.

Pocock, J. G. A. *The Machiavellian Moment: Florentine Political Thought and the Atlantic Republican Tradition*. Princeton, 1975.

Polishook, Irwin H. *Rhode Island and the Union, 1774–1795*. Evanston, Ill., 1969.

Price, Jacob M. *Capital and Credit in British Overseas Trade: The View from the Chesapeake, 1700–1776*. Cambridge, Mass., 1980.

Rakove, Jack N. *The Beginnings of National Politics: An Interpretive History of the Continental Congress*. New York, 1979.

Reed, William B. *Life and Correspondence of Joseph Reed*. . . . 2 vols. Philadelphia, 1847.

Risch, Erna. *Quartermaster Support of the Army: A History of the Corps, 1775–1939*. Washington, D.C., 1962.

_____. *Supplying Washington's Army*. Special Studies Series. Washington, D.C., 1981.

Rogers, Alan. *Empire and Liberty: American Resistance to British Authority, 1755–1763*. Berkeley and Los Angeles, 1974.

Rossman, Kenneth R. *Thomas Mifflin and the Politics of the American Revolution*. Chapel Hill, 1952.

Royster, Charles. *Light-Horse Harry Lee and the Legacy of the American Revolution*. New York, 1981.

_____. *A Revolutionary People at War: The Continental Army and American Character, 1775–1783*. Chapel Hill, 1979.

Russell, Howard S. *A Long Deep Furrow: Three Centuries of Farming in New England*. Hanover, N.H., 1976.

Ryerson, Richard Alan. *The Revolution Is Now Begun: The Radical Committees of Philadelphia, 1765–1776*. Philadelphia, 1978.

Sakolski, A. M. *The Great American Land Bubble*. New York, 1932.

Sanders, Jennings B. *Evolution of the Executive Departments of the Continental Congress, 1744–1789*. Chapel Hill, 1931.

Schwoerer, Lois G. *"No Standing Armies!": The Antiarmy Ideology in Seventeenth-Century England*. Baltimore, 1974.

Sedgwick, Theodore, Jr. *A Memoir of the Life of William Livingston*. . . . New York, 1833.

Sheridan, Eugene R. *Lewis Morris, 1671–1746: A Study in Early American Politics*. Syracuse, N.Y., 1981.

Shy, John. *A People Numerous and Armed: Reflections on the Military Struggle for American Independence*. New York, 1976.

_____. *Toward Lexington: The Role of the British Army in the Coming of the American Revolution*. Princeton, 1965.

Smith, Charles Page. *James Wilson: Founding Father, 1742–1789*. Chapel Hill, 1956.

Spaulding, E. Wilder. *His Excellency George Clinton: Critic of the Constitution*. New York, 1938.

Speck, W. A. *Stability and Strife: England, 1714–1760*. Cambridge, Mass., 1977.

Stillé, Charles J. *Major-General Anthony Wayne and the Pennsylvania Line in the Continental Army*. Philadelphia, 1893.

Stinchcombe, William C. *The American Revolution and the French Alliance*. New York, 1969.

Stourzh, Gerald. *Alexander Hamilton and the Idea of Republican Government*. Stanford, Calif., 1970.

Sydnor, Charles. *Gentlemen Freeholders: Political Practices in Washington's Virginia*. Chapel Hill, 1952.

Thayer, Theodore. *Nathanael Greene: Strategist of the American Revolution*. New York, 1960.

Trussell, John B. B., Jr. *Birthplace of an Army: A Study of the Valley Forge Encampment.* Harrisburg, Pa., 1976.

Van Doren, Carl. *Mutiny in January.* New York, 1943.

———. *Secret History of the American Revolution.* New York, 1941.

Van Dusen, Albert E. *Connecticut.* New York, 1961.

Ver Steeg, Clarence L. *Robert Morris: Revolutionary Financier.* Philadelphia, 1954.

Wallace, Willard M. *Appeal to Arms: A Military History of the American Revolution.* New York, 1951.

Ward, Christopher. *The War of the Revolution.* Edited by John Richard Alden. 2 vols. New York, 1952.

Ward, Harry M. *The Department of War, 1781–1795.* Pittsburgh, 1962.

———. *"Unite or Die": Intercolony Relations, 1690–1763.* Port Washington, N.Y., 1971.

Weaver, Glenn. *Jonathan Trumbull: Connecticut's Merchant Magistrate.* Hartford, 1956.

Weigley, Russell F. *The American Way of War: A History of United States Military Strategy and Policy.* New York, 1973.

———. *The Partisan War: The South Carolina Campaign of 1780–1782.* Columbia, S.C., 1970.

Wells, William V. *The Life and Public Services of Samuel Adams. . . .* 3 vols. Boston, 1865.

White, Philip L. *The Beekmans of New York, 1647–1877.* New York, 1956.

Whittemore, Charles. *A General of the Revolution: John Sullivan of New Hampshire.* New York, 1961.

Wickwire, Franklin B. *British Subministers and Colonial America, 1763–1783.* Princeton, 1966.

Wildes, Harry Emerson. *Anthony Wayne: Trouble Shooter of the American Revolution.* New York, 1941.

Wood, Gordon S. *The Creation of the American Republic, 1776–1787.* New York, 1969.

Zuckerman, Michael. *Peaceable Kingdoms: New England Towns in the Eighteenth Century.* New York, 1970.

ARTICLES

Adair, Douglass. "Fame and the Founding Fathers." In *Fame and the Founding Fathers: Essays by Douglass Adair,* edited by Trevor Colbourn, 3–26. New York, 1974.

Applegate, Howard Lewis. "The American Revolutionary War Hospital Department." *Military Medicine* 126 (1961): 296–306.

———. "The Medical Administrators of the American Revolutionary Army." *Military Affairs* 25 (1961): 1–10.

Banning, Lance. "James Madison and the Nationalists, 1780–1783." *William and Mary Quarterly,* 3d ser., 40 (1983): 227–55.

Bell, Whitfield J., Jr. "The Court Martial of Dr. William Shippen, Jr., 1780." *Journal of the History of Medicine and Allied Sciences* 19 (1964): 218–38.

———. "A Portrait of the Colonial Physician." In *The Colonial Physician and Other Essays,* edited by Whitfield J. Bell, Jr., 5–26. New York, 1977.

Biddle, Henry D. "Owen Biddle." *Pennsylvania Magazine of History and Biography* 16 (1892): 299–329.

Bockelman, Wayne L. "Local Government in Colonial Pennsylvania." In *Town and County: Essays on the Structure of Local Government in the American Colonies,* edited by Bruce C. Daniels, 216–37. Middletown, Conn., 1978.

Bonomi, Patricia U. "Local Government in Colonial New York: A Base for Republicanism." In *Aspects of Early New York Society and Politics,* edited by Jacob Judd and Irwin H. Polishook, 29–50. Tarrytown, N.Y., 1974.

Bowler, R. Arthur. "Logistics and Operations in the American Revolution." In *Reconsider-*

ations on the Revolutionary War: Selected Essays, edited by Don Higginbotham, 54–71. Westport, Conn., 1978.

Bradford, S. Sydney. "Hunger Menaces the Revolution, December 1779–January 1780." *Maryland Historical Magazine* 61 (1966): 1–23.

Bradley, Harold W. "The Political Thinking of George Washington." *Journal of Southern History* 11 (1945): 469–86.

Breen, T. H. "Persistent Localism: English Social Change and the Shaping of New England Institutions." *William and Mary Quarterly*, 3d ser., 32 (1975): 3–28.

Brown, B. Katherine. "The Controversy over the Franchise in Puritan Massachusetts, 1954–1974." *William and Mary Quarterly*, 3d ser., 33 (1976): 212–41.

Buel, Richard, Jr. "Democracy and the American Revolution: A Frame of Reference." *William and Mary Quarterly*, 3d ser., 21 (1964): 165–90.

———. "Time: Friend or Foe of the Revolution?" In *Reconsiderations on the Revolutionary War: Selected Essays*, edited by Don Higginbotham, 124–43. Westport, Conn., 1978.

Cometti, Elizabeth. "Depredations in Virginia during the Revolution." In *The Old Dominion: Essays for Thomas Perkins Abernethy*, edited by Darrett B. Rutman, 135–51. Charlottesville, 1964.

———. "Impressment during the American Revolution." In *The Walter Clinton Jackson Essays in the Social Sciences*, edited by Vera Largent, 97–109. Chapel Hill, 1942.

———. "Inflation in Revolutionary Maryland." *William and Mary Quarterly*, 3d ser., 8 (1951): 228–34.

Countryman, Edward. "Consolidating Power in Revolutionary America: The Case of New York, 1775–1783." *Journal of Interdisciplinary History* 6 (1976): 645–77.

Cunliffe, Marcus. "Congressional Leadership in the American Revolution." In *Leadership in the American Revolution*, 41–62. Library of Congress Symposia on the American Revolution, Washington, D.C., 1974.

Destler, Chester McArthur. "Colonel Henry Champion, Revolutionary Commissary." *Bulletin of the Connecticut Historical Society* 36 (1971): 52–64.

Douglass, Elisha P. "Thomas Burke, Disillusioned Democrat." *North Carolina Historical Review* 26 (1949): 150–86.

Estes, J. Worth. "'A Disagreeable and Dangerous Employment': Medical Letters from the Siege of Boston." *Journal of the History of Medicine* 31 (1976): 271–91.

Ferguson, E. James. "The Nationalists of 1781–1783 and the Economic Interpretation of the Constitution." *Journal of American History* 56 (1969): 241–61.

Ferguson, Isabel. "County Court in Virginia, 1700–1830." *North Carolina Historical Review* 8 (1931): 14–40.

Graeff, Arthur D. "Henry Vanderslice: Wagon-Master 1777–1778." *Historical Review of Berks County* 2 (1937): 67–73.

Greene, Jack P. "Changing Interpretations of Early American Politics." In *The Reinterpretation of Early American History: Essays in Honor of John Edwin Pomfret*, edited by Ray Allen Billington, 151–84. San Marino, Calif., 1966.

———. "The Growth of Political Stability: An Interpretation of Political Development in the Anglo-American Colonies, 1660–1760." In *The American Revolution: A Heritage of Change*, edited by John Parker and Carol Urness, 26–52. Minneapolis, 1975.

———. "Legislative Turnover in British America, 1696 to 1775: A Quantitative Analysis." *William and Mary Quarterly*, 3d ser., 38 (1981): 442–63.

———. "The Role of the Lower Houses of Assembly in Eighteenth-Century Politics." In *The Reinterpretation of the American Revolution, 1763–1789*, edited by Jack P. Greene, 86–110. New York, 1968.

———. "Society, Ideology, and Politics: An Analysis of the Political Culture of Mid-Eighteenth-Century Virginia." In *Society, Freedom, and Conscience: The American Revolution in Virginia, Massachusetts, and New York*, edited by Richard M. Jellison, 14–76. New York, 1979.

Griffenhagen, George B. "Drug Supplies in the American Revolution." *Bulletin of the United States National Museum* 225 (1961): 110–33.

Haber, Samuel. "The Professions and Higher Education in America: A Historical View." In *Higher Education and the Labor Market*, edited by Margaret S. Gordon, 237–80. Berkeley and Los Angeles, 1974.

Handlin, Oscar, and Mary Handlin. "Revolutionary Economic Policy in Massachusetts." *William and Mary Quarterly*, 3d ser., 4 (1947): 3–26.

Harlow, Ralph Volney. "Aspects of Revolutionary Finance, 1775–1783." *American Historical Review* 25 (1929): 46–68.

———. "Economic Conditions in Massachusetts during the American Revolution." *Transactions of the Colonial Society of Massachusetts* 20 (1918): 163–92.

Hart, Charles Henry. "Colonel Robert Lettis Hooper: Deputy Quarter Master General in the Continental Army and Vice President of New Jersey." *Pennsylvania Magazine of History and Biography* 36 (1912): 60–91.

Higginbotham, Don. "The American Militia: A Traditional Institution with Revolutionary Responsibilities." In *Reconsiderations on the Revolutionary War: Selected Essays*, edited by Don Higginbotham, 83–103. New York, 1978.

Hoffman, Ronald. "The 'Disaffected' in the Revolutionary South." In *The American Revolution: Explorations in the History of American Radicalism*, edited by Alfred F. Young, 273–316. DeKalb, Ill., 1976.

Hutson, James A. "The Logistics of Arnold's March to Quebec." In *Military Analysis of the Revolutionary War: An Anthology by the Editors of Military Affairs*, 106–20. Millwood, N.Y., 1977.

James, Mervyn. "English Politics and the Concept of Honor, 1485–1642." *Past and Present*, Supplement 3 (1978): 1–92.

Jameson, Hugh. "Equipment for the Militia of the Middle States." In *Military Analysis of the Revolutionary War: An Anthology by the Editors of Military Affairs*, 121–30. Millwood, N.Y., 1977.

Jensen, Merrill. "The American Revolution and American Agriculture." *Agricultural History* 43 (1969): 107–24.

———. "The Idea of A National Government during the American Revolution." *Political Science Quarterly* 43 (1943): 356–79.

Johnson, Victor L. "Internal Financial Reform or External Taxation: Britain's Fiscal Choice, 1763." *Proceedings of the American Philosophical Society* 98 (1954): 31–37.

———. "Robert Morris and the Provisioning of the American Army during the Campaign of 1781." *Pennsylvania History* 5 (1938): 7–20.

Kaplan, Sidney. "Rank and Status among Massachusetts Continental Officers." *American Historical Review* 56 (1951): 318–26.

Kohn, Richard H. "American Generals of the Revolution: Subordination and Restraint." In *Reconsiderations on the Revolutionary War: Selected Essays*, edited by Don Higginbotham, 104–23. Westport, Conn., 1978.

McLean, David. "Timothy Pickering: Citizen-Soldier of the Revolution." In *Studies on the American Revolution*, edited by Neville Meany, 115–50. South Melbourne, Australia, 1976.

Main, Jackson T. "Government by the People: The American Revolution and the Democratization of the Legislatures." *William and Mary Quarterly*, 3d ser., 23 (1966): 391–407.

Morgan, Edmund S. "The Puritan Ethic and the American Revolution." In *The Challenge of the American Revolution* by Edmund S. Morgan, 88–138. New York, 1978.

Morgan, William James. "American Privateering in America's War for Independence, 1775–1783." *American Neptune* 36 (1976): 79–87.

Morris, Richard B. "Labor and Mercantilism in the Revolutionary Era." In *The Era of the American Revolution*, edited by Richard B. Morris, 76–139. New York, 1939.

Murrin, John M. "The Great Inversion, or Court versus Country: A Comparison of the Revolution Settlements in England (1688–1721) and America (1776–1816)." In *Three British Revolutions, 1641, 1688, 1776*, edited by J.G.A. Pocock, 368–453. Princeton, 1980.

————. "Review Essay." *History and Theory* 11 (1972): 226–75.

Pavlovsky, Arnold M. "'Between Hawk and Buzzard': Congress as Perceived by Its Members, 1775–1783." *Pennsylvania Magazine of History and Biography* 101 (1977): 349–64.

Peck, Linda Levy. "The British Case: Corruption and Political Development in the Early Modern State." In *Before Watergate: Problems of Corruption in American Society*. Studies on Society in Change, No. 4, edited by Abraham S. Eisenstadt et al., 35–49. New York, 1979.

Pocock, J.G.A. "The Classical Theory of Deference." *American Historical Review* 81 (1976): 516–23.

Pole, J. R. "Historians and the Problem of Early American Democracy." *American Historical Review* 67 (1962): 626–46.

Purvis, Thomas L. "'High-Born, Long-Recorded Families': Social Origins of New Jersey Assemblymen, 1703–1776." *William and Mary Quarterly*, 3d ser., 37 (1980): 592–615.

Reed, H. Clay, and Joseph A. Palermo. "Justices of the Peace in Early Delaware." *Delaware History* 14 (1971): 223–37.

Reynolds, Donald. "Ammunition Supply in Revolutionary Virginia." *Virginia Magazine of History and Biography* 73 (1965): 56–77.

Rossman, Kenneth R. "Thomas Mifflin—Revolutionary Patriot." *Pennsylvania History* 15 (1948): 9–23.

Royster, Charles. "'The Nature of Treason': Revolutionary Virtue and American Reactions to Benedict Arnold." *William and Mary Quarterly*, 3d ser., 36 (1979): 163–93.

Salay, David L. "The Production of Gunpowder in Pennsylvania during the American Revolution." *Pennsylvania Magazine of History and Biography* 99 (1975): 422–42.

Schlebecker, John T. "Agricultural Markets and Marketing in the North, 1774–1777." *Agricultural History* 50 (1976): 21–36.

Scott, Kenneth. "Price Control in New England during the Revolution." *New England Quarterly* 19 (1946): 453–73.

Sellers, John R. "The Common Soldier in the American Revolution." In *Military History of the American Revolution: Proceedings of the Sixth Military History Symposium, USAF Academy, 1974*, edited by Stanley J. Underhal, 151–61. Washington, D.C., 1976.

Shalhope, Robert E. "Republicanism and Early American Historiography." *William and Mary Quarterly*, 3d ser., 39 (1982): 334–56.

————. "Toward a Republican Synthesis: The Emergence of an Understanding of Republicanism in American Historiography." *William and Mary Quarterly*, 3d ser., 29 (1972): 49–80.

Shy, John. "The American Revolution: The Military Conflict Considered as a Revolutionary War." In *Essays on the American Revolution*, edited by Stephen G. Kurtz and James H. Hutson, 121–56. Chapel Hill, 1973.

————. "The Legacy of the American Revolutionary War." In *Legacies of the American Revolution*, edited by Larry R. Gerlach et al., 43–60. Logan, Utah, 1978.

Stephenson, Orlando W. "The Supply of Gunpowder in 1776." *American Historical Review* 30 (1925): 271–80.

Thayer, Theodore. "The Army Contractors for the Niagara Campaign, 1755–1756." *William and Mary Quarterly*, 3d ser., 14 (1957): 31–46.

Trumbull, Jonathan. "Joseph Trumbull, The First Commissary-General of the Continental Army." *Records and Papers of the New London County Historical Society* 2, pt. 3 (1897): 329–47.

Watterson, John S. "Thomas Burke, Paradoxical Patriot." *Historian* 41 (1978–79): 664–81.

Wells, Thomas L. "An Inquiry into the Resignation of Quartermaster General Nathanael Greene in 1780." *Rhode Island History* 24 (1965): 41–48.

Wood, Gordon S. "Conspiracy and the Paranoid Style: Causality and Deceit in the Eighteenth Century." *William and Mary Quarterly*, 3d ser., 39 (1982): 401–41.

————. "Rhetoric and Reality in the American Revolution." *William and Mary Quarterly*, 3d ser., 23 (1966): 3–32.

DISSERTATIONS

Carp, E. Wayne. "Supplying the Revolution: Continental Army Administration and American Political Culture, 1775–1783." Ph.D. dissertation, University of California, Berkeley, 1981.

Chase, Philander Dean. "Baron von Steuben in the War of Independence." Ph.D. dissertation, Duke University, 1973.

Fowler, James Henry II. "The Breakdown of Congressional Authority: A Study of the Relations between the Continental Congress and the States, 1780–1783." Ph.D. dissertation, Oklahoma State University, 1977.

Lender, Mark Edward. "The Enlisted Line: The Continental Soldiers of New Jersey." Ph.D. dissertation, Rutgers University, 1975.

McBride, John David. "The Virginia War Effort, 1775–1783: Manpower Policies and Practices." Ph.D. dissertation, University of Virginia, 1977.

Nuxoll, Elizabeth Miles. "Congress and the Munitions Merchants: The Secret Committee of Trade during the American Revolution, 1775–1777." Ph.D. dissertation, City University of New York, 1979.

Patterson, Michael Scott. "From Revolution to Constitution: The Forging of the National Republic, 1776–1787." Ph.D. dissertation, University of North Carolina at Chapel Hill, 1971.

Robinson, Edward Forbes. "Continental Treasury Administration, 1775–1781: A Study in the Financial History of the American Revolution." Ph.D. dissertation, University of Wisconsin, 1969.

Royer, H. H. "The Role of the Continental Congress in the Prosecution of the American Revolution." Ph.D. dissertation, Pennsylvania State University, 1960.

Royster, Charles. "The Continental Army in the American Mind, 1775–1783." Ph.D. dissertation, University of California, Berkeley, 1977.

Van Dusen, Albert E. "The Trade of Revolutionary Connecticut." Ph.D. dissertation, University of Pennsylvania, 1948.

UNPUBLISHED DUPLICATED MATERIAL

Murrin, John M. "Colonial Political Development." Paper read at Oxford University Conference in American Colonial History, August 1981, revised June 1982. Oxford University. Xeroxed.

INDEX

New Jersey tax law, 120; and 9 July 1779 resolution, 122; and private trade, 125; and settlement of accounts, 129, 130, 258 (n. 113); attitude toward Quartermaster Department, 156, 164–65; and patriotism, 157–58, 160; and staff officers' resignations, 158–60, 167; resignation of, 159, 194–95; and esprit de corps of staff officers, 163; and reputation, 163–64; pursuit of fame, 164–65; defends high cost of war, 173–74; and system of specific supplies, 178–79, 180; criticizes state assemblies, 184; recommends sending committee to army, 191; criticizes reform of Quartermaster Department, 192–93; and strengthening powers of Congress, 196, 222; and contract system, 214; denies misuse of public funds, 257 (n. 100); urges Biddle to remain in public service, 263 (n. 58); favors calling convention of states, 270 (n. 43)

Greene, William, 108, 202; and system of specific supplies, 182; disobeys congressional resolve, 184

Greenwich, R.I., 85

Hackensack, N.J., 89

Hamilton, Alexander: and Hughes case, 134; criticizes Congress, 197; and Nationalists' program, 197–99; criticizes states, 198; urges abolition of system of specific supplies, 198; favors strengthening powers of Congress, 222; on sovereignty, 269 (n. 26); favors calling convention of states, 270 (n. 43)

Hamilton, Thomas: and impressment, 88

Hancock, John, 42

Hanover Precinct, N.Y., 116

Hardwick, N.J., 79

Harrington, James, 9

Harrison, Benjamin: criticizes Congress, 30

Harrison, Robert Hanson, 36

Hart, Joseph, 186

Hartford, Conn., 62, 164, 202

Hartford Convention (1780), 204; proceedings of, 203

Harvie, John, 236 (n. 26)

Hay, Udny, 124, 155; and artisans' wages, 63–64; personally finances supply purchases, 71; and impressment, 89, 91, 93, 96; and ancillary supply system, 95–96; defense

against charges of corruption, 114; reaction to 9 July 1779 resolution, 121; and commission system, 129; appeals to patriotism, 160–61; criticizes dismissal of express riders, 174; borrows money, 243 (n. 53)

Head of Elk (Elkton), Md., 212, 213

Heath, William, 208, 215; denounces quartermasters, 58; sent off for supplies, 210–11

Hessian fly, 109

Hide Department, 192

Highlands (N.Y.), 171

Hollis, Thomas, 9

Holt, John, 183

Honor, 159; and staff officers, 155–56; colonial heritage of, 163. *See also* Fame; Reputation

Hooper, Robert Lettis, Jr.: case of, 3–5, 112, 121; accused of fraud, 117; reputation of, 166

Hooper, William, 182

Hopewell, N.J., 89

Hospital Department, 24–25, 31, 41, 191, 201–2; creation of, 25–26; feuds in, 26–28; personnel shortages in, 28; reorganizations of, 37, 38, 49, 201–2, 235 (n. 8); criticism of, 47; and high mortality rates, 47; and corruption, 101; denounced as corrupt, 118; settlement of accounts in, 133; esprit de corps of, 163; and conflict of interest proviso, 200–201; resignations from, 269 (n. 36). *See also* Director-general and chief physician, Hospital Department

Hospital Department (Brit.), 20; regulation of, 27

Hospitals: corruption in, 117

House of Representatives, 134

Hubbard, Nehemiah, 155, 162; threatens to resign, 167

Hudson River, N.Y., 38, 56, 61, 96, 109, 212

Hughes, Hugh, 44, 124, 155, 158, 167; and impressment, 90; rejects nepotism, 123; case of, 134–35; resignation of, 159–60

Humphreys, David, 82

Huntington, Samuel, 90, 120, 182, 184, 192, 203, 208

Hutchinson, Thomas, 21, 58

Impost: proposed by Nationalists, 200–201; Nationalists' attitude toward, 205; inade-